THE LOST WOODLANDS OF ANCIENT NASCA

A Case-Study in Ecological and Cultural Collapse

THE LOST WOODLANDS OF ANCIENT NASCA

A Case-Study in Ecological and Cultural Collapse

by

David Beresford-Jones

A British Academy Postdoctoral Fellowship Monograph

Published for THE BRITISH ACADEMY

by OXFORD UNIVERSITY PRESS

Acknowledgements

This book emerges out of research that I carried out during my Ph.D., funded by the Natural Environmental Research Council (NERC), and a British Academy Postdoctoral Fellowship at the McDonald Institute for Archaeological Research, University of Cambridge. I am grateful to all those institutions for the funding they provided.

While, naturally, I am solely responsible for any weaknesses, this book represents the results of the work and contributions of many others. I would particularly like to thank the following:

The members of the Proyecto de Investigación Arqueológica Samaca who made fieldwork possible and so enjoyable: Mario Advíncula, Tom Birch, Julie-Manon Breuil, Lauren Cadwallader, Isabel Cornejo, Claudia Grimaldo, Mark Oldham, Brian Pitman, Gustavo Ramírez and Leanne Zeki. Most of all to my co-director, Susana Arce Torres of the Museo Regional de Ica and to my valued friends and colleagues, Kevin Lane, Sandy Pullen and Fraser Sturt.

The Instituto Nacional de Cultura, Peru for permissions to carry out fieldwork.

All the members of the George Pitt-Rivers Laboratory for Bioarchaeology, University of Cambridge, past and present, particularly Rachel Ballentyne, Alan Clapham and Lila Janik. Members of the department of Geography, University of Cambridge: Chris Rolfe, Will Fletcher, Phil Hughes, and most of all to Steve Boreham for his time and expertise. Many members and ex-members of the Department of Archaeology, University of Cambridge: Manuel Arroyo-Kalin, Julie Boreham, Elizabeth DeMarrais, Charly French, Paul Heggarty, Alex Herrera, Martin Jones, Karen Milek, David Redhouse and Geraldine Slean.

Carmela Alarcón, Oscar Portocarrero, Wolfgang Stuppy and David Goldstein, for their help in identifying plant fossils; Manuel Gorriti Manchego and Lauren Cadwallader for their mollusc identifications; Helen Lewis for thin section assessments; and Alex Chepstow-Lusty for pollen identifications and much help and advice besides.

Many in Lima and Ica, including Herman Berger, Mariano Cabrera, Rodrigo Nuñez, Tomás d'Ornellas, César Patroni, Félix Quinteros of the Universidad Nacional San Luis Gonzaga de Ica, Peru, Julio Sánchez, Richard Stoddart and, in particular, Claudia Lüthi and Sonya Curasi.

Chapterhead: Detail of Paracas embroidered textile (drawing courtesy of the Brooklyn Museum).

My academic editor, Warwick Bray, for his suggestions on this book, and much help and advice besides; two anonymous reviewers and one anonymous reader; and my copy-editor, Carol Fellingham Webb.

Above all, I owe thanks to my wife, Chloe, and children, Georgia and Arthur, for their patience and understanding; to my friend and collaborator Oliver Whaley of the Royal Botanical Gardens Kew; to all the people, past and present, of the Escuela Libre de Puerto Huamaní, Samaca; and to Don Alberto Benavides Ganoza. *Todo han sido solo posibles gracias a su acogida y visión, una visión que pocos parecen compartir . . .*

los guarangos dejan pasar el sol, pero quitándole el fuego…
[the guarangos let the sun pass, but take out its fire]

José María Arguedas

1. Introduction

In the midst of an ever-greater awareness of how seriously today's industrial society impacts upon our environment, there is a widely held notion that past peoples were not so blind and foolish. Nowhere is this more the case than in the popular perception of the state of the 'New World' on the eve of its conquest by Europe. Epitomised in the popular imagination by films such as *Dances with Wolves*, is an idea that Native American peoples dwelt in Eden, inflicting 'barely perceptible disturbance' as Shetler (1991: 226) would have it, upon its wilderness. For many archaeologists, geographers and other students of the past this is mere myth—coloured, indeed, by strands of our own philosophy dating back to Rousseau's *Discourse on the Origin of Inequality*. For there would seem to be a host of historical and archaeological evidence to refute this 'myth of the ecologically noble savage', as Lentz (2000: 2) calls it. And yet we also have to hand detailed anthropologies and ethno-ecological histories which would seem to lend substance to the 'myth', in the shape of a number of Native American societies whose very worldviews seem conditioned by a sophisticated conservationism. How are we to reconcile these apparent contradictions?

This book presents a new archaeological case of prehistoric human impact on the environment: a study of ecological and cultural change from the arid south coast of Peru, beginning around 700 BC and culminating in a collapse by about AD 1000. Its focus is the lower Ica Valley, today largely depopulated and bereft of cultivation, but whose abundant archaeological remains attest to substantial prehistoric occupations and thereby present a *prima facie* case for changed environmental conditions. This is a place of extreme environmental juxtaposition: one of the world's oldest and driest deserts, crossed by lush riverine oases and sporadically impacted by El Niño floods or long droughts. Archaeological interpretations of culture change here have long relied upon those climatic perturbations. Yet, while the archaeological record that I will present does indeed include new evidence of huge ancient

Chapterhead: Detail of Nasca embroidered textile with birds, carrying in their beaks ant, wasp, beetle, root crops, cactus, fresh water shrimp, snake, chilli pepper, germinating bean, wild tomatoes, fish and possibly cotton, peanut, and achira. The different neck lengths, tail forms and wing markings of the birds suggest different species including finches, parrot, mocking bird, perhaps egret (drawing from Early Nasca Needlework by Alan Sawyer, courtesy of Lawrence King Publishing).

flood events, it also distinguishes more gradual, *human-induced* changes. This case-study contradicts, therefore, the popular myth of the 'ecologically noble savage'. No less interestingly, however, it also records correlations between changes in society and degrees of human impact. We may hope to use these to clear a path through the polemic surrounding this 'myth', by making much more specific inferences about those social and ecological contexts in which significant human environmental impacts in the New World did and did not arise.

That this polemic has political efficacy is hardly to be doubted: witness the furore attending the quincentennial commemoration of Columbus's discovery of the Americas in 1992. Then, the Smithsonian Museum of Natural History mounted a landmark exhibition called *Seeds of Change*, and the museum's deputy director, the botanist S. Shetler wrote in its catalogue: 'Pre-Columbian America was still the First Eden, a pristine natural kingdom. The native people were transparent in the landscape, living as natural elements of the ecosphere. Their world, the New World of Columbus, was a world of barely perceptible human disturbance'(Shetler 1991: 226). In the eyes of many this both articulated and lent credibility to the 'myth of the ecologically noble savage'—a viewpoint best put perhaps by Denevan (1992) and Butzer (1992), in a publication of the Association of American Geographers intended precisely to debunk it (see also Jett and Wood 1992).

For, arguably, there is something inherently patronising in this view of New World peoples as 'transparent in the landscape', which undermines our appreciation of their contribution to the wider story of humanity. As Butzer (1996: 141) puts it: 'to deny that New World peoples humanized and modified the environment, or created their own cultural landscapes, is to reinforce the metaphor of the 17th century preacher, Cotton Mather, who referred to them as primitive savages, blending into the forest like beaver'.

The reality was of course quite the contrary. The New World was home to two of humanity's rare hearths of agriculture and civilisation. The sheer scale of landscape modifications undertaken in the Andes and the sizes and splendour of the cities of Mexico astounded the first Spanish chroniclers, for they were greater than anything that could be seen in Europe. Moreover, the products of millennia of Native American plant manipulation and the subsistence bases of huge pre-Columbian populations—estimated by Denevan (1992: 370) at some 54 million souls—duly became the underpinning for societies elsewhere. Of the fifteen staple food crops that 'really feed' the world population today (Harlan 1975: 233), no fewer than six were domesticated in the Americas: maize, potatoes, beans (of the genus *Phaseolus*), manioc, sweet potato and peanuts (as the source of groundnut oil). Cuisines worldwide were altered by tomatoes, chilli peppers and cocoa, while other important American domesticates include squashes and pumpkins, cotton and tobacco.

Consequently, the New World was no 'pristine Eden': it was mostly, if not entirely, an *artefact*. As Butzer (1996: 142) notes, the first Spaniards encountered deforested landscapes from Mexico to Panama. Indeed, Denevan (1992) presents the evidence that the first Europeans encountered environments altered and managed by people almost everywhere: from the open woodlands of North America; across the fields of maize of Mexico and the

Mississippi; up the serried ranks of terraces that mould the heights of the Andes to the very expanses of Great Prairies of the Midwest and jungles of the Amazon Basin. The origins, then, of the myth of a pristine Eden in the Americas lay in the population collapse that followed the introduction of Old World diseases. So utter was this collapse—the death of 89 per cent of the original New World population by Denevan's (1992: 371) estimate—that many of these environments were left to revert to the state of nature of much later description, such that 'human presence was less visible in 1750 than it was in 1492' (Denevan 1992: 369).

Moreover, there is considerable archaeological evidence that the intensity of some Native American populations and agriculture sometimes had a very deleterious impact on the environment. Pollen and geomorphological records attest to the severity of the deforestation wrought in the first millennium AD by the Classic Maya civilization on the Yucatán peninsula (see for instance Rice *et al.* 1985, Vaughan *et al.* 1985, Abrams and Rue 1988). Episodes of soil erosion provoked by human land use have been documented in various parts of Mexico (Butzer 1996), not least through the sediment records of Lake Pátzcuaro in central Mexico, the heartland of the Tarascan state, a contemporary and adversary of the Aztecs (O'Hara *et al.* 1993). Various lines of archaeobotanical data have recorded irreversible damage, around a millennium ago, inflicted through deforestation of an arid environment: the area around the Chaco Canyon settlements of the Anasazi culture (Betancourt and Van Devender 1981, Samuels and Betancourt 1982, Betancourt *et al.* 1986, Hayes *et al.* 1981). These are but vignettes of a larger story of the ancient human impact on the environment, set out most accessibly by Redman (1999) and Diamond (2005). Perhaps the starkest and most famous example is that of Easter Island, whose Polynesian settlers succeeded in deforesting entirely Rapanui, as they called it, reducing its vast bird population to a single species, and themselves to internecine war, cannibalism and starvation.

As for the Peruvian coast, even to the casual observer it is seemingly apparent that parts have suffered environmental degradation and diminished land use over time. Long-abandoned prehistoric irrigation canals and their associated agricultural systems, preserved in an arid climate, are still to be seen in many Peruvian coastal valleys. Sometimes these lie beyond the limits of modern irrigation, witness both to the engineering ingenuity of their prehistoric builders and to the environmental change that has occurred over time. Parts of the north coast of Peru have been the subject of a number of important archaeological studies (see for instance Farrington 1974, Moseley *et al.* 1981, Pozorski and Pozorski 1982, 2003a, Park 1983). Here, it is estimated that farmers today are able to use only 60–65 per cent of the land that their prehistoric ancestors had under cultivation (Browman 1983, Moseley 1983, Denevan 1992). Yet, the precise reasons for this 'agrarian collapse' and the problems of erosion, river incision, soil salinisation and desertification that underlie it, are still to be properly understood. For as we will see, the original explanation offered for the north coast—tectonic uplift since the construction of ancient systems—has since been called into doubt.

Indeed, as our case-study from the Peruvian south coast will illustrate, few of the archaeological instances of human impact upon ancient environments turn out to be so straightforward as the extreme case of Easter Island. As with any dialectic of a complex past based upon scanty clues left to us in the present, uncertainty attends our interpretations. So, for instance, there is also evidence of a relatively dry period coinciding with the deterioration of the high forest environment inflicted by the Classic Maya (Hodell *et al.* 1995). Was Maya civilisation undone then by the damage that it inflicted on its own environment, or by natural climate change—or indeed by something else entirely? What makes disentangling the respective 'drivers' of change in the past so difficult is, of course, that they will often play out in concert (see for instance Diamond 1994). There are obvious resonances here with our environmental debates in the present. For all the methods of the natural sciences that we might seek to bring to bear on these problems, archaeology—with its primary data excavated and interpreted from differentially preserved contexts—is no 'hard science'. We would only be poor scientists to pretend otherwise. As Butzer (2005: 5) puts it, 'geoarchaeological and bioarchaeological study provides an indispensable foundation—but by itself is unlikely to reveal the cause-and-effect interrelationships of social and environmental variables'. In other words, while the environmental sciences can help us recognise *what* changed, they may tell us little about *why* it changed. The methods of natural science are necessary but insufficient for complete explanation. In trying to answer the questions of when change occurred in the lower Ica Valley, and indeed, how and why it occurred, I will be at pains to avoid glossing over this critical distinction.

For, as far as the 'myth of the ecologically noble savage' is concerned, we also have abundant evidence that much Native American land stewardship did indeed entail extremely sophisticated conservationism. Nowhere is this more poignantly expressed, as Lovell (1992: 437) points out, than in the entreaty to Philip III by the remarkable native Peruvian chronicler Guaman Poma, written between 1585 and 1615:

> Consider these poor Indians and their labours ... that in each town they constructed irrigation canals from rivers or springs, from lakes or reservoirs. In bygone days these were built with so much effort, by hand, and with the greatest skill in the world that it seems that every Indian [who lived] raised up a stone. All this was sufficient for the great many people who then were alive.
>
> And so throughout the kingdom all lands produced food, whether crops were planted in the yungas, or hot lands, or in the desert [oases], or in the rugged mountains of this realm. And the Inca kings commanded that no one should damage or remove one stone, and that no livestock should enter the aforementioned canals.
>
> But now this law no longer applies. And so all the fields are destroyed because of a shortage of water. On account of this the Indians lose their lands, and Your Majesty his royal share, and Holy Mother Church her tithe. For nowadays the Spaniards let loose their animals, their mule trains or their cows, their goats and sheep, and they cause great damage. And they take the water and destroy the irrigation canals so much so that no amount of money could repair them. And the little amount of water that remains, that also is taken from the poor Indians. And so the Indians abandon their towns.
>
> (Guaman Poma de Ayala, cited by Lovell 1992: 437)

The conquistadors themselves were aware of this. Rostworowski (1981: 55; my translation), for instance, cites the melancholic reflections of Pizarro's companion in arms, Mancio Serra de Leguizamo, on the lost 'order and harmony' of the Inca Empire, and on how well its people had managed its 'lands and mountains and mines and pastures and households and woodlands'. We will see as much here in other early Spanish accounts of Peru, some of which, such as those of Cieza de León and Bernabé Cobo, stand as works of considerable sympathy and perception.

More recently, we may read of societies whose very worldviews are conditioned by conservationism, in the detailed anthropologies of Amerindian societies in Amazonia by Balée (1994) and Descola (1994), and in the ethnohistories of other parts of the New World, including the Sonoran Desert of North America, which we will explore in some detail here. Balée (1994: 116), for instance, observes that for the Ka'apor, a Tupi-speaking group from the Brazilian state of Maranhão, 'management' of the forest means its manipulation so as to bring about 'a net environmental diversity greater than that of so-called pristine conditions'. The origins of agriculture itself in the Americas, likely lie in precisely such management of jungle lowlands (see for instance Pearsall and Piperno 1998).

Indeed, Descola's (1994) study of the Achuar, a Jivaroan group living on the Ecuador–Peru border, reveals how the very bifurcation between 'nature' and 'culture' also owes far more to our own philosophical tradition than it does to the worldviews of those societies. For the Achuar see themselves as in no way seperate from nature. And while there might appear to be a number of glaring differences between these recent Amazonian contexts and those of our case-study here on the ancient south coast of Peru, some of those differences turn out to be less obvious on closer inspection. Balée (1994: 116) concludes that whether a society is 'in or out of equilibrium with Amazonian environments may be understood in terms of fundamental differences between stateless (egalitarian) peoples and those incorporated into a nation-state society'. Clearly, however, this is to see contrasts between the extremes of what is really a very long and graded continuum. What is more instructive is to seek instances of different degrees of environmental impact along that scale of social complexity, much of which lies in the realm of prehistory, and hence archaeology. Indeed, it is precisely this perspective — over the passage of time — that 'historical ecology', advocated by Balée (1994: 1) and others, aspires to take. Moreover, historical ecology seeks to avoid 'culture' and 'environment' becoming 'alienated subject and object' as Balée (1994: 1) puts it, by focus 'on a relationship, not an organism, species or society'. This seems to me a very sensible approach and I attempt to adopt it into this archaeological case-study of the lower Ica Valley, by focusing on human–plant *relationships* and how they changed through deep time.

I will begin this case-study in Chapter 2 by looking at the peculiar desert environment of the Peruvian south coast. We will then go on to explore the archaeology of the lower Ica Valley in Chapter 3. This is based upon many seasons of archaeological fieldwork with the purpose of gathering different datasets with which to reconstruct geomorphological, ecological and land-use changes in the Samaca and Ullujaya basins. I will run through the rich archaeological record in these basins from the Early Horizon (*c*.750 BC) through to the Inca Late Horizon that ended abruptly with Spanish conquest in AD 1532, as revealed through detailed archaeological survey and excavation. Chapter 4 will set out the geomorphological history of the basins of the lower Ica Valley — those processes of erosion and deposition which have formed and destroyed their archaeological record, and indeed given rise to today's landscape there. Chapter 5 will then examine the ancient plant and other remains recovered from our excavations. Organic remains enjoy extraordinary preservation in this hyperarid climate, and can provide us with both information on the human use of plant resources and proxy indicators of changed environmental conditions.

In Chapter 6 I will begin to look beyond the lower Ica Valley to trace the old and gradual story of deforestation through the wider archaeological record for the south coast, the Spanish chronicles and administrative records of the region, and recent memory. Yet we can only understand the consequences of that deforestation through a proper appreciation of the ecology of the 'keystone' species of the south coast: the huarango — a tree of the genus *Prosopis*. So, in Chapters 7 and 8 I will explore this through the botanical and agroforestry literature, and our own studies of today's riparian dry forest ecology on the south coast of Peru. We will see that the huarango is a remarkable leguminous hardwood that can live for more than a millennium, providing an (almost) unfailing resource of food, forage and fuel — the 'staff of life' for the inhabitants of the Peruvian south coast. More subtly — and no less importantly — it also integrates various parts of a fragile south coast desert ecosystem. In Chapter 9 I will embellish this by defining and justifying a limited analogy with the ethnoecology of the Sonoran Desert in North America.

In conclusion, I will attempt to synthesise these various parts of the story so as to incorporate the relationship between humans and plants — in particular the huarango — much more fully into archaeological interpretations of the Peruvian south coast. I will also seek to make specific inferences about those social and ecological contexts in which significant human environmental impacts here did, and did not, arise. Fortunately for this purpose we have a very useful framework set out by Butzer (1996, 2005), for the Mediterranean:

> The Mediterranean ecosystem is the product of millennia of co-evolution between the environment and human activities, but traditional land use has been conservative and ecologically adaptive, despite sporadic disequilibrium. The deviations from the norm pose a number of testable hypotheses for further examination, not only in the Mediterranean region but also in other areas such as the New World.
>
> (Butzer 1996: 141)

I will seek to test these hypotheses in the case of the long trajectory of human–plant relationships recorded in the archaeological record of the lower Ica Valley.

The *sine qua non* of my archaeological approach here is that if we wish to study ancient human ecology, then we must try to understand properly the wider elements of that ecology. We are, as Hodgson (2001: 2) puts it plainly, 'part of the natural ecosystem, whether we like it or not'. The prehistoric inhabitants of the lower Ica Valley doubtless understood this immutable truth far more profoundly than we can ever hope to. That I wish to adopt this into my research design does *not* necessarily make my interpretations environmentally deterministic. On the contrary, it allows for more informed discrimination between human agency and environmental response.

For the environment of the south coast of Peru is not simply a static background canvas upon which to paint our archaeological interpretations. Its woodlands—described by Vázquez de Espinosa (1942 [1629]: 485) in the seventeenth century as 'impenetrable at many points . . . with many savage wild animals . . . so thick that the highway is the only way to get through them and one sees nothing but woods and sky'—are gone. They have been replaced by the broad fields of agro-industry, saline soils, shifting dunes and degraded *monte* scrub. This modern landscape influences, in unwarranted ways, archaeological interpretations, which have also relied too heavily on climatic factors such as El Niño, to proffer entirely environmentally determined explanations of cultural change. We will see that there is evidence that gradual, *human-induced* changes exposed the south coast landscape to the effects of El Niño perturbations, long *before* Europeans arrived in Peru.

2. The South Coast Desert

Our area of interest here — the basins of the lower Ica Valley on the Peruvian south coast — lies within one of the world's oldest and driest deserts. We will start by examining the causes of that desert's age and extreme aridity — 'first the strange sea, the cause of it all', as von Hagan (1961: 16) suggests. But the climate, geology, geomorphology and hydrology of the south coast are further distinguished from the rest of the Peruvian coast. We will go on to explore those peculiarities of the south coast since they underlie the particular sensitivity of its human ecology. Yet we will also begin to see how coloured by the effects of long human impact are our archaeological impressions of the south coast's 'limitations'. For in fact — thanks to those factors of climate and geomorphology that we will explore here — its riparian valleys are among the most potentially productive in the world.

The Peruvian Coastal Desert

The Peru–Chile Desert, or Atacama, of which the Peruvian south coast is part, extends for more than 2,000 kilometres from around 30 °S to 5 °S in a very long strip of western South America, confined between the Pacific Ocean on the one hand and the Andean cordillera on the other. As von Hagen (1961: 16) describes: 'the mountains loom up out of the desert like dry bones; the whole aspect of it in its entire length is hollow and fainting'. For a tropical coast, it has an extremely peculiar climate — annual precipitation rarely exceeding 25 mm (see for instance Petrov 1976, Cooke *et al*. 1993). Yet this aridity is not due to any lack of humidity. For like all tropical coasts this desert's air is pregnant with water vapour. Rather, its almost complete lack of rainfall is due to extreme atmospheric stability caused by interactions between the south-east Pacific trade winds and the Andean cordillera. So the roots of the Peru–Chile Desert lie in its geology, and those of its great age, in its geological history.

Chapterhead: Nasca black-slipped ceramic bottle showing llamas tethered amid forms reminiscent of a huarangal (drawing courtesy of Ann Peters).

Geological history

The continental margin of western South America is one of the world's major convergent plate boundaries. As the oceanic, so-called 'Nazca Plate' is subducted beneath the South American continent it has thrown up one of the most extreme geographical dislocations on earth. On the east of this margin the Andean cordillera rises abruptly to heights of more than 7,000 metres, while offshore to its west, the Peru–Chile marine trench descends to depths beyond 7,600 metres below sea level.

Most of this topography has been shaped by the plate boundary during the most recent geological era, the Cenozoic (Dunbar *et al.* 1990). The main uplift of the central Andes was complete by the early Miocene epoch, some 20 million years ago. This is still a geologically active region with frequent subduction zone earthquakes. Yet, since the Andean pediplain has suffered remarkably little erosion since the late Miocene, it seems unlikely that there has been significant uplift during the Quaternary (Cooke *et al.* 1993, Wells and Noller 1999).

Since it is this topography that causes its aridity, the Peru–Chile Desert is thought to be very old. Arid conditions have prevailed since the late Eocene with the onset of hyperaridity by the middle to late Miocene, some 15 million years ago (Alpers and Brimhall 1988). Indicative of this great age are extensive sodium nitrate deposits, which occur in horizons several metres thick across parts of the desert surface. Very soluble, these nitrate salts can persist only in an almost complete absence of significant rainfall (Böhlke *et al.* 1997, McKay *et al.* 2003). Thus their occurrence in such quantities indicates that extreme aridity has persisted here for as long as 10–15 million years (Cooke *et al.* 1993). Indeed, isotopic analyses confirm that these deposits date from the Miocene (Böhlke *et al.*1997). They were once extensively exploited for fertilizer — the economics of which triggered the 'War of the Pacific' between Chile and Peru in 1879. And small-scale mining operations of sodium nitrate deposits continue today along the edges of the lower Ica Valley of the Peruvian south coast, our area of interest here.

The Peru–Chile Desert is, therefore, like the Namib of south-west Africa, a so-called 'core-desert' of great age, in which climatic change has been quite limited throughout the Quaternary. It occupies, however, a very different latitude to the Namib. Unlike in any other tropical coastal region, arid conditions extend northwards, almost to the Equator.

Causes of aridity

These geological facts orient this Pacific littoral along a north-west to south-east direction, which coincides with the direction of the south-eastern Pacific trade winds. These are channelled north by the Andes and drive a cool ocean current — the Humboldt, or Peruvian Current — up this coast in huge, unhurried rollers, causing cold up-welling from the deep submarine trench beneath. This brings to the surface nutrients that support a huge phytoplankton biomass: the base of one of the world's richest marine food chains and the subsistence basis of the first sedentary societies along the Peruvian coast (see for instance Quilter 1989, Dillehay *et al.* 2004). Indeed—perhaps uniquely worldwide—they formed the foundations of the first complex societies in the Andes (Moseley 1975).

These trade winds thereby create a cold, moist marine air layer along this coast. Meanwhile, the air above the marine layer is warmed by tropical sunshine. The result is temperature inversion: a rigid stratification of coastal air masses that prevents the convective air currents that would normally cause rainfall—producing 'dry' oceans and arid desert coasts (Prohaska 1973). At the same time, the Andes block from the Pacific coast the moist easterly tropical air masses of the Intertropical Convergence Zone over the Amazon Basin. So also do these trade winds, channelled by the Andes, displace climatic conditions more typically associated with low latitudes, northwards by around 15° of latitude towards the Equator. As Prohaska (1973: 96) notes, this 'persistence of inversion and its equatorward extension is extraordinary anywhere on earth, let alone in tropical latitudes'.

Despite its persistence, however, the structure of this temperature inversion varies markedly from summer to winter. Since it is a function of both subsidence-induced adiabatic heating from above and cooling below, variation in the inversion depends on surface and upper air conditions, both of which are a direct consequence of trade-wind intensities. These in turn depend upon the changes in pressure that occur throughout the entire area of tropical South America south of the Equator.

During winter, from May to September, the inversion layer is deep and steady onshore trade winds blow in humidity off the ocean. The air trapped beneath the inversion layer is saturated with moisture and skies are covered by a blanket of unrelenting stratus cloud, absorbing all sunshine. Winter temperatures—averaging 15 °C in Lima—are consequently almost 10 °C cooler than equivalent tropical latitudes (Prohaska 1973). Nocturnal cooling produces the phenomenon of drizzling fogs (*garúa*), although the amount of actual precipitation resulting on the coast itself is negligible. However, on the hills (or *lomas*) of the coastal hinterland at the contact zone where the Andes rise into the inversion layer base, there is a nearly continuous drizzle. Combined with reduced evaporation loss due to the stratus cover, this gives rise to areas of ephemeral, xerophytic fog-drip vegetation. Since vegetation itself is a fog catcher, once its growth starts, the soil beneath receives several times more water than would have been produced on a barren slope. Thus, in this environment, vegetation acts not as a water-consuming, but as a water-*producing* factor: something that has ramifications for the ecological changes we seek to track here. As this occurs *lomas* areas blossom with intense green meadows and pasture. But, as summer begins from October to December, the stratus cover and its *garúa* fades and so too does the *lomas* vegetation, until the landscape is once more barren desert.

Summer proper prevails from January through April. The trade winds persist, albeit with less intensity, and inversion is almost continuously manifest. Rainfall remains negligible. Yet the inversion layer now lies closer to the surface and is much thinner. Skies clear and temperatures are now only some 3°C cooler than comparable tropical latitudes (Prohaska 1973). Water vapour is still trapped beneath the inversion layer and the coastal air is sultry. Some high clouds spill over the Andes as moist easterlies over the Amazon Basin rise to great heights and wrap the Andean peaks in towering *foehen-walls* of cloud, which may be visible from the Pacific. The rainfalls that, together with summer glacial melt, feed the seasonal rivers which drain the eastern slopes of the Andes and run west down to the Pacific, are therefore usually not of a Pacific origin, but spill-over of the intensive summer precipitation along the windward, eastern slopes of the Andean cordillera and the Amazon watershed (Prohaska 1973).

These are the controls then that determine the peculiarities of the Peruvian coastal climate for its tropical location: its absence of precipitation, large annual and small daily temperature variations, and, during the dry season or hemispheric winter, its high relative humidity and extensive cloudiness. On the south coast, however, this climate is considerably altered because of variations in these controls. Here it is hotter and drier still, with almost year-round sunshine and a much stronger wind regime. The reason for these variations is that the desert hinterland on the south coast, lying between the Pacific and the Andean foothills, is much wider than along the rest of the Peruvian coast. This in turn is due to the particular geological characteristics of the south coast region: once again the consequence of geological fate.

The Ancient Landforms: the Geology of the South Coast

The tectonic processes of subduction that have raised the Andean cordillera have also formed a series of so-called 'forearc basins' extending along this plate boundary. These contain deep, stratified sedimentary sequences, dating up to the Eocene (Dunbar et al. 1990). Most lie just offshore. Yet unusually on the south coast, the forearc basin known as the 'Pisco Formation', or colloquially as the 'Tablazo de Ica', lies onshore, as a great expanse of sedimentary rock some 70 kilometres wide east to west and extending some 100 kilometres north to south.

Over millennia the south coast rivers that drain the eastern Andean highlands have incised their courses deep into this sedimentary tableland. Its topography is therefore typical of so-called 'basin-range' deserts — one of two main types of desert based on topographical architecture. While most of the world's deserts, typified by the Sahara, are so-called 'shield and platform' deserts and have a topography of vast plains and huge shallow basins, 'basin-range' deserts, by contrast, occur in relatively active tectonic areas and have topographies dominated by alternating mountains and basins, with a much higher ratio of mountains to plains. They are therefore characterised by enclosed drainage systems (Cooke *et al.* 1993). Meanwhile, the surface of the Peruvian south coast desert has been scoured by more than 20 million years of aeolian erosion in a relentlessly arid climate. This has exposed rock strata from the Miocene through to the Eocene, filled with the fossils of the ancient seabed of those epochs. They are therefore highly calcareous. Figures 2.1 and 2.2 show the south coast of Peru from Landsat 7 photographs and mark points of particular interest that we will visit in more detail throughout.

Figure 2.1. The south coast of Peru

Between the sedimentary Tablazo and the ocean lie the ranges of the Coastal Cordillera, formed from the ancient igneous rock of the coastal batholith. Dating back more than 600 million years these are the very basement of the Andes themselves. Rich in iron and other minerals, they make vivid red and dark purple splashes of rock and sands where they are exposed across the desert tableland. These ancient but very hard rock formations still retain considerable altitudes, rising abruptly out of the Pacific all along the southern littoral—they profoundly affect the climate of the south coast.

Figure 2.2. The lower Ica Valley and lower Río Grande de Nazca, identifying various places mentioned in the text

Hyperaridity: the South Coast Climate

On the south coast the effects of the inversion layer that dictates the peculiar climate of the Peruvian coast are blocked from extending into the interior hinterland by this Coastal Cordillera. From the lower Ica Valley the clouds of the inversion layer can be seen banked up and spilling over the seaward horizon of the Lomas de Ullujaya, which rise to almost a thousand metres along the coast. The fog-drip, *lomas* vegetation associated with winter *garúa* is therefore found along their seaward heights. Inland, the wide desert hinterland of the Tablazo de Ica is consequently less influenced by the 'abnormalities' of the Peruvian coastal climate and is much more typical of a sub-tropical desert.

The skies of the south coast are rarely covered by the constant stratus cloud of winter. The sun is visible all year round and the interior deserts of Ica and Nazca experience 350–360 days of sunshine per year. So, while in Ica there is an average of 7.73 hours of sun per day over the whole year (Table 2.1), in the valley of Chincha—just 100 kilometres to the north but typical of the usual Peruvian coastal climate—this average is a mere 1.76 hours.

Constant, year-round sunshine makes the south coast valleys much hotter, and their air drier, than the rest of the coast. Intense sunshine during the day, dry soils and intense heat loss at night cause much more extreme daily and seasonal temperature fluctuations. In the Samaca Basin of the lower Ica Valley we have recorded diurnal variation in the ambient air temperature during winter from 4 °C at night to 35 °C at midday. Such daily temperature ranges are likely among the highest anywhere on earth (Prohaska 1973).

Table 2.1. Temperatures and hours of sunshine in the middle Ica Valley

Month	Maximum temperature (°C)		Minimum temperature (°C)		Average monthly temperature (°C)	Total hours of sunshine per month
	Average	Absolute	Average	Absolute		
January	30.9	35.0	18.7	16.9	24.8	250
February	31.3	36.2	19.2	18.5	25.0	200
March	31.2	35.9	19.3	15.2	25.3	259
April	30.3	34.9	17.3	11.8	23.9	280
May	26.4	33.8	13.6	6.2	20.0	278
June	24.7	31.0	12.7	3.8	18.7	196
July	23.6	32.0	11.4	4.2	17.5	215
August	24.5	29.9	11.2	5.0	17.6	232
September	25.0	30.2	11.1	7.2	18.6	235
October	26.3	32.9	13.4	8.5	19.8	285
November	28.2	32.2	14.4	10.0	21.4	221
December	30.0	33.8	16.9	12.6	23.5	171
Yearly average	27.6	33.2	15.0	10.0	21.3	7.73 (per day)

Source: SENAMHI-Ica 1997 and 1998. Averages from 1992 to 1998. Recorded at Tacama station, middle Ica Valley.

Table 2.2. Average annual rainfall along a transect up the Ica Valley

Location		Altitude (metres a.s.l.)	Average annual precipitation[a] (mm)
Ocucaje	Lower coastal valley	320	0.3
City of Ica	Middle coastal valley	410	2.8
Huamani	Upper coastal valley	800	14.8
Mullichimpana	Andean foothills	1,800	79.6
Acora	Andean foothills	1,800	195.7
Santiago de Chocorvos	Andean highlands	2,500	181.4
Tambo	Andean highlands	3,250	250.3

Source: ONERN (1971).
Notes: [a] Over five-year period, 1964–9.

Rainfall, such as it is along the Peruvian coast, varies with altitude and with latitude. Moving north, closer to the tropical Ecuadorian climate, precipitation increases slightly. On the south coast it virtually never rains. The average annual precipitation at Ocucaje in the lower Ica Valley is just 0.3 mm. Further inland, however—and increasing with altitude—precipitation does occur from that sometime spill-over from Amazonia (Table 2.2).

Air humidity in the coastal valleys of Ica and Nazca is lower than the extremely high figures experienced year round on most of the Peruvian coast. Nonetheless, the air, particularly at night and in the early mornings, is still humid compared with most desert regions owing to the persistent winds blowing along the river valley courses from the sea. The air humidity in the town of Ica in the middle Valley varies between 57 per cent and 78 per cent over the year (SENHAMH-Ica 1997, 1998) and humidity increases markedly down the valley with proximity to the sea. Yet because of the strong winds and constant sunshine, evaporation rates are very high. The evaporation rate recorded, for example, at Pampa Villacurí means that a single hectare area of surface water loses almost 22,000 cubic metres of water per year.

Strong winds are the other characteristic that defines the climate of the south coast. These winds blow persistently from the south-east (Parker Gay 1999). They originate with the same south-east trades that affect the entire Peruvian coast, but are greatly augmented and swung westward by a 'sea-breeze' front as sunshine warms the wide desert hinterland along the south coast during the day, creating extreme temperature differences between the land and the sea (McCauley *et al.* 1977). In the lower Ica Valley the wind speed profile, daily duration and direction are extraordinarily strong and uniform. Mornings are still, but by afternoon and until sunset, the wind picks up. These winds are particularly strong during September through to November when the trade wind intensities combine with the effects of summer insolation (Parker Gay 1999). Wind velocities in the Samaca Basin were measured continuously over seven months to January 2005 by a Davis cabled weather station. The average monthly wind speeds recorded varied between 32.3 kph (for October

Table 2.3. Average wind speeds recorded in the Samaca Basin, lower Ica Valley

	Jul	Aug	Sept	Oct	Nov	Dec	Jan	Average
Maximum wind velocity (kph)	75.66	112.68	115.92	93.24	101.16	82.08	82.08	
Average wind velocity (kph)	28.03	28.83	28.35	32.29	30.16	27.05	26.93	28.80

Source: Alberto Benavides G. & Ing. César Patroni, Samaca, Ica.

2004) and 27 kph (for December 2004). Maximum gusts recorded varied between 116 kph and 82 kph, respectively. Indeed, the overall continuous *average* wind speed for this whole period in the basin was 28.8 kph (Table 2.3). As we will see shortly, the landscape itself here stands in testimony to the great strength and stability of this wind regime.

South Coast Geomorphology: the Regional Scale

In an ancient and hyperarid climate with negligible rainfall over millennia, even during major El Niño events, there are on the south coast only two natural agents of geomorphological change: the rivers and the wind.

The role of rivers

The only sources of water in this coastal desert environment are the rivers, which arise in the Andean highlands and flow westwards into the Pacific. Along these rivers are the 'riparian' oases—the verdant corridors that conjoin mountains and sea. Outside the ephemeral blooming of *lomas* vegetation at higher elevations, life and human settlement, both ancient and modern, are restricted to these riparian valley bottoms. Their edges are starkly defined against the barren desert, often by the edge of an outermost irrigation canal tracing the contact between river basin alluvium and bedrock or dune sands (Figure 2.3B).

Typically, major Peruvian coastal rivers emerge from steep, deeply incised channels running straight to the sea across a narrow coastal plain, at most 50 kilometres wide. Since sea levels stabilised—around five thousand years ago—these rivers have deposited broad, fan-shaped delta complexes whose distal edges extend up to 8 kilometres into the sea (Wells and Noller 1999). But on the south coast, the Ica and Río Grande river systems show a very different geomorphologic configuration. This distinction, as with the area's climate, arises because of the widening of the south coastal desert caused by the uplifted sedimentary rock plateau of the Tablazo de Ica.

In its upper reaches in the Andean foothills, the Río Ica flows south-west like most Peruvian coastal rivers. It emerges on to the coastal plain just 48 kilometres south-east of

A Canyon through Lomas de Ullujaya, lower Ica Valley
B Riparian basin, Chiquerio, lower Ica Valley
C Mouth of Río Ica (March 2006)

Figure 2.3. The role of the rivers on the south coast

the Río Pisco, its northern neighbour. Yet then it is diverted to run south parallel to the coast for some 150 kilometres, through a series of wide basins that it has incised into the sedimentary desert tableland. These alternate with narrows and canyons, which occur where the river encounters remnants of the hard and ancient igneous rock of the Andean basement. The last of these downstream is a long canyon cut through the thousand-metre high *lomas* de Ullujaya that run along the Pacific littoral (Figure 2.3A). Finally the river emerges to the sea, now far south of the mouth of the Río Pisco, but almost within sight of the mouth of the Río Grande de Nazca (see Figure 2.1). The Río Grande system likewise comprises ten separate streams which, blocked from the sea by the Coastal Cordillera rising to 1,791 metres at Cerro Huaricangana, converge to form a single outlet to the sea. So, neither the Ica nor the Río Grande drainage has a wide alluvial delta. Rather, their mouths are mere patches of marsh that emerge from narrow canyons to the sea (Figure 2.3C) and the rich alluvial sediments they carry are deposited within the series of wide basins along their long courses.

These alluvial basins are full of traces of their ancient inhabitants and archaeologists have long contrasted the valleys with the broad floodplains and wide ocean frontage of the other valleys of the Peruvian coast (Silverman 1993: 3–8). Kroeber (1944: 25), for instance, notes that 'the amount of cultivatable land in Ica and Río Grande valleys is strictly limited, and however dense the population, it could never have been very great absolutely'. Kosok (1965: 51), meanwhile, describes the Río Grande de Nazca drainage as 'minute, isolated valleys that lie scattered over one of the world's driest deserts'. Engel (1981: 11) likewise observes that whereas the northerly valleys, 'though short, end up in broad cones with space for ample farmland and for numerous settlements and dense settlements', in the Ica and Nasca drainages, 'the plots where farming could be practiced here are not found near the sea, but inland'.

The role of the wind

The extraordinary wind regime of the south coast has etched its effects upon the landscape on vast scales (see Figure 2.2). These include dune fields and yardangs.

Yardangs (a Turkmen word co-opted into geomorphology) are wind-abraded ridges aligned with the wind. They vary greatly in dimension but in classic form have a steep, windward 'prow' with a long, gentle lee slope (Cooke *et al.* 1993) and they arise only in unidirectional (or 'unimodal') wind regimes. The yardangs of the Tablazo de Ica are truly enormous – kilometres long and hundreds of metres high (Figure 2.4A). Indeed these 'mega-yardangs' are testimony both to the strength and stability of the wind regime here and to the great age of this desert (McCauley *et al.* 1977).

Although the Peru–Chile Desert generally has rather few areas of dunes (Cooke *et al.* 1993), the south coast is exceptional. Great expanses of the Tablazo are covered with barchan dune fields, along three principal 'wind currents', channelled by topography into the Ica Valley (Parker Gay 1999; see Figures 2.1 and 2.4C). Wherever the unidirectional winds encounter hills or rock outcrops, anchored dunes have formed. Some are of great size. A dune known as Cerro Blanco, for instance, rises to more than a thousand metres over the town of Nazca: high enough for its summit to sustain *lomas* vegetation. Finer wind-entrained particles are deposited all the way up the Andean footslopes to altitudes of 2,500 metres, forming extensive accumulations of loess (Eitel *et al.* 2005, Mächtle *et al.* 2006). Loess deposits in the Quebrada de Cansas in the Ica Valley are up to six metres thick and cover some 30,000 hectares (Wellmann 1998).

The Rivers of the South Coast

A final characteristic of the Peruvian south coast, and one to which archaeologists also often draw attention, is the apparently poor hydrology of its rivers. Menzel *et al.* (1964: 5) for instance describe the Río Ica as 'one of the poorest in water of all the major rivers of

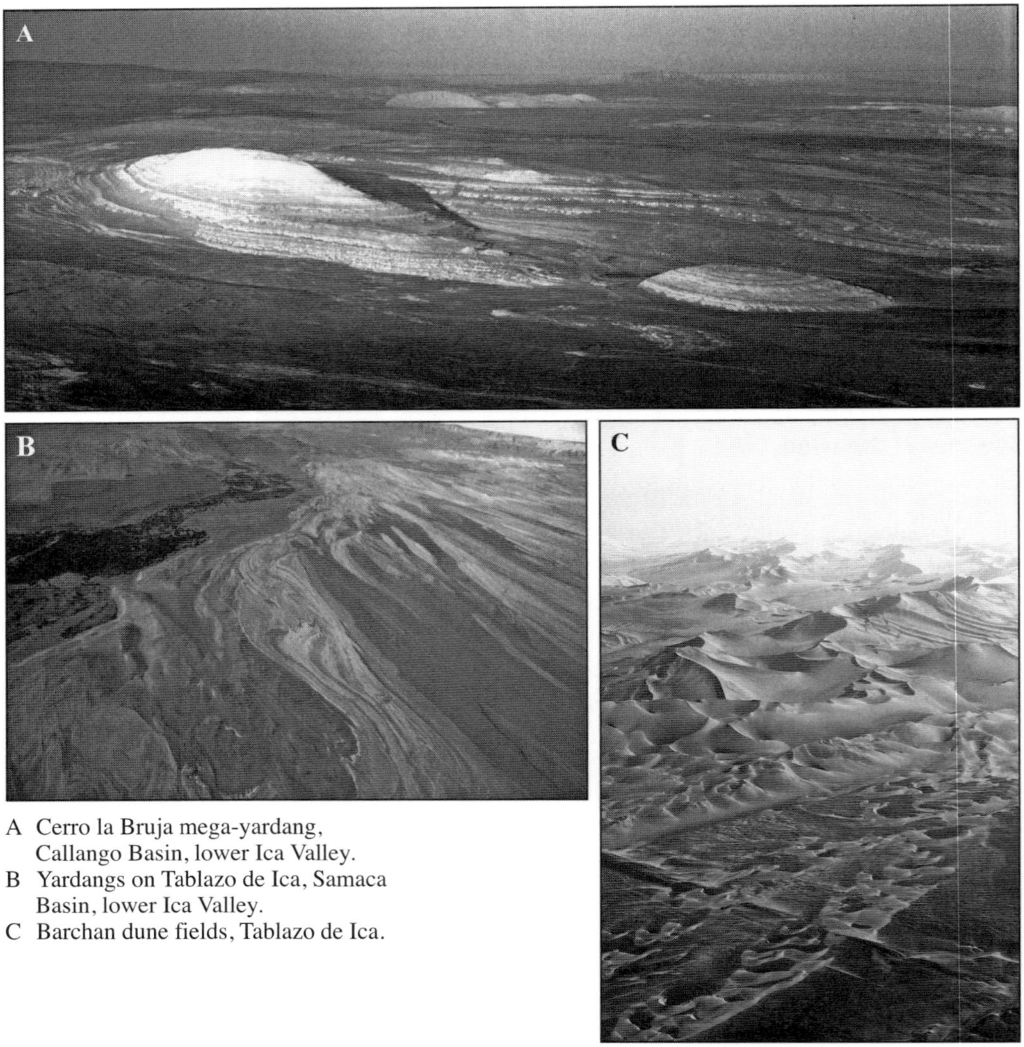

A Cerro la Bruja mega-yardang, Callango Basin, lower Ica Valley.
B Yardangs on Tablazo de Ica, Samaca Basin, lower Ica Valley.
C Barchan dune fields, Tablazo de Ica.

Figure 2.4. The role of the wind on the south coast

the Peruvian coast'. Meanwhile, Silverman and Proulx (2002: 44) note that the tributaries of the Río Grande de Nazca 'suffer frequently from scarce water and a variable water regime . . . when water does flow, the volume is far below that of other valley systems further to the north' (see also Craig and Psuty 1968: 60). These comparisons with the well-watered, wide valleys of the north and central coasts frequently colour interpretations of the south coast archaeological record. Yet, as we will see, some of this owes more to impression than to fact.

Surface flow

In common with almost all coastal rivers, the rivers of the south coast have as their sources the limited summer rainfall that occurs above 2,000 m on the western Andean watersheds and snow melt into lakes in the high sierra. Surface flow is therefore seasonal, water appearing in January and lasting until March or April. The south coast rivers have very few high altitude lakes in their catchments. Indeed, the Río Ica has none. This lack of natural reservoirs certainly exacerbates their erratic flow—increasing the severity of both periodic floods and droughts. Droughts of up to seven years in duration have been recorded in the Ica Valley and the Río Grande de Nazca drainage during the past century (Wellmann 1998) and, as we will see later, there is evidence of even harsher droughts in prehistoric times.

Table 2.4 compares the hydrological data for the rivers of the south coast since 1922 with those of the valleys of Chincha and Pisco to the north. They show precisely why the impression arises that the hydrology of the south coast rivers is far poorer than that of their immediate northern neighbours. For the average annual surface flow of the Río Ica over this period was only 257 million m^3 per annum, considerably less than half that of the Río Pisco and the Río San Juan of the Chincha Valley to the north. Figure 2.5A meanwhile shows how the annual flow of the Río Ica has oscillated erratically about that average (with a standard deviation of over 150 million m^3).

The picture of surface flow for the Río Grande de Nazca is more complicated because this river consists of ten separate tributaries. Although these are individually small, their combined total average annual surface flow of 764 million m^3 is in fact quite substantial. Moreover, other data shown in Table 2.4 imply that the single observation of river surface flow is of only partial use in comparing water availability between these dryland valleys.

Firstly, regardless of their seeming hydrological poverty, the actual number of hectares under agriculture and urban populations supported today in the southern river valleys is broadly the same as for their northern neighbours. This is because, as with many dryland river systems (see for instance Graf 2002), a substantial—and by definition difficult to quantify—amount of river flow is sub-surface. Moreover, the total catchment areas for the Río Ica and Río Grande are larger than those of rivers to the north. And the very distinct geomorphological configurations of the south coast river valleys mean that this sub-surface flow and groundwater storage is, relatively, much more significant than in the Chincha and Pisco valleys.

Sub-surface flow

As we have seen, the Río Ica and the Río Grande de Nazca are blocked from the sea by the uplifted formations of the Tablazo de Ica. This same topographic peculiarity diverges these rivers into much longer courses than their northern neighbours and creates, in effect, a vast natural dam—which preserves high groundwater levels. So these southern rivers *lose* little

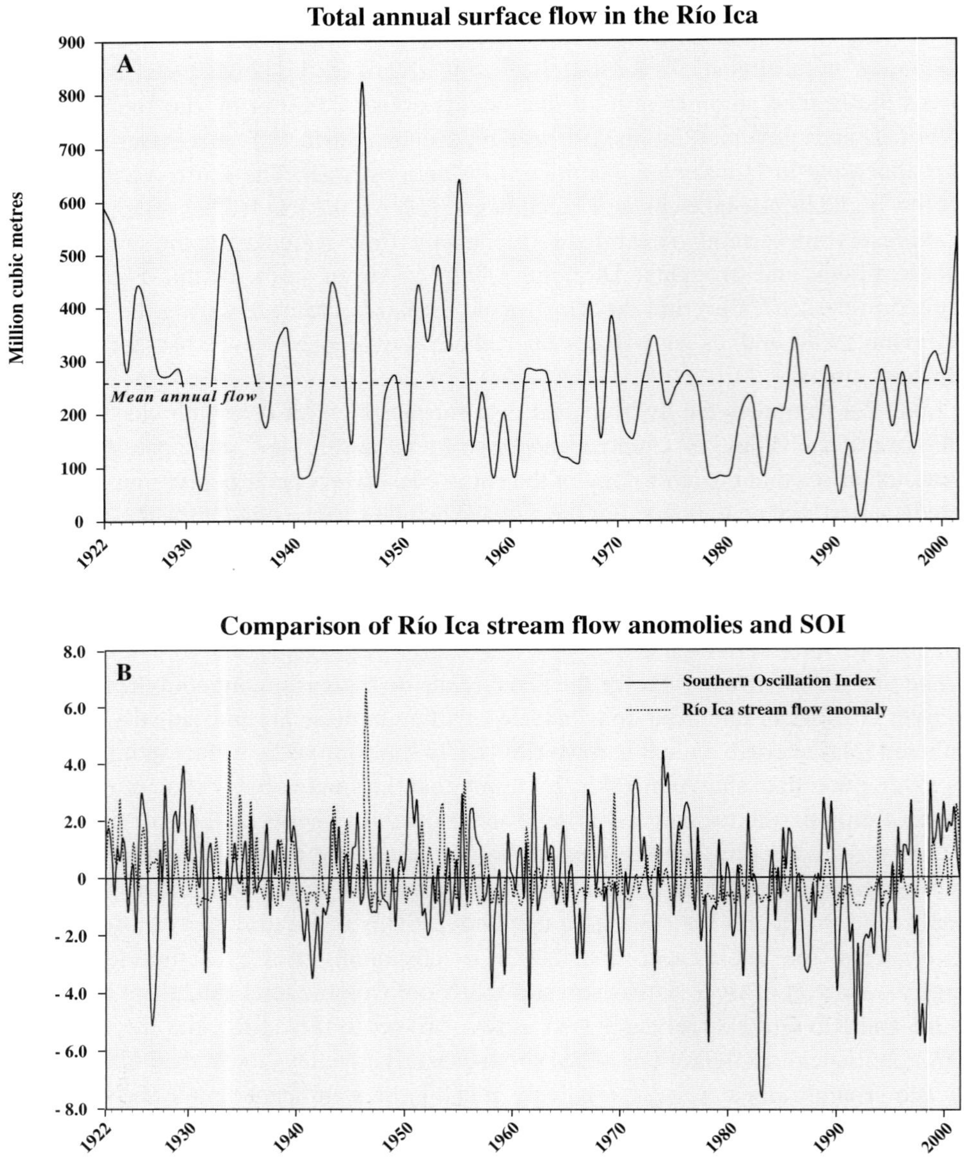

Sources: SENAMHI–Ica (1997, 1998, 2002).

Notes:

A Annual total surface flow in the Río Ica (months of January to April) measured at Achirana gauge.

B Comparison of variations in the Southern Oscillation Index (SOI) and annual Río Ica stream flow anomalies (months of January to April), where:

$$\text{Flow anomaly}_{(\text{month } x)} = \frac{\text{Flow Velocity}_{(\text{month } x)} - \text{Average Flow Velocity}_{(1992\text{–}2001)}}{\text{Average Flow Velocity}_{(1992\text{–}2001)}}$$

Figure 2.5. Historical Río Ica hydrology

Table 2.4. A comparison of the hydrologies of the rivers of the south coast with their northern neighbours

Valley	River	Total catchment area (km^2)[a]	Catchment area above 2,000 m (km^2)[a,b]	Natural reservoir volume[a] (million m^3)	Average annual surface flow (million m^3)	Maximum annual flow (million m^3)[c]	Minimum annual flow (million m^3)	Area under irrigation (hectares)[a]	Urban population[a]
Chincha	San Juan	4,082	2,475	95	567[d]	2,326[d]	91[d]	30,000	200,000
Pisco	Pisco	4,438	3,100	50	845[e]	1,623[e]	446[e]	24,850	–
Ica	Ica	7,437	1,807	0	257[f]	823[f]	5[f]	30,000	300,000
Nazca	Santa Cruz	437	–	–	5[a]	–	–	1,843	
	Grande	1,820	–	–	514[a]	–	–	2,875	45,000
	Palpa	643	–	–	45[a]	–	–	927	12,000
	Viscas	845	–	–	47[a]	–	–	1,272	
	Ingenio	1,660	–	–	98[a]	–	–	3,177	
	Socos	134	–	–	1[a]	–	–	103	
	Sub-total Río Grande upstream of Río Nasca	**5,539**	**–**	**–**	**710**	**–**	**–**	**10,197**	**57,000**
	Aja	513	–	–	24[a]	–	–	3,332	
	Tierras Blancas	508	–	–	11[a]	–	–	2,937	
	Taruga	385	–	–	3[a]	–	–	1,899	
	Chauchilla	321	–	–	1[a]	–	–	2,762	
	Las Trancas	797	–	–	15[a]	–	–	3,833	
	Sub-total Río Nasca	**2,524**	**–**	**–**	**54**	**–**	**–**	**14,763**	
	Total Río Grande	**8,083**	**–**	**–**	**764[a]**	**–**	**–**	**24,960**	**57,000**

Notes: [a] Source: Wellmann (1998).
[b] i.e. receiving significant precipitation.
[c] Quantifications of river flows are based upon flow velocity (m^3/s). During floods this is impossible to measure directly. Thus, velocity figures derived during flood periods and then multiplied by time duration are subjective.
[d] Source: SENAMHI Chincha. Unpublished data. Measurements 1922–1980.
[e] Source: Tahal (1969).
[f] Source: SENAMHI-Ica. Measurements 1922– 2001.

water to the sea. While the Río Chincha, for example, discharges around 420 million m^3 of flow to the sea in normal years — and up to 2,000 million m^3 in flood years — surface flow in the Río Ica may not reach the sea at all, as water tables in the many basins along its long course are replenished.

The significance of these groundwater horizons in Ica is demonstrated by the discrepancy between the average river surface flow of 257 million m^3 recorded at the Achirana flow station at the head of the valley, and the actual annual consumption of water in the valley of around 740 million m^3 (Wellmann 1998), the difference being accounted for by the extraction of groundwaters. These comprise both the underflows of the surface watercourses and also other 'autonomous' water supplies which flow through the fault complexes of Cretaceous shists and Miocene strata which make up the bedrock of the southern river valleys.

One of the few of these sub-surface flows to have been well studied is that of the so-called Río Seco in Ica (Taltasse 1973). The sources of the Río Seco are the same highland headwaters as for the Río Ica, but they eventually follow the axis of geological fault complexes in the more conventional east to west direction of coastal rivers, rather than being diverted south like the main course of the Río Ica. The Río Seco therefore flows under the Pampas of Lanchas and Villacurí, effectively linking the Ica and Pisco drainages (see Figure 2.1 above). Water temperature and the chemical composition of its groundwater horizon clearly distinguish it from the waters of the Río Pisco (Taltasse 1973). And its sub-surface flow is estimated at around 70 million m^3 per annum (Tahal 1969 cited in Wellman 1998).

Today, the course of the Río Seco is marked only by patches of huarango trees — which, as we will see, have very deep roots — across the Pampas of Lanchas and Villacurí. In the early 1960s, and 'contrary to all expectations' (Taltasse 1973: 109), wells dug in the Pampa of Villacurí promptly produced copious water. Today, some 75 million m^3 of water per annum is pumped from this groundwater horizon to supply agro-industry (Wellmann 1998). Yet, the Río Seco subterranean water source had long been exploited, even in historical times. In the fifteenth century the Jesuit Order had, for example, produced grapes for wine in a series of 'delightful' lagoons along its course on the Lanchas Pampa through sunken field agriculture (Sánchez Elías 1957). There is even some suggestion that, until a series of earthquakes between 1644 and 1687, there had been surface flow in the Río Seco, arising effectively as a branch of the Río Ica at Cerro Prieto, and flowing westward to enter the sea at the Paracas peninsula (Wellmann 1998).

Such sub-surface water horizons underlie all the Río Ica drainage. They are many and complex. Well-diggers report encountering multiple horizons, which occur as waters become trapped above impermeable calcrete layers. Autonomous groundwater drains are encountered at up to 120 metres depth. In the basins of the lower Ica Valley, the water table usually lies at only around 4 metres beneath the surface. Here, water can often be seen flowing, when higher up, in the city of Ica itself, the riverbed is quite dry. Inevitably groundwater resources are very difficult to quantify. In the 1970s the Peruvian Ministry of Agriculture estimated the total sub-surface flow in the Ica drainage to between 300 and 330 million m^3

per annum (ONERN 1971). Combined with the underflows of the Río Seco, this conservatively puts the total average annual Río Ica hydrology at some 630 million m^3.

Sub-surface water flows are also a defining feature of the Río Grande de Nazca drainage and their importance has long been appreciated by its inhabitants (see Silverman and Proulx 2002: 205–214 for a review). Indeed, Silverman (1993: 12) observes that Cahuachi—the principal Nasca Period archaeological site on the Río Nasca—is known locally as the 'place where water appears'. She notes that, 'even during the dry season there were always points of permanent seepage'. Proulx (in Silverman and Proulx 2002: 212) reports that residents of Usaca on the Río Poroma hear 'the sound of a waterfall below them'. Moreover, sub-surface water has been exploited for centuries here through systems of vertical shafts known as '*ojos*' (eyes), often linked by subterranean filtration galleries and reservoirs (Schreiber and Lancho Rojas 1995). Some of this system is still in use in Nazca today. Indeed, some argue that orientation of the ancient and famous 'Nazca Lines' is associated with sub-surface water flows in the transmissive faults underlying the Pampa de San José (Johnson cited in Silverman and Proulx 2002: 185–19).

So *in toto*, the hydrologies of these south coast rivers are not necessarily for poorer than those of their northern neighbours. The natural dam of the uplifted Tablazo de Ica preserves substantial sub-surface water resources from being lost to the sea. This groundwater storage smoothes out some of the effects of a highly erratic river flow. Like huge sponges, the basins of the Río Ica and Río Grande drainages have groundwater horizons lying just beneath their surfaces, and all down their very long diverted courses, riparian oases flourished and cultivation was possible.

There is also little doubt that this sub-surface supply has been over-exploited in recent decades. Since the peak of its exploitation during the 1960s the total area of land irrigated and cultivated in the Ica Valley has fallen by around 9,000 hectares. Of a total of 900 tubular wells recently inventoried by the Ministry of Agriculture in the Ica drainage, only around 350 are in regular use, extracting some 300 million m^3 of water per annum (Wellmann 1998).

History of El Niño in the Ica Valley

Now and again the peculiar climatic regime of the Peruvian coast is disrupted by the ocean–atmosphere perturbation of the El Niño Southern Oscillation (ENSO) phenomenon (or as it is more widely known, just El Niño). During these events, ocean temperatures are raised by a warm equatorial counter-current, which first appears during the month of January. The effects of El Niño are complex and vary greatly along the Peruvian coast. In general, major events warm sea surface temperatures, disrupting the maritime food chain, bring torrential rainfall to the north coast and dramatically increase precipitation on the high seaward mountain slopes throughout the Andean cordillera, causing rivers to flood.

During 1997/8 an El Niño event occurred with particular impact on the south coast. The entire town of Ica suffered an inundation of more than two metres in depth (Figure

2.6B). Skies were often dark, with occasional lightning flashes and bursts of light rainfall —so unusual that they caused hysteria. Nonetheless, even during this so-called 'Super El Niño' event in the lower Ica Valley itself no significant rainfall was recorded.

The history of El Niño is a matter of considerable interest and its past duration, intensity, extent and frequency the subject of much research and debate (see for instance Thompson *et al.* 1985, 1995, Rollins *et al.* 1986, DeVries 1987, DeVries and Wells 1990, Sandweiss *et al.* 1996, Moy *et al.* 2002). Some of this debate revolves around our ability safely to associate flood deposits observed in the geomorphological record with past El Niño events (as employed for instance by Wells 1987, 1990, DeVries *et al.* 1997, Keefer *et al.* 1998, Wells and Noller 1999).

Ortlieb and Vargas (2003), for instance, review various attempts to link debris-flow deposits in the stratigraphy of coastal valleys with ENSO past occurrences. They conclude (2003: 48) that 'in coastal southern Peru, debris-flow activity is not straightforwardly related to ENSO conditions'. Their study pertains mainly to the early Holocene, but it includes also an analysis of the recent historical stream flow of the Majes Valley on the central Peruvian coast. They argue that this record shows no clear-cut correlation with historical El Niño events. This serves as a caution against the facile assumption that flood deposits are per se indicators of past El Niño events, or indeed, that their impacts may easily be generalised across different valleys (see also Eitel and Mächtle 2009). Archaeologists are occasionally guilty of such simplifications.

Figure 2.5B shows a comparison between anomalies in the Río Ica stream flow and the Southern Oscillation Index (SOI) since 1922 ('anomalies' here being defined as degree of divergence from the average stream flow). Major positive or negative perturbations in the SOI are associated with El Niño (warmer seas and more rainfall in the foothills) or La Niña (colder seas, no rainfall), respectively, on the coast of Peru. The comparison uses the available data—over a relatively short time period. It also ignores the complications arising from phasing: SOI perturbations taking some months to translate into surface flow in the Río Ica. The comparison shows that the relationship between anomalies in the Río Ica stream flow and the SOI is indeed far from straightforward. Yet the two datasets do demonstrate significant correlation (Beresford-Jones 2005). It is therefore reasonable to assume that, in the case of the Río Ica at least, flood deposits of a certain size can be associated with past El Niño events.

Revaluating South Coast Limitations

The distinctive climate, geomorphology and hydrology of the river valleys of the south coast have profound implications both for their riparian ecologies and for agricultural productivity on their rich alluvial soils. Importantly, they call into question archaeology's insistence on interpreting their prehistoric past in terms of 'constraints' and 'restrictions', for this is not well substantiated by the actual physical conditions of the south coast.

A 180° panorama of the Río Ica in the Samaca Basin, lower Ica Valley during the 1997/8 El Niño.
B City of Ica in April 1998.
C Incision in a Late Intermediate Period archaeological site H-8 in the Samaca Basin made by the Río Ica during the 1997/8 El Niño (see D below).
D Aerial view of the lower Samaca Basin in June 1999 showing the effects of the 1997/8 El Niño flood, identifying various archaeological sites mentioned later in the text.

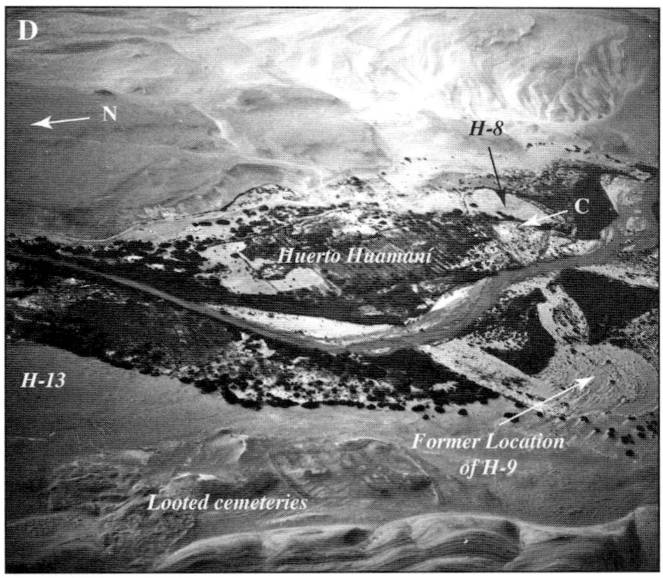

Figure 2.6. The 1997/8 El Niño event in the Ica Valley

Annually replenished, the alluvial sediments of these valleys are extremely fertile. Their very dry climate greatly restricts insect and disease impact on crops. The measure of 'thermal integration' (accumulated degrees Celsius per day), or so-called 'heat units', is crucial to agriculturalists because its corollary is photosynthesis and the number of agricultural cycles that can be maintained year round. The average thermal integration over the year for

Ica is 3,900 degrees per day, while for Nazca it is 4,460. These are amongst the highest in the world (Wellmann 1998: 44). Thus, depending on the crop, between two and four harvests each year can be obtained. The comparable figure for the Chincha Valley just to the north is only 2,250 degrees per day. So, it is hardly surprising that when large Chilean agro-industrial concerns began large-scale investments in Peru during the early 1990s, they chose first the Ica Valley. Industrial-scale production of tomatoes commenced in 1993. Within four years, using year-round cropping on a 120-day cycle, production levels were attained of 65 tonnes per hectare per annum, comparable to the highest in the world in Chile and Israel (Wellmann 1998).

While the soils and climate of the south coast rank amongst the most productive in the world, the region's obvious limitation is that of water availability. Yet, as we have seen, when sub-surface flows are properly incorporated, the hydrology of the south coast rivers is not far poorer than that of their northern neighbours. And, although the many alluvial basins of the south coast rivers are individually smaller than those wide deltas to the north, there are many of them, down much longer courses, and they lose much less of their erratic water supply to the sea. Moreover, while our area of interest here—the lower Ica Valley—has most certainly been hyperarid for many millennia, recent studies in Palpa, Nazca offer intriguing hints of wetter periods during prehistory in the Andean foothills, from whence of course river flows on the south coast arise (Eitel and Mächtle 2009).

What is true, however, is that many of the physical characteristics of the south coast, such as its very strong sun, extraordinary wind regime and highly erratic river surface flow, define sharp and critical ecological and geomorphological thresholds. Consequently, degradation through El Niño perturbations—or indeed human impact—is more easily provoked. As we will see, it is within this dynamic physical context that proper consideration of the role of humans and their cultural trajectories within a wider ecology becomes so important.

3. A Lost Landscape:

Ancient Settlement of Samaca and Ullujaya

The Lower Ica Valley

Today, casual impressions of the south coast desert are determined by the route of the Pan-American highway. Travelling south along this artery of the Peruvian coast one swings inland as the coastal plain widens south of the Pisco Valley, along the edge of the Andean foothills to leave the great expanse of the Tablazo de Ica between the road and the sea (see Figure 2.2). Presently, one crosses the Pampas of Villacurí, among the wide fields of agro-industry that are the business of Ica today, and thence into the urban ribbons strung along the course of the highway and into the town of Ica itself. This is the middle Ica Valley.

Founded in 1563, Ica is no longer the small town of historical description, sleeping under a hot desert sun amid the shade of woodlands of huarangos and fruit trees. In little more than a single lifetime it has changed beyond recognition. Today it is a sprawl of gimcrack housing and dusty fields sown with plastic bags: an agricultural boom-town, to which thousands, driven by rural poverty and terrorism in the Ayacucho sierra, have flocked to seek new livelihoods. Outside the city, the vast empty pampas have been converted into endless expanses of agro-industrial monocrops through relentless pumping of groundwater from great depths. We will return to this history of change in the middle Ica Valley in Chapter 6. But, as we saw earlier, the Río Ica — quite unlike other rivers of the Peruvian coast — is diverted by the Tablazo de Ica to run parallel to the sea and our interest here lies much further on, down that long course, into the lower Ica Valley.

South of Ica, the Pan-American highway follows the river through the villages of Tate, Santiago and so forth that now all merge one into the other along its route. Then, as the river turns south into the last verdant basin of the middle Ica Valley — Ocucaje — the highway

Chapterhead: Detail of Nasca embroidered textile showing a figure holding a germinating bean and maize stem with a cat headdress, from which emerge a root crop, cf. sweet potato, and an inflorescence in which two animals appear to be feeding (drawing courtesy of the Brooklyn Museum).

parts company with it and emerges on to the barren desert pampa to begin its way south to Nazca. The road down into the lower Ica Valley turns off here—little more than the palimpsest of tyre tracks made by itinerant fishermen, charcoal burners, small-scale nitrate miners and others, whose business takes them south to the lower reaches of the river or the sea. Although, as the condor flies, it is only some 70 kilometres from the highway to the sea, on the ground the road winds interminably among the great windblown yardangs of the Tablazo, along the eastern edge of wide basins scooped out of the desert tableland by the river. It takes some four or five hours for a stout vehicle to reach the ocean.

About halfway down the valley are the basins of Samaca and Ullujaya: our focus here. The lower Ica Valley, as it is generally defined archaeologically (see for instance Massey 1991, Cook 1999), comprises the basins downstream of the Chiquerío batholith outcrop, principally Callango, Ullujaya and Samaca. Downstream of Samaca, the river enters the long canyon cut through the thousand-metre-high *lomas* de Ullujaya and Amara, which run along the Pacific littoral (see Figure 2.1), before it enters a last wide basin, Montegrande, and thence the sea.

These huge basins of the lower Ica Valley present a rather striking contrast to the urban bustle and extensive agriculture of the middle valley, for they are almost entirely desertified and mostly empty of people and cultivation. Although there is some agriculture in Callango, and indeed recently efforts have being made to rejuvenate Ullujaya and Samaca, these are only exceptions that prove a rule: today, human settlement is concentrated in the middle Ica Valley (see Figure 2.1). So was it during the fifteenth century when the Spanish founded the city of Ica there. And yet the archaeological record suggests that this was not always the case.

For, as Massey (1991: 317) notes, the middle Ica Valley was intensively settled rather late in the long trajectory of south coast prehistory—'during the Late Intermediate with the expansion of the Chirana irrigation canal from the upper valley to the zone of Tacaraca-Ica Viejo, the Ica-Inca capital in the upper middle valley'. Prior to this it was the *lower* Ica Valley that was the site of most human settlement, and, as we will see, its archaeological remains attest to substantial prehistoric populations.

Figure 3.1 shows the Callango Basin today. It seems scarcely credible from its presently impoverished condition that, during the first millennium BC, this basin was likely the centre of human settlement in the Ica Valley and the location of—among others—two large habitation sites, known as Animas Bajas and Animas Altas, covering 50 and 100 hectares, respectively (Massey 1991). But the Callango Basin is huge, with traces of its lost vegetation extending over some 3,600 hectares. Ullujaya and Samaca are somewhat smaller, but nevertheless substantial, basins and, if anything, show even greater ecological degradation. The lower Ica Valley thereby presents a *prima facie* case for dramatically changed ecological and landscape conditions.

This has long prompted archaeologists to speculate on how environmental conditions may have changed. Strong, for instance, made a brief excursion down the valley in 1941, observing that:

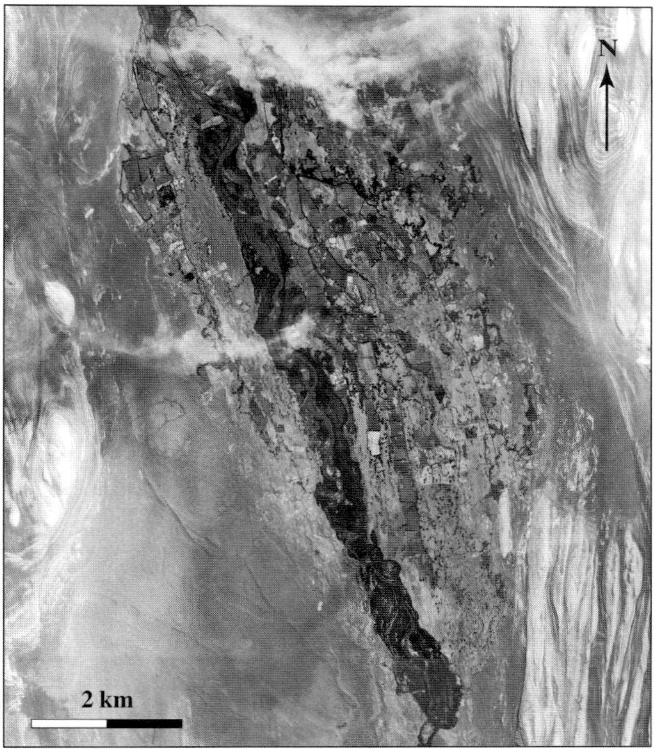

Figure 3.1. The Callango Basin, lower Ica Valley

> It is already apparent that in earlier times this part of the Ica valley was thickly populated. Today, owing to the almost complete diversion of the water of the Ica river in the upper part of its drainage area, the lower portions of the valley below Ocucaje are desolate and largely without habitants. Even the most cursory examination indicates that this was not always the case. (Strong *et al*. 1943: 23)

Much later, Massey (1991: 317) made an archaeological survey of the Callango Basin, warning that 'it is necessary not to judge prehistoric settlement decisions by modern conditions of the valley, which has undergone dramatic changes in appearance and land use within the last fifty years'.

During the late 1980s a large-scale archaeological survey was conducted of the entire course of the lower Ica Valley by Anita Cook, Miguel Pazos and other colleagues (Cook 1994), which aimed to identify the location, approximate size and time period of all the archaeological sites in the lower valley. Cook (1999: 65; my translation) observes of the lower Ica Valley that 'today's ecological conditions show very poor conservation and do not necessarily represent the conditions of the past'.

The Cook survey provides a useful background for our own archaeological investigations, which have a rather different purpose. Our focus was smaller scale, higher resolution survey of parts of the Ullujaya and Samaca basins chosen precisely because they exhibit clear evidence of environmental degradation and diminished land use over time. We aimed to trace changes in geomorphology, ecology and land use and, by examining these alongside the sequence of human occupation and social change revealed through archaeology, to try to answer the questions of *when*, *how* and indeed *why* such changes took place. For, preserved precisely because of their subsequent abandonment, these basins have a very remarkable archaeological record (Figure 3.2). As Rossel Castro (1977: 59; my translation) puts it, 'in Samaka and Ullujaya one may find all the strata of the civilisations of Ica. This little-known region is of great importance to the field of archaeology.'

Archaeological Investigations In the Samaca and Ullujaya Basins

The archaeological investigations reported here were the collaboration of very many people (see Acknowledgements). In particular they owe everything to the founding by Alberto Benavides Ganoza in Samaca in 1994 of an experiment in traditional agriculture, the Escuela Libre de Puerto Huamaní—or 'Huerto Huamaní' (Benavides Ganoza 2004)—in which I was fortunate to participate; and to my co-director for subsequent fieldwork—Susana Arce Torres of the Museo Regional de Ica.

Our rubric was that advocated by Butzer (1982) of archaeology as human ecology. Since fields and canal systems are environments modified by humans, they are 'anthropogenic' in the same sense as, say, an ancient habitation site. This approach avoids the essentially arbitrary distinctions between so-called 'on-site' and 'off-site' locations. Indeed, even entire degraded landscapes may be artefacts. Our methodology combined geomorphological and archaeobotanical approaches. Understanding geomorphological change is a requisite for interpreting the extant archaeological record and indeed to understanding why the landscape itself looks as it does today. This will be the task of Chapter 4. Archaeobotany meanwhile offers direct and indirect insight into ecological change through analysis of vegetation changes in the wider landscape and the proxy indications of human diet. These will be discussed in Chapter 5. Here we will review the archaeological record encountered today in the lower Ica Valley. As we will see, aside from its intrinsic archaeological interest, careful consideration of this record allows us to *date* processes of landscape change.

This archaeological record was examined through fieldwork over five years, which included detailed survey to produce very accurate three-dimensional maps of the topography and archaeological and landscape features of the Ullujaya and Samaca basins, and excavation to define and date archaeological features such as habitation sites, platforms, relict canal fragments and so forth (for further details on excavation and survey methodology see Beresford-Jones *et al.* 2004, 2009b, Beresford-Jones 2005).

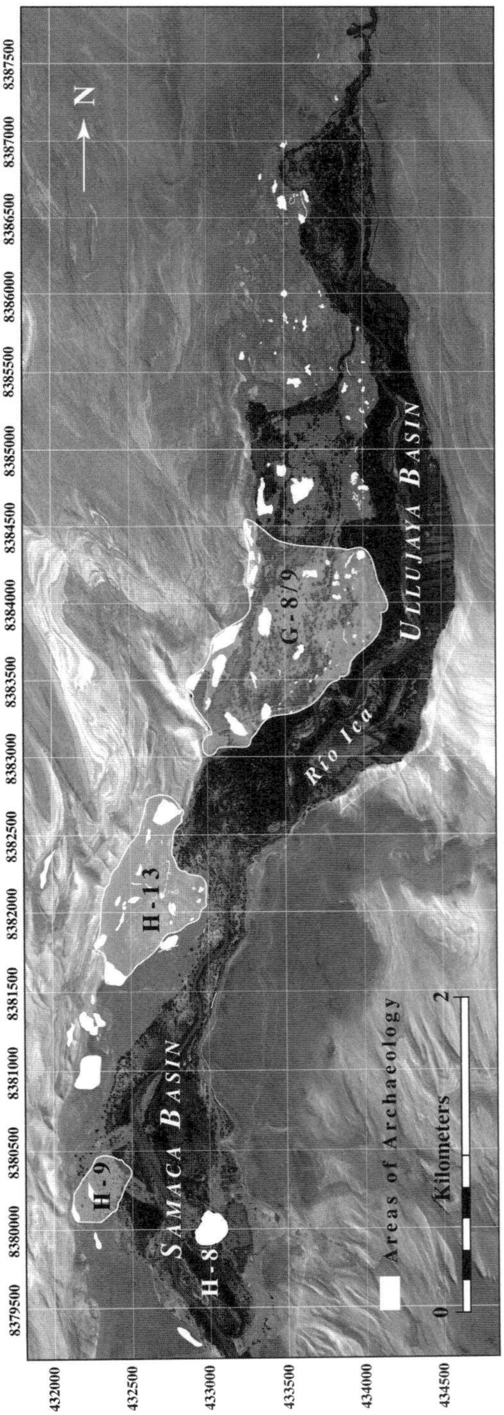

Figure 3.2. Map of area of investigation: the Ullujaya and Samaca basins of the lower Ica Valley

Horizon (Menzel 1967, Isbell 1988, Schreiber 1992, 1999, 2001). Menzel's (1967) ceramic typology for Wari has become, as Isbell (2001: 52; my translation) notes, 'one of the most consolidated . . . of all Andean prehistory' and its relative chronology would have us believe that the rise and fall of the Wari Middle Horizon were swift. As Schreiber (1992: 276) puts it, 'each phase of the Middle Horizon 1B, 2A and 2B, is estimated to have lasted only about 50 years . . . if this is accurate, the Wari Empire lasted only about 150 years'. Yet in the face of mounting C^{14} evidence, this view is now being abandoned. As Cook (2004: 158) summarises: 'instead of a 200-year span (approximately AD 650–850) during which time the empire flourished, the time frame has doubled (approximately AD 550–1000)'. Such earlier dates put the start of the Middle Horizon well back into the period we would call 'Nasca' on the south coast following the nomenclature of the Dawson seriation.

The archaeological evidence indicates millennia of interactions between the south coast and its immediate sierra hinterlands: Ayacucho. At the dawn of the Wari Middle Horizon, however, there was a significant shift in the intensity of those interactions. The ceramic typology of the later Nasca Phases seems to reflect a splintering of the earlier, conservative Nasca artistic canon that had been shared across the many, small, scattered basins of the south coast river systems (Silverman and Proulx 2002: 252). The material culture of the south coast just prior to the Middle Horizon — so-called 'Nasca 8 and 9' — has little in common with the preceding ceramic phases of the Early Intermediate. Indeed, the occurrence of particularly 'Nasca 9' far afield from the south coast is sometimes taken as evidence of 'Nasca-influence', although evidence for the precise direction of this influence is largely lacking. Certainly, however, the later Nasca Phases represent the first evidence of the widespread movement of people and ideas that was to receive its ultimate expression in the Middle Horizon.

The millennium or so which precedes the Nasca Period on the south coast (the so-called Early Horizon) is divided according to ten phases of the 'Ocucaje' ceramic sequence made by Menzel *et al.* (1964) and named after the Ocucaje Basin, which lies only some 30 kilometres upstream from our area of interest. Uncertainties of detail similar to those for Nasca also attend this ceramic seriation (see for instance Massey 1991, Silverman 1991, Unkel and Kromer 2009).

For all these reasons we will take a conservative approach to dating by means of decorated ceramics in the lower Ica Valley. For the detail of these sequences we will use Menzel *et al.* (1964), Pezzia Assereto (1968) and Cook (1999) for the Ocucaje Phases of the Early Horizon. For the subsequent Nasca Periods of the Early Intermediate we draw upon Pezzia Assereto (1968), Proulx (1968, 2006), Silverman (1993), Hecht (2009) and Browne (personal communication). For the Middle Horizon we follow Menzel (1967), Pezzia Assereto (1968) and Kroeber and Collier (1998); and for the subsequent Late Intermediate Period we use Pezzia Assereto (1968), Menzel (1976) and Marcus (2008).

For our interpretations, however, we will rely only upon broader categories. Thus we define 'Early Nasca' here as Dawson Phases 2 to 5 and 'Late Nasca' as Dawson Phases 6 to 7. Dawson Phases 8 and 9 meanwhile are assigned to the Middle Horizon. This approach

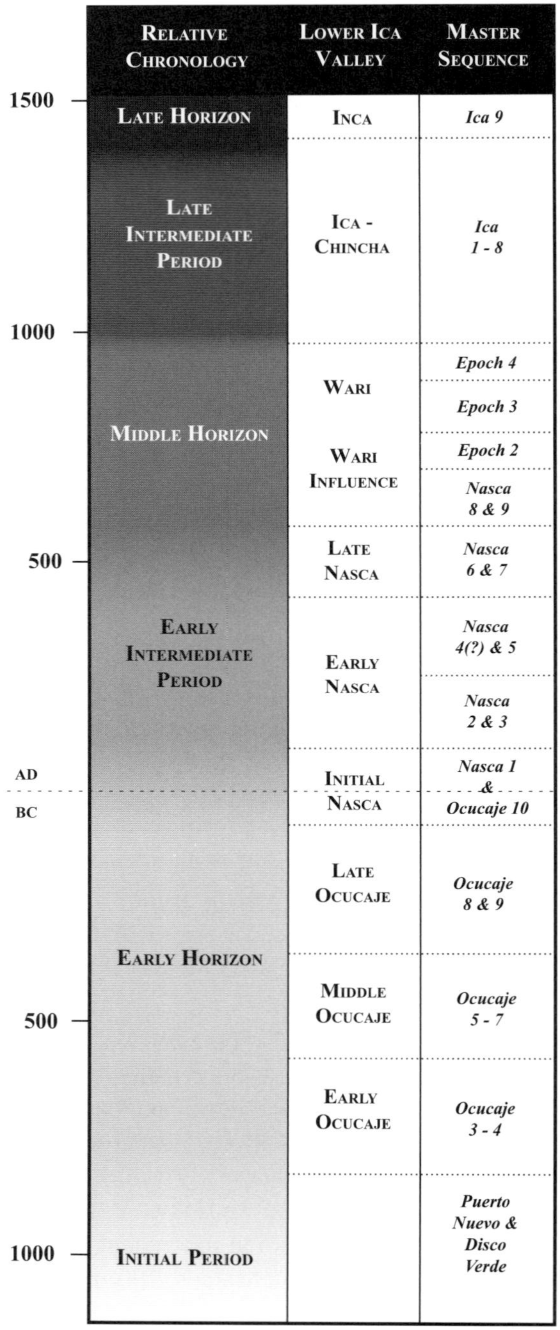

Source: Based on Silverman (1993: 31), Hecht (2009: 230), Unkel & Kromer (2009: 243).

Figure 3.3. Perhistoric chronology of the south coast, Peru also conforms to that recently defined by Hecht (2009) based upon excavated, radiocarbon-dated materials from Palpa, Nazca, although only occasionally will we feel the need to discriminate between his Early and Middle Nasca in our lower Ica Valley contexts.

After all this discussion of their uncertainties, it is important to keep a sense of proportion about the problems of dating using the Ica Valley ceramic typologies. For, notwithstanding their occasional serious shortcomings of detail, their validity is well established in the broad, and very useful for our purposes here of tracing ecological and cultural changes —within a relatively widely defined temporal framework.

Human Settlement Patterns in the Lower Ica Valley

We turn now to the rich archaeological record itself of the Ullujaya and Samaca basins. Despite its austere condition today, the lower Ica Valley is full of the traces of considerable prehistoric human occupation. The Cook survey describes twenty-four areas of archaeological remains in the Ullujaya Basin and fourteen in Samaca (Cook 1994: 133–74). In Ullujaya, for instance, Cook records two large areas of archaeological remains as 'G-8' and 'G-9', defined separately only because they are now divided arbitrarily by a modern road (Cook 1994: 141). Together, they cover more than 100 hectares. In Samaca, meanwhile, 'H-13' is recorded over almost 50 hectares. These extensive testaments to ancient occupation were the particular focus of our high-resolution archaeological survey and targeted excavations. Both H-13 and G-8/9 occupy the surfaces of the relict river terraces, which define much of the landscape of these basins today. Today these are largely barren — although there is some patchy vegetation on Ullujaya G-8/9 as a consequence of a canal cut during the 1950s as part of an effort to grow cotton here (Plate 1). As we will see, however, there is copious evidence that this was not always the case.

Unsurprisingly, G-8/9 and H-13 are revealed, not so much as individual archaeological sites, but as the now-faint traces of multiple occupations over considerable time. They are conglomerates of the remains of human settlement: made up of mounds, fragments of enclosures, platforms and buildings of adobe brick or stone, rubbish middens, ancient floors of post-holes, hearths, cemeteries, and remnants of the ancient agricultural landscape in the form of relict canal courses (Plate 1). We will use the names of G-8/9 and H-13 here as a useful shorthand for the relict river terraces of Ullujaya and Samaca, respectively, on which is situated much of the archaeology revealed by our survey. And we will explore this archaeological record by gradually peeling back the remains of more recent time periods to reveal those of more remote time depths.

The archaeology of later prehistory

The best preserved archaeology in the lower Ica Valley dates, naturally enough, to the later periods of prehistory: the Late Intermediate Period and the Inca Late Horizon, which established its brief but brilliant suzerainty over the south coast for less than a century and half before the Spanish arrived. During the Late Intermediate Period a rich and populous society, sometimes called 'Ica-Chincha', flourished on the south coast, defined by finely made ceramics and tapestry-weave textiles with intricate repetitive patterning. This was a time during which the southern Andean region was broken up into 'an almost unbelievable number of small political units', as Rowe (1946) puts it. Ica-Chincha was larger than most—extending between the south-central coast valleys of Nazca and Cañete—yet it was still a regional polity. Rostworowski (1989) notes its opulence, at the time of its incorporation into the Inca Empire. Pedro Pizarro learnt from conversations with the Inca himself that the *Señor de los Llanos*—the Lord of Chincha—was the Inca's closest friend and ally, who could put to sea 'a hundred thousand rafts' (Rostworowski 1989: 218). Sixteenth-century sources analysed by Rostworowski (1989: 219) describe Chinchano traders carrying out their business all along the Pacific coast. So the south coast in general enjoyed considerable power and prestige during these later periods, based largely it seems upon commerce and marine resources.

The single most conspicuous archaeological site in the lower Ica Valley is a large mound recorded as 'H-8' (Cook 1994: 166) in the lower part of the Samaca Basin on the east bank of the Río Ica (Plate 1). H-8 is preserved almost in its entirety: some 2.5 hectares of complex adobe architecture with its huarango door posts still *in situ*. Surface remains date H-8 to the Late Intermediate through to the Late Horizon and perhaps into the early Colonial Period. A sister site, recorded as 'H-9' on the opposite bank of the river (Cook 1994: 166–7), was largely destroyed by the enormous flood in the valley during the 1997/8 El Niño (see Figure 2.6D). We have not yet undertaken excavation in H-8, but, when the 1997/8 flood destroyed H-9, it also cut a steep section along the western edge of H-8 (see Figure 2.6C), which reveals no underlying stratigraphy dating to earlier time periods. Together, these two sites represent the later prehistoric occupation in the lower Ica Valley.

Yet the first striking observation about the archaeology of the Samaca and Ullujaya basins is that H-8 and H-9 are the only significant occupations in these basins that date to these later periods of prehistory (Plate 1). Late Intermediate material culture is encountered in profusion either in the immediate vicinity of H-8 and H-9 within the river floodplain, or in some cemetery contexts. Elsewhere it is inevitably scarce and limited to a few ceramic fragments.

These Late Intermediate settlements lie amid the lush riparian vegetation *within* the current river floodplain. Indeed, the damage to them by the river during the 1997/8 El Niño was precisely a consequence of their proximity to today's river course. By contrast, earlier settlements within the areas of H-13 and G-8/9 are atop the higher relict river terraces, mainly along the west bank of the Río Ica. These terrace surfaces are now largely bare of vegetation and subject to the scouring effects of the region's extraordinary wind regime. Aside from cemetery contexts, archaeology from periods after the Middle Horizon is conspicuous by its almost complete absence from the relict terrace surfaces of the lower Ica Valley.

An archaeological survey of H-8 leads to the impression that its resident populations had a somewhat specialised lifestyle. Most of its surface area is given over to very well-preserved adobe enclosures containing enormous quantities of marine and terrestrial molluscs. Indeed, the sheer proportion of this material relative to the size of the site, and the fact that molluscs appear to be grouped by type within particular enclosures, lends to H-8 all the appearances of a way-station at which marine products were gathered and processed, before transport by llama caravans on to the higher reaches of the Ica Valley, where by this time most of the population lived. This suggestion awaits further investigation.

What is clear, however, is that Late Intermediate settlement in the lower Ica Valley is concentrated on just two sites, within the current river floodplain, founded there without antecedents, and is absent from the huge, barren terrace surfaces on which the archaeology of earlier time periods is found in abundance. This leads to the inescapable conclusion that major landscape change here happened *before* these later periods of prehistory.

The archaeology of the Middle Horizon

As we have seen, the archaeological record of the Middle Horizon, which preceded the Late Intermediate Period, shows some degree of unity across great expanses of the central Andes. And while archaeologists have advanced contrasting interpretations of what driving processes lay behind the Middle Horizon, at least a partial consensus has been established: 'most researchers agree that Wari was an expansive state, an empire that consolidated power rapidly', as Cook (2004: 146) puts it.

The Wari heartland lay in the Ayacucho highlands of the south-central Andes, centred on the vast eponymous urban centre there. The consensus would have Wari expanding rapidly out of this region during its so-called Epoch 1B, to control directly all the central and southern coast between Chancay (just north of Lima) and Acarí (south of Nazca), and the Peruvian highlands over an even greater extent, from Ancash to the Cuzco region (see for instance Menzel 1967: 147, D'Altroy and Schreiber 2004). The evidence for Wari's early domination of the south coast during this period is particularly clear (see for instance Schreiber 2001), unsurprisingly, since the Ayacucho highlands are its immediate hinterland. It may then be no accident that archaeologists of the south coast have been among the most consistent advocates of Wari as a military expansionist empire. The archaeological record here during the Middle Horizon—as represented by iconography, burial forms and skull deformation—shows very little influence from the Early Intermediate or 'Nasca' styles that preceded it (Isla 2009). As Rowe (1956: 148) observed more than fifty years ago, the Middle Horizon 'apparently marks the virtual replacement of one culture by a radically different one on the south coast'.

In the basins of the lower Ica Valley, however, the material culture of the Middle Horizon shows little of the refined ceramic tradition sometimes associated with Wari expansion elsewhere. In general, it comprises a corpus of thick-walled ceramics of crude paste and decoration, which stands in marked contrast to the elaborate fineware of the

Intermediate periods that both preceded and followed it (see for instance Pezzia Assereto 1968, Kroeber and Collier 1998, Menzel 1967; and see Figure 3.4D).

There are considerable archaeological remains dating to the Middle Horizon in the Samaca and Ullujaya basins but, curiously, most of these appear in mortuary contexts (Figure 3.5). Cemeteries from all the time periods we will discuss here are found in the Ullujaya and Samaca basins. They have all been brutally looted in the recent past by *huaqueros*, sometimes using bulldozers. Indeed, looting continues to this day (*El Comercio* 1999). While some professional looters (or '*huaqueros*') have better experience of context and material culture than most archaeologists, the criminality of their activity renders this knowledge obscure — and ultimately lost. So while huge numbers of beautiful ceramics and textiles from the ancient tombs of the south coast reside today in museum collections worldwide, few of these mortuary contexts have ever been properly described, let alone scientifically excavated (Isla 2009). For the lower Ica Valley itself we have little more than the observations of Alejandro Pezzia Assereto (1968), from his years as conservator of the Museo Regional de Ica, and Alberto Rossel Castro (1977). Theirs are invaluable perspectives because so many of the mortuary contexts they describe are now destroyed. Together with the detritus left by *huaqueros*, their descriptions allow us — to some extent — to date cemeteries despite their highly disturbed state.

Like other cemeteries, those of the Middle Horizon are found usually high on the footslope along the margins of these basins and inevitably on the west side of the river — perhaps because they were thereby upwind of settlements. Several, however, are also found on the relict terrace of Ullujaya G-8/9. These are sets of large (up to seven by two metres) rectangular, funerary chambers, cut into the duracreted terrace surface, often lined with adobe brick and some with fragments of their huarango pole roofs still in place (Features 208, 752, 755 on Figure 3.5 and see Figure 5.3). These gallery tombs — known locally as 'barbacoa' — contained multiple burials wrapped in huge quantities of raw cotton (Isla 2009, Pezzia Assereto 1968: 246–7). In addition there are smaller, circular pit chambers of individual burials but perhaps of different dates. For while the fragments of material culture scattered about these areas are predominantly Middle Horizon, there are also substantial materials from the preceding Late Nasca Period, and some from the Late Intermediate. Indeed, it seems quite evident despite the upturned condition of mortuary contexts that both Middle Horizon and Late Intermediate occupants of these basins often chose to bury their dead among those of the earlier Late Nasca Period (Plate 1).

By contrast, sites of clear Middle Horizon settlement in the Ullujaya and Samaca basins are rather few (see Figure 3.5). We examined one of these in some detail through excavation: a large mound, almost fifty metres long and standing almost three metres above a surrounding flat landscape of the barren relict terrace of Samaca H-13, forming one of the most predominant features on Samaca H-13 ('mound 23', see Figure 3.4, and Beresford-Jones 2005 and Beresford-Jones *et al.* 2009b for more detail).

The surface of this mound was densely covered with large Middle Horizon Epoch 2 ceramic fragments (or sherds), while all about it on the hard surface of the terrace were

A View south across Samaca H-13 showing mound 23 before excavation.
B Bas of southern profile of mound 23 excavations showing nabkha contexts (S.U. 60) underlying Middle Horizon midden contexts (S.U. 51/54).
C Modern nabkha formation in the Samaca Basin.
D Selected decorated fragments – mound 23 surface context. Middle Horizon – Epoch 2.

Figure 3.4. Excavation of mound 23, Samaca H-13: a Middle Horizon midden mound on a relict nabkha

mixed scatters of sherds from much earlier time periods: Early Nasca and even Early Horizon. We have come to understand that many of these terraces of the lower Ica Valley—exposed to centuries of a powerful unidirectional wind regime—are *deflated* landscapes. Indeed, this much is evident in the extensive scatters of sherds from various epochs that now lie mixed upon their surface. Since those ceramics long pre-date the Middle Horizon, we excavated mound 23 in the hope that it might harbour a preserved stratigraphy which would offer insight into the sequence of human occupation on H-13. While this turned out

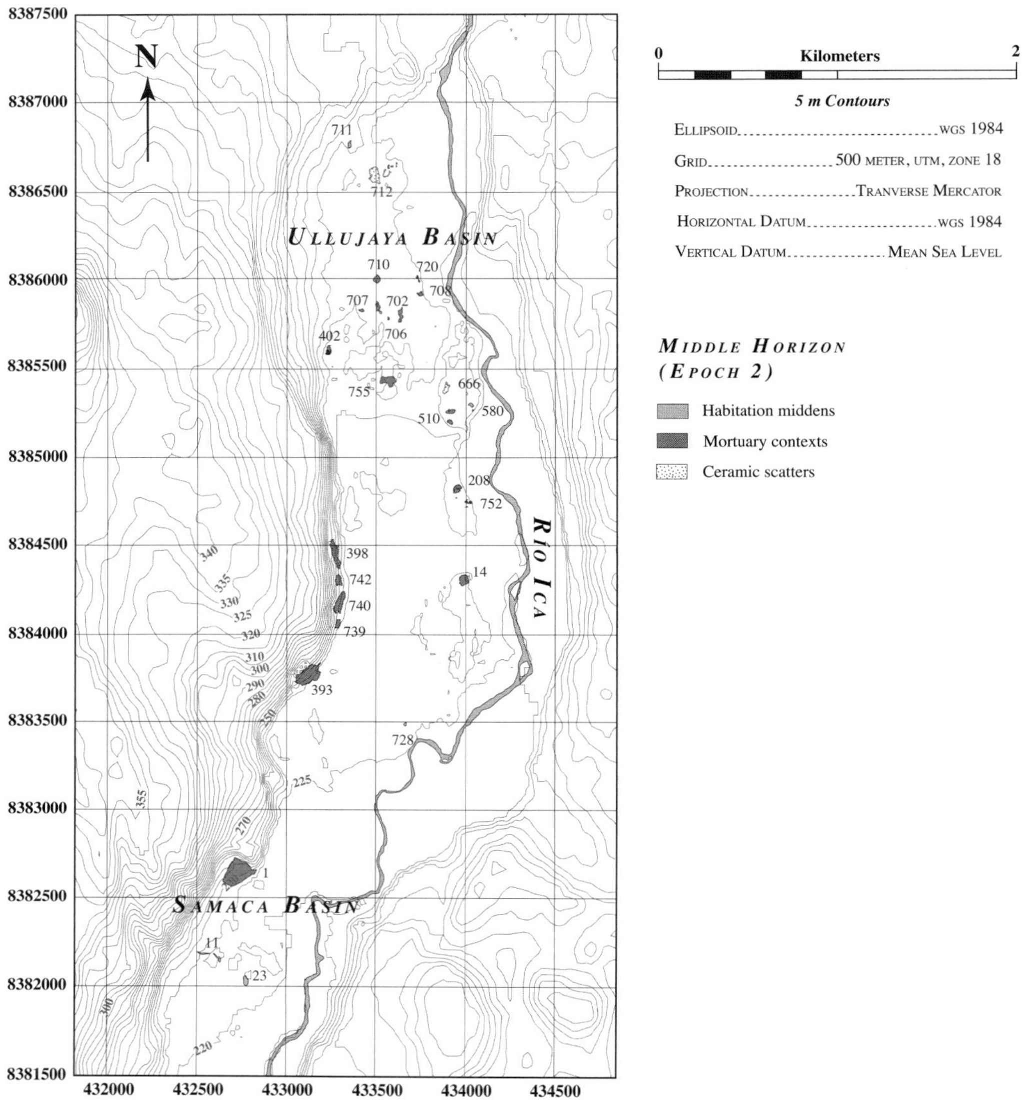

Figure 3.5. Map of the Middle Horizon archaeology of the Ullujaya and Samaca basins

not to be the case, the underlying structure of mound 23 was no less significant for our understanding of landscape change in the lower Ica Valley.

The upper deposits of mound 23 were full of the detritus of human activity, including Middle Horizon Epoch 2 sherds, charcoal, mollusc shells, textile fragments and lithics, including obsidian, a material of distant highland origin (see Figure 5.6 and Burger *et al.* 1998). As we will see in Chapter 5, flotation of these deposits also yielded copious amounts of plant remains and other archaeobotanical data for the Middle Horizon period. What was most obvious, however, even during excavation, was that these deposits contained enormous quantities of desiccated huarango tree litter. Indeed, as the amounts of midden materials decreased rapidly down the profile of the mound, so did the proportion of this tree litter increase. The lower levels of mound 23 consisted of unconsolidated fine sands in graded beds interspersed with lenses of this dense huarango tree litter. This is *in situ poña*, the thick layer of litter that carpets the desert under a huarango tree. This pattern of deposition leads inexorably to the identification of mound 23 as a relict nabkha — a so-called 'phytogenic' mound that forms through the gradual deposition of windborne fine sands about a tree. These are common features of some desert landscapes — and can be seen today in the lower Ica Valley (Figure 3.4C). Other clues included a large bowl of sandy fill in the excavation where the tree had once stood, and several large tree roots. The size of this tree-throw, and of mound 23 itself, speaks of a very large huarango, in whose shade the Middle Horizon inhabitants of Samaca H-13 chose to carry out all those activities leading to the formation of a midden there.

The extant form of Middle Horizon mound 23 — standing amid a surrounding deflated landscape covered with the sherds of earlier epochs — is due to its more recent age, the binding effects of nabkha formation and to the sheer density of heavy ceramic and lithic midden materials on its surface. The fact that it is a relict nabkha, in and of itself, has important consequences for our interpretation of how change occurred in the lower Ica Valley. Finally, large though mound 23 may be as a nabkha, it is nonetheless the remains of a fairly insubstantial human settlement, relative to other archaeological remains in these basins. Its middens do not overlie deeper layers of occupation from earlier time periods and, as we will see in Chapter 5, their archaeobotanical data reveal some rather particular forms of subsistence.

In short then, archaeological investigations reveal rather few settlements in the Ullujaya and Samaca basins and yet considerable evidence for burials here during the Middle Horizon. A sizeable Middle Horizon occupation is reported from just upstream in the Callango Basin at Casa Vieja (Roque *et al*. 2003, Cook and Parrish 2005). Middle Horizon burials are located both along the western edges of the basins and also on the flat surface of the G-8/9 relict terraces. This is strong evidence that, by this time, these terraces were high above the water table, outside the active river floodplain and thus beyond the area of productive agriculture. As we will see later, this had not always been so. But, by the Middle Horizon, and indeed during subsequent periods of prehistory, much of the wide landscape of the Ullujaya and Samaca terraces had become a place where people came to bury their dead.

The archaeology of the Late Nasca Period

The Middle Horizon was preceded on the south coast by Late Nasca, a time for which the wider archaeological record would seem to reflect great changes in society. As we saw earlier, the Nasca ceramic typology becomes particularly complicated during the Late

Nasca Period: a conservative canon of Early Nasca fractures into sub-styles, and new iconography appears including clear depictions of warriors and other militaristic themes. Instances of the taking of trophy heads, both actual and iconographic, increase in the record, witness to internecine struggle between different groups that made up Nasca society (Silverman 1993: 334, Tomasto 2009). Meanwhile, the themes of the natural and agricultural worlds that so distinguish earlier Nasca iconography become rare (see for instance Silverman and Proulx 2002, Hecht 2009). Moreover, the evidence for Late Nasca social rupture goes well beyond iconography. The preeminent Early Nasca centre of Cahuachi on the Río Nazca was abruptly abandoned just before this time and this turmoil presages the dawn of the Middle Horizon, whose archaeological record we have just examined.

The basins of the lower Ica Valley contain numerous Late Nasca archaeological remains (Figures 3.6 and 3.7). Indeed, together with those of the Early Nasca Period, these are the most significant traces of human occupation on the relict terraces of Ullujaya and Samaca. Outside of the much later sites of prehistory such as H-8, the few remains of what might properly be termed 'architecture'—both of large, rectangular adobe blocks and of large field stones, set into adobe mortar—date to the Late Nasca Period. These consist of the foundations of some quite substantial constructions: enclosures and platform features. There are also substantial remains of Late Nasca settlement in the form of large midden mounds, particularly in one cluster on Ullujaya G-8/9, and many looted tombs with Late Nasca remains, often mixed with Middle Horizon materials, which lie along the western flanks of these basins and, sometimes, on the surface of their relict terraces. We investigated some of these features through excavation.

The first of these was a large mound known locally as *La Campana* ('the bell') on account of its prominent shape in the Ullujaya landscape (Figure 3.7). From afar *La Campana* (or mound 1, Ullujaya G-8/9) is a dark shade of red on account of the sheer density of Late Nasca sherds on its surface. It is the most conspicuous of several Late Nasca midden mounds in this vicinity, sitting in the centre of a conglomeration of smaller mounds to the south (Features 7–10) and a large mound to the north (Feature 37). During the latter half of the last century there were substantial earth movements in this area linked with attempts to grow cotton, which have disturbed many of these sites. Abandoned modern fields lie all about here so that some of these mounds may once have been more contiguous. Yet mound 1 is still an *in situ* archaeological site with fragments of adobe walls visible within it. We excavated here, primarily to extract an archaeobotanical record from its very well-preserved organic remains (Figure 3.7B). Our excavations also confirmed that mound 1 dates only to Late Nasca, for its lower levels preserved no earlier archaeological strata.

We also made several excavations in two adobe architectural features just to the south on Ullujaya G-8/9: a large platform 23 and a smaller platform 3 (Figure 3.7A and D). Platform 3 had been built on top of the course of a relict canal fragment (canal 4). Excavation of this platform revealed signs of habitation in the form of dispersed midden materials: camelid bone, molluscs, charcoal and some Late Nasca and plainware pottery sherds. This rather curious arrangement of a large Late Nasca platform constructed directly

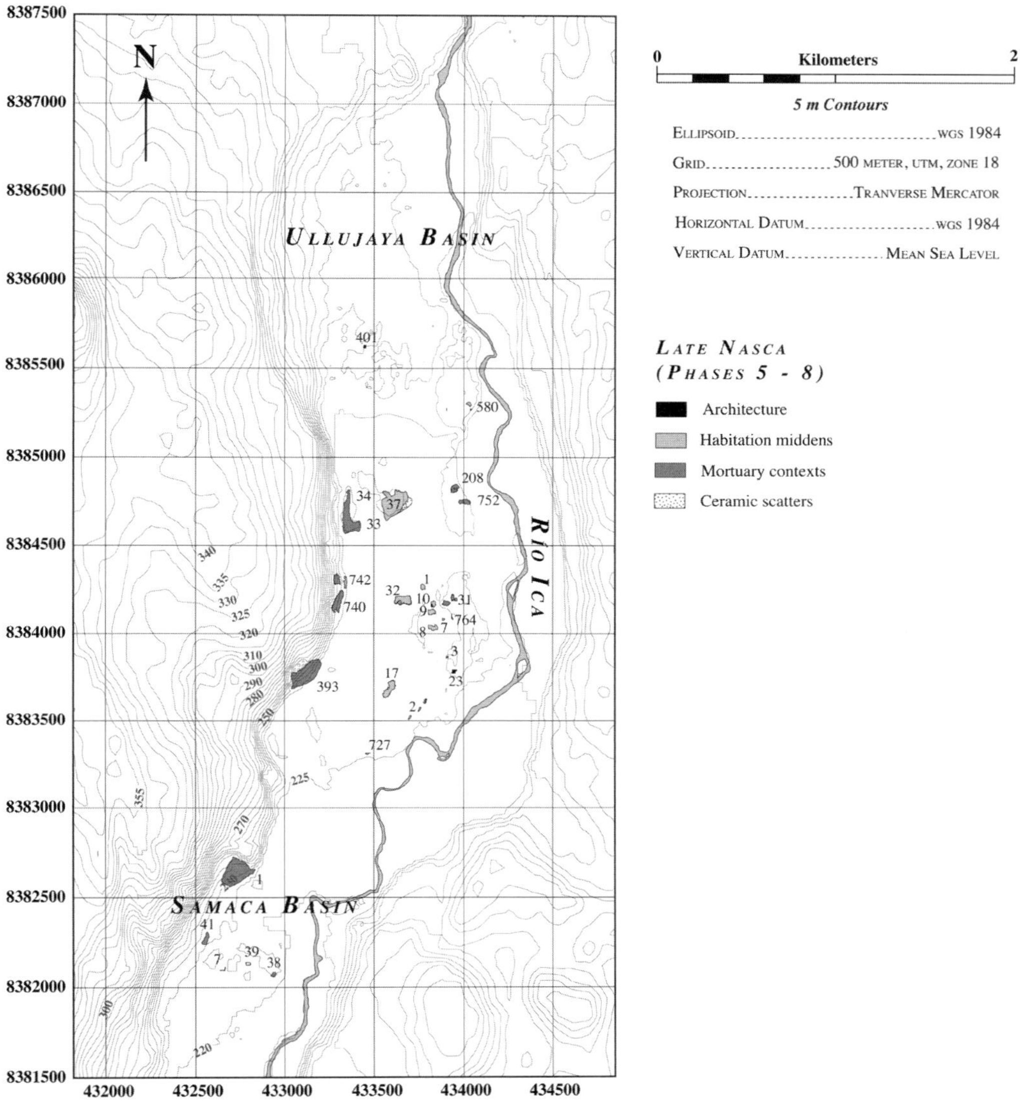

Figure 3.6. Map of the Late Nasca archaeology of the Ullujaya and Samaca basins

across the course of a canal is a characteristic of several parts of the archaeological landscape in these basins and can be seen elsewhere on Ullujaya G-8/9 and on Samaca H-13.

There are substantial fragments of relict canal 4 still remaining across the Ullujaya G-8/9 landscape (canal fragment 11, for example, is almost certainly part of this same original course). A long fragment standing some 2 metres above today's land surface emerges from beneath platform 3 and runs across a sandy bowl to the west and below the second

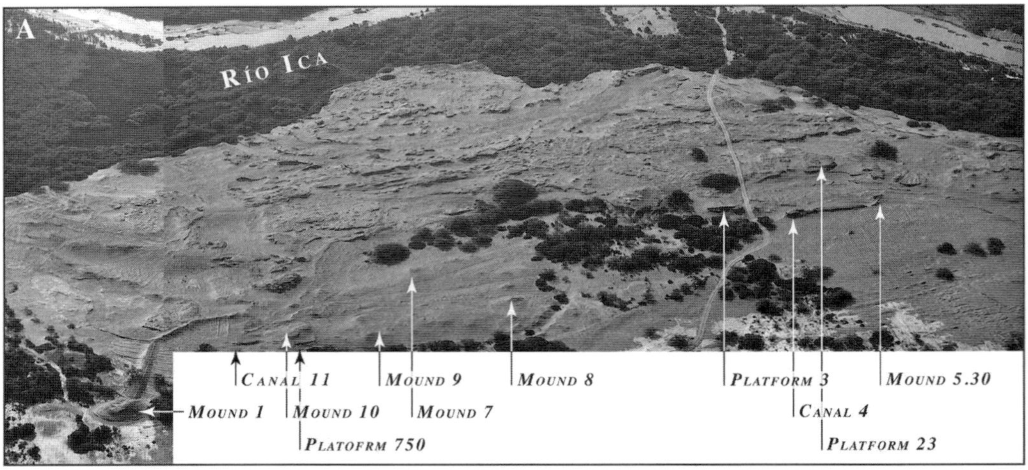

A Aerial view to south-east across Ullujaya G-8/9 showing Late Nasca features.
B Dense midden deposits in Ullujaya G-8/9 Late Nasca mound 1.
C View north-west of Late Nasca Ullujaya G-8/9 mound 1 ('La Campana').
D View north of Ullujaya G-8/9 Late Nasca platform 3.

Figure 3.7. Selected Late Nasca archaeolgical features of Ullujaya G-8/9

Late Nasca feature (platform 23), which has protected the canal from the force of the unimodal wind in these basins. The archaeology thus reflects a long process of landscape deflation, which we will examine further in the next chapter.

Platform 23 meanwhile is substantial, measuring some 20 metres along a side. It was constructed by infilling with adobe rubble a rectangular enclosing wall to create a flat platform. This wall was over a metre and a half thick and built of very large, irregular blocks of duracrete or adobe, set into an adobe mortar. Yet the platform had been created by remodelling an earlier, more elaborate construction, for excavations revealed the remains of another building which had previously stood within its massive enclosing walls. Those walls also retain fragments of plaster on their inner surface and a narrow, well-used entrance on the north side. That inner building was contemporary with the outer walls and was circular, with a diameter of around 10 metres (Figure 3.8B). The remains of a hearth and sparse midden materials indicated that this had been a space in which people lived. There was also evidence that this inner building had been burnt: a thick layer of ash in the area of its wall and in the stratigraphy of the bank outside (Figure 3.8C). All the sherds from the inner building, and from its subsequent infilling to create a platform, date from various phases of the Late Nasca Period (Figure 3.8D).

Just below platform 23 was a small mound densely covered with sherds and, like platform 3, sitting atop the course of relict canal 4. In section this mound (Feature 5.30) showed thick, dense black and orange lenses in a highly disturbed stratigraphy in section (Figure 3.8E). While it is notoriously difficult to identify evidence of warfare in the archaeological record, this section, and indeed the ash layer in platform 23 itself, offers the impression of destruction events. Moreover, the construction of a massive wall about a lighter habitation structure on mound 23 suggests fortification.

What our investigations clearly reveal are, firstly, that at times during the Late Nasca Period—just as in the following Middle Horizon—the relict terraces of the lower Ica Valley were suitable places to bury the dead. Secondly, large tracts of the centre of Ullujaya G-8/9 were given over to settlement during this period—represented by the extensive cluster of habitation middens about *La Campana*. There are many more remains of Late Nasca settlement in these basins than there are for the subsequent Middle Horizon. Thirdly, certain buildings—such as the one under platform 23—were utterly remodelled during the same Late Nasca Period, after which they had held some quite different function. Finally, and rather obviously, many of the large canals still visible in this landscape operated no more, or were long out of operation, following the Late Nasca date of construction of several platforms on top of their courses.

The archaeology of the Early Nasca Period

Early Nasca, as defined here (Dawson Phases 2 to 5), is that period which falls within the first five hundred years of the Early Intermediate. Its iconography celebrates the 'abundance of all life forms', as Silverman (1993: 323) puts it: the fecundity of nature and

A View east of Ullujaya G-8/9, platform 23, under excavation.
B Buried floor beneath platform 23, showing post holes of inner building.
C West-facing section of Trench 1 in platform 23, showing platform fill (S.U. 2031); ditch (v–x) and bank (xii) with ash layer (iv) and buried floor (S.U. 2032) of inner building.
D Selected ceramic finds from fill (S.U. 2031 and S.U. 2022) and buried floor (S.U. 2019) of platform 23. Late Nasca.
E North-facing section of Ullujaya G-8/9, mound 5.30 showing disturbed contexts.

Figure 3.8. Excavation of Late Nasca platform 23, Ullujaya G-8/9 agriculture on the south coast rendered through a beautiful corpus of slip-painted ceramics and intricate needle-knit and stem-stitch embroidered textiles (see the illustrations on the opening page of each chapter and, for instance, Sawyer 1997 and Isla 2009). For reasons that will become evident later I will evoke the term 'riparian consciousness' for this canon. Moseley (1992: 190) uses the term 'corporate style' to describe Early Nasca iconography, and offers a pithy reading of its wider archaeological record: 'individuality—with cultural coherence, but without large scale or integrated power—were hallmarks of Nasca society'.

To date there have been few archaeological excavations of Early Nasca settlements on the south coast (but see Vaughan 2010). Partly this is because investigations have concentrated, naturally enough, on the monumental Early Nasca ceremonial site of Cahuachi on the Río Nasca. But it is also because—as our investigations in the lower Ica Valley illustrate—these settlement sites seem almost invisible, being small and built of ephemeral materials. The first expressions of Early Nasca began some two millennia ago, and the long exposure of this archaeology to the effects of wind and twentieth-century agriculture are very evident in the Ullujaya and Samaca basins. Yet there are still significant vestiges of the Early Nasca occupation here, including the remains of a once-extensive relict canal system (Figure 3.9). There are, in addition, some looted burials.

Early Nasca settlement sites on the relict terraces of Ullujaya and Samaca are manifest in the form of remnants of preserved floors identifiable by arrangements of post-holes, together with numbers of clay-lined circular pits of about one metre in diameter whose interiors are oxidised to bright orange by fire (so called 'fired-earth pits'). These are the remains of buildings which very likely looked much like those of Huerto Huamaní today—constructed of wooden posts with walls of woven heavy grass then plastered with mud (known as '*quincha*' construction). Floors in Huerto Huamaní are 'made ground', dampened daily to keep dust down and of course walked upon. With time this produces a very hard floor from the fine sediments of the lower Ica Valley. These ancient Early Nasca floors survive only in fragments as platforms standing slightly above a surrounding landscape that has been blown away (Figure 3.10B). They can be dated to the Early Nasca Period by sherds scattered about them and visible in their wind-exposed edges. There are particular concentrations of these Early Nasca settlements on various parts of Ullujaya G-8/9, including a large mound Feature 21, which we investigated in more detail. Since mortuary contexts are looted it is difficult to draw definitive conclusions from them. Yet the apparent imbalance between settlement and cemetery remains which we noted earlier for the Middle Horizon appears again for the Early Nasca Period: this time, however, in reverse. If so, it may be that people were being buried elsewhere at this time.

The function of the many fired-earth pits associated with these floors, in which fires were clearly set over considerable time, remains obscure. They may have been cooking hearths, but in survey these pits are concentrated along relict canal courses and excavations of better-preserved examples produced many heavy, burnt fragments of ceramic, which may have been added to achieve the fine control of temperature necessary for firing

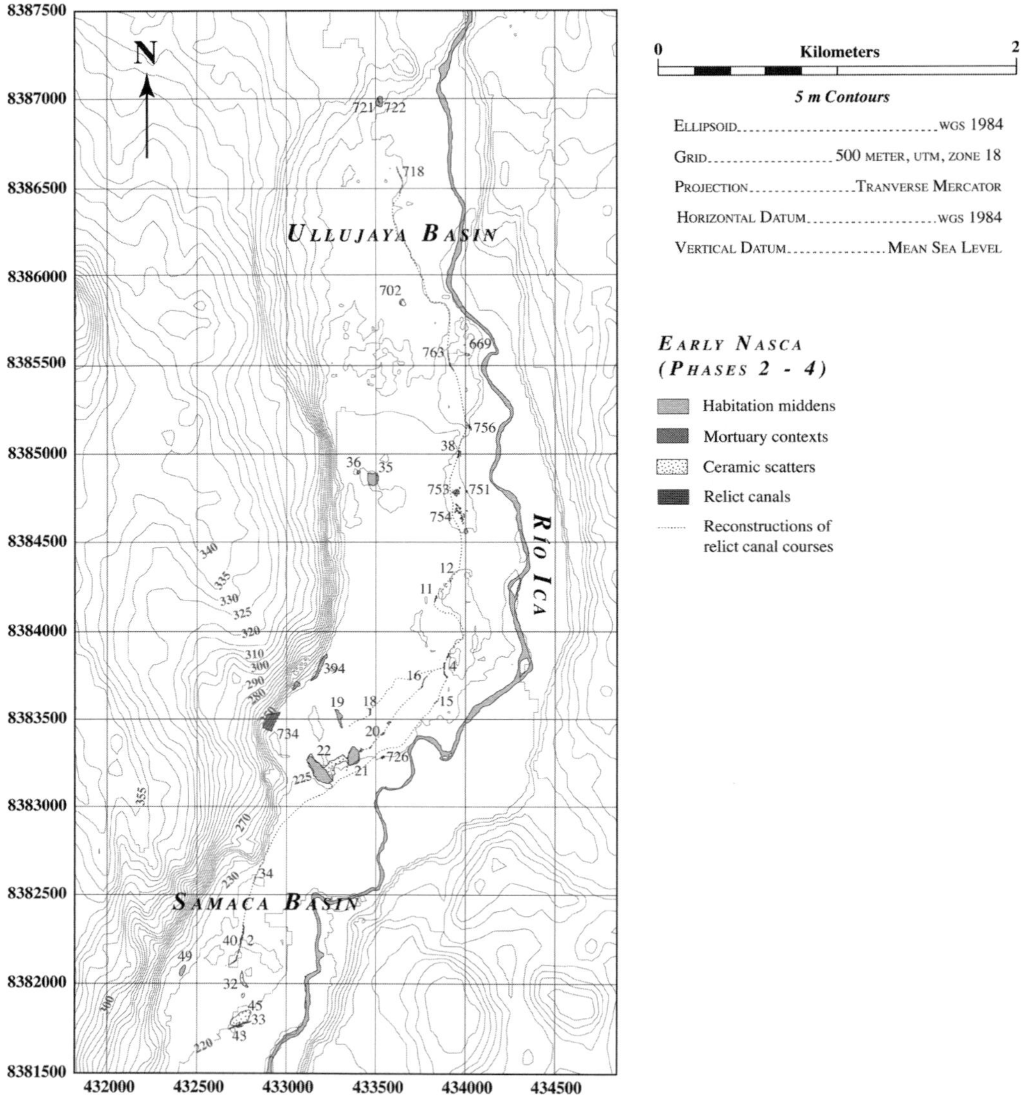

Figure 3.9. Map of the Early Nasca archaeology of the Ullujaya and Samaca basins

ceramics (Figure 3.10C). Today, craftsmen making exact replica ceramics use a small fire of just these dimensions. Moreover, the desert hereabouts is 'painted' with the colours of white, yellow, pink and red sedimentary bedrocks, which can be ground into the colours of Nasca slip-decoration. Indeed, in 1952 Rossel Castro saw grinding stones in Ullujaya with precisely such coloured sediments, which led him to the view that this was a centre of ceramic fabrication (Rossel Castro 1977: 58).

There are also several large mounds in a group at the southern extreme of Ullujaya G-8/9, the surfaces of which are covered with Early Nasca sherds (Features 21 and 22). As with other parts of this landscape there have been earth movements in this area in recent times and a modern road truncates both these mounds. Attempts to clean a section of this road cut through mound 21 revealed little underlying archaeology and exposed only very dispersed midden materials in an unconsolidated sandy matrix. The course of a small relict canal passing close by mound 21 can be traced across several remaining fragments in the Ullujaya G-8/9 landscape and we made excavations to expose profiles of this canal on the southern flank of mound 21. Sherds from within the sediments of the bottom of this relict canal were, like those on the surface, Early Nasca (see Figure 3.14F). These excavations also revealed that the Early Nasca surface overlay a much denser midden

A and B Views south across fragment of early Nasca floor 751, Ullujaya G-8/9, with post holes, fired-earth pits and clay-lined pits.
C Fired-earth pit under excavation on Samaca H-13 adjacent to relict canal 40.

Figure 3.10. Selected Early Nasca floor features from Ullujaya G-8/9

deposit. Indeed, the canal course itself had been cut into that midden, which contained materials dating back to a much more remote period of archaeology in the lower Ica Valley: the Chavín Early Horizon.

Yet, the small canal fragment next to mound 21 is only one of very many remains of ancient canals surviving on the relict terraces of the lower Ica Valley (Figure 3.11). Unlike the mound 21 canal, however, almost all of these are visible today as raised courses running high above their surroundings. At some locations the surfaces of these canal courses lie more than two metres above the land surface on their immediate flanks. This is evidence of the considerable deflation that the terraces have experienced since the time when these canals were in operation for, as we will see in the next chapter, it is a classic *inversion* of relief, whereby wind erosion has left features such as canals, once cut into the land surface, as upstanding features. The ancient canals themselves are preserved by calcrete enrichment along their courses, deposited over time by the water they once held. But fragments of canals are only preserved where their orientations coincide with that of the prevailing wind. When a canal's original course took it perpendicular to the wind, it no longer survives. Nonetheless, those original courses can still be tracked across the landscape for, even when destroyed, detailed three-dimensional landform modelling sometimes reveals traces of relict courses in the topography of these terraces and existing fragments can be matched together on the basis of their dimensions, directions and the surveyed heights of their courses (see Figures 3.9 and 3.11). Indeed, our survey suggests that these relict canal fragments were all once part of the same contemporary system.

We excavated several of these canals, in particular the remains of two large examples: Feature 4 on Ullujaya G-8/9, underneath the Late Nasca platform 3 just discussed, and Feature 40 on Samaca H-13 (Figure 3.12). These were difficult to excavate because their courses are indurated and very hard. Calcite cementation often extended to more than three metres beneath the canals, evidence that they were in operation for considerable periods of time (Beresford-Jones *et al.* 2009b).

The dimensions of both relict canal 4 on Ullujaya G-8/9 and canal 40 on Samaca H-13 are those of a principal supply canal, from which many other, smaller off-take canals supplied water to irrigate particular parts of the agricultural landscape, or what Moseley *et al.* (1983: 316) define as a 'Class 1' canal. Although these fragments lie almost two kilometres apart, the difference between their respective course heights (2.07 m, implying a gentle gradient of one in one thousand) would have sustained perfectly what Moseley *et al.* call a 'sub-critical flow regime', necessary for flow without erosion in such unlined canals. This, together with their similar dimensions, strongly suggests that they were once part of the same canal system.

The large profiles excavated in canal 4 revealed what had once been a substantial canal in use for a long period of time, with many courses of water-lain sediments superimposed one on top of the other and separated by the cuts and recuts from the episodes of regular cleaning, necessary with such unlined canals and during which sediments were removed and dumped along the canal banks (Figure 3.12C). All the identifiable sherds from within these courses were Early Nasca.

A View of Samaca H-13 along the course of relict canal fragment 40.
B Relict canal fragment 33, Samaca H-13.
C View north of relict canal fragment 4, Ullujaya G-8/9, with platform 3 built across its course in the background.
D View south of relict canal fragment 34, on the very edge of the Samaca H-13 terrace. Its course has been cut by an incursion and down-cutting by the river in the past, creating the new floodplain visible in the background.
E Relict canal fragment 11 on Ullujaya G-8/9. Note that our survey data suggest that fragments 11 and 4 on Ullujaya G-8/9, and 34 and 40 on Samaca H-13, were all once part of the same, primary canal course.

Figure 3.11. Selected Early Nasca relict canal fragments from Ullujaya G-8/9 and Samaca H-13

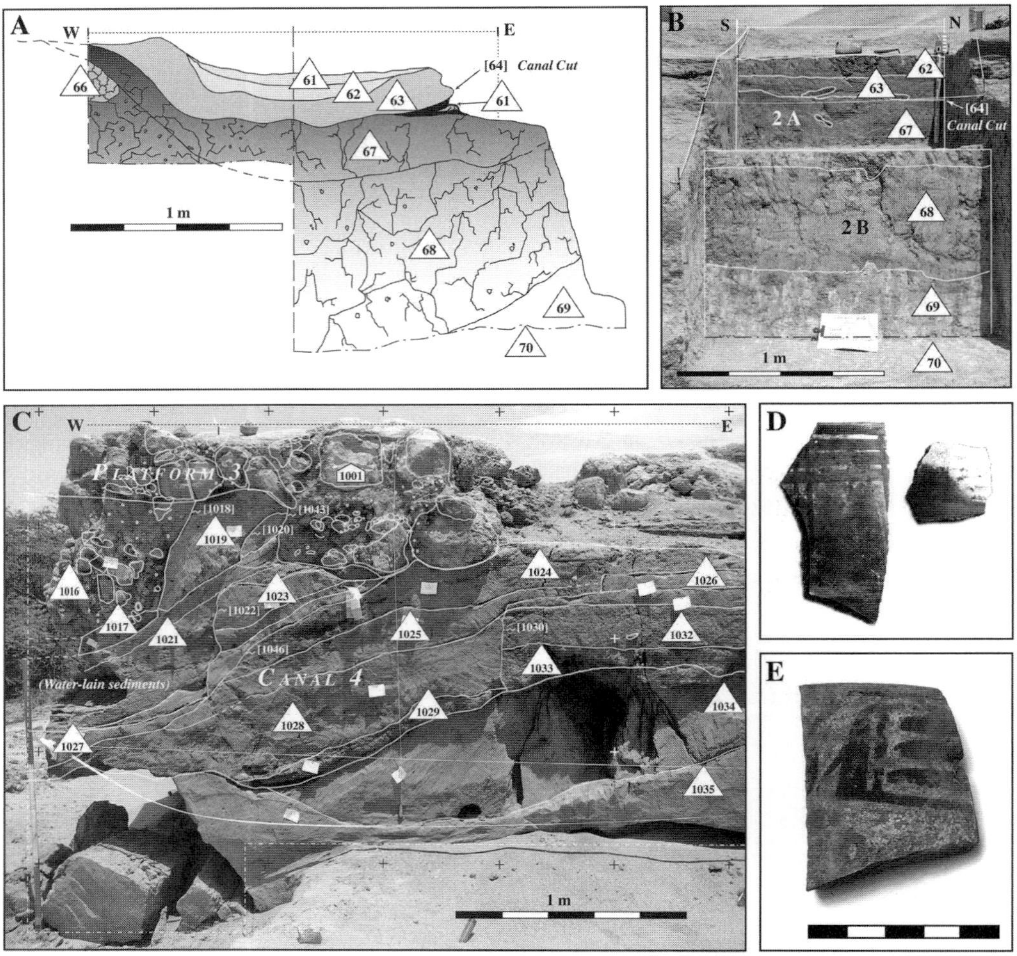

A South-facing profile of relict canal 40, Samaca H-13 (Test Pit 2), showing original canal course (S.U. 61–3).

B East-facing profile of relict canal 40, Samaca H-13 (Test Pit 2), showing calcrete to depth (S.U. 69).

C South-facing profile of Ullujaya G-8/9 platform 3 on top of course of relict canal 4, showing original canal course (S.U. 1021 and S.U. 1027) and multiple canal recuts ([1022], [1046], [1030], etc.).

D Exampes of water-stained decorated ceramic fragments from within course of relict canal 33, Samaca H-13. Early Nasca.

E Example of decorated ceramic fragment from S.U. 1027, within water-lain deposits of Ullujaya G-8/9, relict canal 4. Early Nasca.

Figure 3.12. Excavations of relict canal features from Ullujaya G-8/9 and Samaca H-13

Early Nasca pottery was also noted embedded in the exposed sections of other canals in the lower Ica Valley, including relict canal 33 on Samaca H-13, and in canals 12 and 38 on Ullujaya G-8/9. All of these fragments show extensive black oxide staining suggestive of long immersion in water (Figure 3.12D and E). Dense scatters of Early Nasca fragments were also encountered in close association with these and other canal fragments. And a midden ('Feature 43')—dating to the Early Nasca Period—was excavated alongside canal 33 on Samaca H-13 (see Figure 3.11B), to which we will return in the next chapter since it has particular importance for our geomorphological investigations.

The precise dating of features such as canal systems, in use over extended time periods, is problematic. A date inferred from a particular find in such a feature proves only that it was in use at that particular time and says little about when it was first built, or indeed ceased to be used. Nonetheless, if various lines of data can be brought together from the survey of an entire landscape then some fairly secure inferences can be made about dating. In the lower Ica Valley the evidence is that these canal fragments are all relicts of the same contemporary system and further suggests a *terminus ante quem* for this system at around the end of the Early Nasca Period. We have yet to find archaeological materials from later time periods associated with any of these relict canals. Moreover, some have Late Nasca platforms constructed across their courses, rendering them inoperable by that time. We may therefore safely conclude that these are the remains of a canal system that dates to no later than the Early Nasca Period.

The archaeology of the Early Horizon

The oldest archaeology we have yet encountered in the Ullujaya and Samaca basins dates to the Early Horizon, the first period for which the archaeological record shows clear evidence of some form of Pan-Andean integration, this time centred on the monumental site of Chavín de Huantar in Ancash, north-central Peru.

Sunk in far deeper recesses of Andean prehistory, there is even more uncertainty about the precise nature of the Early Horizon than there is for the Middle Horizon. Most archaeologists see it as the expression of a proselytising cult, radiating out from (or in towards) the monumental site of Chavín de Huántar (see for instance Burger 1993, Kembel and Rick 2004). Some would even deny its very existence as a 'Horizon' (for example, Pozorski and Pozorski 1987). But in a lucid defence, Burger (1993: 74) concludes that 'the Chavín horizon is not a stylistic chimera as some have contended, but a real pattern'. And looking at some of the iconography from our excavations in the lower Ica Valley—here some six hundred kilometres as the condor flies from Chavín de Huántar—one can see his point.

There is also ongoing debate about the precise dates of the Chavín Early Horizon (see for instance Rick 2008 and Burger and Salazar 2008) and, as we saw earlier, some uncertainties over parts of the long, corresponding Ocucaje ceramic sequence in Ica. The Ocucaje materials that we will see here belong to the earlier phases (3 and 4) of that sequence, dating to around 750 BC (Kaulicke, personal communication). While some chronological details remain to be resolved, these are classified here simply as Chavín Early Horizon.

Remains of Ocucaje Period settlement in the Ullujaya and Samaca basins are few. The largest, habitation Feature 1004 (Plate 1), dating to Late Ocucaje Phases 9/10, lies high up the edge of the Samaca Basin at over 300 m a.s.l. This location — far above the traces of later settlements and well over a hundred metres above the current vegetated river floodplain — suggests a radical change in the geomorphology of the basin and diminution of the vegetation extent within it, since this ancient time. Lower down on the relict terraces of H-13 and G-8/9 most of the Ocucaje materials recorded in consist only of a few scatters of sherds, usually in mixed assemblages with Early Nasca sherds (Figure 3.13). However, excavations in the vicinity of the Early Nasca canal adjoining mound 21 in Ullujaya revealed a rare discovery: an Early Horizon habitation midden, apparently well preserved in this otherwise much deflated landscape.

Mound 21 was covered with numerous Early Nasca sherds, as was the surface around the relict canal, which was a hard crust of compacted silty-sand, probably alluvium periodically cleared from the canal course. Our excavations exposed two sections across either end of this canal and showed that the sediments along the bottom of its course contained Early Nasca materials. Beneath this surface silty crust we encountered archaeological contexts of a very different kind: roughly horizontal layers of unconsolidated fine sands, the uppermost levels of which contained more Early Nasca Period ceramics. At greater depth these layers contained dense lenses of charcoal and large amounts of marine and terrestrial molluscs and other domestic debris. The pottery associated with these deeper midden deposits was Early Horizon: Ocucaje Phases 3 and 4 (Figure 3.14).

These middens were preserved beneath the indurated sediments of the small Early Nasca canal, which much later, had been cut through them. Such well-preserved stratigraphy is very rare in the lower Ica Valley for, not only has the wind usually deflated most of the original contexts of the relict terraces, but also settlement locations would seem to change from one period to the next. Yet this seems not to have been the case between the Early Horizon and Early Nasca Period. Early Horizon remains are scanty in the Ullujaya and Samaca basins (see Figure 3.13) and so it would be easy to over-interpret this single midden, but it is also noticeable that where Ocucaje sherds are found in scatters on deflated surfaces, they are often mixed with Early Nasca materials.

Much larger-scale Early Horizon habitation sites have been reported in Callango (Massey 1991, DeLeonardis 1977, 2005) and also at Cerro Uhle in Ocucaje (Menzel *et al.* 1964). Indeed, as we saw earlier, Massey's survey argues for the lower Ica Valley being the focus of settlement at this remote time. In the broader context, the sites in Ullujaya are minor settlements. Nonetheless, our excavations are significant because they are among the first on the south coast to carry out flotation and archaeobotanical analyses on an undisturbed Early Horizon midden, in secure stratigraphic association beneath Early Nasca deposits. We will examine those analyses and their implications in Chapter 5.

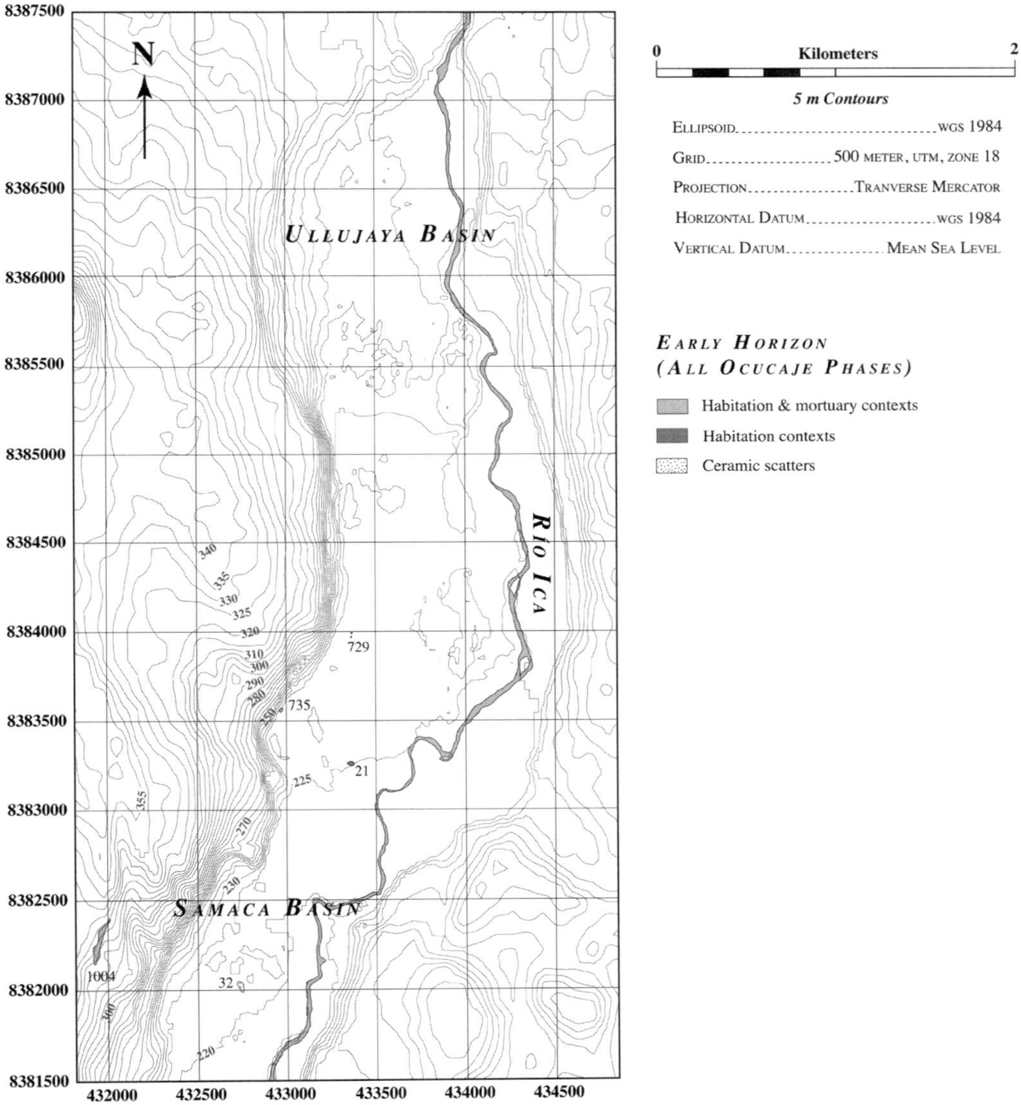

Figure 3.13. Map of Early Horizon archaeology of the Ullujaya and Samaca Basins

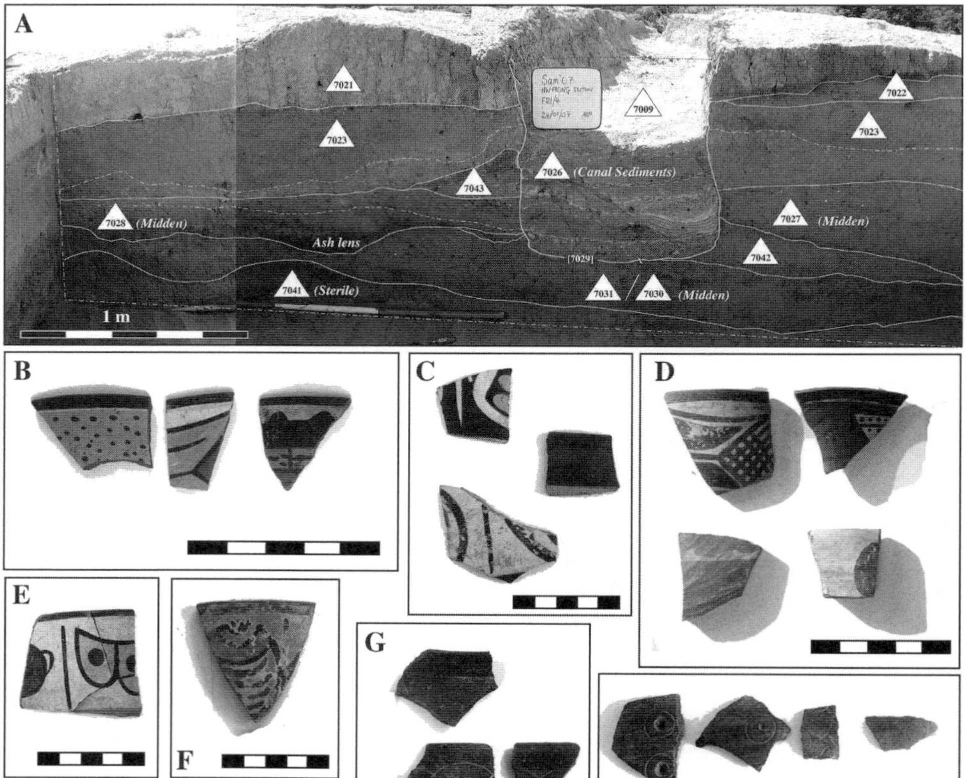

A North-west-facing profile of excavation F21/4 in Ullijaya G-8/9 mound 21, showing Early Nasca surface and canal cut into underlying Early Nasca and Early Horizon midden contexts.

B Early Nasca ceramic fragments from the surface of Ullujaya G-8/9, mound 21.

C and D Early Nasca ceramic fragments from excavcation of F21/3, midden context (S.U. 7006: equivalent to S.U. 7023 in Figure 3.15 A).

E Early Nasca ceramic fragments from excavation of F21/4 silty crust (S.U. 7021).

F Early Nasca ceramic fragments from excavation of F21/4 within canal sediments (S.U. 7026).

G and H Early Horizon ceramic fragments from excavation F21/4 midden contexts (S.U. 7027).

I Early Horizon bowl fragments with Chavín feline (Ocucaje Phase 4) from excavation F21/3 midden contexts (S.U. 7020: equivalent to S.U. 7028 in Figure 3.15).

Figure 3.14. Excavation of an Early Nasca canal cut into an Early Horizon midden context on mound 21, Ullujaya G-8/9

The Archaeological Story of the Ullujaya and Samaca Basins

To summarise the story told by the archaeology of the Ullujaya and Samaca basins, settlement sites from the later periods of south coast prehistory lie within the current Río Ica floodplain. For this reason they were badly damaged by the 1997/8 El Niño floods (which demonstrates incidentally that those floods were the most severe in the Ica Valley during the past millennium). In contrast, the largely barren, duracreted relict river terraces of these basins preserve a palimpsest of the imprints of much earlier human occupation, back over some two millennia before about AD 1000. The fact that there is no evidence of human occupation or use of these relict terraces, except as cemeteries, after around AD 1000 is strong evidence indeed that they were largely abandoned landscapes by that date.

Of course, similar ancient high-energy river events could have removed or buried any settlements older than AD 1000 that once lay within today's active floodplain. Nonetheless, it is clear that settlements of the preceding Middle Horizon on the relict terraces themselves are scarce, restricted to insubstantial sites on the nabkhas that build up under large isolated huarango trees, in a landscape already subject to incipient wind erosion.

We have examined the nature of the damage done by natural and human agencies to the archaeological remains on these terraces (the so-called 'taphonomic' factors). Nevertheless, precisely because they have long since been abandoned, these terraces preserve a very remarkable archaeological record. Indeed, for much of the past millennium and a half they were regarded as appropriate places to bury the dead, for their surfaces show the remains of tombs from all the epochs of prehistory that followed the Late Nasca Period. An apparent imbalance between poverty of settlement and profusion of mortuary contexts for the Middle Horizon might have several explanations, the most straightforward of which is that people were brought here to be buried from farther afield. Pragmatically this was because these terraces were—by then—high and dry and beyond the reach of the water table or of productive agriculture and were also on the west bank of the Río Ica, upwind of settlement. Yet there may well have been other, more enigmatic reasons for choosing to bury the dead on these relict terraces. For it must have been even more evident then than now that in remoter times people had lived upon and farmed these relict river terraces—the Middle Horizon and Late Intermediate landscape of the *dead* is set amidst the traces of a Nasca landscape of the *living*.

By contrast, the remains of Early and Late Nasca settlement on the G-8/9 and H-13 terraces are substantial despite millennia of wind deflation, which has blown away much of their original stratigraphy and left mixed scatters of ceramic fragments upon their surfaces. Some of the heavier sandy products of that wind erosion have been deposited in climbing dunes anchored against the western flanks of parts of these basins, which, as we will see in the next chapter, bury and preserve fragments of their ancient surface. Elsewhere, the bones of an entire ancient agricultural landscape have been left visible through an inversion of topography, whereby features such as ancient canal courses, once cut into the land surface, are preserved by their evaporitic duracretes as upstanding features. These canals operated across these terraces during the Early Nasca Period, but, by Late Nasca times platforms were built—seemingly almost on purpose—across their courses and this system was no longer operational. Indeed, Late Nasca archaeological remains hint at those convulsions, which we read from a wider archaeological record, to have been gripping society around this time.

Finally, there are traces of earlier occupations in these basins dating back to the Early Horizon more than two millennia ago. These are apparently few and small in the Ullujaya and Samaca basins. Nonetheless, while the settlements of later time periods occupy unique places in this landscape, Early Nasca occupations seem to be located in the same places as their Ocucaje predecessors, which leads us to infer some continuity between those long time periods.

So the archaeological record of the Ullujaya and Samaca basins provides us with tantalising intimations of dramatically altered local ecological conditions, the precise causes of which we will investigate in forthcoming chapters. Moreover, it provides us with a temporal framework by which we may hope to date those processes of landscape change, which we will turn to next through the geomorphological record of these basins.

4. Tracing Landscape Change:

The Geomorphological Record

Geomorphology — the study of those processes of deposition and erosion by which wind and river have shaped the landforms of the lower Ica Valley over time—was the foundation of our investigations. Why? Because the geomorphological record reveals why the landscape looks as it does today and how its archaeological record has been formed, and often, destroyed. So, only by understanding these processes of geomorphological change may we interpret the extant archaeological and landscape features, identify the most prosmising areas for excavation, and begin to reconstruct prehistoric human land use and impact.

We began our investigations, therefore, with a detailed geomorphological survey along a transect across the upper part of the Samaca Basin, which included the area of H-13. This transect was chosen because it was more or less representative of the landforms encountered throughout the basins of the lower Ica Valley. For H-13 is an excellent example of those wide expanses of relict river terrace that characterise these basins today and show clear evidence of environmental degradation and diminished land use. Our purpose was to describe and characterise the sediment and soil sequences along this transect, so as to gain insight into the differential processes of deposition and erosion through alluvial and aeolian action over time in the basin.

Fortunately for this purpose, the Peruvian south coast is a very dry 'basin-range' desert with a topography characterised by enclosed drainage systems. These basins make for well-defined and convenient landscape units within which to study the key geomorphological agents that affect a lowland valley system and thereby influence its human–environment interactions (French 2003). Moreover, in a climate of zero rainfall there are effectively only two natural agents of geomorphological change, the wind and the river, each of which acts in well-defined—and roughly opposite—directions. In this chapter we will review the results and interpretations of our geomorphological survey, which included:

Chapterhead: Rollout drawing of Nasca ceramic depicting desert foxes and cacti cf. *Neoraimondia arequipensis*, endemic to the south coast and which flowers just prior the arrival of river water (drawing courtesy of the British Museum).

1. The definition of the basic geomorphic units across the lower Ica Valley;
2. Investigating the character of the relict river terraces of H-13 and G-8/9, which underlie most of their archaeology;
3. Understanding the extent of landscape and ecological change across the Samaca and Ullujaya basins, as revealed by buried ancient land surfaces; and,
4. Evaluating those contexts from which archaeological and archaeobotanical data were extracted and subsequently analysed.

Some technical jargon becomes unavoidable here since certain terms convey precise meanings within the discipline, although we will seek to explain these (and see, in particular, Cooke *et al.* 1993 and Goldberg and Macphail 2006 for useful definitions and explanations). It may be worth starting by clarifying briefly an important distinction between 'soils' and 'sediments', for this is widely overlooked, even by archaeologists whose business is conducted in them.

Sediments are materials of different grain size (sands, silts and clays), deposited mainly by agents such as water or wind (so-called 'clastic' sediments), but also by other chemical and organic processes (Goldberg and Macphail 2006: 11–27). Soils, by contrast, are the result of those sediments being subject to various *soil-forming* processes (Goldberg and Macphail 2006: 42–71). So, as Goldberg and Macphail (2006: 46, emphasis added) explain, while 'a sediment has a *dynamic* history, which encompasses erosion, transport, and deposition over a landscape or area … in contrast, a soil is *static* in that it has formed *in situ* through various weathering and biological processes'. These *in situ* processes differentiate a soil into 'horizons' and this is commonly used to distinguish them from sediments. As we will see, however, in the arid, alluvial context of the lower Ica Valley, this distinction is rarely clear. In fact, the vast majority of materials in these basins are sediments (and archaeological contexts themselves are composed usually not of soils but of sediments deposited by humans). Usefully then, analysis of sediments can offer information about their *history*. Soils, meanwhile, being formed only under circumstances of stability, are rare in the contexts of the lower Ica Valley. Their occasional occurrence here therefore tells its own important story.

We begin with a brief outline of the methods used in carrying out the survey and subsequent laboratory analyses.

Methods

Our geomorphological study was carried out along a systematic transect of thirty-one survey pits dug 25 metres apart, proceeding due west between the sedimentary base rock edges of the upper Samaca Basin (Figure 4.1). Detailed descriptions were made in the field of the soil and sediment profiles exposed in these pits following Hodgson (1974) and using Munsell (2000).

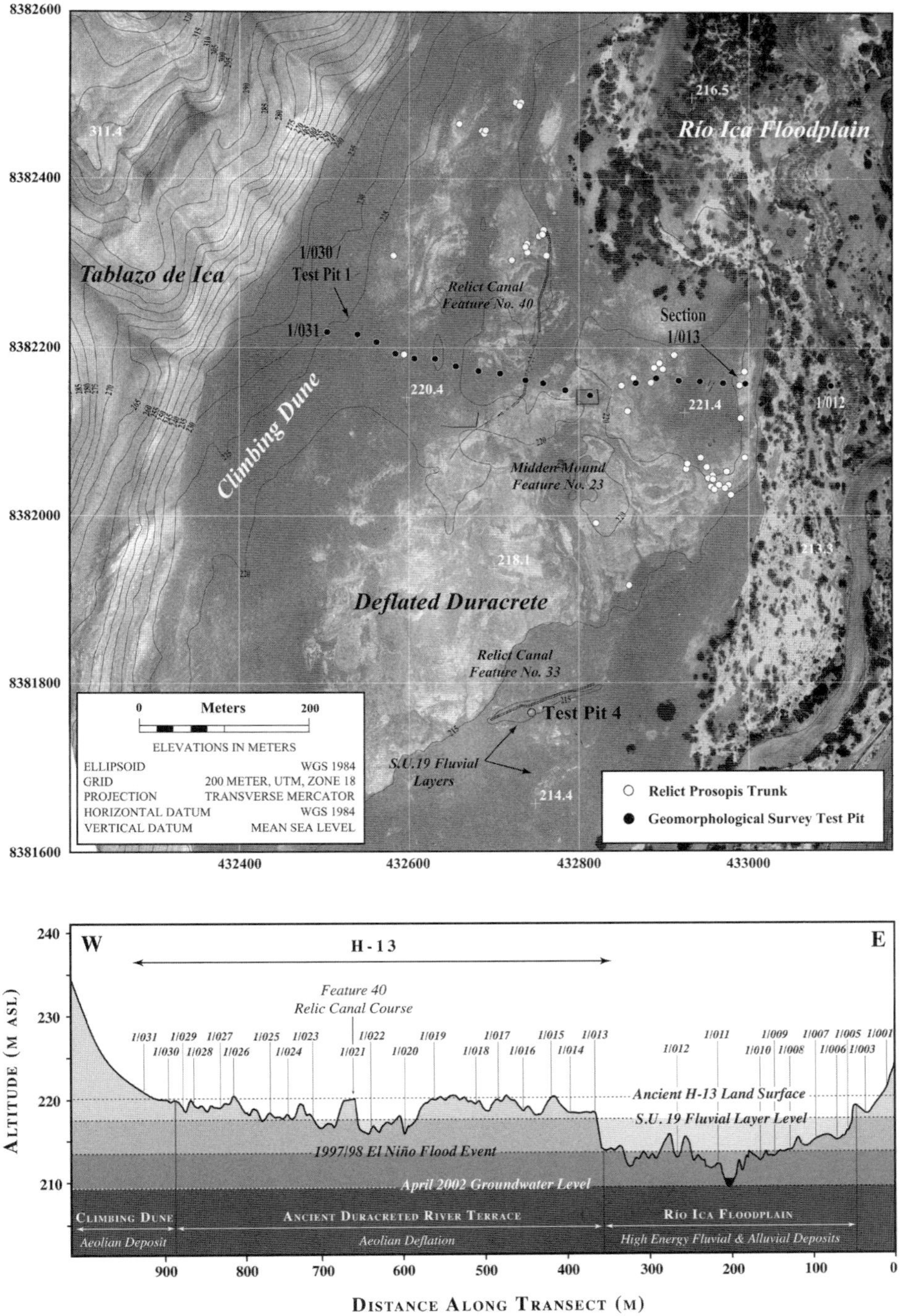

Figure 4.1. Map and profile of geomorphological survey transect across Samaca H-13

Bulk samples were collected from selected layers for the following subsequent analyses in the laboratory: (1) magnetic susceptibility (or 'Mag Sus'), following Bennett *el al.* (1990); (2) loss-on-ignition (or 'LOI'), following Bengtsson and Enell (1986); (3) electrical conductivity (or 'EC'); and (4) grain-size analysis using a Malvern Mastersizer 2000 laser particle sizer (Beresford-Jones 2005 and Beresford-Jones *et al.* 2009a for further details, including protocols). Targeted monolith samples were also taken and thin sections produced from them in the laboratory (after Murphy 1986), for subsequent analysis (following Bullock *et al.* 1985).

Measuring loss-on-ignition following the progressive heating of a sample to different temperatures provides proxy measures of some of its components. LOI at 105 °C is a measure of water held within the pores of a sample and, in sediments such as these with little clays, can be used as a proxy for moisture content. LOI at the higher temperature of 550 °C, provides a measure of organic carbon matter content of the sample, while LOI at 950 °C is a measure of its calcium carbonate content (see Beresford-Jones *et al.* 2009a for a justification of the accuracy of this method in the particular context of the lower Ica Valley). Electrical conductivity meanwhile provides a total measure of all the soluble salts in a sample (the more salts, the greater the EC). Magnetic susceptibility measures the amount of magnetic minerals present in a sample. Mag Sus may be enhanced because of burning and other human activities, biological activity and pedogenesis, or because of exposure to the air. Grain-size analysis measures the proportions of all particle sizes within a sample, from coarse sands through finer silts to the smallest clay particles. Larger particles naturally require more energy to move than finer ones, so the shape of a grain-size profile of a sample offers information on its environment of deposition. While none of the properties measured by these analyses can be used per se to reach definitive conclusions, read together they offer much information about past environments, as we will see.

Basic Geomorphic Units

Moving from east to west along the transect, our survey defined four basic geomorphic units across the Samaca Basin, as follows:

Firstly, a short footslope at the eastern end of the transect covering about 100 metres whose surface is covered with colluvium: materials that have fallen or been blown from the edge of the basin. These consist of poorly sorted coarse to medium sands and small rocks, and they gradually diminish westwards. They overlie those deposits that characterise most of the rest of the basin: shallow layers of massive, very well-sorted fine sands, indicative of wind (aeolian) deposition; and deeper layers of well-sorted, massive, hard silty-clay loam with varying degrees of calcium carbonate concretion and iron staining, indicative of river (alluvial) deposition.

Secondly, the current floodplain of the Río Ica, which is around 300 metres wide along the transect, and is the only part which has vegetation today, in largely degraded riparian associations (Figure 4.2A). As we have seen, the seasonal flow of the Río Ica is highly erratic and varies greatly from year to year. During flood events the river becomes laterally unstable, experiencing a rapid change from meandering to braided flow. This is typical of many dryland rivers, which change from one form to another and back again (so-called 'compound' rivers). In flood, river braids can come to fill all the available space between low terraces (Graf 2002, Schumm 2003). So, in our context here, 'floodplain' means the entire area influenced by the lateral instability of the river during these high-energy events.

The river's erratic discharge gives rise to a complex, 'first-order' topography in its floodplain. Vertical accretion occurs as overbank river flows deposit fine-grained materials in horizontal beds. Lateral accretion occurs in cross-bedded forms, as coarse materials are deposited in lag deposits by exceptional river flows. After flooding, as the river gradually returns to meandering flow, the many minor channels of the braided system become filled with fine sediments. As we will see, these processes are highly influenced by the occurrence and nature of riparian floodplain vegetation.

The disturbed geomorphology of the floodplain reflects these high-energy flood events, including of course that of the 1997/8 El Niño. The floodplain consists of massive, laminated silty-clay crusts of fluvial and alluvial deposition (known locally as *yapana*), overbank deposits of interbedded fine layers of medium to fine sand with well-rounded rocks along several channel beds, newly stabilised dunes and incised channel walls at the edge of the river thalweg. At the time of the survey in April 2002 groundwater levels were encountered at 209 metres a.s.l. This groundwater is full of dissolved salts, has a saline taste and a high pH of 9. The 1997/8 El Niño left overbank flood deposits up to 213.3 metres a.s.l. (see Figure 4.1). Unsurprisingly, archaeological remains are scarce within the floodplain area.

Thirdly, more than half a kilometre of the transect is defined by the relict river terrace of H-13. This terrace stands around 5 metres higher than the floodplain and 10 metres higher than the current Río Ica thalweg. It is totally barren of vegetation. Most of the archaeology of these basins is found across the surface of this terrace and the equivalent terrace in Ullujaya, G-8/9. These terraces are characterised by the prevalence of hard, compacted pans, typical of arid environments in which water loss through evapotranspiration has exceeded water input. These form as salts of differential solubility—but particularly those of calcium, which are relatively insoluble—become concentrated in particular horizons.

We will examine the sediments that make up the relict H-13 terrace in detail shortly, but in general they consist of even, parallel beds of well-consolidated, blocky silty-clay loams, interleaved with structureless, well-sorted, fine sandy loams and massive, well-sorted, very fine sandy loams. In certain layers calcrete cementation forms very hard, petrocalcic desert duracretes, which have a profound effect on the land surface of the relict river terraces of the lower Ica Valley. The high, unvegetated relict terraces are exposed to the full force of the very strong, unimodal wind regime of the region, which has deflated their surfaces over time, creating a so-called 'flat-iron' topography (see Figure 4.2C). The effects of this aeolian deflation of the H-13 and G-8/9 landscape are evident in frequent palimpsests of multiperiod surface scatters of pottery sherds, and complex 'second-order' landforms created by a classic

A Río Ica thalweg.
B Edge of relict terrace H-13 at Section 1/013.
C 'Flat-iron' topography of deflated duracrete surface of H-13 relict terrace.
D Climbing dune at western end of transect with excavation of 1/031 in progress.
E Aerial view from the west of geomorphological survey transect across Samaca H-13 with main geomorphic units and views of transect marked.

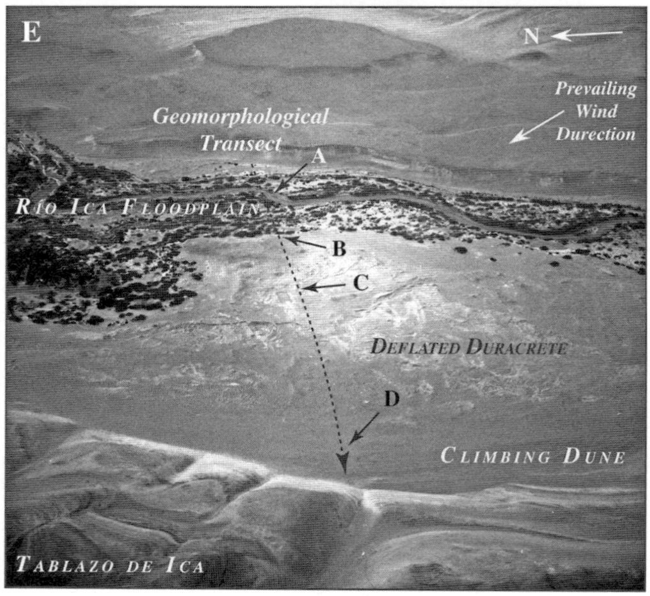

Figure 4.2. Views of the geomorphological survey transect across Samaca H-13

inversion of relief, whereby features such as canals, which were once cut into the land surface, are preserved by duracrete enrichment as upstanding features above the deflated surrounding landscape (Maizels 1988, Cooke *et al.* 1993: 305–6; and see Figure 3.11).

Lastly, the western end of the transect lies across a large dune, blown by the unimodal wind regime to become anchored upon the sedimentary rock slope along the western flank of the basin (a so-called 'climbing dune'; see Figure 4.2D). This part of the transect is particularly important for our purposes here since the deposits of the climbing dune bury and seal ancient land surfaces, which are elsewhere lost across the surface of the relict terraces of the lower Ica Valley because of wind deflation.

There is a clear distinction between the poorly consolidated, coarse to fine sands in graded bedding of the dune and the underlying ancient surface, which is marked by frequent cultural remains such as midden materials and sherds. Underneath, the deposits of the ancient surface are massive, moderately well-consolidated, moderately sorted layers of fine sandy-silt loam, and hard, consolidated, brown silty-clay with a well-developed blocky structure. We will also return to look at these in more detail shortly.

Relict River Terraces

The edge of the relict terraces of the lower Ica Valley is defined by a steep, five metre high embankment, incised by the river at some point in the past (Figure 4.2B). On the survey transect, some three metres of this profile at the edge of H-13 were cleaned, described and subsequently analysed in detail as 'Section 1/013'. The top of the embankment at this point lies at 218.79 metres a.s.l. (see Figure 4.1). This profile represents the deeper-time history of the H-13 relict terrace prior to the deposition of those archaeological materials dating from the Early through to the Middle Horizon, which are found scattered across its surface.

The 1/013 section is characterised by distinctive surface and sub-surface horizons in repeated sequences. Distinguishing soils from sediments in this arid environment is not straightforward because sequences of alluvial and aeolian sedimentation will produce bedding that closely resembles the soil horizons that form through the *in situ* processes of pedogenesis. Indeed, as Cooke *et al.* (1993: 51) note, 'processes of sedimentation and pedogenesis are frequently superimposed'. Those processes include sub-surface enrichment from inputs of fine aeolian dust and processes associated with fluctuations in groundwater levels, including the differential distribution of salts of varying solubility and clay illuviation (Cooke *et al.* 1993: 51). Many of these are interrelated and some can be associated with human activity. Flooding, for instance, can of course be caused by irrigation, while human-induced changes in vegetation cover can alter aeolian deposition, as well as leading to carbonate mobilisation in the soil (Goudie 1973). All together, they often give rise to complex profile sequences whose underlying causal processes are not easy to disentangle.

Secondary calcium carbonate enrichment is a common feature of arid zone soils, and is the defining characteristic of the H-13 relict terrace. Very tough, calcium carbonate enriched 'duracrete' horizons are known as calcretes, or *calíche* on the south coast of Peru and elsewhere. Most calcrete horizons in arid area soils are pedogenic: their formation and development are influenced by factors including the texture of the host material, the partial pressure of carbon dioxide in the soil air, the rate of supply of calcium, amount of infiltrating water, the profile age and the climatic history of the region (Cooke *et al.* 1993: 56–60, Goudie 1973, 1983).

Estimates of the age of duracretes vary widely. Most are thought to be very ancient: from ten thousand years old to as far back as the Miocene (Cooke *et al.* 1993: 61). Yet duracretes formed from floodwaters may develop quite quickly (Machette 1985), and the sheer preponderance of calcrete deposited to a depth of more than three metres, observed in the base of relict canals during excavation (Figure 3.11) strongly suggests that at least some of the duracrete of the relict terraces of the lower Ica Valley is due to to human manipulation of floodwaters during our archaeological time periods. Since the region's hyperarid climate has persisted for millions of years, duracrete formation during the archaeological time spans of interest here cannot easily be explained by climate change in the immediate vicinity. However, any long-term variations in seasonal rainfall on the distant Andean foothills (Eitel *et al.* 2005, Mächtle *et al.* 2006) would have affected groundwater levels in the lower Ica Valley. Here, as in many North American deserts (Machette 1985 and Schlesinger 1985), the primary source of calcium carbonate enrichment is likely dust from winds blowing for millennia over the highly calcareous, sedimentary formations of the Tablazo de Ica.

Beneath its uppermost layer (of 0 to 42 cm), the 1/013 profile shows a series of clear episodic sequences down (B-B' on Figure 4.3). These sequences can be seen in the field and are also reflected in the data from laboratory analyses of the profile and in its grain-size profiles (Figure 4.4). They repeat to depth throughout the entire section (see Beresford-Jones *et al.* 2009a for further details). Each episode consists of:

1. Thin, brown silty-clay loams (e.g. layers 42 to 48 cm, 65 to 73 cm and 83 to 90 cm), with sub-angular blocky structures, numerous ferric mottling and calcite nodules, with relatively high loss-on-ignition (LOI) readings at 550 and 105 °C, and relatively high levels of electrical conductivity (EC) and magnetic susceptibility (Mag Sus). These layers have bimodal grain-size profiles skewed towards finer materials of silts and clays.
2. Underlying, relatively thin, light olive brown, structureless sandy loams (e.g. layers 48 to 53 cm and 73 to 75 cm), with very low LOI readings at 550 and 105 °C and low levels of EC and Mag Sus. These layers are moderately well sorted with grain-size profiles skewed towards coarser materials.
3. Underlying, relatively thick, light yellowish-brown, massive sandy loams (e.g. layers 53 to 65 cm and 75 to 83 cm), with intermediate LOI readings at 550 and 105 °C, and intermediate levels of EC and Mag Sus. These layers have grain-size profiles that are also skewed towards coarser materials, though less so than 2.

These sequences represent the history of the H-13 terrace when it was part of the active river floodplain in the distant past. Episodic, seasonal flood deposition of alluvial silts and

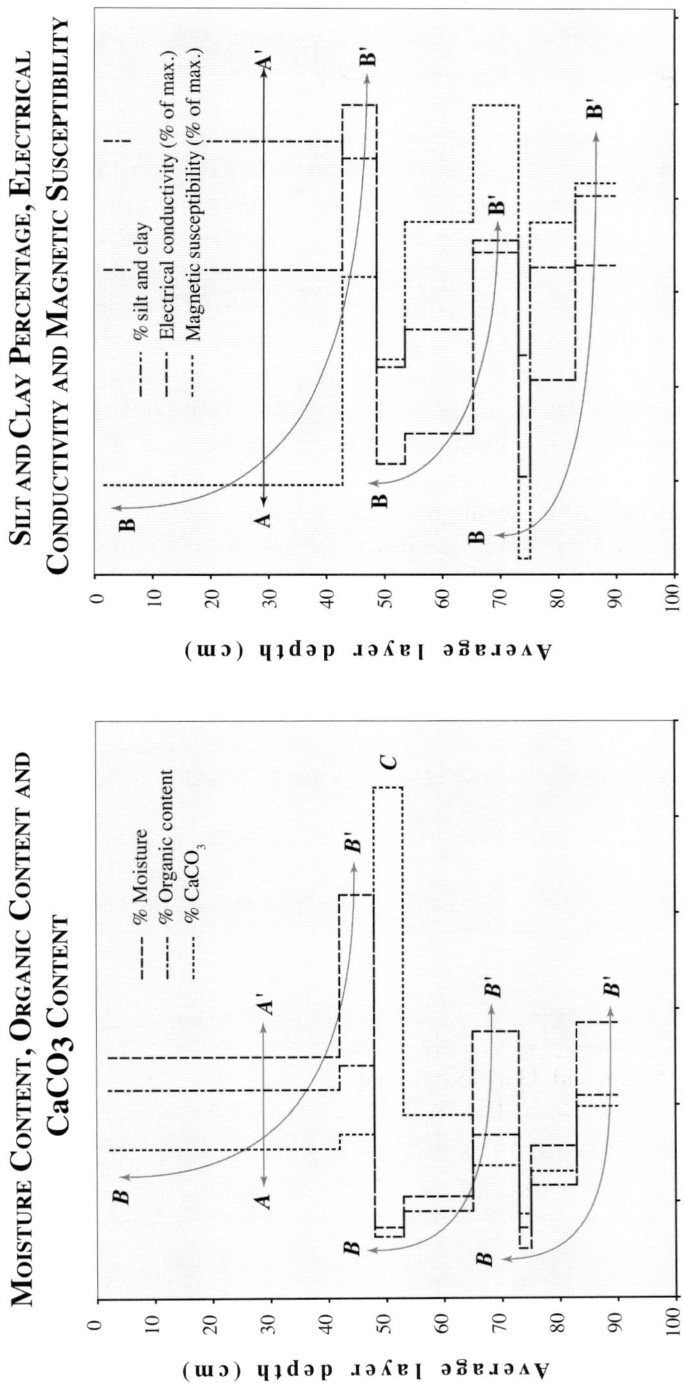

Figure 4.3. Variations of several lines of data with depth in Section 1/013

clays (1. above and B' in Figure 4.3) was followed by subsequent dry periods with aeolian deposition of well-sorted fine sands in varying energies (2. and 3. above and B in Figure 4.3), as seasonal riparian vegetation gradually became established upon damp alluvium (see Figure 4.7).

Mag Sus measurements are very high in alluvial layers and very low in aeolian layers (Figure 4.3), and yet Mag Sus does not correlate significantly with percentage of silt and clay across the whole 1/013 section. This indicates both that alluvial flood deposits remained exposed prior to their gradual burial by aeolian deposits, and also that alluvial layers experienced biological activity as plants grew on the damp alluvium.

Sharp discontinuities in moisture indicated by LOI at 105 °C down the profile confirm the current 'standstill' condition of the H-13 terrace system in this hyperarid environment. Hydrological continuity or ongoing capillary action from the basin water table is very unlikely up a profile which has thin, dry layers with more than 50 per cent sand and large amounts of pore space, but with only about 1 per cent moisture (e.g. 73 to 75 cm).

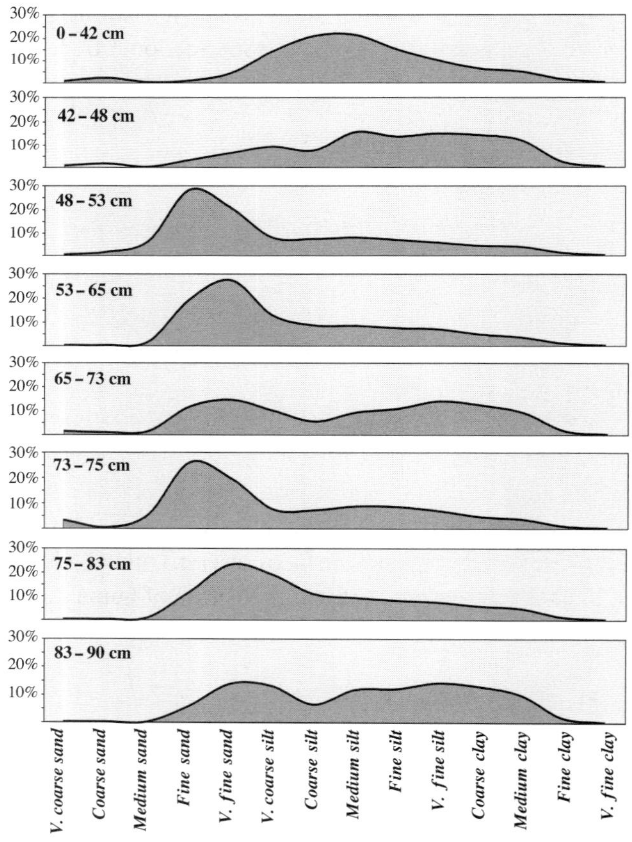

Figure 4.4. Grain-size profiles down geomorphological survey Section 1/013

Measures of organic content by LOI at 550 °C are very low throughout Section 1/103, which is to be expected in sediments of clastic origin and with only incipient soil formation in an arid environment. Nonetheless, the organic matter contents of the ancient alluvial layers (B' in Figure 4.3) of around 4.5 per cent are significantly higher than those of other layers and are fairly typical for alluvial silts. In most soils organic content is typically a measure of their productivity. Yet these alluviums—as, for instance, on the Nile—are extremely fertile. This is because their productivity has little to do with their organic content and everything to do with their annually replenished content of mineral nutrients.

Although measures of calcium carbonate content by LOI at 950 °C generally vary in accordance with the observed episodic sequence, there are notable exceptions. These include a very high calcite content of layer 48 to 53 cm and a white petrocalcic K horizon of almost pure calcrete at 240 to 245 cm. This indicates that calcite enrichment is largely the product of processes of secondary enrichment (Goudie 1973, Raghavan *et al.* 1991), which suggests that groundwater levels in the basin were once much higher than those that persist today, some 10 metres beneath the standstill condition terrace.

EC provides an overall measure of soluble salts. While it is strongly positively correlated with percentage of silts and clays in the samples from Section 1/013, their calcite contents are not. This indicates that calcrete formation here does not conform straightforwardly to the model proposed by Gile (1966, Gile *et al.* 1997), in which laminations form as water through-flow is channelled over a plugged, fine-textured hardpan. However, another factor behind the calcite enrichment of the relict terraces of the lower Ica Valley may be previously extant vegetation. Many of the calcrete horizons across today's barren surface of H-13 and G-8/9 are full of calcite rhizoliths and huarango leaf litter pseudomorphs (Figure 5.2) and calcite nodules are observed within and below the alluvial layers of Section 1/013. These may indicate drawing of groundwater up-profile by roots (Goldberg and Macphail 2006: 69). Moreover, as we will see in Chapter 8, removal of vegetation may itself lead to a concentration of calcite because of changes in carbon dioxide partial pressures in the rhizosphere.

The uppermost part of the 1/013 stratigraphy (0 to 42 cm) is, however, quite different to these underlying floodplain sequences. This thick, upper layer of pale brown, massive silty-clay with frequent ferric mottles is significantly less sorted and has a symmetrical grain-size profile about a median, medium silt: very distinct from its underlying layers (Figure 4.4). Since a relict canal system runs across the surfaces of H-13 and G-8/9 these distinctions of layer 0 to 42 cm are likely to be the result of the imposition of human control upon the energies of the underlying episodic floodplain regime, bringing with it agriculture and incipient pedogenesis.

Although of considerable thickness, this uppermost layer is nonetheless clearly truncated at its top, since it is evident that the surfaces of the relict terraces of the Ullujaya and Samaca basins have undergone severe wind deflation over time. We can determine the original land surface of these terraces from the extant form of their archaeology. For instance, the average height of the course of canal 40 across H-13 is 220.06 metres a.s.l., while its maximum height is 220.88 metres a.s.l. This means that the original surrounding land surface of the H-13 terrace lay at around 220.5 metres a.s.l. The average height of the deflated flanks of this canal lie at 218.55 metres a.s.l. This is almost coincident with the top of Section 1/013, and it implies some two metres of deflation since the canal was abandoned. Thus, the 0 to 42 cm layer observed today in Section 1/013 has been truncated by this depth and represents only the bottom part of the original surface profile of the terrace, when relict canal 40 was in operation.

The amount of entrainment of grains by wind, and thus of aeolian deflation experienced in a particular environment, is of course a rather complex function of wind speed, surface conditions, including vegetation cover, and grain size and cohesion—which in turn depend upon properties such as moisture and salt enrichment (see for instance Maizels 1988, Fryberger and Dean 1979, Cooke *et al.* 1993). But since, as we saw in Chapter 3, the date by which the H-13 relict terrace was completely abandoned by vegetation can be determined through various lines of archaeological data to around the end of the Middle Horizon—a millennium ago—we can go on to estimate the average rate at which the stable, unimodal wind regime of the region is deflating these relict terraces. This is useful because, as Cooke *et al.* (1993: 263) observe, 'there are few reliable measurements of rates of transport in the field'. Assuming a deflation depth of 2 metres, the total volume of material removed from the surface of the H-13 terrace, much of it deposited in the climbing dune anchored on the western edge of the basin, can be estimated to total some 377,000 m^3. The flank of the terrace perpendicular to the unimodal Samaca wind direction is around 1,100 metres in length (see Figure 4.1), which implies an average deflation rate of around 0.31 m^3 (m width)$^{-1}$ yr^{-1}: or, by around 2 mm depth per year.

Buried Ancient Land Surfaces

Since most of the surfaces of the relict terraces of the lower Ica Valley are deflated by the wind they offer few prospects for the preservation of deep stratigraphies relating to archaeological time periods. However, at the westernmost extreme of our geomorphological transect, where it encounters the climbing dune deposited against the edge of the basin, we did find sealed, and thereby preserved, land surfaces beneath those dune deposits (Figure 4.1).

Survey Pit 1/030 (or 'Test Pit 1'): buried soils

Survey Pit 1/030 was located at the very base of the climbing dune at 219.89 metres a.s.l. The altitude of the bottom of this pit was therefore roughly that of the top of Section 1/013, about half a kilometre away, across the relict terrace H-13. This survey pit was later expanded to become Test Pit No. 1 (Figure 4.5).

Uniquely in all the profiles recorded along the geomorphological survey transect, that of Survey Pit 1/030 contained evidence of a buried *soil* horizon. The profile of 1/030 comprised: (1) a surface layer (0 to 33 cm) of unconsolidated, graded sands—the aeolian

A View south of expanded Survey Pit 1/030 as Test Pit 1 under excavation.
B Human footprint in surface of S.U. 5 in Test Pit 1.
C Western profile of Test Pit 1 with thin section monolith sampling marked.

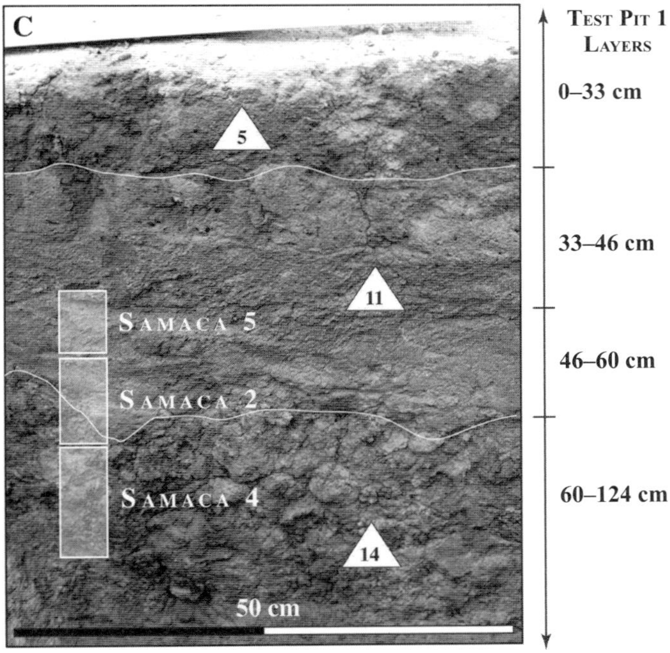

Figure 4.5. Context and details of geomorphological survey Test Pit 1/030

deposits of the climbing dune; overlying (2) a sequence of moderately well-consolidated and moderately-sorted sandy and silt loams (33 to 46 cm and 46 to 60 cm); over (3) a brown, well-developed, blocky-structured, sandy silt loam (60 to 124 cm). In the field this latter layer appeared to be a buried soil horizon.

Monolith samples were therefore taken from the interfaces across layers 46 to 60 cm and 60 to 124 cm, and thin sections were prepared from these monoliths for micromorphological analysis to refine the characterisation of this profile (Beresford-Jones *et al.* 2009a). This analysis showed that the upper part of this profile, immediately beneath the dune deposits, was alluvium arising from low-energy flooding, with some aeolian input. The thin sections prepared from these monoliths had a well-accommodated, sub-angular blocky microstructure with short thin planar voids filled with 'dusty' clay inclusions of illuvium (that is to say, materials dispersed by water vertically within the profile). They also showed polyconcave voids, suggesting soil collapse related to water saturation, and iron mottles and manganese nodules were associated with these cracks and channels. The fine groundmass of their deposits was moderately striated and stained with oxidised iron, characteristics typical of fine sediments undergoing shrink–swell processes caused by periodic wetting and drying.

The thin section from below these was quite different and confirmed its identification as an old soil horizon. Its fabric was light brown, much more stained with amorphous organic matter than the iron-stained fabrics of the overlying sections. Coalesced crumb peds and microaggregates suggested reworking by soil fauna for some time. Although organic materials within this thin section were depleted through oxidation, they nonetheless still made up almost one quarter of its area. Its sandy loam texture was much more mixed than that of the layers above. The more organic and mixed nature of this layer indicates that it was once a proper soil horizon, lying beneath multiple low-energy, alluvial deposits.

At some time in the past, this whole sequence became petrified into its current standstill condition and, in due course, was overlain by the aeolian deposits of the climbing dune. Since wind deflation of H-13 has removed its once extant stratigraphy, only isolated fragments of this soil layer are observed outside the area sealed by the dune, most notably along parts of the eastern flanks of relict canals, which are protected from the effects of the wind by the canals themselves.

The significance of this identification of alluvial deposits, overlying a once organic, buried soil horizon, is perhaps best appreciated in Figure 4.5A. For this profile lies today in the midst of a barren landscape, more than half a kilometre distant from, and about five metres above, the edge of the current riparian Río Ica floodplain. Indeed, as Survey Pit 1/030 was expanded to become Test Pit 1 and its unconsolidated climbing dune deposits were brushed away, a remarkably preserved footprint was found on the underlying surface of the hard silt-loam (33 to 46 cm, also called Stratigraphic Unit 5, or 'S.U. 5' in Test Pit 1). This footprint is further, and rather poignant, evidence that S.U. 5 was an ancient surface, buried and protected by the climbing dune. And when that person stepped upon that surface, it was moist (Figure 4.5 B).

Survey Pit 1/031: gradual aeolian deposition

Survey Pit 1/031 marked the western limit of the transect, 25 metres further up the ascending face of the climbing dune from 1/030, at a surveyed altitude of 222.43 metres a.s.l., and some 2.5 vertical metres higher than the dune surface at 1/030 (Figures 4.1 and 4.2D).

The upper layer of 1/031 of 0 to 64 cm consisted of light brownish grey, unconsolidated fine to coarse sands in a graded bedding—the aeolian deposits of the climbing dune. Most analyses of the sediments of this profile showed no clearly discernible repeating sequences (like those of 1/013, for instance) and the profile showed no evidence of alluvial deposition. Indeed, the bottom of Survey Pit 1/031 lay around half a metre higher than the surface at 1/030, and was therefore well above the level of alluvial deposition recorded in that survey pit. However, grain-size profiles record a gradual increase in the proportion of coarse materials up the profile (Figure 4.6). Larger particles requiring more energy to move them than finer ones, this pattern indicates a steady increase in the energy of deposition by the wind.

Beneath its seal of dune deposits, interspersed among the upper parts of its sequence, was frequent evidence of human activity, including significant amounts of charcoal and an

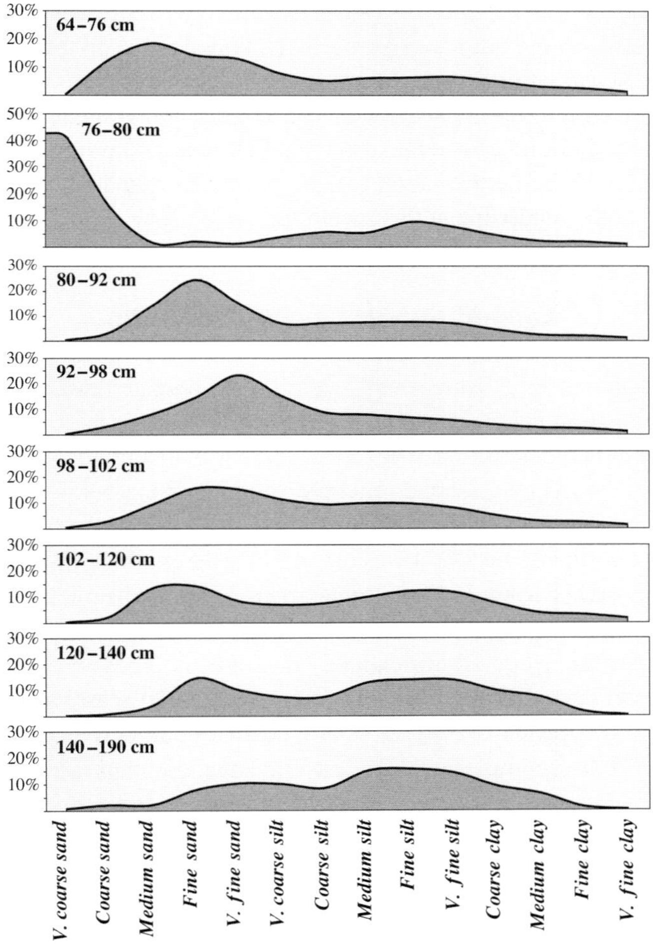

Figure 4.6. Grain-size profiles down geomorphological survey Test Pit 1/031

in situ hearth. Some Early Nasca (Phases 2/3) ceramic fragments in the 76 to 80 cm layer date it to the Early Intermediate Period. Layer 92 to 98 cm was that of the *in situ* hearth, which unsurprisingly showed high readings for carbonates, electrical conductivity and magnetic susceptibility (Beresford-Jones *et al.* 2009a).

Organic matter readings increased down the profile until depths of 140 cm and show very high levels for arid area sediments (e.g. 10.4 per cent for layer 98 to 102 cm). This was because proportions of desiccated huarango tree litter (*poña*) increased to this depth down the 1/031 profile. The sheer preponderance of this fossil tree litter is strong evidence of huarangos once growing in this immediate vicinity, and its excellent preservation confirmed that these deposits lay above the sequences of high pH floodwater wetting and drying that characterise the layers of 1/030, some 2.5 metres lower down on the surface of H-13. We will return in Chapter 5 to the significance of other archaeobotanical data extracted from Survey Pit 1/031.

These data indicate that the deposits of Survey Pit 1/031 represent surfaces upon which accumulations of aeolian materials were progressively deposited on the western flank of the basin in a unidirectional wind regime. Moreover, there was a gradual increase over time in the energy of deposition of these particles by the wind, as the graded sand aeolian deposits of the climbing dune built up. Since the lower Ica Valley has constantly experienced strong winds for millennia, the best explanation for this pattern is a gradual change in exposure to that wind regime of the landscape at this location.

Ancient Fluvial Layers and El Niño

Elsewhere in the landscape of Samaca H-13, excavation revealed further information about the geomorphological processes that underlie change in the basins of the lower Ica Valley. Most notably, these included the excavation of 'Test Pit 4' in a midden mound (Feature 43), alongside a relict canal 33 on a second relict river terrace, lying below the main expanse of H-13 but also now barren and deflated by wind erosion (see Figure 4.1).

The excavated profile of Test Pit 4 was capped by a 30 cm thick layer (called 'S.U. 19'). S.U. 19 was composed of irregularly orientated peds of well-consolidated, very fine clayey silt. Its bottom 10 cm showed frequent lenses of very fine sand, usually occupying the interstitial areas between the irregularly orientated fine silt peds. These are the features of a fluvial, overbank flood deposit—the fertile alluviums deposited seasonally by the river. The local name for these deposits is *yapana*—the Quechua noun derived from the verb *yapa*, meaning to replenish or 'top-up' (Paul Heggarty, personal communication). For annual alluvial inundations of *yapana* are indeed 'top-ups' of fertility and moisture in the lower Ica Valley.

As the river subsides, the alluvium carried by it settles out from suspension in the standing waters of overbank floods—larger, heavier particles first, and smaller, lighter particles last— giving rise to a typical 'fining-upward' sequence of grain sizes. These *yapanas* dry out very slowly because their surfaces are sealed to evaporation by the very finest silt and clay particles. This top-up layer of very fertile *yapana* will thus usually retain its moisture long enough for a variety of quick-growing crops, such as maize, to be sown, brought to maturity and harvested. As the *yapana* dries, desiccation cracks and fissures open in the upper silt layers. Fine sands reworked by the wind are deposited within these voids. If exposed for any time, the dry, well-consolidated peds of the *yapana* layer become broken up into smaller, randomly orientated peds through disturbance by animals, germinating plants and the effects of wind erosion. Figure 4.7 shows this sequence over the six months following the 1997/8 El Niño event in the Samaca Basin.

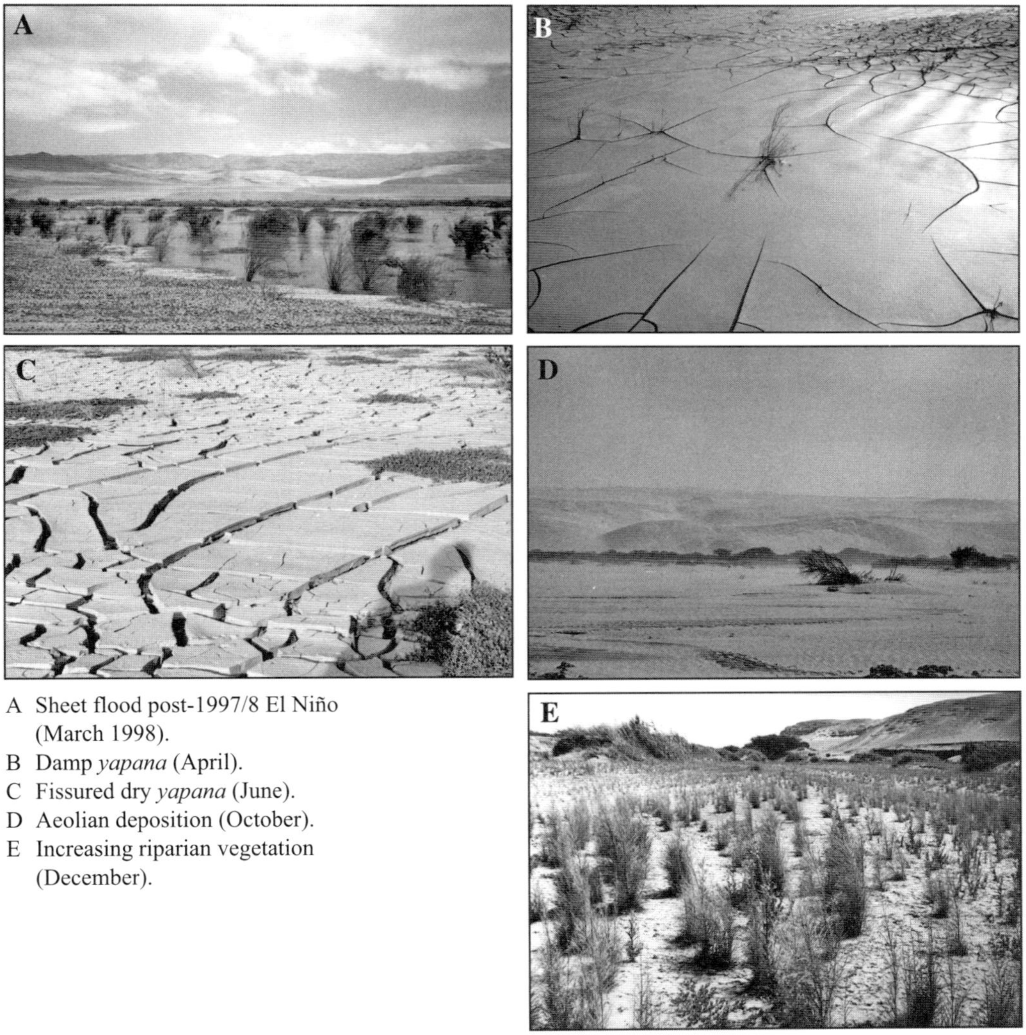

A Sheet flood post-1997/8 El Niño (March 1998).
B Damp *yapana* (April).
C Fissured dry *yapana* (June).
D Aeolian deposition (October).
E Increasing riparian vegetation (December).

Figure 4.7. The floodplain sequence today in the Samaca Basin, lower Ica Valley

A View east across Samaca H-13 showing mound 43 context.
B South-facing profile of Test Pit 4 showing fluvial (*yapana*) layer (S.U. 19) and Early Nasca midden deposits (S.U. 20), 27/28 and 40) with dominant charcoal layers. Note *in situ* Early Nasca ceramic fragment at base of S.U. 27/28.
C Detail of *yapana* cap on mound 43 prior to excavation, showing midden contexts immediately beneath with terrestrial mollusc (Fam. Bulmulidae) shells and charcoal lenses.
D Another fragment of the S.U. 19 fluvial layer in mound 46.
E Early Nasca (Phase 5) ceramic fragments from Test Pit 4, midden contexts (S.U. 40).

Figure 4.8. Context and details of Test Pit 4 and S.U. 19 flood layer

S.U. 19 appears identical to the deposits left by the extensive sheet flooding observed in the lower Ica Valley during the recent 1997/8 El Niño event. Of course, layers of *yapana*, even ones as thick as S.U. 19, cannot be simply taken as indicators of past El Niño events. Yet, as we saw in Chapter 2, there is a very good correlation between river flow and the Southern Oscillation Index in the Ica Valley. It may therefore be assumed that flood deposits of a certain size may be indicative of past El Niño events. The question remains, of course, as to precisely what size of flood deposit indicates an ancient El Niño flood, as opposed to merely a particularly strong river flow.

In fact, the size and position in the landscape of the S.U. 19 *yapana* layer do strongly suggest that it was indeed the product of a major ancient El Niño event akin to that of 1997/8. Firstly, the current surface of S.U. 19 in Test Pit No. 4 lies at 216.5 metres a.s.l., or around 6.5 metres higher than the Río Ica thalweg today (Figure 4.1). Secondly, S.U. 19 has long been exposed on the surface of mound 43. Elsewhere, other fragments of this ancient fluvial catena at precisely the same altitude are evident at scattered points across the deflated H-13 landscape. Preserved from the truncating effects of wind erosion, some of those layers are no less than 60 cm thick (Figure 4.8D). By contrast, the *yapana* levels of the 1997/8 El Niño flood—demonstrably the largest flood in these basins in the past millennium—reached only 213.3 metres a.s.l. across the equivalent profile in the Samaca Basin. Conservatively, this is some 3.5 vertical metres lower than the level of the S.U. 19 flood. By all these measures, the ancient flood that deposited S.U. 19 was a gigantic one.

Moreover, we can to some extent date the S.U. 19 flood, for the *yapana* cap in Test Pit 4 sits directly on top of a series of archaeological midden contexts containing mollusc shell, animal bone, charcoals and various plant macrofossils (Figure 4.8C). This midden also contained distinctive, slip-decorated Nasca 5 ceramic fragments (S.U. 27 and 40, Figure 4.8E). Thus, the S.U. 19 flood event occurred sometime after Nasca 5, towards the end of the Early Intermediate Period.

We will return to consider the significance of the S.U. 19 fluvial layer, and our other geomorphological data here, for our model of landscape change for the lower Ica Valley in Chapter 10. In the meantime, the story it tells is as follows.

Tracing Landscape Change

Today, the floodplain of the Río Ica in the Ullujaya and Samaca basins is narrow. It has a highly disturbed geomorphology—with overbank deposits, silty-clay alluvial crusts and newly stabilised dunes of remobilised riverbed deposits—indicative of laterally unstable, high-energy flood events. At some time in the past the river has incised into its floodplain, exposing the five metre embankment and creating the H-13 and G-8/9 relict terraces.

The deep-time history of these terraces, as recorded in Section 1/013, shows repeated episodes of flooding—with the deposition of alluvial silts—followed by dry periods—with increased aeolian inputs of well-sorted fine sands. During this time these terraces were part of the active river floodplain. Yet the uppermost part of the Section 1/013 sequence reflects a very different environment: one under a controlled energy regime indicative of human influence and control over the process of episodic sedimentation and of pedogenesis. This is quite unsurprising in view of the Early Nasca canal system preserved across the surface of the H-13 and G-8/9 terraces.

Sediments in these terraces are indurated with various salts and have a high pH of 9. The groundwater today in these basins is slightly saline, with the same pH. EC (and thus pH) levels increase up the sequence of alluvial layers in Section 1/013 (Figure 4.3). So these terraces—petrified into a 'standstill' condition by river down-cutting—preserve evidence of the gradual accumulation of salts that often occurs through irrigation of low-lying areas. Elsewhere, this has long been put forth as one explanation of civilisation 'collapse' in several arid regions: for the Ur dynasty in Mesopotamia (Jacobsen and Adams 1958), and for the Hohokam (Redman 1999)—those quintessential irrigators of another arid American riparian system, whom we will meet in Chapter 9. Today salinisation, due to irrigation, is a problem affecting huge areas of formerly productive agricultural lands in arid regions.

Once river entrenchment had occurred, these terraces became entirely degraded landscapes without any vegetation cover. In time they were completely exposed to the effects of the region's extraordinary wind regime. The process of aeolian deflation had begun. The presence of different degrees of secondary calcium carbonates in the terraces—in part due to human floodplain management and irrigation—and the subsequent exposure of these deposits by deflation, created a complex second-order landform with inverted relief. So features cemented with calcite such as canal courses survive today standing above the deflated relict terrace surfaces, while artefacts spanning some two millennia, from the Early through to the Middle Horizon, have been left as mixed assemblages scattered across them. As we will see in Chapter 10, these archaeological data can be used to date approximately these processes of geomorphological change.

The products of that deflation have been deposited by a unidirectional wind regime as a climbing dune, anchored against the western flank of these basins. This deposition has buried, and thereby preserved, a portion of the ancient land surface along that western edge, encountered in Survey Pits 1/030 and 1/031. Those excavations provide evidence about the extent of alluvial deposition and organic-rich soil horizons once present on these terraces, and thus of the dramatic scale of landscape and ecological change in the lower Ica Valley.

The proximate reason for the abandonment of these relict terraces was river entrenchment. Yet the ultimate cause that exposed these landscapes to that impact remains to be properly discerned, for many of the changes recorded in the extant landscape of the lower Ica Valley are the products of *anthropogenic* geomorphology.

5. Tracing Human Ecology:

The Archaeobotanical and Malacological Record

One of the most striking features of the archaeology of the Peruvian coast is its seemingly almost miraculous preservation of organic remains. In most archaeological contexts artefacts such as textiles and baskets, the detritus of food preparation, and indeed the bodies of the ancient inhabitants themselves, quickly succumb to inevitable decay. What remains for archaeologists to recover is merely the inorganic skeleton of life's rich pattern, or a microcosm of plant remains preserved by the happenstance of charring. Not so on the south coast of Peru. In a land of virtually no rainfall, if organic materials are deposited above a fluctuating and alkaline water table, they may be preserved in a desiccated and yet otherwise unchanged condition for millennia. Here the problem is rather the opposite: how to 'separate the wheat from the chaff' in the sheer volumes of organic remains that can be recovered from some contexts.

The purpose of our archaeobotanical work was to reconstruct the human utilisation of plants in the past. Much of our focus in excavation was on archaeological middens—the rubbish of ancient settlement. This is because they offer a record of human ecology, not least of changing human diet as evidenced in food refuse. Indeed, while the beautiful artefacts of the ancient inhabitants of the south coast are renowned worldwide through museum collections of looted mortuary contexts, remarkably little is yet known about how these people actually *lived*. As Silverman and Proulx (2002) put it, Nasca society still largely remains 'invisible in life as it was visible in death'. Seemingly humble rubbish deposits offer us unique insight into past lifeways. They also turn out to be proxy indicators of changing ecological conditions in the basins of the lower Ica Valley.

Aside from their hyperarid climate, two other features of these basins are fortunate for our purpose here. Firstly, as we saw in the last chapter, potential agents of natural geomorphological change here can be reduced to two: the river and the wind. These two high

Chapterhead: Detail of Nasca embroidered textile showing pacay (*Inga feuillei*) tree growing through a pampas cat that holds in its paw a bean pod. The pacay, like the huarango, is a legume tree that improves soil quality (drawing courtesy of the Brooklyn Museum).

energy agents operate in easily definable directions and have done so continuously over great time-depths. This is convenient for our consideration of all those processes that influence the deposition of plant and other fossil materials and thereby bias the archaeological record which remains for us to study: the so-called 'taphonomic' processes. Secondly, the ecology of this region is peculiarly sensitive. When ecological or geomorphological thresholds are breached in these riparian desert ecosystems, change can become complete and irreversible. As Cooke *et al.* (1993: 45) put it, 'as a consequence of the critical nature of these thresholds, degradation is more easily provoked in arid than in humid soils'. Moreover, deserts—especially hyperarid ones such as that of the south coast of Peru—are regions of sharply defined boundaries: between verdant riparian vegetation and absolute desert; between well-drained and poorly drained soils and sediments; and between sediment deposits and weathered, bare rock basin mantles. So the imprints of past change are more easily discernible here than they might be in other more climatically and ecologically varied environments. We begin with a brief outline of our methods.

Methods

Any archaeological record—even one enjoying the remarkable preservation conditions of the lower Ica Valley—offers only a fragmented and partial picture of the past. Archaeologists try to mitigate these weaknesses through careful selection of excavation contexts and sampling strategies. Most importantly, however, since each archaeological dataset has its own strengths, weaknesses and taphonomic considerations, they seek to use as many lines of data as possible. Interpretations based upon so-called 'multi-proxy' data will always be more interesting and secure than those offered by any one single dataset.

Today, as we have seen, almost the entirety of the ancient river terraces H-13 and G-8/9 is devoid of vegetation. And yet geomorphological analyses reveal that within this desolate landscape are buried fragments of ancient, once organic soils. Here we will focus upon several lines of archaeobotanical data, which will help further elaborate a picture of landscape change in the lower Ica Valley. The *sine qua non* for reconstructing a history of ecological change, or of human use and manipulation of an ecosystem, is an understanding of today's plant distributions and having to hand a modern reference collection by which to identify archaeobotanical remains. The rich and beautiful riparian ecology of the south coast will therefore be the subject of forthcoming chapters.

In the hyperarid climate of the lower Ica Valley well-preserved ancient plant remains range in size from entire tree trunks to microscopic pollen grains. Huge macrofossils such as tree trunks can of course be surveyed and their distribution mapped. Smaller plant macro- and microfossils need to be excavated and extracted undamaged from their archaeological contexts for their subsequent identification in the laboratory.

Flotation in the field using a simplified version of the standard Cambridge Flotation Tank (see Beresford-Jones 2005 for further details) proved an extremely effective way of extracting desiccated organic remains undamaged from the dry and friable sediments of the lower Ica Valley. Samples of uniform, eight-litre volumes from selected archaeological deposits were floated and their contents separated into 500 mm and 2.0 mm light fractions using a sieve deck. These flotation samples were subsequently sorted and identified in the laboratory using a modern reference collection and available literature (see in particular Martin and Barkley 1961, Sagástegui 1973, Pearsall 1980, Gunn and Ritchie 1988, Brako and Zarucchi 1993, Gentry 1996, Brack Egg 1999, and see Beresford-Jones 2005 for further details). Marine and terrestrial molluscs, crustaceans and echinoderms were separated in heavy fractions and identified. Meanwhile, sediments for pollen analysis were prepared in the laboratory following Berglund and Ralska-Jasiewiczowa (1986).

Relict Tree Trunks

By far the plainest evidence of landscape change in the Samaca and Ullujaya basins comes in the form of relict tree trunks scattered over the most desolate parts of their windblown terraces (Cook 1999: 65): 396 of these were recorded, stretching across H-13 and G-8/9 (Figure 5.1), but usually clearly associated with the higher, deflated duracrete surfaces of these terraces. Exposed to the long effects of wind abrasion, these relict trunks are very worn but several were excavated to ascertain for certain that they were *in situ* tree trunks (Figure 5.2). All showed the distinctive very hard, fine-grained wood and contorted growth characteristics of the huarango. Many were hundreds of metres from the current vegetated river floodplain, some up to a kilometre distant. The highest relict trunk ('T15' on Figure 5.1) was recorded at 233 metres a.s.l. on Samaca H-13, some 25 metres above the current groundwater level.

There are, however, many other indications of ancient trees growing on these terraces. Great expanses of these terraces have been deflated into a 'flat-iron' topography by the effects of wind erosion, which has exposed the edges of many thick sections of duracrete. These reveal relict tree roots and even the imprint of ancient tree litter. The huarango deposits huge quantities of this *poña* litter of leaves and twigs. Over time calcium carbonate replacement has created so-called 'pseudomorphs' of this tree litter, so fragile that they cannot be excavated, other than by the infinitely delicate hand of the wind. And where the wind has exposed thick sections of duracrete, these reveal intricate *poña* pseudomorphs across a truly basin-wide scale (Figure 5.2).

The distribution of all these relict tree trunks and wide expanses of *poña* pseudomorphs offers a clear impression of a once much-wider riparian floodplain in these lower Ica Valley basins, but the question is, of course, how old they are. The trunks themselves have not been radiocarbon dated. Yet, given that as we will see, the huarango may live for more than a millennium, there may be little point in doing so. We will return to consider this matter in our concluding chapter.

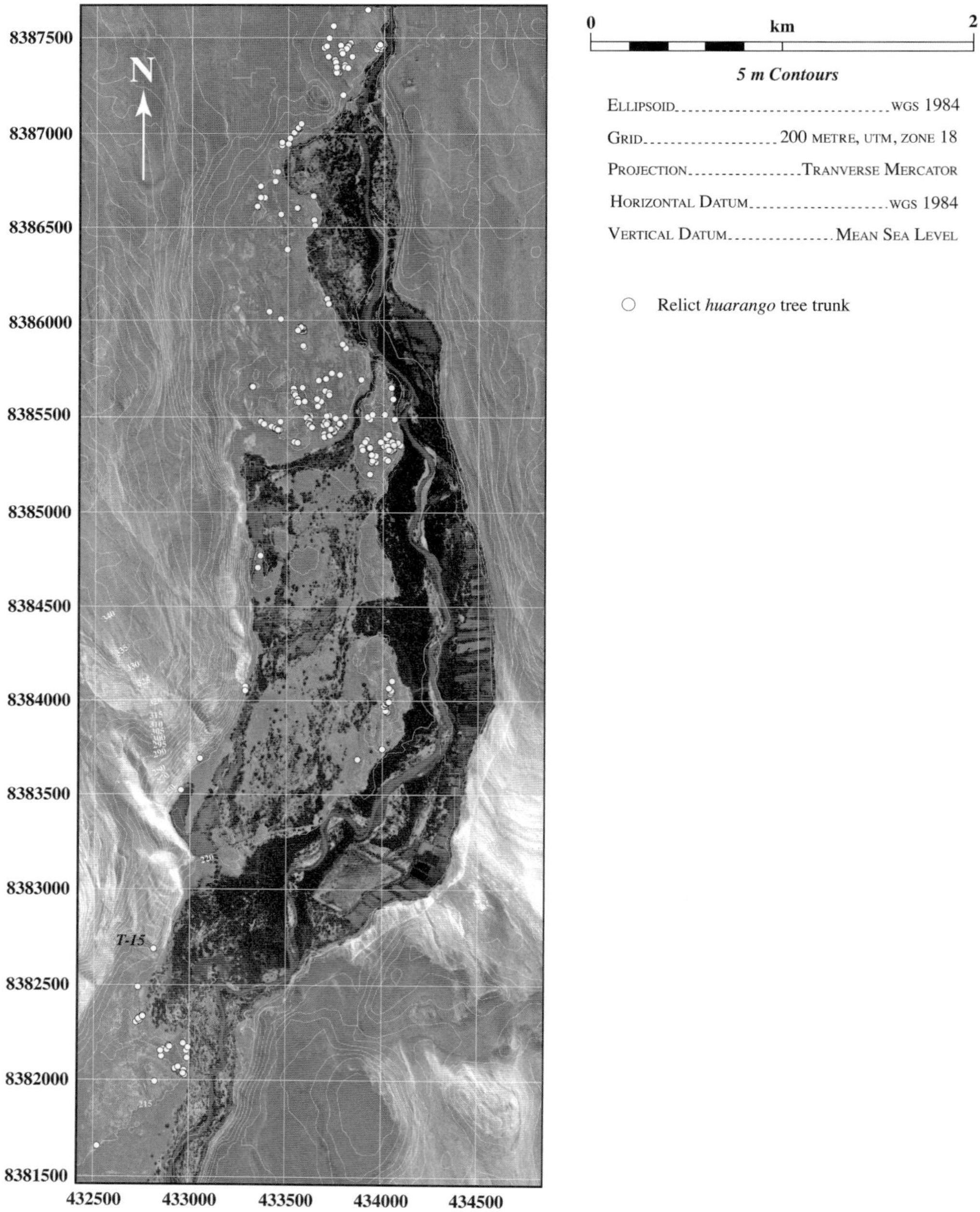

Figure 5.1. Map of relict huarango tree trunks of the Samaca and Ullujaya basins

A H-13 relict huarango trunk exposed by recent civil engineering work on Ullujaya G-8/9.
B and D Relict huarango trunks under excavation on Samanca H13 (T10–Test Pit 8, T14–Test Pit 7, respectively).
C–F Selected relict huarango trunks from H-13 and G-8/9 showing long effects of wind abrasion.
G Calcite huarango leaf litter pseudomorphs and rhisoliths exposed by wind erosion in H-13 calcretes.
H Detail of G.

Figure 5.2. Selected huarango tree trunks and other remains from the Samaca H-13 and Ullujaya G-8/9 terraces

Prehistoric Human Ecology

What then of the archaeobotanical and malacological evidence coming from human habitation sites excavated on the relict river terraces of H-13 and G-8/9? Tables 5.1 summarises the archaeobotanical data from all our excavations to which we will refer throughout the subsequent discussion. The forty-six archaeological contexts analysed—totalling almost four hundred litres of samples—have been arranged into chronological order according to their material culture associations. Their plant remains have been grouped according to their ecological associations:

Group A the trees of the riparian woodland, dominated by huarango;
Group B the shrubs and herbs of riparian woodland and woodland edges;
Group C the so-called 'agrestal' weeds associated with areas of agriculture and other human disturbance;
Group D the riverine plants of water courses and pools;
Group E the grasses of open areas;
Group F the cultivated plants of the agricultural landscape; and finally,
Group G those wood charcoals, charred parenchyma remains and other flowering plant fragments that could not be further identified.

Table 5.2 shows the marine and terrestrial mollusc and other marine foods recovered from the heavy fractions of the products of flotation of selected lower Ica Valley contexts. We will refer to all these here as 'malacological' data for the sake of convenience, although crustaceans and sea urchins are, of course, not molluscs. Again, these are arranged into chronological order according to their material culture associations.

Recall that all these data come from flotation samples of a uniform size and are therefore in a broad sense comparable. Yet we will resist what Hubbard and Clapham (1992: 117) rightly call the 'Pavlovian urge to quantify', for, as they observe, quantification beyond that justified by context or taphonomy 'degenerates into nonsense'. Plant materials in Table 5.1 and malacological remains in Table 5.2 are therefore classified according to their occurrence in the assemblages of the different archaeological contexts as 'some' (fewer than 10 items), 'moderate' (between 10 and 100), and 'abundant' (more than 100). Those logarithmic categories make for valid comparisons by smoothing out some of the possible vagaries arising from sampling, sorting and counting large amounts of remains from archaeological contexts with different taphonomic histories. In particular, Table 5.1 also shows at the bottom the occurrence of heavy fraction materials in all these contexts since these provide a measure of the relative density of these various midden contexts. These will be very useful in seeking to compare contexts across time.

In the Chavín Early Horizon

As we saw in Chapter 3, the earliest contexts that we excavated and analysed dated from the Early Horizon: those midden contexts from mound 21, Ullujaya G-8/9 that contained Chavín ceramic fragments (Ocucaje Phases 3 and 4), in a clear stratigraphic association beneath a later Early Intermediate Nasca occupation and canal cut. Dating to around 750 BC these are likely among the oldest midden contexts yet scientifically analysed in the Ica Valley (see also DeLeonardis 1997: 558–9). And, strikingly, these ancient remains contain no plant domesticates (Group F in Table 5.1), other than cotton (*Gossipium barbadense*) fibres and seeds.

Cotton (*Gossipium* sp.) is a shrub native to tropical and subtropical dryland watercourses worldwide and, uniquely among major crops, seemingly underwent independent domestication processes in the Old World and the New. *Gossipium barbadense*, the cotton domesticated on the coast of Peru (varieties of which are known as 'extra long staple', 'Sea Island' or 'Egyptian' cotton), is one of the first plants recorded in the earliest sedentary human occupations here, for the lines and nets used to harvest the area's bountiful marine resources (Dillchay *et al.* 2007). So ubiquitous does cotton become in the middens of the incipient complex societies of the Peruvian coast that the term 'Cotton Pre-ceramic' was coined for the end of that long period (see for instance Moseley 1975). Since *Gossipium* occurs as part of the natural vegetation of these riparian valleys in wild, feral and landrace forms, the shift between its use as a gathered, 'wild plant' resource and as a cultivated plant lies along a long continuum of human–plant co-evolution (Westengen *et al.* 2005: 393). With time, the fabric technologies of fishing evolved into weaving. And much later, by the time of the Early Horizon, all of the structural innovations that characterise the extraordinary Andean textile tradition had been developed (see for instance Conklin 2008). Indeed, cotton textiles are some of the most famous examples of that Chavín material culture, to which the mound 21 contexts so clearly relate (see Figure 3.14I). Although few Chavín textiles have been scientifically excavated, most are from the south coast and many reportedly from Samaca, Ullujaya and Callango in the lower Ica Valley (Brugnoli and Soledad 1991, Burger 1992: 198, Roe 2008). The cotton plant itself is clearly depicted in the iconography of some of these textiles (see for instance, Conklin 2008: 265).

Unlike the protein fibres of wool, cotton is not easily dyed. Along the Peruvian coast, however, cottons were developed in an extraordinary array of natural colours. Fibres in two different colours, white and beige, were identified in the Early Horizon contexts of mound 21. And although most of the corpus of Chavín textiles in existence have their 'art' made by painting on to a plain-weave cotton fabric, others use textile structures such as so-called 'warp wrapping' of these natural cotton colours to form their designs (Conklin 2008: 264).

Cotton being the only identifiable cultivated plant in these Early Horizon contexts begs the obvious question of what these people were eating, to which the answer, it seems, was predominately food from the sea. The Ullujaya Basin perfectly fits Kroeber's (1944: 24) characterisation of the region as 'coastal but not maritime', for it is separated from the sea by the Lomas de Ullujaya, rising to almost a thousand metres high. The ocean does not feel close. It is a long walk of at least two days to reach the mouth of the Río Ica by following its course south through the hot and contorted canyon of its lower reaches. Yet, walking west across the aptly named Pampa Correviento over a 600 metre pass in the *lomas*, a fit person

Table 5.1. Archaeobotanical remains from excavations in the Samaca and Ullujaya basins

KEY
- Some (<10 items)
- Moderate (10-100 items)
- Abundant (> 100 items)

				MIDDLE HORIZON							LATE NASCA											
				H-13 MIDDEN F 11			*H-13 MIDDEN MOUND F 23*				*G-8/9 MIDDEN MOUND F 1*											
			Excavation	*Pit 1*			*Pit 5*				*Pit 1*							*Pit 2*				
			Stratigraphic Unit	*5*	*11*	*17*	*32*	*42*	*48*	*51*	*3001*	*3002*	*3003*	*3004*	*3006*	*3007*	*3011*	*3012*	*3013*	*3015*	*3016*	*3017*
LIGHT FRACTIONS (2 mm & 500 μm)		FAMILY	COMMON NAME																			
Ⓐ	*Prosopis* sp. leaf rachis and leaflets (*Poña*)	Mimosaceae	*Huarango*	Some		Moderate	Some	Moderate	Abundant	Abundant	Moderate	Moderate	Moderate	Moderate	Moderate	Abundant	Moderate	Moderate	Moderate	Moderate	Moderate	Moderate
	Prosopis sp. pod fragments	Mimosaceae	*Huarango*				Some	Moderate		Some		Some		Some								
	Prosopis sp. seed	Mimosaceae	*Huarango*				Some				Some	Moderate		Some	Some						Some	
	Salix sp. leaf	Salicaceae	*Sauce*									Some										
Ⓑ	*Indigofera* sp. (cf. *truxillensis*) seed	Papilionoideae	*Tintillo*															Some			Some	
	Baccharis salicifolia flower	Asteraceae	*Chilco*																			
	Asteraceae Type *Pluchea/Tessaria* sp. achene	Asteraceae								Some												
	Asteraceae Type *Spilanthes* sp. achene	Asteraceae								Some												
	cf. *Spilanthes* (Syn. *Acmella*) sp. achene	Asteraceae	*Frailecillo*																			
	Galvezia sp. seeds	Scrophulariaceae																				
	Verbena sp. (cf. *litoralis*) fruit	Verbenaceae											Some									
	Argemone subfusiformis seed	Papaveraceae	*Cardosanto*											Some								
	Chamaesyce hypericifolia seed	Euphorbiacae	*Golondrina*											Some							Some	
	cf. *Urocarpidium* seed	Malvaceae																				
	Desmodium sp. seed	Papilionoideae	*Patita de Pero*																		Some	
Ⓒ	*Crotalaria* sp. seed	Papilionoideae	*Cascabelillo*			Some		Some	Some													
	Boerhaavia erecta achene	Nyctaginaceae	*Pega pega*					Some		Some												
	Amaranthus sp. (cf. *spinosa*) seed	Amaranthaceae	*Yuyo*	Some				Abundant	Abundant	Abundant		Moderate	Some	Some	Some			Some				
	Alternanthera sp. flower	Amaranthaceae	*Leche leche*									Some		Some								
	Chenopodium sp. seed	Chenopodiaceae	*Paico*			Some		Some	Some	Some												
	Chenopod or *Amaranth* seed	Cheno/Amaranth									Moderate	Some	Some		Moderate			Some		Some	Some	Some
	Portulaca/Sesuvium sp. seed	Portulacaceae	*Verdolaga*	Some		Some		Abundant	Moderate	Abundant	Some	Moderate	Moderate	Moderate	Moderate		Some		Some		Some	
	Polygonum sp. achene	Polygonaceae		Some		Some			Some									Some				
	Solanum sp. seed	Solanaceae							Some	Some	Some											
	Solanum sp. seed (small morphology)	Solanaceae	*Tomatillo*				Some	Some	Moderate	Moderate	Some	Some	Some	Some				Some	Some	Some	Some	
	Lippia (Syn. *Phyla*) *canescens* fruit	Verbenaceae	*Panadero*	Some		Some		Some	Moderate	Some		Some		Some								
Ⓓ	*Juncus* sp. seed	Juncaceae							Some	Some												
	Cyperus sp. achene and glumes	Cyperaceae						Some	Some	Some	Some										Some	
	Cyperus sp. stem	Cyperaceae										Abundant		Abundant	Some			Abundant				
	Cyperus sp. seed	Cyperaceae							Some		Some											
	Scirpus sp. *achene*	Cyperaceae						Some	Some	Some												
Ⓔ	*Cenchrus* sp. seed coat	Poaceae	*Pega pega*				Some															
	Cenchrus sp. flower	Poaceae	*Pega pega*								Some			Some	Moderate						Some	
	Setaria sp. seed	Poaceae																				
	Andropogon (*Syn. Bothriochloa*) sp. seed	Poaceae									Some											
	Eriochloa sp. spikelet	Poaceae										Some										
	Sub-family Paniceae seed	Poaceae																				
	Sub-family Paniceae stem	Poaceae										Some										
	Phragmites australis stem	Poaceae	*Carrizillo*				Moderate		Moderate		Some	Some	Moderate	Abundant								
	Gynerium sagittatum stem	Poaceae	*Caña brava*				Moderate		Some			Abundant	Moderate		Some							
	Grass fragments	Poaceae		Some	Some	Some	Moderate	Some	Abundant	Moderate	Some	Some	Some	Some					Some	Some	Some	
Ⓕ	*Gossypium barbadense* fibre & capsule	Malvaceae	*Algodon*				Moderate	Some	Moderate		Abundant	Abundant	Abundant	Abundant	Abundant			Moderate		Some		
	Gossypium barbadense seed	Malvaceae	*Algodon*				Moderate				Some	Some		Moderate		Some		Some				Moderate
	Gossypium barbadense peduncle fragments	Malvaceae	*Algodon*									Some	Some	Moderate								
	Zea mays stalks	Poaceae	*Maíz*									Abundant		Abundant	Some							
	Zea mays cobs	Poaceae	*Maíz*								Some	Moderate		Some				Some			Moderate	
	Psidium guajava seed	Myrtaceae	*Guayaba*				Some			Some	Some			Some				Some	Some			
	Inga feuillei leaf fragments	Mimosaceae	*Pacay*				Moderate	Some	Abundant	Some		Some						Moderate		Some	Some	Some
	Phaseolus vulgaris seeds & pods	Papilionoideae	*Fréjol*								Some	Moderate	Some									
	Phaseolus lunatus seeds & pods	Papilionoideae	*Pallar*								Some	Some	Some	Some	Some							
	Arachis hypogaea shell	Fabaceae	*Maní*								Some											
	Erythroxylum coca seed	Erythroxylacae	*Coca*				Some					Some										
	Capsicum sp. seed	Solanaceae	*Aji*								Some	Moderate			Moderate							
	Canna edulis flower	Cannanaceae	*Achira*									Some										
	Lagenaria siceraria seed, leaf & flower	Cucurbitaceae	*Mate*									Some		Abundant							Some	
	Cucurbita sp. seed	Cucurbitaceae	*Zapallo*							Some		Some		Some	Some							Some
Ⓖ	Unidentified dicot. stems										Abundant	Abundant	Abundant	Abundant	Abundant	Abundant	Abundant	Abundant	Abundant	Abundant	Abundant	Abundant
	Unidentified dicot. seeds			Moderate		Some	Moderate	Moderate	Some	Some												
	Charcoals				Moderate	Abundant	Abundant	Abundant	Abundant	Abundant	Abundant	Abundant	Abundant	Abundant	Abundant	Abundant	Abundant	Abundant	Abundant	Abundant	Abundant	Abundant
HEAVY FRACTION *(Measure of midden density)*	Ceramic fragments			Some	Some	Some	Moderate	Some	Moderate	Some	Moderate	Abundant	Abundant	Moderate				Moderate	Moderate		Moderate	
	Molluscs			Some	Some	Some	Moderate	Moderate	Moderate	Moderate	Moderate	Moderate		Moderate	Some			Some	Some		Some	
	Animal bone			Some			Moderate	Moderate	Some	Some	Moderate	Moderate	Moderate	Moderate				Moderate	Moderate		Moderate	
	Lithics										Moderate	Moderate	Moderate									
	Textile fragments & spun yarns						Some	Some	Some		Some	Some										

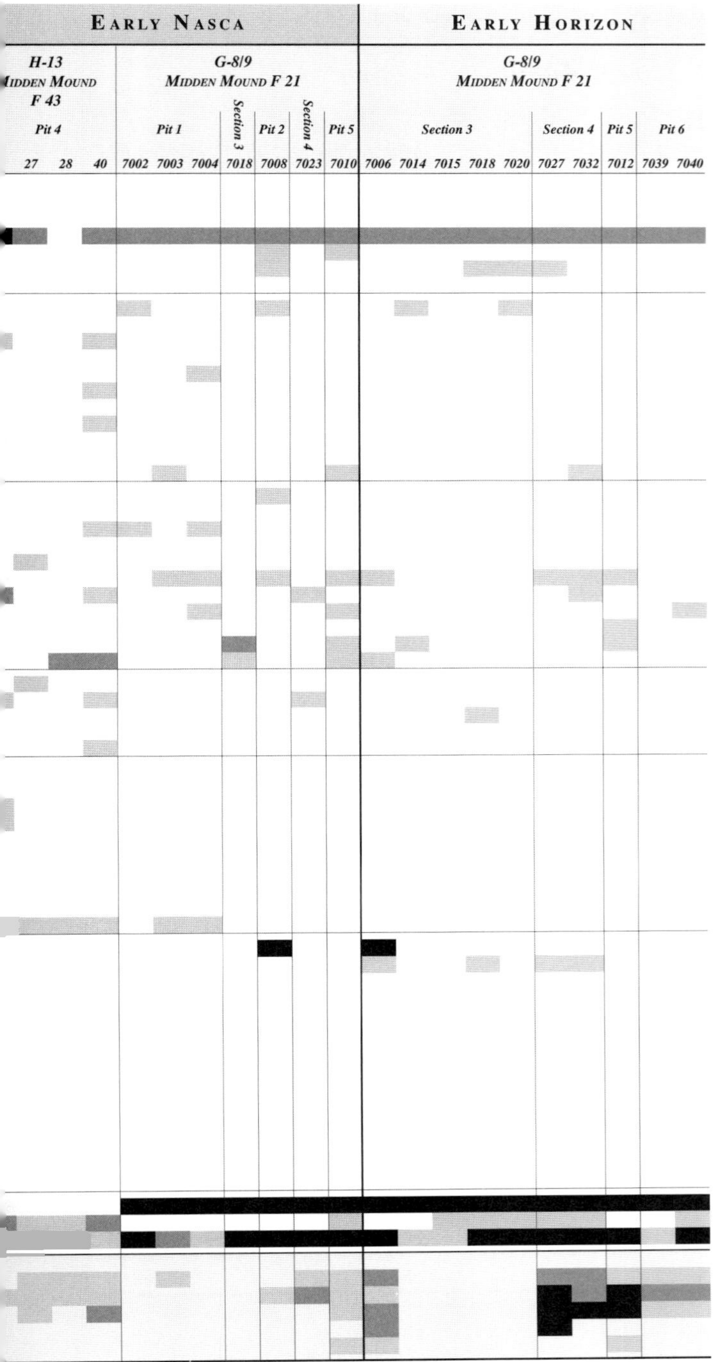

Identifications by Carmela Alarcón, David Beresford-Jones and Oscar Portocarrero

Table 5.2. Malacological remains from excavations in the Samaca and Ullujaya basins

Key: Some (<10 items); Moderate (10–100 items; Abundant (>100 items)

	Middle Horizon			*Early Nasca*		*Early Horizon*
	H-13 Midden F11	*H-13 Midden Mound F23*		*H-13 Midden Mound F43*		*G8/9 Midden F21*
	Pit 1	*Pit 5*		*Pit 4*		*Section 4*
	5	*32*	*48*	*27*	*40*	*7027*
Heavy fraction (2mm)						
Echnioderms						
Tetrapygus niger spines		Some				Abundant
Tetrapygus niger spines						Abundant
Marine crustacea						
Crab claw fragments						Some
Fam. Balanidae				Some		
Unidentified crustacea fragments	Some	Some				
Freshwater crustacea						
Cryphiops caementarius		Some		Some		
Mollusca						
Chitons						
Fam. Chitonidae		Some	Some			
Gastropods						
Concholepas concholepas	Some		Some			
Tegula sp.		Some	Some			Some
Fisurella sp.	Some	Some				Some
Fam. Acmaeidae		Some	Some			
Bivalves						
Cumingia mutica				Some		
Choromytilus chorus			Some		Some	
Brachidontes sp.						Moderate
Perumytilus purpuratus	Abundant	Abundant	Moderate	Some		Abundant
Semimytilus algosus	Some	Moderate	Some			
Aulacomya ater		Some	Some		Some	
Mesodesma donacium	Some					
Mulinia edulis						
Terrestrial gastropods						
Fam. Bulimulidae	Moderate	Moderate	Moderate	Moderate	Some	Moderate
Unidentified mollusc fragments	Some	Some		Some		Moderate
Total mass (g)	5.4	26.9	13.5	4.8	6.8	244.2

Identifications by Manuel Gorriti, Lauren Cadwallader and David Beresford-Jones may reach the vast Playa Lomitas in only eight hours (see Figure 2.2). And these Chavín deposits contain abundant vestiges of such journeys.

As Table 5.2, shows these dense Early Horizon middens are dominated by sea urchin (*Tetrapygus niger*) shells and spines and by the shells of three types of small mussels (Figure 5.3). They also have large numbers of land snail shells (Fam. Bulimulidae), which live exclusively in the *lomas*. The range of species in these contexts is more limited than those of later periods that we will examine shortly. In particular, the Early Horizon occupants seem to have had a preference for smaller, lighter kinds of shellfish. There may be many reasons for that choice, but ease of foraging and transport—presumably without the aid of llama caravans—would seem likely to be among them. At the same time, these marine foods seem to make up a huge proportion of the total midden. Although comparative quantifications of such data need to be treated very cautiously, the total masses of the heavy fractions in Table 5.2 show how the mound 21 Early Horizon middens are around *ten times* richer in heavy marine and terrestrial remains than those same volume samples recorded from other, later archaeological contexts.

Turning to the other remains in these Early Horizon contexts shown in Table 5.1, along with a dearth of identifiable domesticated plants compared with other, later archaeological

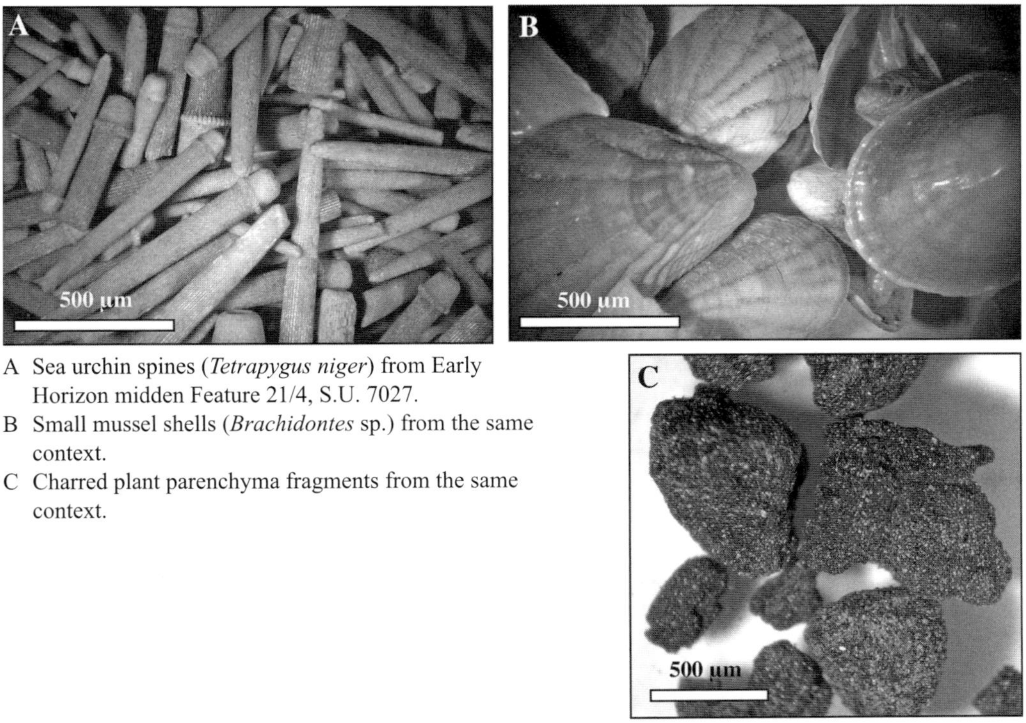

A Sea urchin spines (*Tetrapygus niger*) from Early Horizon midden Feature 21/4, S.U. 7027.
B Small mussel shells (*Brachidontes* sp.) from the same context.
C Charred plant parenchyma fragments from the same context.

Figure 5.3. Selected marine food recovered from the Early Horizon midden context (S.U. 7027) of mound 21, Ullujaya G-8/9

contexts, there are no grasses of open areas (Group E) and very few of the weeds associated with human disturbance or agriculture (Group C). They also included very few plant macrofossils from Group B: the shrubs and larger herbs that grow in clearances and along the edges of the south coast riparian woodland. There are copious charcoals and some charred remains of parenchyma—the storage cells of plants found in greatest concentrations in their roots, seeds and fruits (see for instance Hather 2000)—which indicate that some plant foods were being consumed. There are also many desiccated huarango *poña* remains and charred leaflets and, indeed, seeds, which may indicate that the pods were being eaten.

As we have seen, the remains of Early Horizon settlement are seemingly scarce in the Ullujaya and Samaca basins. Our data from the rich Early Horizon midden contexts of mound Feature 21 come together with that observation to paint a picture of an occupation at this time of a relatively small group of people, subsisting mainly on the smaller and lighter species of marine and terrestrial molluscs and sea urchins gathered, and moved from distant locations, but consuming also some gathered food plants including huarango fruit. They were, it seems, undertaking floodplain cultivation of cotton, but within an otherwise relatively undisturbed riparian woodland.

In Early Nasca

Early Nasca (Dawson Nasca Phases 2 through 5) represent the majority of the Early Intermediate Period in the lower Ica Valley—the first five hundred years or so of the Common Era. Data from several deposits dating to these times were analysed, including other middens from mound 21, Ullujaya G-8/9, lying stratigraphically above those we have just discussed for the Early Horizon, and also from mound 43 on Samaca H-13.

The relative density of the various midden contexts analysed is perhaps best reflected by the frequency of their heavy fraction finds, shown at the bottom of Table 5.1. These show that these Early Nasca middens were very *sparse* relative to those of other time periods in pottery, molluscs and other indicators of human activity. Table 5.1 also shows that these Early Nasca middens were empty of obvious plant domesticates, bar cotton. Yet we must read interpretations of human ecology from such sparse contexts with great caution, for as always in archaeology, absence of evidence is not evidence of absence. And other lines of data seem to indicate a rather fully developed agricultural landscape in these basins during this time.

Table 5.2 also shows that the remains of both marine and terrestrial molluscs in these Early Nasca contexts are relatively few in quantity in comparison to both earlier and later periods: another indication of the scattered taphonomic condition of these middens. Despite their scantiness in overall midden remains relative to the Early Horizon contexts, Table 5.1 shows that these Early Nasca context nonetheless included significantly *more* remnants of grasses (Group E) and woody shrubs like *Galvezia* sp. and *Tessaria/Pluchea*, typical of open areas of riparian vegetation (Group B). They also had considerably more remains of weedy herbaceous plants (Group C) than those earlier remains. Several of these will prove significant in our discussions here, but plant remains of two similar genera—chenopods and amaranths—are of particular interest.

Seeds of various *Amaranthus* and *Chenopodium* species are all small, circular-lenticular and shiny black in colour (see Figure 5.8 below). Since these can be difficult to distinguish we sometimes have deemed it prudent only to identify to the level of chenopod *or* amaranth (see Beresford-Jones 2005 for further details and modern reference material against which these were made). These genera of plants are so-called 'halophytes', originally evolving in saline river estuary environments, which adapts them perfectly to those areas whose ecologies have been disturbed by settled human presence. Consequently, they have followed hand-in-hand the steady colonisation of the landscape worldwide by human agriculture. Chenopods, amaranths and indeed all the weedy species of Group C are found growing abundantly amid and along the edges of the modern fields of Huerto Huamaní in Samaca. These 'agrestal' weeds are the classic indicators of the clearances and disturbances that come with agriculture.

Like the Early Horizon contexts, the Early Intermediate contexts of G-8/9 mound 21 contained seeds of the 'Tintillo' shrub, *Indigofera* (cf. *truxillensis*). This is a plant from which an intense blue dye may be obtained from the leaves, through a particularly obscure, unpredictable and complex process (see for instance Zumbühl 1979: 31–2, Stone-Miller 1992: 17, 20). Early Intermediate south coast textiles are remarkable among the vast corpus of later, pre-Hispanic Andean textiles for their extravagant use of the colour blue (see for instance Stone-Miller 1992: 165–7), often for the whole of a large plain-weave textile then fringed with the most intricate polychrome needle-knit borders depicting flowering plants and hummingbirds (see for instance Stone-Miller 1992: 72–91 and Sawyer 1997). These ancient seeds hint also at ecological change, for, not only does blue become ever rarer in later period textiles, in our later archaeological contexts there are no *Indigofera* remains. *Indigofera* thrives in the shade of riparian woodland. And, while it is still present—albeit uncommon—elsewhere on the south coast, we have yet to encounter a single plant growing in the lower Ica Valley today (Whaley *et al.* 2010b).

Again these deposits also included moderate numbers of huarango leaflets and leaf rachis fragments (Figure 5.4). Indeed, as we will see, macrofossil remains of huarango were the single common denominator of all the archaeological contexts analysed in G-8/9 and H-13. Particular botanical features allow these and other huarango remains to be identified as *P. pallida* forma *pallida* (following Harris *et al.* 2003) or, as preferred here, *P. limensis* (following Mom *et al.* 2002). These will be elaborated on in Chapter 7, but they include leaflet shape, size and surface morphology, an absence of thorns, pod size and shape, and the number of interfoliar glands per rachis.

The archaeobotanical assemblage from the H-13, mound 43 midden are also noteworthy for two other reasons. Firstly, despite the huge S.U. 19 flood layer that overlies them, described in the preceding chapter, they contained well-preserved desiccated plant remains. This is strong evidence that a flood event was a very rare, or even unique, event at this point in

A Examples of the dessicated huarango (*Prosopis limensis*) leaf rachis (no thorns, single interfoliar gland) from Test Pit 4, S.U. 40 in mound Feature 43, Samaca H-13.
B Example of dessicated huarango (*Prosopis limensis*) leaflet (6 mm long, 2 mm wide) from the same context.
C Water boatman exoskeleton from Test Pit 4, S.U. 27.
D Fragments of freshwater shrimp (*Cryphiops caementarius*) from Test Pit 4, S.U. 20.

Figure 5.4. Selected macrofossil remains from the Early Nasca midden contexts of mound 43, Samaca H-13

the landscape, since otherwise constant wetting by alkaline waters would quickly have degraded these plant macrofossils. Secondly, obligate wetland plants such as *Juncus* sp. and Cyperaceae, water boatman insect exoskeletons, a freshwater mollusc shell and fragments of freshwater shrimp (*Cryphiops caementarius*) were also recovered from these middens (Figure 5.4). These all contribute to the interpretation that these Early Intermediate middens were indeed contemporaneous with the relict canal 33 running alongside. So our archaeobotanical data come together with the evidence we saw earlier to date the relict canal system of relict lower Ica Valley terraces to the Early Nasca Period: the most straightforward evidence of a formerly extensive agricultural landscape in the Ullujaya and Samaca basins at that time.

In Late Nasca

Late Nasca (Dawson Nasca Phases 6 and 7)—the last two or three hundred years of the Early Intermediate Period, ending around AD 600—represent the most abundant archaeological remains in the basins of the lower Ica Valley. A rich archaeobotanical dataset was analysed from various Late Nasca contexts including in particular the midden mound 1, Ullujaya G-8/9.

As Table 5.1 shows, the contexts of mound 1 were much more abundant in midden materials generally than those analysed for the Early Nasca Period. We may therefore be more confident in their reflections of human ecology during the Late Nasca Period. They contained the remains of the complete suite of south coast plant domesticates (Group F), including cotton and gourd (*Lagenaria siceranea*), together with the domesticated food plants of maize (Figure 5.5), beans (*Phaseolus lunatus* and *Phaseolus vulgaris*), pumpkin (*Cucurbita* sp.), peanut (*Arachis hypogaea*), achira (*Canna edulis*), the fruit trees *pacay* (*Inga feuillei*) and guava (*Psidium guajava*), and chilli seeds (*Capsicum* sp.). This last cultivar is a member of Solanaceae—a large family of plants that counts among its members many of those New World plant domesticates whose worldwide impact has been most profound. They include the potato (*Solanum tubersosum*), chilli peppers (various *Capsicum* species), tomatoes (*Lycopersicon* sp.) and tobacco (*Nicotiana* sp.): all plants with vestiges of a general feature of the Solanaceae family—toxicity. Indeed, in addition to these, a number of other important New World domesticates including the sweet potato and manioc also derive from families of plants that include many toxic and psychoactive relatives. As Jones (2009) notes, the ancient American hunter-gatherers who began the long process of co-evolution with plants of these families were plainly very astute botanists, perhaps as a consequence of their long adaptations to the cold deserts of Siberia and Beringia from whence they came.

Unfortunately, however, the Solanaceae family frustrates archaeobotanists because seeds of some of its different genera can be difficult to distinguish (see Figure 5.8 below, Martin and Barkley 1961 and Beresford-Jones 2005 for more detail). And many wild Solanaceae plants grow as weeds today in the fields of the south coast, including those of the genera *Solanum*, *Datura*, *Nicotiana*, *Lycopersicon*, *Physalis* and *Lycium*. Indeed, Solanaceae is the fourth most common family in our modern plant collections on the south coast. A few of these, very common in the fields of Huerto Huamaní, Samaca, produce huge quantities of tiny, delicious tomato fruits (*Solanum pimpinellifolium* and *S. peruvianum*—known as tomatíllo, see Sagástegui 1973: 377–82). The quantities of various morphology *Solanum* seeds in our Late Nasca and other contexts—many with coprolite encrustations—are good evidence that they were part of the human diet, a matter we will return to shortly. The very toxicity of others may have conferred upon them other, extramundane uses: the fruit of *S. nigrum* for instance contains powerful alkaloids and is poisonous to livestock, although it is used as an anaesthetic (Sagástegui 1973: 377–82). *Datura* meanwhile is powerfully psychoactive (see for instance Schultes 1972: 46–51). But, because of the uncertainties in identifying ancient Solanaceae seeds, we have conservatively elected to lump all these under *Solanum* in Group C—weedy plants associated with agriculture.

Indeed, Late Nasca contexts in the lower Ica Valley are part of a seemingly clear trend in Table 5.1 of increasing intensity of those agrestal weeds (Group C), through the various

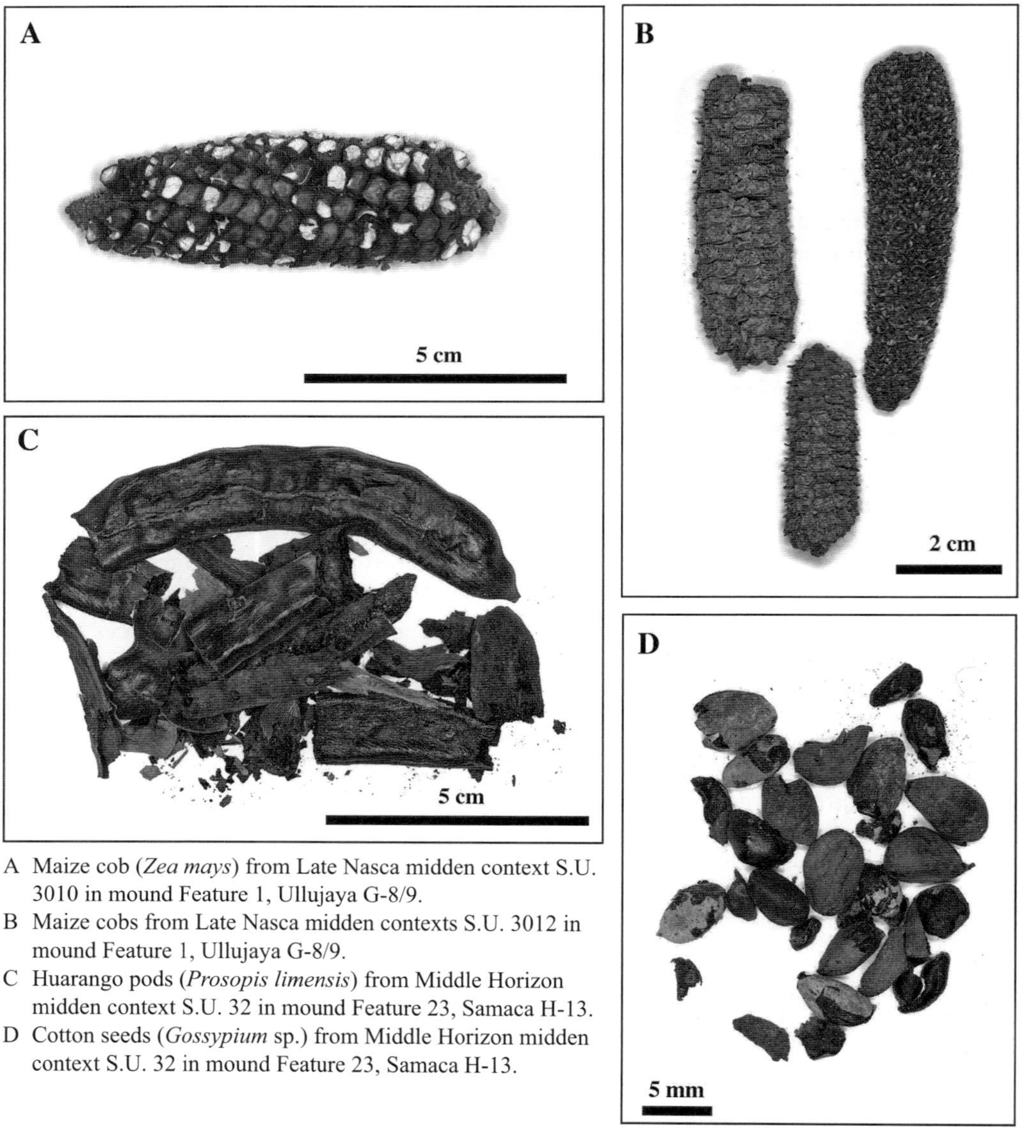

A Maize cob (*Zea mays*) from Late Nasca midden context S.U. 3010 in mound Feature 1, Ullujaya G-8/9.
B Maize cobs from Late Nasca midden contexts S.U. 3012 in mound Feature 1, Ullujaya G-8/9.
C Huarango pods (*Prosopis limensis*) from Middle Horizon midden context S.U. 32 in mound Feature 23, Samaca H-13.
D Cotton seeds (*Gossypium* sp.) from Middle Horizon midden context S.U. 32 in mound Feature 23, Samaca H-13.

Figure 5.5. Selected most common plant finds from excavations in the Samaca and Ullujaya basins

archaeological periods analysed. At the same time, those other indicators of open-area disturbance to riparian woodland, grasses (Group E) and shrubs (Group B), also appear to increase steadily. Together with domesticated plant remains, what we seem to be witnessing in our archaeobotanical record is a gradual increase in the amount of agriculture being carried out over time in these basins. Moreover, along with the aforementioned chenopods and amaranths, *Sesuvium* (Syn. *Portulaca*) is another classic halophyte, particularly well adapted to saline conditions. So the increasing amounts of *Sesuvium* in this record suggest also an increasing salinity, often a consequence of long-term irrigation of low-lying landscapes.

In the Middle Horizon

As we have seen, there are simply no settlement remains on the relict river terraces of Samaca and Ullujaya after Epoch 2 of the Middle Horizon. In and of itself, this alerts us to the fact of critical change during this period from around 800 to 1000 AD. Yet we need to look to other data to answer the more subtle questions of how and why that change happened, and the archaeobotanical data from our Middle Horizon contexts point to the culmination of all those trends that we have traced across earlier time periods. Those of mound 23 on Samaca H-13 were particularly revealing.

As we saw earlier, mound 23 was revealed to be an Epoch 2 Middle Horizon midden sitting atop a relict nabkha. Its upper deposits were full of the rubbish of human settlement: copious marine and terrestrial mollusc shells, lithic flakes, partly spun cotton and even desiccated human coprolites (Figure 5.6). As shown at the bottom of Table 5.1, these middens were as dense as those of the preceding Late Nasca Period, and our flotations of these contexts also yielded copious amounts of plant remains. Their suite of cultivated plants (Group F), however, was far more limited—a matter to which we will return shortly, for they were no less interesting for our purposes here. Most obviously the lower contexts of midden mound 23 contained enormous quantities of desiccated huarango tree litter.

As the amount of Middle Horizon midden material decreased down the stratigraphy of the mound, so did the proportion of this tree litter increase—to some 40 per cent by volume in the lower levels. As we saw earlier, this is *in situ poña*: the thick layer of tree litter that carpets the desert under huarango trees. Those older tree remains were preserved as calcified pseudomorphs with the wide expanses of duracrete that form much of these relict terraces and formed as these terraces dried out. Mixed with the material culture of the Middle Horizon, however, these remains are desiccated in contexts that stand above that ancient water table. High on the deflated terrace of H-13, mound 23 has been exposed to the full force of the region's extraordinary wind regime for a millennium since the passing of the Middle Horizon. Yet it is still almost 50 metres long: dimensions which speak of a nabkha that built up under the canopy of a very large tree over a considerable period of time. Indeed, the lifespan of a large huarango might easily have exceeded the duration of the entire Middle Horizon.

What then of the rest of the rich assemblage of plant remains from the midden contexts of mound 23 shown in Table 5.1? It contained abundant fibres of cotton, some of which were partly spun into yarn, a few pumpkin (*Cucurbita* sp.) seeds, and remains of those same fruit trees which we encountered earlier in Late Nasca deposits: leaf fragments of pacay (*Inga feuillei*) and guava (*Psidium guajava*) seeds. It also included moderate numbers of coca (*Erythroxylum* sp.) seeds (Figure 5.7). This latter conjunction of plant remains is perhaps rather remarkable.

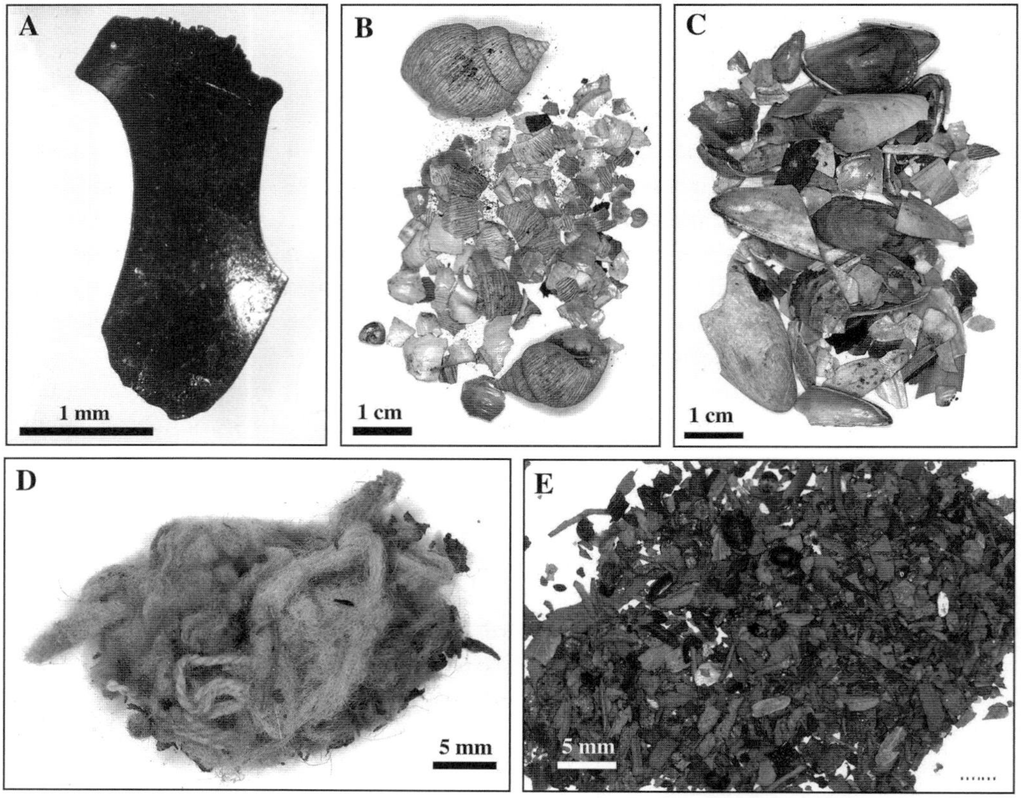

A Obsidian flake from heavy fraction of Middle Horizon mound 23 Samaca H-13 midden context S.U. 42.
B Land snail shell (Fam. Bulimulidae) from mound 23, S.U. 48.
C Various marine mollusc shells from mound 23, S.U. 48.
D Partly spun cotton fibre (*Gossypium* sp.) from mound 23, S.U. 32.
E 500 µm flotation sample from mound 23, S.U. 51 prior to sorting showing dominance of hurango *poña.*
F Broken dessicated human coprolite from mound 23, S.U. 41 containing masticated huarango pod fragments and seeds (marked 'i.').

Figure 5.6. Selected midden materials from the Middle Horizon contexts of mound 23, Samaca H-13

Coca is a plant whose long cultural significance in the Andes is today desecrated through the illegal extraction of a single alkaloid constituent of its leaves—cocaine. Its leaf, used as a mild stimulant, is found in south coast archaeological contexts but only becomes relatively common in the Middle Horizon. Prior to this very few coca leaf remains have been found and only in very Late Nasca Phase 8 contexts at the major site of Cahuachi (Piacenza 2005). Iconographic representations of coca chewing are likewise restricted to Late Nasca (Silverman and Proulx 2002). The plant therefore seems to have been first used on the south coast rather late, around about the time that the Wari Empire was beginning its expansion into the region, and the coca seeds in this Middle Horizon midden fit that chronology. In fact, Schreiber (1999, 2001) has argued that Wari's expansion out of the Ayacucho highlands was driven, at least in part, by seeking new locations for coca cultivation.

Today coca—predominately *Erythroxylum coca* var. *coca*, or 'Huánuco coca'—is grown at high altitudes on the eastern slopes of the Andes above a thousand metres. Yet at the time of the Spanish conquest coca consumption was far more widespread, including all over Caribbean South America and into the Isthmus of Panama (Warwick Bray, personal communication). Indeed, another species of coca, *Erythroxylum novogranatense*, is more flexible in

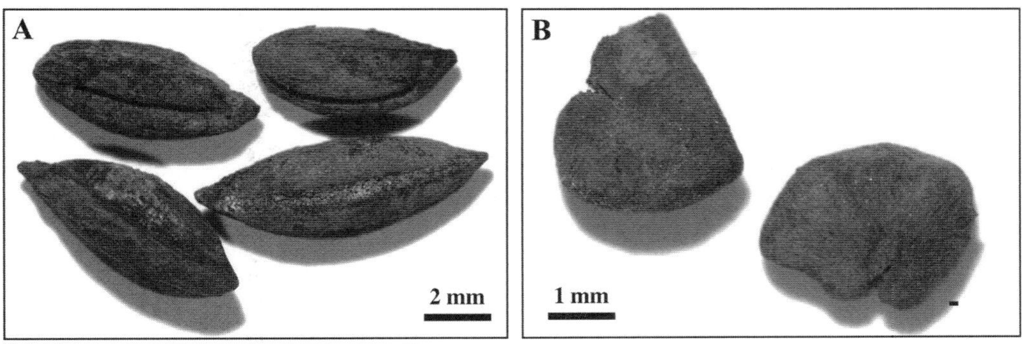

A Selected *Erythroxylum* sp. (coca) seeds from Middle Horizon midden mound 23. Samaca H-13, S.U. 32.
B Selected *Psidium guajava* (guava) seeds from the same context.
C Detail of *Inga feuillei* (pacay) leaf fragment example from the same context.

Figure 5.7. Coca cultivation?: a plant assemblage from a Middle Horizon midden context (S.U. 32) of mound 23, Samaca H-13

its adaptation and can be grown as low as sea level. In 1875 it was propagated successfully in the Far East and for this reason is sometimes known as 'Java coca'. Since the work of Plowman (1979, 1984), in particular, a variety of this species (var. *truxillense*, or 'Trujillo' coca) has been recognised growing on the Peruvian coast. The range of this drought-resistant coca is put historically as '*Chaupi Yunga*': an ecozone that, according to Netherly (1988: 264), lies 'between hot and cold', and whose definition varies with latitude. Rostworowski (1989: 245, 246) puts it between 200 and 1,200 metres, in areas free of cold sea mists. Coca, like coffee, is cultivated in the shade of larger trees (see for instance Plowman 1984). And Rostworowski (1989) cites various sixteenth-century sources which describe Pacific coastal plantations of *E. novogranatense* growing under the protective shade of two species of fruit tree in particular: pacay and guava. A 1559 document, for instance, describes Quivi in the Chillón Valley: 'they harvest nothing from these lands save coca but here they have trees of guabas and guayabas and they don't sow or harvest maize because this land is only for coca' (Rostworowski 1989: 252; my translation). This coastal variety of coca was prized by the Incas above all others for its superior taste (Netherly 1988).

It would certainly be precipitous to draw definitive conclusions from this anthropogenic assemblage from a single Middle Horizon midden. Nonetheless, its conjunction of coca seeds (rather than leaves) together with guava and pacay remains in the same stratigraphic unit (S.U. 32) is, to say the least, striking in light of Rostworowski's historical documentation. The lower Ica Valley lies at the lower end of the altitude range specified by Rostworowski and is considerably lower than Pataraya, the site which Schreiber speculates may represent a Wari coca plantation in Nazca. Yet, as we have seen, its climate of year-round sunshine is rather peculiar for the Peruvian coast and is, indeed, more typical of the *Chaupi Yunga*. Conceivably then, this assemblage might be the remains of a relatively local source of coca cultivation. Moreover, several of the *relaciónes* cited by Rostworowski (1989: 243) describe coca being produced together with cotton—another plant for which we have abundant evidence of production in the lower Ica Valley. This Middle Horizon midden was also full of cotton fibre, seeds, capsule fragments and leaves, and looted Middle Horizon tombs in the lower Ica Valley contain vast quantities of raw cotton fibre.

Be that as it may, these archaeobotanical remains certainly point to *changed* ecological conditions. For neither coca, nor indeed the large, simple-leafed fruit trees of pacay and guava—whose remains are so profuse in both Early Intermediate and Middle Horizon middens—can be grown easily today anywhere in the lower Ica Valley, because of its wind regime (Alberto Benavides, personal communication). If the occurrence of any one of this intriguing conjunction of plants represents local cultivation, then local ecological conditions—specifically, the wind protection and sub-canopy microclimatic alteration effected by a much more extensive woodland canopy—must have changed dramatically in the Samaca and Ullujaya basins.

What is otherwise most noticeable about these Middle Horizon middens is their relative dearth of cultivated foods. For while they contained large quantities of marine and terrestrial molluscs and, indeed, a significantly wider range of gathered marine foods than preceding time periods (Table 5.2), aside from pacay, guava and a few pumpkin seeds, their food plant assemblage contained no obvious cultivars. Archaeobotanical remains from the Middle Horizon site of Casa Vieja upstream in Callango offer an interesting contrast, for its contexts included the full range of typical south coast crops including maize, beans, potato, sweet potato and yucca (Roque *et al.* 2003, Cook and Parrish 2005).

Desiccated human coprolite fragments were also extracted by flotation from the deposits of midden mound 23, offering direct evidence of what people were eating. These contained clearly visible evidence of the consumption of huarango pods (Figure 5.6). But many of the other plants identified shown in Table 5.1—including *Solanum*, *Sesuvium*, *Amaranthus*, *Chenopodium*, *Crotalaria* and *Lippia*—also showed evidence of coprolite encrustation (Figure 5.8). In fact, the importance of all these genera as gathered, *wild* plant foods is well documented in the ethnobotany of other arid American environments. Indeed, the most abundant plant genera in these Middle Horizon contexts virtually mirror the list of those wild plant food sources most valued by the peoples of the North American Sonoran for their combination of common occurrence and nutritional properties (omitting only certain important Sonoran cactus species). Even the pumpkin seeds recorded here are not necessarily indicative of cultivation, for zapallo (*Cucurbita maxima*) grows uncultivated as a 'volunteer' plant in the Samaca Basin today. The starchy rhizomes of plants in the *Scirpus*, *Cyperus*, *Boerhaavia* and *Phragmites* genera are also recorded as providing food in New World deserts (Holden 1991, Rea 1997 and Hodgson 2001). Of all the plants recorded in the mound 23 contexts, only four have no potential as a food source: cotton, the grasses of *Gynerium sagittatum* and *Cenchrus echinatus* and *Juncus* sp. of the Cyperaceae family.

Of course, many of these plants were recorded also in our Early Intermediate midden deposits. In Chapter 9 we will examine the agriculture of parts of the Sonoran Desert, in which these agrestal weeds were encouraged within fields precisely because they were an all-important, additional food source. Of these gathered wild foods, however, by far the most important was the fruit of *Prosopis*. Even for the consummate agriculturalists of the Sonoran river basins, *Prosopis* was the single most important food. At Casa Vieja in Callango, notwithstanding its full suite of cultivated food plants—including the paramount American cereal, maize—the most abundant food plant recorded in its Middle Horizon contexts was 'the fruit and seeds of *Prosopis*' (Roque *et al.* 2003: 36). As we will see in the next chapter, this same importance is reflected in Silverman's (1993) archaeobotanical data from Cahuachi, Nazca (see also Piacenza 2005), and in the ancient remains of many agricultural societies in the Chilean Atacama Desert (Kautz 1980, Holden 1991, Holden and Núñez 1993). In fact, the pre-eminence of *Prosopis* pods as food, that we will evoke by ethnobotanical analogy with the Sonoran is to be found reflected in almost all the available archaeobotanical data from the Peruvian south coast and Chile.

Taken alone, it might be all too easy to over-interpret the archaeobotanical data that we have discussed here for the Middle Horizon and earlier periods. Coming from ancient midden contexts they offer a window into the past that is both partial and anthropogenically biased. The relative proportions in the coprolite-encrusted plant assemblage of midden

A Dessicated *Amaranthus* sp. seeds with coprolite encrustations from Samaca H-13, mound Feature 23, Middle Horizon midden contexts (S.U. 48).
B *Sesuvium* (*Portulaca*) sp. from the same context.
C *Chenopodium* sp. from the same context.
D *Solanum* sp. (cf. *pimpinellifolium* or 'tomatillo'), from the same context.
E *Lippia* (Syn. *Phyla*) sp. from the same context.

Figure 5.8. Selected agrestal weed macrofossils from Middle Horizon midden contexts in mound 23, Samaca H-13 mound 23, together with its wide range of molluscs from the ocean and *lomas*, would certainly seem to suggest that gathered, *wild* plant foods were particularly critical to human diet during the Middle Horizon in the Samaca Basin. But we began this chapter with the observation that interpretations derived from multi-proxy data are inherently more reliable than those from any one dataset. So we turn next to another archaeobotanical dataset with its own particular strengths and weaknesses: the pollen record of the Samaca Basin.

The Pollen Record

Although good pollen preservation is reported in other arid locations (see, for instance, Fish 1985, Gilbertson *et al.* 1994), there are rather few precedents for successful pollen extractions from the Peruvian coast (Weir and Eling 1986, Wells and Noller 1999). This is because appropriate contexts need to be selected very carefully. Many samples from the lower Ica Valley contained very little preserved pollen. Archaeological middens proved barren, probably because the formation of their anthropogenic deposits was not conducive to pollen deposition in the first place. Also, any deposits exposed to a high pH, fluctuating groundwater table in the past yielded little, or no, preserved pollen (see Beresford-Jones 2005 for more details). Nonetheless, we did succeed in extracting well-preserved pollen from certain Samaca Basin contexts, for reasons which become clear in their particular geomorphological circumstances.

One sequence of consecutive stratigraphic units on Samaca H-13, in particular, yielded a revealing pollen record: that of Test Pit 1/031. As we saw in the previous chapter, that excavation was under a climbing dune anchored on the western flanks of the Samaca Basin in a unidirectional wind regime. Grain size and other geomorphological analyses revealed that under the unconsolidated sands of the dune were a series of so-called 'aggrading aeolian deposits': surfaces deposited over time by a wind of progressively greater energy. In time these ancient surfaces were buried and sealed under the climbing dune itself, which built up as the wind gradually deflated the surface of the relict terrace H-13. Similarly, we obtained a decent pollen extraction from stratigraphic unit 33–46 cm in Test Pit 1/030, the layer immediately beneath the dune deposits, on which a human footprint provided the most poignant evidence of a buried preserved ancient land surface, associated with Middle Horizon material. From these buried surfaces good pollen concentrations were extracted of between 15,200 and 99,300 pollen grains per cm^3.

A pollen record naturally has its own taphonomic peculiarities, which we need to keep in mind when reading it for reconstructing ecological change (for some pertinent South American examples see Monsalve 1985, Chepstow-Lusty *et al.*1998, Chepstow-Lusty and Winfield 2000, Paez *et al.* 2001 and Weng *et al.* 2004). Different plants vary enormously in their production of pollen, according to whether they disperse their pollen using the wind—so-called 'anemophilous' pollen, which is generally very small, produced in vast numbers and spread over great distances—or by insects—so-called 'entomophilous' pollen, which is generally heavy and sticky, produced in far fewer numbers and moves not far from the parent plant (unless it adheres to an insect and so never enters the pollen record). Moreover, once deposited, pollen can be moved again, resulting in so-called 'secondary deposition'. Deriving a once-extant vegetation from relative amounts in a pollen record is thus rarely straightforward.

We will consider this further in our discussions here, but we start by recapitulating that there are only two possible agents of secondary deposition in the lower Ica Valley: the wind blowing uniformly from the south-west from the sea and the flow of the river in more or less in the opposite direction. As Figure 5.9 shows, the location of Test Pit 1/031 in the landscape was, therefore, an effective trap for wind-borne pollen blown across H-13—and for entomophilous plant taxa in its immediate vicinity. It lies above and beyond the reach of the river, which is after all, why it retains a useful pollen record. Moreover, downstream and upwind of the Samaca Basin the river enters a long canyon to the sea. So there are rather limited possibilities for contamination of the 1/031 record by exotic pollen brought in from

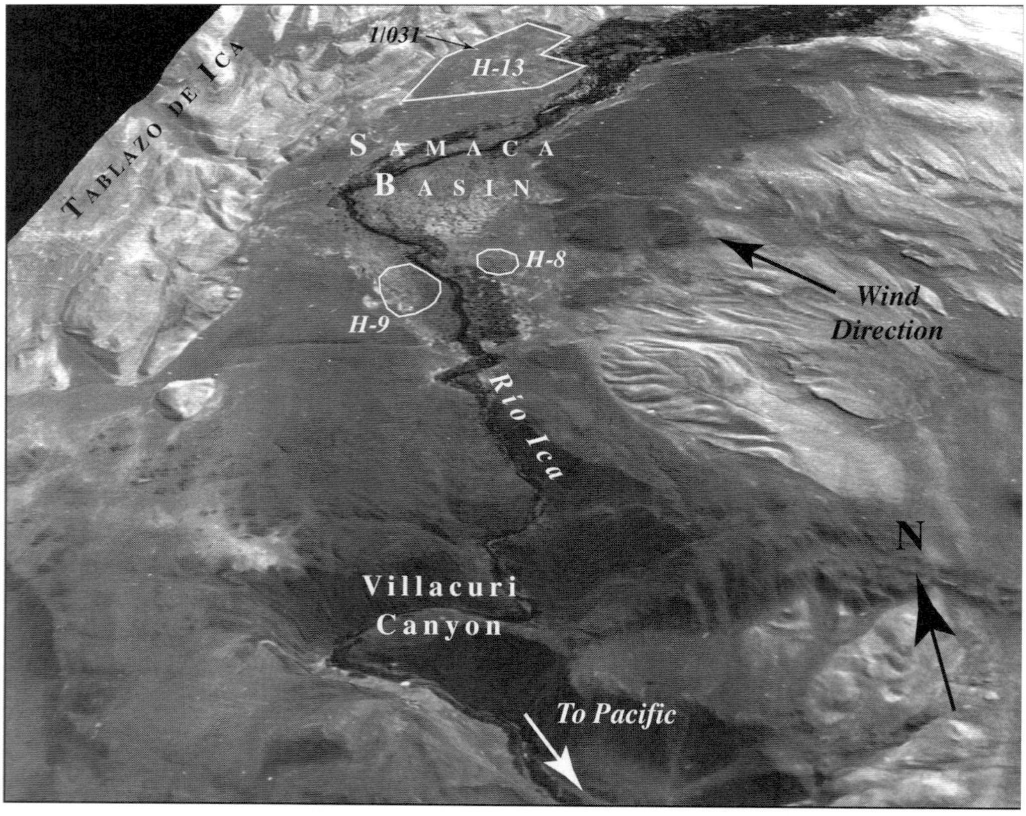

Figure 5.9. The location of the 1/031 pollen sequence on a large-scale digital elevation model of the Samaca Basin

outside the vicinity of the basin itself, and indeed, there are only very tiny percentages of obvious exotics in this record. In due course, the 1/031 sequence was buried and sealed by the aeolian graded sand deposits of the climbing dune.

As we will explore in more detail in Chapter 8, there is still one remaining fragment of 'old-growth' huarango woodland on the south coast today in the Quebrada Usaca on the Río Poroma, Nazca. By making pollen extractions from the floor of this woodland we were able to prepare modern pollen rain reference samples, with which to compare our ancient pollen record from Test Pit 1/031. These Usaca modern analogue samples were dominated by *Prosopis* sp. pollen (more than 75 per cent), with significant amounts other legume tree pollens, including *Acacia* sp., Papilionoideae and Caesalpiniaceae. They also included pollens of willow (*Salix* sp.), the Asteraceae family and *Ephedra* sp., and small amounts of grass, Cyperaceae and chenopod/amaranth pollen.

Prosopis produces a lot of pollen. Yet it is entomophilous — large and sticky and adapted for dispersal by insects. So its occurrence in any pollen record testifies to trees growing in the *immediate* vicinity. Chenopods and amaranths, meanwhile, the pre-eminent weedy flora of disturbed, anthropogenic areas like today's Huerto Huamaní fields, produce high volumes of anemophilous pollen (which cannot be distinguished beyond the level of chenopod/amaranth). Thus, the very high percentages of huarango pollen, rather fewer of other legume trees, willow and Asteraceae shrubs, and very low volumes of chenopod/amaranth and grass pollen are all together perfectly reflective of the relatively undisturbed state of the Usaca forest fragment, and, naturally enough, similar to the modern plant collections we made in the Quebrada Usaca. The only small disparity between our modern pollen analogue and our plant collections is the occurrence of *Ephedra* sp. in the former. But this primitive Gymnosperm — supremely adapted to arid areas — occurs widely in the coastal Andean foothills above 500 metres (Brack Egg 1999) and it produces high volumes of anemophilous pollen. So its exotic presence in the modern Usaca pollen assemblage is unsurprising.

Figure 5.10 then shows the pollen sequence from the various contexts of Test Pit 1/031, in order of increasing depth, and thus age. As we have seen, Early Nasca pottery sherds in an upper layer (76 to 80 cm) give a rough chronological framework for the rest of the sequence. Figure 5.10 compares this pollen record, firstly to the average of the pollen preparations of modern samples taken from the floor of the Usaca woodland fragment and, secondly, to the single successful pollen preparation from the 'footprint' layer of Test Pit 1/030, which was associated with Middle Horizon archaeological materials. The results are quite revealing.

The rich *Prosopis*-dominated (70 per cent) pollen assemblage recorded for the bottom of the 1/031 sequence (layer 140 to 190 cm) is very similar to that of the modern forest floor of the Usaca fragment. Desiccated huarango *poña* was also recorded in the sequence of contexts from Test Pit 1/031. Both pollen and *poña* thus point to trees once growing in this immediate vicinity, which, let us recall, is today in the midst of a barren landscape, far from the vegetated river floodplain (Figure 5.10). *Prosopis* pollen declines steadily up the

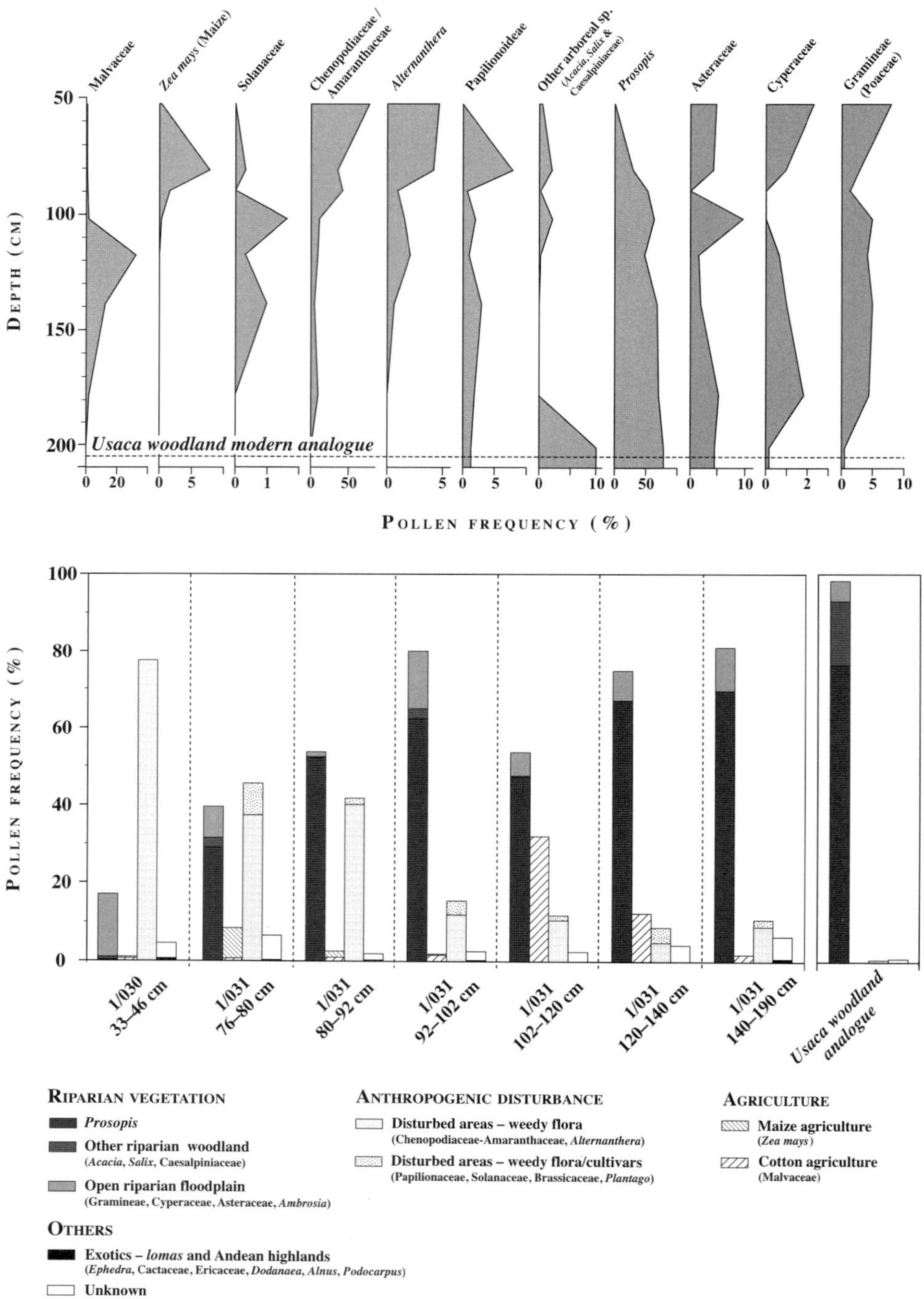

Figure 5.10. A pollen sequence from Samaca H-13

sequence, as pollen from cultivated plants appears and increases. The earliest of these are large, broken pollen fragments from the Malvaceae family which appear to be of cotton. Cotton was, of course, the only cultivar identified our earliest midden contexts dating to the Ocucaje Phases 3 and 4 of the Early Horizon. Further up the sequence, however, pollen appears of maize (*Zea mays*) and of the Papilionoideae family, which may be beans.

Self-pollinating maize produces a very low pollen rain of very large, easily identified grains, which are never dispersed very far from the plant at all (see for instance Weir and Eling 1986). Indeed, studies show that only about 1 per cent of the pollen rain immediately beneath a modern maize field is made up of *Zea* pollen grains (Martin 1963). So the seemingly modest occurrence of maize in these contexts is actually evidence of maize growing in significant quantities in the immediate vicinity. Maize pollen reaches a maximum in the Early Nasca layer 76 to 80 cm: the same period during which, as we saw earlier, a canal system was in operation and imposing on the terrace of H-13 a deposition regime of controlled energy quite distinct from the preceding, episodic floodplain clastic deposition. This layer was extraordinary for the high abundance of complete maize grains (Beresford-Jones *et al.* 2009b).

As *Prosopis* pollen declines steadily up the 1/031 sequence, pollen of chenopods/amaranths—those halophytic pioneers of open ground that are markers of anthropogenic disturbance and also of degraded riparian vegetation—steadily increases. Since chenopods and amaranths are wind pollinated, its occurrence here suggests a wider-scale ecological change upwind across the Samaca Basin. In the Middle Horizon contexts of 1/030, these have come to dominate the pollen assemblage entirely, while *Prosopis*, other tree species, and maize and cotton have all but disappeared. In short then, the pollen record shown in Figure 5.10 reflects a gradual replacement of huarango woodland with cultivation and anthropogenic disturbance on H-13, culminating in a landscape entirely dominated by halophytic weeds.

Tracing Human Ecology

As we have seen, the various lines of data from which we have tried to read a changing human ecology in the Ullujaya and Samaca basins each have their own strengths and weaknesses. In particular, they each suffer from particular taphonomic bias—obvious cases in point being that Early Nasca middens were relatively sparse, and that different plants produce very different volumes and types of pollen. Our focus is also blurred by the inevitable imprecision and limitations of each methodology. Moreover, these data must be interpreted according to context: plant macrofossils were extracted from ancient rubbish middens—which are by definition anthropogenic assemblages. The pollen record, on the other hand, better reflects the wider environment.

And yet aggregated and arranged as the plant macrofossil data are in Table 5.1—by time along one axis and by major ecological group down the other—a clear overall pattern may still be discerned. Figure 5.10 attempts the same for another dataset: the plant microfossil remains of pollen—producing another pattern, which we can superimpose on the first. Malacological data in Table 5.2, meanwhile, embellish our resulting picture of human ecology.

Table 5.1 shows an overall increase in intensity of agriculture over time—that is, until the Middle Horizon. Cotton is the first cultivar in these plant remains, present from the first Early Horizon contexts right through to the Middle Horizon. By Late Nasca the full suite of south coast cultivars is recorded. Indeed, cultivated plants (Group F) increase across the record, until the Middle Horizon when they collapse, in range at least, to a very narrow suite of cultivars. At the same time, agrestal weeds (Group C) associated with agriculture also increase steadily. By the Middle Horizon they dominate the assemblage. Increases of halophytes, such as chenopods, amaranths and, in particular, *Sesuvium*, suggest a gradual increase in salinity with time. Other indicators of open-area disturbance to riparian woodland, grasses (Group E) and shrubs (Group B), also increase, though shrubs too have become rare in the Middle Horizon. *Indigofera*, a shrub that thrives in the shade, is present in early periods but gone by Late Nasca. It does not grow at all today in the lower Ica Valley. Nor indeed do certain other cultivars, such as guava and pacay, which are common in the ancient middens. And, most striking of all, the pollen assemblages shown in Figure 5.10 show precisely the same trends as those in the plant macrofossil data—once their respective taphonomic differences are taken into account. The data of Table 5.2, meanwhile, show that gathered, marine and terrestrial malacological foods were extraordinarily important to the subsistence of Early Horizon inhabitants. And while they remain part of diet through time, they return to their former pre-eminence in the Middle Horizon, some two millennia later.

Indeed, the only real exception to this excellent correlation between plant macro- and microfossil data is from those of trees—predominantly huarango. For while the desiccated and charred remains of huarango maintain a fairly constant intensity across time in the macrofossil remains of Table 5.1 (Group A), in the pollen record they fall from levels almost the same as those of a modern analogue, the forest floor of the Usaca old-growth woodland, to almost nothing. Yet this serves only to emphasise the importance of huarango resources, and shade, to human ecology: matters we will explore further in the next chapters. For the plant remains in Table 5.1 are of course from anthropogenic contexts. And the huge amounts of huarango *poña* in the Middle Horizon midden of mound 23, Samaca H-13, are merely further confirmation of our identification of it as a relict nabkha—a place where people gathered under the canopy of a single, isolated tree, amid a landscape already undergoing *gradual* change under the hand of the wind. We will return in our final chapter to attempt to weave these threads of human ecology into other lines of data.

6. Deforestation

The loss of riparian woodland recorded in the archaeological and geomorphological records of the basins of the lower Ica Valley is but one, early part of a larger and still ongoing, history of the deforestation of the coast of Peru. This is an old and gradual story that can be read through the Spanish chronicles, administrative records and recent memory. The twentieth century witnessed its vertiginous acceleration. On the south coast, the story is now all but complete. For its sensitive ecology, adapted to the niche of marginal desert lands, the consequent environmental change is profound. The seeds of much of this change were sown by the cultural cataclysm that followed European conquest, as Mancio Serra de Leguizamo (cited by Rostworowski 1981: 55; my translation), companion-in-arms of the conquistador Pizarro, reflected in his memoirs of the lost 'order and harmony' of the Inca Empire, and of how well its people had managed its 'lands and mountains and mines and pastures and households and woodlands'.

This chapter will follow the traces of this tale here, beginning in the deep past with the archaeology of the south coast, beyond the lower Ica Valley. We will then turn to historical documentation, firstly to review the uses of *Prosopis* by humans on the coast of Peru and in arid lands elsewhere in South America, before finally returning to focus on the south coast to examine the historical record of deforestation there.

Prosopis in the Archaeology of the South Coast

The most famous expression of pre-Hispanic culture on the south coast of Peru is the so-called 'Nazca Lines'—the great landscape of geoglyphs marked upon the surface of the Pampa de San José in the Rio Grande drainage. Serious interpretations of this extraordinary artefact, which can only be properly seen from the air, concur in identifying it as a sacred landscape: a palimpsest of ritual pathways along which people processed in musical rites of

Chapterhead: Detail of Paracas embroidered textile showing figure carrying beans and root crops (drawing courtesy of Ann Peters).

fertility and water supply (see for instance Urton 1990, Reinhard 1993, Silverman and Proulx 2002). Most are lines and huge trapezoids. Those that are figurative, depicting plants, birds and animals, are clearly those of Early Intermediate Nasca iconography. One of the great ground figures on the Nazca pampa (Figure 6.1) is frequently interpreted as being of the huarango tree (Rossel Castro 1977, Reinhard 1993, Ormeño Iglesias 1995). And as Reinhard (1993: 50) observes of the several plant geoglyphs, 'all of these, in this desert climate, can be interpreted in terms of fertility'.

And yet, beyond this possible representation of the tree on the Pampa de San José, depictions of it within the famously naturalistic corpus of Nasca iconography are few. We will see why this should be so in Chapter 9, for we are offered a clue by the rich ethnobotanical history of another environment in which the genus is critical to human ecology: the south-western United States. In the meantime, archaeology's attention to the genus *Prosopis* on the south coast of Peru has been almost, but not entirely, limited to its use as a construction material.

Yacovleff and Herrera's (1934: 291) monumental compendium of the ethnobotany of pre-Hispanic Peru provides the first detailed mention of trees of the genus *Prosopis*. They quite correctly identify the trees on the beautiful Moche fine-line ceramic depictions of deer hunts as *Prosopis juliflora*. And they make reference to the use of algarrobo in the roofs of

Figure 6.1. The 'huarango' geoglyph on the Pampa de San José, Nazca (drawing by Oliver Whaley) and ancient huarango in Usaca

tombs and the frequency of its occurrence as posts carved with human faces ('*cabezas de palo*'), found marking grave lots on the south coast (Figure 6.2D).

Indeed, the use of *Prosopis* wood for construction timbers is seemingly almost as ancient as sedentary society itself on the Peruvian coast, since it is identified in the construction of Huaca Prieta in the Moche Valley on the north coast and one of the earliest known sites of the pre-Ceramic Period at around 2,500 BC (Strong and Evans 1952). In an arid climate, artefacts of *Prosopis*—one of the world's hardest timbers—enjoy quite remarkable preservation. Distinctive Y-shaped huarango posts (known as '*horcones*'), once commonly found in south coast archaeological sites, are so durable here that they are continually reused, even in modern buildings. Indeed, commercialisation of these ancient timbers is today a minor industry in the towns of Ica and Nazca. In 1997 a four metre high *horcone* cost around four soles (equivalent to around one pound sterling), though their prices have now risen with a diminishing supply.

Many artefacts found in the lower Ica Valley are fashioned from the distinctive fine-grained wood of the huarango. These range from tiny spinning bobbins to agricultural tools and *in situ horcone* door posts in the two Late Intermediate sites of H-18 and H-9 in the Samaca Basin (Figure 6.2). There are also great quantities of timbers in the cemeteries that line the western flanks of these basins (Figure 6.3). Extensive looting briefly exposes the many timbers used in their construction, mainly as roofing beams. Tragically these tomb timbers cannot be quantified as a line of data, for, not only are their contexts so upturned, but also, they seldom last long—presently being hauled off for firewood. Yet we have observed some huge huarango trunks in these looted cemeteries (Figure 6.3A). Indeed, most of them have far larger proportions than any trees living today in the lower Ica Valley.

One of the first large-scale archaeological surveys of the south coast region was by the great American anthropologist Alfred Kroeber, in the Río Grande drainage in the 1920s and and 1940s (Kroeber 1944, Kroeber and Collier 1998). His observations are particularly important because, as Schreiber (1998: 270) notes, nearly half of the sites he investigated have since been destroyed. Kroeber's reports make dozens of references to tombs roofed with 'huarango poles', including some quite substantial timbers (see for instance Kroeber and Collier 1998: 57–60) and also a 'walled and palisaded enclosure' of huarango timbers (see also Pezzia Assereto 1968: 183, 247, Rossel Castro 1977: 143, 162–3, for illustrations of the use of huarango poles in tombs from the Early Intermediate through to the Late Intermediate on the south coast). But, by far the most remarkable site reported by Kroeber in our context here, is that of La Estaquería, on the Río Nasca, upriver from the principal archaeological site of the Early Nasca Period—Cahuachi.

La Estaquería

Kroeber described Estaquería as he found it in 1926:

> Here . . . is a large Nazca cemetery, from several parts of which rise planted huarango or algarroba trunks, mostly forked at the top. In one spot an array of these is set on a low adobe platform, twelve

A and B Agricultural tools made of huarango from Late Intermediate sites H-8 and H-9, Samaca, Museo del Sito, Huerto Huamaní.

C *In situ* huarango door posts (*'horcones'*) in Late Intermediate site H-8, Samaca Basin.

D Late Intermediate Period huarango grave marker, reportedly from Ullujaya, Museo del Sito, Huerto Huamaní.

Figure 6.2. Selected huarango artefacts from the Samaca Basin, lower Ica Valley

A A very large huarango trunk around one and a half metres in diameter inside a looted Middle Horizon cemetery Feature 398, Ullujaya G-8/9. Note the huge quantities of raw cotton.

B and C Exterior and interior, respectively, of a looted Middle Horizon 'barbacoa' gallery tomb with huarango roof beams in cemetery Feature 398, Ullujaya G-8/9.

D Looted Middle Horizon cemetery Feature 406 on Ullujaya G-8/9. A few huarango roof timbers and vast quantities of raw cotton lie strewn in the vicinity.

Figure 6.3. The looted cemeteries of the Ullujaya Basin in October 2006

> rows of twenty logs each, about two meters apart, plus an annex on the west of smaller posts—a most impressive sort of wooden Stonehenge . . . my doubts increased whether, even in the rainless climate of Nazca, posts could remain solid and standing for four hundred years since the Inca, let alone the five or six hundred more since the Nazca culture. It is true that the algarrobo—a mesquite—and the also leguminous huarango have an incredibly hard, dense wood, and that under a cover of sand, timbers of them are frequently preserved even in Nazca graves. But would they stand up for centuries in the blinding light and occasional sandstorms of the region? . . . the whole situation seemed insoluble. But on seeing the squared algarrobo lintels over the gates at Chancaillo (Casma Valley) still carrying their loads of stone, I concluded that the Estaquería columns were presumably also pre-Spanish; and so they are put on record here. (Kroeber 1944: 27)

Some of the Estaquería cemetery posts were carved with human faces and serpentine figures (Rossel Castro 1977, Lancho Rojas 1998, Silverman 1993). The precise age of La Estaquería is still debated, although its pre-Hispanic antiquity is not. Strong carried out limited excavation and radiocarbon dating there (AD 1050), concluding it was Late Nasca (Strong 1957). While it is set amidst what was clearly an Early Nasca cemetery, it seems to post-date the nearby Cahuachi site (Silverman 1993). By the time Strong worked there in 1952 only forty-seven posts remained. Today, no more than half a dozen huarango posts remain, the rest having been stripped from the site for sale as 'art', construction poles or even burning into charcoal (Figure 6.4).

Cahuachi

Downriver from La Estaquería is Cahuachi, first investigated scientifically by William Strong, who carried out excavations there in 1952. Owing to his untimely death only a preliminary report was published (Strong 1957), though it makes numerous mention of the use of 'algarrobo' timbers in construction of the site. Strong described the site as 'the greatest, and probably the main capital site of the Nazca civilization in the time of its own peculiar florescence' (Strong 1957: 32). And this view of Cahuachi as manifestly the most important Nasca Period site has not changed with modern investigations (Silverman 1993: xi). Yet, thanks to the work of Helaine Silverman and Guiseppe Orefici, we now know that Cahuachi was not the capital city of an expansive state, as was once supposed (Rowe 1963, Lumbreras 1974). Their re-evaluations of the function of Cahuachi are central to our understanding of the nature of the society that built it and was responsible for the distribution of the essentially homogeneous Early Intermediate Nasca style throughout the region (see in particular Silverman 1993). Part of Silverman's interpretation incorporates the huarango in ways that go beyond the prosaic for the first time.

Cahuachi covers 150 hectares, of which 'around 25 hectares are covered by some 43 adobe brick mounds of greatly varying size and internal complexity; laid out in association with a series of plazas, patios and forecourts' (Silverman 1993: 87). Vast cemeteries surround the site, which have been heavily looted over the years. More than 21 kilograms of perfectly preserved plant remains were recovered during Silverman's excavations at Cahuachi, among which were 'industrial' plant species such as cotton; edible plants, such as

A and B The Late Nasca archaeological site of La Estaquería, on the Río Nasca photographed by Alfred Kroeber in 1942 (Kroeber 1944: 27), 'a most impressive sort of wooden Stonehenge'.
C and D La Estaquería in 2002.

Figure 6.4. La Estaquería, on the Río Nasca

maize, peanuts, beans, squash and potato, and edible fruit remains, including avocado, peppers and huarango. Indeed, 34 per cent of the total weight of edible plant remains recovered was huarango fruit (known as *huaranga*). Maize remains (at 38 per cent) were the only more significant component. Furthermore, *Prosopis* seeds were present in human coprolites. Silverman (1993: 293) comments that: 'except for the abundance and presumed important role of huarango in the early Nasca diet at Cahuachi, there are no real surprises in the botanical remains'. Yet Angel Maldonado had long since come to the same conclusion, based upon his observations of Strong's 1952 excavations in Cahuachi. For Donaire

Vizarreta (1998 [1959]: 199; my translation) relates conference proceedings from 1952 in which Maldonado reports that these revealed human excrement in quantity full of huarango seeds: 'providing irrefutable proof that its ancient inhabitants had used huarango fruits for food'.

Most of Silverman's *huaranga* remains were recovered from a single feature: a large, square enclosure covering 225 square metres. Silverman (1993: 174–94) calls this the 'Room of Posts', since twelve vertical huarango posts had been implanted in its floor, nine of them about a low platform at its centre. Seemingly, there was no evidence that these posts had supported a roof. In fact the 'Room of Posts' bears little resemblance to any other archaeological feature at Cahuachi: the only other comparable site in the region is that of La Estaquería. And Silverman's interpretation of this enclosure is key to her subsequent interpretation of the nature of the Cahuachi site and Nasca society.

For Silverman and Orefici's (Orefici and Drusini 2003) excavations at Cahuachi belie former descriptions of it as a great city. They show that its mounds are the product of major construction and remodelling, and that while they show numerous evidence of offerings of ceramics, plants and animals, they have little of populous habitation. Furthermore, in striking contrast to the vast adobe platforms of the contemporary Moche on the north coast, Cahuachi's architecture consists of diverse mounds with no single architectural focus, constructed upon natural hills. It is, as Silverman (1993: 336) puts it, 'monumentally unmonumental'. Instead, following a model suggested by Shimada to characterise other great Andean coastal ceremonial centres, Silverman (1993: 300–43) proposes that Cahuachi was a sacred pilgrimage and burial place for a number of independent societies, which shared a single cultural and religious tradition. As Shimada (1991: liv, cited in Silverman 1993: 322) defines this model, 'peripherally situated settlements . . . had a set of long-term social and ritual obligations to the religious centre . . . the nucleus [was] a centre not in terms of population density or size but rather in terms of interaction'. And Silverman goes on to suggest that these south coast societies were individual kinship groups akin to the foundational unit of traditional Andean society: the ayllu.

Huarango and the ayllu?

Some bemoan a tendency by Andean archaeology to project ethnohistorical or even ethnographic models far back into the ancient past, and certainly the precise definition of the ayllu may have varied considerably across time and space. Nonetheless, this 'earth-cell commune', as von Hagan (1961: 35) calls it, was woven into the entire social fabric of the Inca Empire (see for instance Rowe 1946, Johnson and Earle 1987, Conrad and Demarest 1984). Indeed, so fundamental is the ayllu, within a conservative and resilient Andean tradition—qualities which, of course, convey historical continuity—that some see its traces far back in the archaeological record of the very earliest complex societies on the Peruvian coast (see for instance Burger 1992). The ayllu is a kin-based, endogamous social group, defined by its claimed descent from a single ancestor, and who hold land communally. Today, as at the time of the Inca, its members have reciprocal obligations to one another and work together on larger corporate projects such as irrigation canals and agricultural terracing.

Ancestor worship is intimately related to the concept of the ayllu. During the Inca period this became elaborated into the 'panaqa' institution, whereby mummified dead rulers were maintained in full splendour, consulted as oracles and participated in rituals, amidst their former household ayllus (Conrad and Demarest 1984). Some scholars see evidence for ancestor worship of great antiquity in Peru, dating back to before 3500 BC (see for instance Vreeland and Cockburn 1980, Arnold and Hastorf 2008). On the south coast, this evidence includes the communal graves of the Cabeza Larga Necropolis cemetery site on the Paracas peninsula (see for instance Silverman and Proulx 2002: 214–21, DeLeonardis and Lau 2004). Others argue that the practice evolved only during the Early Intermediate Period (Isbell 1997). Yet, either way, ancestor worship would seem to have been a fundamental aspect of Early Intermediate south coast society.

Silverman interprets the Room of Posts as a sacred precinct associated with ancestor worship. Its walls had been repeatedly and carefully plastered and painted with red pigments showing indistinct tracings of Nasca iconography. Before abandonment it had apparently been carefully interred with clean sand brought some distance from the riverbed. Numerous offerings were deposited within this sand, including *Spondylus* shell, maize, peppers, late Nasca ceramics and the large cache of *Prosopis* fruit. Radiocarbon dating on the remains of the huarango posts themselves give dates of between AD 40 and AD 150, although, given the durability and consequent frequent reuse of its timbers in this arid environment, and that, as we will see, the tree itself may live for more than a millennium, these may be of limited use for the accurate dating of the Room of Posts itself. More significant, however, is a radiocarbon date from the cache of *huaranga* fruit itself, which gives a date of AD 830, the very end of the Early Intermediate and consistent with finds of Nasca 8 ceramics in the Room. Silverman (1993: 193) cautiously suggests that the huarango posts in the enclosure may have been 'ancestor posts'—totemic representations of the founding ancestors of Nasca ayllus—and, that 'Nasca society may have been using the huarango as a metaphor, similar to the biblical tree of life.' She cites various elements of evidence for this interpretation, and indeed also proposes it for the site of La Estaquería.

As we have seen huarango posts carved with human features, or unelaborated but of the same shape, are distinctive features of south coast mortuary furniture. Kroeber and Strong reported them as grave markers in the huge Nasca cemeteries around Cahuachi and La Estaquería. Furthermore, as Silverman (1993: 191) notes, Zuidema (1972) has interpreted one of the principal images of the Nasca iconographic canon as representing the ayllu founding ancestor. And in some depictions this image appears to grasp one of these forked posts (Zuidema 1972: 192). The mound in which the Room of Posts enclosure is situated has suffered some of the most severe looting of the whole of Cahuachi, which strongly suggests that it once included numerous important burials. Silverman (1993: 192–3) also cites the ethnographic work of Shernbody, which documents cultivated trees as a representation of ayllu ancestors in some Andean traditions: 'some ayllus represented their original ancestors in the form of *mallki* or trees. A large old tree would be a symbol of a long life and a fruit tree, of a fructiferous life. The *mallki*-ancestors had these attributes.' Silverman herself is very careful with her interpretations of the Room of Posts, calling these tenuous suggestions (Silverman 1993: 193). But her hypothesis that the huarango was a metaphor for ayllu society and that the huarango posts were totemic representations of ayllu ancestors is lent considerable credibility by the ecological information that we will review in Chapter 8. Moreover, it is also strengthened by the ethnohistory of Ica.

Father Rossel Castro (1954, 1968) records many *iqueño* ethnohistorical details including the fact that, at the time of the Spanish conquest, there were three *cacicazgos* (macro-social grouping under a *cacique* leader) in the Ica Valley, which became *repartimientos* under Spanish rule. These were the Urin Ika, the Anan Ika and the San Juan de Urin-Ika. Each of these was subdivided into groups of ayllus, called *Huarangas*, because they comprised around a thousand households each (the word 'huaranga' meaning a thousand in Quechua). The Urin-Ika, for instance, comprised the Kollana-Huaranga, the Tallana-Huaranga, the Toma-Huaranga, the Achira Huaranga, the Pallana-Huaranga and the Loka-Huaranga (Rossell Castro 1954: 44).

On the south coast, trees of the genus *Prosopis* are of course known as huarango. The popular etymology of this name is that it derives from the tree's immense longevity of up to a thousand years, though in fact such an age would test the most resilient of folk memories. Alternatively, the name might conceivably derive from its association with the ayllu clan groupings that Silverman suggests. For strikingly, as we will see in Chapter 9, many peoples of the North American Sonoran Desert also had clans or lineages named for *Prosopis* (mesquite), which had totemic significance. And Ormeño Iglesias records the following myth of Ica, related by an *iqueño* in his late seventies, Don Luis Oculmana Mendoza:

> In the past Ica was an old town of good people. So said our grandparents. For many generations they had work and suffering.
>
> One day when they were wandering vexed with hunger, they saw a pichingo crossing the sky with the flower of a huarango in its beak. This was what they had been waiting for. Quickly they gathered the strongest men and followed the bird along the pampas of Huayurí; but they could not find it.
>
> Time passed and on the day that the oldest men died, they saw the pichingo again carrying the flower of the huarango. This time they lost no time and walked along the dunes leading to the sea where they saw the sparrow in a contorted tree full of foliage. It was the huarango. When they reached the tree they saw that it was fertile, full of fruit with many yellow pods spread out in its shadow. Regretting they could not take them, for they had brought no sacks, they decided to eat them. The small quantity of pods that they could take home were received well and sown in many places.
>
> In each place where huarangos grew, they founded new towns and as the fruit they ate contained seeds, they left them without knowing and later the pampas were full of *huarangals*.
>
> And they honoured this huarango that gave them shade and food as the tree of life, the plant representing hope, born in the deserts, as hard as its seeds. And as in these times people were healthy and wise they called themselves children of the noble huarango, the origin of their dynasty. As they grew in numbers and culture the cacicazgos were divided into pachacas, and these in turn into chuncas. (Ormeño Iglesias 1995: 253; my translation)

Prosopis in Historical Documentation

Historical sources offer us a rich vein to mine for information on past lifeways. For descriptions of pre-Hispanic life we rely upon the Spanish and *mestizo* chroniclers, writing soon after the passing of the Inca Empire. These accounts were of course recorded through the distorting prism of the conquistadors' own worldview, but a few stand as works of considerable sympathy and perception. First among these, both in its time of writing and in its eloquence, was Cieza de León's *La Crónica del Peru*, written in 1553. Almost exactly a century later, Bernabé Cobo's great work, the *Historia del Nuevo Mundo*, synthesised his own close observations with earlier works to produce one of the most balanced early chronicles. Legal documents and administrative records ('*relaciónes*') of the early Spanish colony offer their own details, which have been sifted through by the great Peruvian historian María Rostworowski, among others. We will draw upon all of these—and, in particular, upon Rostworowski's seminal work *Recursos Naturales Renovables y Pesca* (1981)—to extract an account of the role that *Prosopis* played in the daily lives of the inhabitants of the Peruvian coast and, more tangentially, of other arid South American lands over the historical past. Since our ambition here is strictly ethnobotanical, we will be spared some of the pitfalls of more onerous historical interpretation. Finally, we will review these accounts with, naturally, particular focus on the south coast of Peru, for the glimpses they afford of its long-lost woodland landscapes.

The historical record of *Prosopis* uses

Many of these historical accounts make mention of the use of *Prosopis* resources. In Quechua, the native language family of the Andes and still, by number of speakers, our greatest surviving link to speech in the New World before the European conquest, the name of trees of the genus *Prosopis* is '*Thaccu* or *Taco*' (Yacovleff and Herrera 1934: 291), more properly written *thaqu* (Layme Pairumani 1997). According to D'Antoni and Solbrig (1977: 191) this means 'the tree' or 'the one', which would certainly be indicative of its importance and cultural antiquity, if it were better justified with appropriate linguistic citation. A rather more prosaic etymology likely lies in the word for 'red' (Paul Heggarty, personal communication), which, in turn, would be due to the vivid colour of its heartwood thanks to its very high content of tannins. In the now extinct language of the north coast of Peru known as 'Mochica' or 'yunga', *Prosopis* was called *ong* (Rostworowski 1981). As we have seen, the name used on the south coast—huarango, or *guarango*—is clearly of Quechua origin (Vildoso 1996). Elsewhere on the Peruvian coast, and more widely in South America, *Prosopis* is commonly known as 'algarrobo'. This arrived with the Spanish, who called the tree *el algarrobo de las Indias*, because it resembled the algarrobo, or carob tree, of the Mediterranean—a similar legume, but belonging in fact to the genus *Ceratonia* (for example Vildoso 1996, Pasiecznik *et al.* 2001). Indeed this was the beginning of a long subsequent history of confused *Prosopis* nomenclature, as we will see in Chapter 7.

Yet Cobo, with typical Jesuit perspicacity, was not misled:

> In Peru [there are] five or six species of trees known as guarango which produce edible fruits similar to the algarrobos [of Spain]. The Spanish call the one that produces the best fruits by the name of 'algarrobo de las Indias', but it is different from the one in Spain. The fruits of the guarango are good eating and the Indians make flour and bread from them. In some areas, the natives have little sustenance other than these fruits.

He goes on to describe the use of the distinctive sap of *Prosopis*:

> This tree exudes a certain black resin from its branches, which as it runs to the ground congeals, sometimes in great quantities and in the valleys they use this to decorate ceramics, because heated with water it makes a very black ink, which after being left to cool cannot be erased or rubbed off with water or anything else. (Cobo 1956 [1653]: 124; my translation)

Cieza de León (1995 [1553]: 203; my translation) likewise notes that 'they use the fruits and roots [of *algarrobo*] like we figs and raisins'. And Oviedo's *Historia Natural y General de las Indias* of 1535 (cited in Yacovleff and Herrera 1934: 291; my translation) relates how Almagro's ill-fated expedition south to conquer Chile depended for long periods on algarrobo fruits: 'in these villages there were many of these algarrobo fruits from which honey and bread was made to sustain the people'. The expedition suffered starvation on its return north because the algarrobo fruit crop of the previous year was gone and the new crop had not yet matured. For forty days the conquistadors lived on ten previously collected algarrobo fruits per person a day, an allotment each had to share with his horse. Oviedo also reports that the peoples of the Atacama ate maize for six months of the year and sustained themselves on *Prosopis* fruits for the rest of the year (D'Antoni and Solbrig 1977).

Prosopis woodlands on the coast, as we will see in more detail shortly, once supported large numbers of deer, birds and other game, which also provided food. In Peru there are two types of deer: a now rare coastal species (*Odocoileus virginianus*), called *lluychu* in Quechua; and that of the high sierra, *taruca* (*Hipocamelus antisensis*). Rostworowski (1981) reports that the meat of the latter, like that of the wild camelid vicuña, has a disagreeable flavour due to its diet of *ichu* grass. *Lluychu*, by contrast, feeding frequently on sweet *Prosopis* fruit, apparently has a fine taste.

Cobo also relates that *Prosopis* leaf litter was used by the Indians as fertiliser (Rostworowski 1981). Indeed, this leaf litter—*poña*—is still collected and used as an organic fertiliser by rural people on the Peruvian coast. Today *Prosopis* is also an important source of fuel and construction material, and still also of some food products. The beer—*chicha de huarango*— is prepared from *Prosopis* fruits on the south coast in December (see for instance Silverman 1993: 194), while cottage industries also produce *algarrobina* syrup and a sweet flour from *huaranga* for both local and national consumption (see for instance Grados and Cruz 1996).

Prosopis was also an important source of food for both agricultural and hunter-gather societies in semi-arid north-west Argentina. D'Antoni and Solbrig (1977: 192–5) offer a useful review of its historical ethnobotany in the region. Another Jesuit chronicler, Pedro Lozano (cited in D'Antoni and Solbrig 1977: 193) reported in the sixteenth-century, for instance, that here there are 'an infinite number of *algarrobos* some of which are called *zorruna* and which are not eaten but given to the animals, and others which are edible . . . of two species, one is quite juicy, another white and drier. Both are ground and from the flour, bread is made which in Tucumán is called *patay* . . . they also make wine from *algarrobos* which is called *chichi*.' The Spanish called these people *algarroberos* for their habit of abandoning their work in the fields of the Europeans once the time came to harvest *Prosopis* fruits. Likewise, the diverse peoples of the semi-arid Chaco region 'highly prized the fruits of algarrobos because the native peoples depended on them in former times for sustenance during parts of the year' (D'Antoni and Solbrig 1977: 193). The Ashlushlay, Lengua, Pilagá and Mbaya peoples all prepared flour from *Prosopis* fruit from which they made *patay* bread. The high nutritional value and calcium content of *patay* was particularly important for children and accounted for the lack of disease associated with hypocalcemia, even in periods of famine. Today *patay* is still eaten commonly in Andalgalá. And, as on the coast of Peru, these peoples also used the fruit to prepare sweet syrup and alcoholic *chicha* (or '*aloja*'). Indeed, the significance of *Prosopis* to the peoples of the Chaco is implicit in the name for one season of their calendar of five: the 'season of algarrobo, chañar and mistol' (D'Antoni and Solbrig 1977: 194). As we will see in Chapter 9, this naming of seasons for *Prosopis* finds an echo in other arid American lands for which we have a rich historical ethnobotany.

The historical record of *Prosopis* woodlands

Bernabé Cobo (1956 [1653]: 124; my translation) wrote that the valleys of the Peruvian coast in which 'the algarrobos or guarangos are most abundant are those of Ica, Nasca, Guambacho, Casma, Chicama, Guadalupe and Catacos'. But it is in Cieza de León's *La Crónica del Peru* that we find the earliest and most eloquent descriptions of the these valleys of the desert coast:

> As fresh and luxuriant as sprigs of basil . . . with woods and glades full of birds of many types, great numbers of pigeons, turtledoves, turkey hens, pheasant, partridge and many deer . . . In the thickets of the valleys are algarrobos and fruits like those of Spain.
>
> (Cieza de León 1995 [1553]: 203; my translation)

Cieza's narrative described the woodlands of many valleys during his first journey south along the coast in 1547. Of the valley of Motupe he wrote, 'the algarrobos and other trees extend over a great stretch thanks to the humidity they find under their roots', and of Tucumé, 'also wide and pretty and full of groves and woodlands' (1995 [1553] 204–5; my translation). He found the valley of Paramonga, 'no less delightful than the rest . . . we saw nothing more than abandoned woodlands and groves' (1995 [1553]: 210; my translation). He described the valley of Pachacamac, today drowned in Lima shanty town sprawl, 'as fragrant and full of woodlands as its neighbours', and the Valley of Mala as 'full of dense glades and groves'; Guarco (now Cañete) was 'large and wide and full of orchards [with] canals of water running under the shade of its groves and woods' (1995 [1553]: 215–16; my translation). Arriving on the south coast itself, Cieza wrote of the valley of Ica that 'it is no smaller and less populous than the rest . . . there are in this valley great thickets of algarrobo woodlands and many orchards of the fruit trees that I have described, and deer, pigeons, turtledoves and other game' (1995 [1553]: 221; my translation). And from Ica his coastal journey continued on to end in the 'beautiful valleys and rivers of the Nasca'.

The valley of Ica began to be populated by Spanish conquistadors around 1535 and the town of Ica was founded in 1563 (Vildoso 1996). An anonymous sixteenth-century document cited by Sánchez Elías (1957: 23, my translation) states that the site was chosen for its richness in 'fields, farms and timber to be had' and because of its copious subterranean water supply. In 1574 López de Velasco (cited in Vildoso 1996: 37; my translation) described the valley's 'large orchards and woodlands for timber'. Another of the great early *cronistas*, Bartolomé de las Casas (cited in Yacovleff and Herrera 1934: 291; my translation) described Ica in 1550 as a valley very rich in algarrobos. Indeed, in his discussion of the Aymara etymology of the name Ica, Cerrón-Palomino (2008: 364; my translation) cites Martín de Murúa, writing in 1613 that 'the Spanish called it *Valverde* on account of its verdure'.

Rostworowski (1981) traces in the early colonial documents many references to woodlands (or '*huarangals*') of Ica, some extensive enough to carry their own names, such as that of Ximata, in the district of San Martin. She cites, for instance, the original land distribution (the *Repartición*) amongst the Spanish carried out by Maldonado de Torres in 1594, defining a *huarangal* of 60 fanegadas adjoining the Tinquina bridge; while a legal document of 1603 concerns the ownership dispute over woodlands in Tacama and refers to the lands thereabouts as extensive forest of huarango. Martìn de Morúa (cited in Rostworowski 1981: 56; my translation), meanwhile, chronicles Ica in 1600 as 'surrounded all about by trees that they call huarangos, and we algarrobos'. Calancha (cited in Sánchez Elías 1957; my translation) similarly described the town in 1639 as 'surrounded by wooded countryside of trees known in these parts as guarangos, of hard wood, and tall, growing sideways as contorted mountains'.

At this time, in the sixteenth and into the seventeenth century, the old 'royal road of the Incas' followed, more or less, the route of today's Pan-American highway from Pisco through Ica and on to Nazca (von Hagen 1961: 131). By all account it was then a pleasant road to travel. De las Casas described it in 1550: 'the whole road was enclosed on both sides with fruit trees placed there to provide on the one hand shade for travellers, and on the other, food for the poor carrying nothing to eat. And these trees were especially garrobos, whose fruit is similar to our garrobos, out of which they make bread of a certain kind.' Cobo (1956 [1653]: 124; my translation) described an algarrobo forest growing across 'all the desert from Pisco to Ica and also up until Nazca'. Further down the Río Ica the woodlands continued—evidenced, for instance, by a property title of 1647 cited by Rostworowski (1981: 59; my translation), which sets out this land as 'covered with guarango forest', and extending from the Ocucaje Basin down the river to the Callango Basin, 'until the royal road of dunes which runs to the valley of Guayurí' (today called Palpa). Yet of all these accounts of old Ica, perhaps the most striking is that of Vázquez de Espinosa (1942 [1629]: 485), who described the woodlands about the town of Ica as 'impenetrable at many points . . . with many savage wild animals'—stretching for five leagues along the road from Ica to Nazca—'so thick that the highway is the only way to get through them and one sees nothing but woods and sky'. For today this, and indeed all these seventeenth-century descriptions of Ica, seem almost incredible. The historical record of deforestation about the city in the middle Ica Valley tells us why.

Deforestation

Exploitation of *Prosopis* woodlands

Initially, coastal forests provided hunting opportunities for the Spanish conquerors. The quantities of deer on parts of the coast up until the eighteenth century were such that traps had to be prepared to protect crops (Martínez Compañón 1778; cited in Rostworowski 1981). Europeans rapidly introduced other animals, particularly pigs and goats, which could be sustained upon *Prosopis* fruits. Cobo relates how great numbers of such livestock could live upon algarrobo fruits, which 'were as nutritious as any grain' (1956 [1653]: 125; my translation). In Ica itself this led to the development of a flourishing tanning and soap industry, which lasted until the end of the eighteenth century and exported its products as far as Panama. Following its first foundation, the town of Ica was repeatedly and almost completely destroyed by an unfortunate sequence of three devastating earthquakes in 1644, 1647 and 1687 (Sánchez Elías 1957). And documentation of its continual rebuilding on new sites makes many references to use of huarango wood. Huge huarango timbers were used, for example, in the raising of two towers of the cathedral (Vildoso 1996).

Indeed, the newly founded colonial cities required great quantities of timber for their construction and fuel. Rostworowski (1981) relates that as early as 1535 the council of Lima was sounding the alarm at the extent of deforestation about the city and issuing orders for the planting of new trees. The order was repeated the following year, presumably because it was not being followed. By 1569, Salazar de Villasante was observing that the country around Lima had been completely stripped of trees for three leagues (17 kilometres) around. Stiff penalties were imposed on anyone caught making charcoal or chopping down trees within four leagues of the city: '50 pesos for the Spaniard, 10 days in jail for the Indian; and 30 pesos or 100 lashes for black slaves' (Rostworowski 1981: 64; my translation). A century later, the *Relación* of 1683 was complaining that the population of Chancay Valley, just to the north of Lima, was 'provisional, serving for little more than the supply of algarrobo charcoal to Lima' (Rostworowski 1981: 65; my translation). Today there are, of course, no *Prosopis* woodlands in Chancay.

By the nineteenth century, there were constant and numerous references in shipping manifests to the transport of algarrobo charcoal from all along the coast to Lima (Rostworowski 1981). Towards the end of that century railways were being constructed, including a number of lines along the coast. These connected Ica and Pisco, Lima and Chancay and other coastal routes. Long defunct and covered with desert sands, little trace of these lines exists today. But *Prosopis* wood provided the sleepers for the lines and fuelled the boilers of their steam locomotives for decades before their demise (Vildoso 1996). The twentieth century witnessed exploitation of dwindling *Prosopis* coastal woodlands at vertiginous rates. They were consumed as domestic fuel, in brick-making furnaces and charcoal production, as fuel for railways, and cleared for the expansion of agriculture. Conservative estimates for the areas of coastal woodlands cleared for these purposes between 1950 and 1980 are put at some 200,000 hectares (Grados and Cruz 1996). And by the end of the twentieth century populations along the coast had exploded as rural people left the sierra to seek easier lives or to escape terrorism. Lima, a city of around 250,000 in 1900, now has a population of some 9 million, around half that of the whole country. Peru's relative economic condition declined steadily over the century thanks to poor and corrupt governance and the country now has one of the lowest consumptions of electricity per capita in Latin America. Kerosene and firewood satisfy much domestic energy demand. The story of the south coast itself then is but a vignette of a wider tale of exploitation to satisfy immediate ends in ignorance, or regardless, of long term costs: in short the rape of the land and its people that defined Peru's colonial history, and whose resonances continue to play out today.

South coastal deforestation

North of the city, the forest between Pisco and Ica described by Cobo, Vázquez de Espinosa and others in seventeenth century has disappeared almost within living memory. Vildoso (1996: 61) describes the 'immense stretch' of huarango woodland that stretched across most of the Villacurí pampa, lying between the Pisco and Ica river valleys. Older *iqueños* can still recall the railway that ran between Ica and Pisco until the 1950s, its sleepers cut from, and its boilers fired off, huarango timber from Villacurí (Vildoso 1996). Indeed, an elderly lawyer, César Jerónimo, cited by Vildoso (1996: 62; my translation), describes how in the fifties, extracted huarango trunks and roots lay in 'veritable cemeteries' in the desert about the city. By the 1990s Villacurí had all been reduced to a few scatters of solitary huarangos in the midst of a desert of shifting dunes. In the past decade, however, much of it has been converted by agro-industrial concerns into huge fields of monocultures. These are fed on fossil groundwaters pumped from boreholes sunk well over a hundred metres down into the pampa, whose depths are increased year by year, as this last and most ancient resource of Ica is run down, and used to cultivate asparagus for export.

South-east of Ica, the last extensive huarango woodlands in the middle Ica Valley were chopped down in the middle of the twentieth century. A woodland near Santiago was destroyed and sold as charcoal in 1945 by a resolution of the Ministry of Public Works (Rostworowski 1981). That woodland covered more than 63 hectares and had around 1,700 trees, all of them more than three hundred years old. Rostworowski (1981) cites the written complaint of an agricultural engineer, Noriega, arguing that the result of this order would be desertification, since only these large old trees had roots sufficiently deep to extract subsurface water in the area. His protest was ineffectual, of course. An estimate for the *explotación* of an old *huarangal*, Potrero de la Beneficiencia in Santiaguillo, Ica, from the 1950s illustrates the fate of Ica's *huarangals* from 1930 to 1955. For this entire woodland (Figure 6.5) was converted in a single operation into 30,000 sacks of charcoal—an unimaginably enormous quantity in today's terms, as we will see shortly—as well as 15,000 *cabezales*, 45,000 *postes de plan* and 15,000 *piés de gallo*: the various pieces of timber architecture for grape vines (Nana Soldi, personal communication). Indeed, this story of the sale of entire woodlands by landowners for their one-off, wholesale conversion into charcoal is repeated over and over again across the south coast valleys at this time. To the east of the city, the areas of Yauca del Rosario, Tingue and la Pampa de los Castillos were once covered by large *huarangals* used by their residents for foddering animals. It has all now been converted to large-scale agriculture (Vildoso 1996: 61). Agricultural expansion accounted for much of the removal of woodland in the middle Ica Valley. In 1890 there were only some 9,000 hectares under cultivation. Today that figure stands at more than 40,000 (see for instance Vildoso 1996, Wellmann 1998). The story of Nazca is similar. Silverman (1993: 13) records that 'my older workers recalled that in their youth (the 1930's and 1940's) the narrow valley floor around Cahuachi was covered by *monte* including huarango . . . over the years the hardwood huarangos have been cut down and burned for fuel or made into charcoal'.

While we have plotted a seemingly steady, overall course through the historical record of deforestation of the middle Ica Valley, ecological change is of course seldom entirely one directional. Throughout the New World ecologies returned to apparently 'pristine' conditions after the terrible collapse in native populations that followed the introduction of Old World diseases (Denevan 1992). Cook (1981) estimates the pre-conquest population of Peru at nine million souls. By 1620 it had fallen by some 93 per cent to around 600,000. On the Peruvian coast native populations 'were almost completely wiped out' (Cook 1981: 114). Subsequently, coastal populations recovered quite rapidly, but such a catastrophic decline must have led to some considerable recovery of riparian woodlands of the south coast, not least in our area of main interest here, the lower Ica Valley. But the context of the south coast desert, with its critical ecological and geomorphic thresholds, is a peculiar one. In places here deforestation turns out to be irreversible. Moreover, the lifespan of its keystone tree species—the huarango—is measured in centuries. Together, these set a ratchet on the process of deforestation here, irrespective of periods of recovery. We will examine the ecological and phenomenological consequences of this process in forthcoming chapters.

In the lower Ica Valley, there is evidence that during the historical period some recovery took place, precisely because it had long been abandoned to substantial settlement. The basins of the lower Ica Valley, Callango, Ullujaya and Samaca, being most isolated from the historical population centres in the middle of the valley, were the last to suffer the final stages of deforestation in the twentieth century. Yet, their wide relict river terraces—H-13 in Samaca and G-8/9 in Ullujaya—have never seen any return to a forested landscape.

Figure 6.5. Huarango woodland in Santiaguillo, middle Ica Valley in 1948 (photographs courtesy of Nana Soldi)

In the past fifty years the remaining woodlands of these basins have suffered what Vildoso (1996: 63; my translation) rightly calls 'violent deforestation'.

The owner of the *huarangal*s of Callango, Sebastián Barranco, sold them in the late 1930s. Donaire Vizarreta (1998 [1959]: 199; my translation) reports his reluctance in realising the sale, 'when he knew that the purchaser would destroy the forests that he so loved'. Yet sell them he did, before leaving for Europe, so repeating that story of the south coast at this time—entire woodlands being burnt wholesale to charcoal. Strong's (Strong *et al.* 1943: 23–4) report on his subsequent excursion down the valley in 1941 is revealing: 'en route to the mouth of the Ica river we stopped at the Hacienda of Callango, formerly owned by Dr Barranco and now the centre for extensive charcoal burning operations in the almost unpopulated lower Ica valley . . . the extensive charcoal burning is further stripping an already eroded and desolate dry country'. Downstream of Callango—Ullujaya and Samaca—Strong reported that 'the country of the lower Ica Valley is very rough, with alternate desert, steep ridges and dense algarrobo thickets'.

Those thickets are also now gone. The Ullujaya and Samaca basins were purchased by Don Pedro Cabrera in the 1950s and cleared of forest for cotton agriculture. Attempts to dam the Río Ica to provide water for this enterprise, however, were deposited in the sea by successive El Niño floods. By the time General Velasco launched his radical agrarian reform in 1969, the large properties of the lower Ica Valley were not even deemed worthy of seizure and repartition. Today, most of these basins are little more than patchy *monte* scrub and dunes. Velasco's reforms ushered in the final chapter of the story of south coast deforestation, for, as so often, well-meaning agrarian reform had only the effect of destroying the resources they were seeking to redistribute. Those few landowners who had resisted the short-term profits offered by burning entire woodlands into charcoal lost their lands. Instead, they became the 'property of the state'. Burning *Prosopis* into charcoal on the coast of Peru has long been illegal without a permit issued by the Instituto Nacional de Recursos Naturales (INRENA). But what meaning does such protection have in a context stripped of social contract by corruption and grinding poverty? In 2007 INRENA had not a single vehicle with which to extend the reach of state protection across the scattered valleys of the south coast. Demand for charcoal is high in urban markets with burgeoning populations, where it is burnt on barbeques or in popular *pollo a la brasa* (barbequed chicken) restaurants. Charcoal burning is conducted with virtual impunity in the properties of the state along the Peruvian coast and every dry season the lazy grey plumes of its smoke rise into the blue skies of Ica and Nazca. An informed estimate of the illegal production of charcoal today is between 1,250 and 2,800 sacks (or between 32 and 73 tonnes) per year for the Ica and Nazca valleys combined (Oliver Whaley, personal communication): a paltry enough quantity next to those extraordinary charcoal operations of the 1940s and 1950s, yet more than enough to threaten the remaining scraps of old-growth woodland left here, as we will see in the next chapter. When we asked the elderly *carbonero*, the late Don Philipe Bartolomé, how many huarango trees he had chopped down in the lower Ica Valley over his long life, he could only sigh and say that 'it must have been a million'.

Figure 6.6. The Samaca Basin in September 1998 (photograph courtesy of Claudia Lüthi)

7. The Huarango:

The Genus *Prosopis* on the South Coast

How may we unravel the profound consequences to human ecology of the long and gradual story of deforestation that we have traced through the archaeology and history of the south coast of Peru? Naturally, we should start by better understanding the tree that, along with humans, dominates its riparian ecology: the huarango. These are a species of the genus *Prosopis*, one of the most common plants found along the watercourses of New World deserts and members of a family of nitrogen-fixing, bean-producing plants — the legumes — whose importance to humankind is second only to that of the cereal grasses and with which our relationship is, if anything, even older.

Fortunately for our purposes, because of its importance in arid environments, *Prosopis* has been widely studied by agroforesters, botanists and ecologists. We can draw upon this work to supplement our own observations in the last fragments of old-growth woodland that remain on the Peruvian south coast. Today, as we will see, perceptions of the genus are deeply divided between appreciation of its value on the one hand, and intense dislike of it as a thorny, invasive weed on the other. In this chapter we will sift through the reasons for this and a history of misidentification, so as to identify the particular characteristics of the huarango and, thereby, its true value as a human resource in the past. Indeed, we will go on to construe that thousands of years of co-evolution with humans have left their mark on the tree's form on the south coast of Peru.

Problems of Taxonomy

The quarter of the earth's land surface that is sub-tropical and dry is dominated by trees of two genera: *Acacia* and *Prosopis* (Geesing *et al*. 2000). These nitrogen-fixing, semi-deciduous, drought-resistant trees occupy more than three million square kilometres

Chapterhead: Detail of Paracas embroidered textile (drawing courtesy of Ann Peters).

(Pasiecznik *et al.* 2001: 2). Both *Acacia* and *Prosopis* are of the same sub-family, Mimosoideae, having small, compound leaves and producing small flowers clustered into inflorescences, within the family Leguminosae (or Fabaceae), whose members are popularly known as legumes, since they produce seeds in legumes or pods. Plants of this large family, whose seeds are relatively rich in protein and include lentils, peas and beans, have an importance to human diet second only to the cereal grasses (see for instance Vaughan and Geissler 2000: xviii). And the time-depth of our relationship with them, and in particular the tree legumes, stretches far back into our hunter-gatherer past (see Jones 2009 and, for the significance of *Prosopis* in very early human diets in Mesoamerica, Smith 1967: 241, Flannery 1968, Callen 1969: 239).

While more than a thousand species of *Acacia* are recognised worldwide, *Prosopis* is but a small genus—represented by only some forty-four species. It is also predominantly an American genus, 90 per cent of its species being native to the New World (Simpson and Solbrig 1977, Catalano *et al.* 2008). Yet the taxonomy of *Prosopis* is still confused and subject to ongoing revisions.

This complicated taxonomy (or 'systematics') arises precisely because of the adaptive flexibility necessary to inhabit arid environments. Most *Prosopis* species, and even individuals, show great plasticity in form (or 'phenotype'), in response to environmental fluctuations (Ibrahim 1992). Furthermore, species frequently hybridise because they are genetically polymorphic, meaning that they have few chromosomal differences (Solbrig *et al.* 1977). These flexibilities convey the advantages of relatively quick physiological and morphological adaptation for plants living in the patchy habitats and climatic unevenness of deserts (see for instance Harris and Cambell 1981). But for botanists concerned with classification, they make for complication. Indeed, Pasiecznik *et al.* (2001: 2) describe the history of the nomenclature of *Prosopis* as 'one of conflicting definitions and changing systematics leading to great confusion in the definitions of species'.

As we have seen, these first confusions began in Peru when the Spanish conquerors called the tree *el algarrobo de las Indias*, because it resembled another legume, the carob tree of the Mediterranean basin (*Ceratonia siliqua*). 'Algarrobo' is today the vernacular name for trees of the genus *Prosopis* throughout South America. The name 'huarango' is restricted to the Peruvian south coast, although, again confusingly, on the north coast this is the common name for another Mimosoideae tree, *Acacia macracantha* (see for instance Brack Egg 1999: 13). In the United States, meanwhile, various *Prosopis* species are known as 'mesquite'.

Scientific classification of *Prosopis* began with Linnaeus, who assigned the name in 1767 to the single species of which he was aware: *P. spicigera* (now synonymous with *P. cineraria*), one of the few Old World species (Fagg and Stewart 1994). The derivation of the name *Prosopis* is 'towards abundance', from the ancient Greek 'pros' for towards; and 'Opis', wife of Saturn and the goddess of abundance and agriculture (Pasiecznik *et al.* 2001: 19). It is purely serendipitous for our purposes here that 'towards agriculture' would be an equally satisfying etymology.

Burkart (1976) subsequently divided the genus *Prosopis* into five distinctive groups of species or 'sections'. Within these, species can be very similar and frequently hybridise. By far the largest is section *Algarobia*, which includes more than half the New World species of the genus, and wherein most taxonomic confusion lies. This led Burkart to believe that *Prosopis* is an old genus, separated into principal lineages, within which episodes of isolation have produced partial speciation (Burkart and Simpson 1977). Thirty-five of the forty-four species recognised are native to South America, which suggests that this was the plant's place of origin (see for instance Burkart and Simpson 1977, Pasiecznik *et al.* 2001). Indeed, this is confirmed by the latest molecular phylogeny studies (Catalano *et al.* 2008), which date the origin of the genus to the beginning of the Oligocene, some 34 million years ago, and link its subsequent spread and divergence to an expansion of arid conditions over this great time-depth.

The history of *Prosopis* classification in Peru mirrors its wider problems, as Díaz Celis (1995: 47; my translation) summarises: 'the systematic treatment of the algarrobo in Peru has been variable and confused'. This history can be followed through the work of MacBride (1943), Weberbauer (1945), Burkhart (1976), Burkhart and Simpson (1977), Ferreyra (1987), Díaz Celis (1995), Pasiecznik *et al.* (2001), Mom *et al.* (2002) and Harris *et al.* (2003) (and see Beresford-Jones 2005 for a comprehensive review).

Rather unsurprisingly then, difficulties with *Prosopis* taxonomy abound also in the archaeological literature. Yacovleff and Herrera (1934: 291) originally identified artefacts of 'algarrobo' wood as *Prosopis juliflora*. Towle (1961: 56), likely following MacBride (1943), considered this identification mistaken, claiming that '*juliflora* does not occur in Peru' and that the Peruvian equivalent is *P. chilensis*, 'a plant very similar to *P. juliflora* and often confused with it'. And most archaeological authors continue to follow Towle in identifying materials as *P. chilensis* (see for instance Menzel *et al.* 1964, Shimada and Shimada 1985, Silverman 1993, Cook 1999, Silverman and Proulx 2002).

Scrupulously, these identifications are almost certainly incorrect. *P. chilensis* is, in fact, one of the more distinctive *Prosopis* species in its live condition, by virtue of its larger leaf morphology (Pasiecznik *et al.* 2001: 33). None of the many trees that we observe on the south coast of Peru today show the *P. chilensis* leaf type (Whaley 2004, Beresford-Jones 2005). Following Burkart and Simpson (1977), Díaz Celis (1995), Pasiecznik *et al.* (2001) and Harris *et al.*'s (2003) systematics, and in agreement with most other current taxonomic authorities, they would be identified as *P. pallida* (H. and B. ex. Willd.) H.B.K. (cf. Piacenza 2005).

Recently, however, Mom *et al.* (2002) published the most authoritative description yet of the *Prosopis pallida* populations of Peru. Their morphological analysis calls for the current classification of *P. pallida* to be differentiated into two species and in so doing they reintroduce the binomial originally used by Bentham (1875), and subsequently discarded by Burkhart (1976), of *P. limensis*. Mom *et al.*'s (2002: Fig. 3) description of the form of *P. limensis* is the most accurate that we have seen for the trees of the valleys of Ica and Nazca (Whaley 2004, Beresford-Jones 2005, Whaley *et al.* 2010b). Indeed, Mom *et al.* (2002: 44) assign the name *P. limensis* to all the *Prosopis* collections they examine from the south coast which include specimens from Ocucaje, Ica and Jumana and Poroma, Nazca. The type specimen assigned the name *P. limensis* by Bentham is held in the herbarium of the Royal Botanical Gardens. It is identified only as from 'Lima' — hence the name assigned by Bentham — yet this may well only be the place from which it was shipped. And its morphology fits Mom *et al.*'s description for the rehabilitated *P. limensis* binomial (Oliver Whaley, personal communication).

So, while I will continue here to use the encompassing binomial *P. pallida* — or the wider so-called '*P. juliflora–P. pallida* complex' (and see Pasiecznik *et al.* 2001 for background on this useful identification class) — for the purpose of corresponding with the existing botanical literature, the more precise classification of the huarango of the south coast should almost certainly be *P. limensis* (Whaley *et al.* 2010a: 14). The distinctive features defined by Mom *et al.* (2002: 43–4) as defining *P. limensis* — the huarango — include its well-developed brachyblasts with distinctive resin ducts; leaves with very many, very small leaflets (less than 7 mm long); and long, straight, yet also wide yellow pods. They are noted in the desiccated *Prosopis* macrofossils recorded during our archaeological investigations (see Figure 5.4).

Indeed, archaeological wooden artefacts from anywhere along the coast of Peru are rather unlikely to be of *P. chilensis* (Molina) Stuntz, which is restricted to isolated populations in higher altitude, dry intermontane locations, mainly in the south of the country (Burkart and Simpson 1977, Díaz Celis 1995, Brack Egg 1999, Pasiecznik *et al.* 2001), and much more likely to be of the so-called '*P. juliflora–P. pallida* complex'. The botanist Fortunato Herrera was certainly well aware of this when he originally identified coastal algarrobos as *P. juliflora* (Yacovleff and Herrera 1934), since he had already identified the *Prosopis* of the high intermontane valleys as *P. chilensis* (Díaz Celis 1995).

Fortunately, however, such specific identifications are unnecessary for many purposes of archaeological interpretation. For all of them fall into Burkart's section *Algarobia*, whose members show strong similarities, even at the very detailed botanical levels of wood anatomy, protein and enzyme characteristics, leaf physiology, and DNA (Pasiecznik *et al.* 2001: 28). Consequently, their ecological characteristics are broadly similar and, as Felgar (1977: 150) puts it, 'ethnobotanically it is both convenient and realistic to treat the North American members of the section *Algarobia* as a unit'. Indeed, within the *P. juliflora–P. pallida* complex itself, these similarities are so marked that species are, as Harris *et al.* (2003: 154) note, 'difficult to distinguish even for those with considerable experience in semi-arid forestry'. Here, therefore, we may use appropriately selected data from studies of the species of section *Algarobia* — and particularly from the *P. juliflora–P. pallida* complex — to help understand the ecological importance and ethnobotany of the huarango on the south coast of Peru. Nonetheless, more specific identifications will still be necessary for some of our purposes here.

Until very recently, for instance, many North American authors continued to follow Bentham (1875) in assigning the one binomial *Prosopis juliflora* to all the plants long since ascribed by Burkhart to thirty different species within the New World section *Algarobia* (Fagg and Stewart 1994, Pasiecznik *et al.* 2001). Trees of this section, and in particular of the *P. juliflora–P. pallida* complex, have been introduced to many exotic locations because of their ecological and resource value in arid environments, such that today they are effectively pan-tropically distributed (Figure 7.1; Fagg and Stewart 1994, Pasiecznik *et al.* 2001). Yet, all too often, inappropriate taxonomic classifications followed these introductions and thence were perpetuated in those exotic habitats. As Pasiecznik *et al.* (2001: 21) caution, 'initial misidentification without correction can be repeated continually'.

Sifting through these identifications is important because modern impressions of the genus are deeply divided. For, while *Prosopis* has long been greatly valued *within* its native ranges, exotic trees assumed to be '*P. juliflora*' are now regarded as a serious invasive pest in others, such as parts of India, the Sudan and Australia. Indeed, local distaste finds expression in their names: 'viper', 'bastard thorn' and dangerous thorn' in the Sahel (Butterfield 1996); 'Mexican thorn' in Ascension Island; 'white man's thorn' in Senegal; 'Syrian thorn' in Iraq; and *vilayati babul* ('foreign thorn') and *ganda babul* ('mad thorn') in India (Pasiecznik *et al.* 2001).

Yet these names would seem quite incongruous to those who live with the genus on the south coast of Peru, where the predominant form of the huarango has no thorns. Forms of the tree with and without thorns are recognised locally as *macho* (male) and *hembra* (female), respectively (Donaire 1998: 199). But thorny trees are rare and they mostly are only saplings. On the north coast, meanwhile, Ferreyra (1987) and Díaz Celis (1995) also recognise two forms of *P. pallida*: forma *armata* with thorns and forma *pallida* without. And in countries to which plants of known Peruvian *P. pallida* origin have been imported, such as Hawaii, Brazil and Haiti, *Prosopis* trees are also known as thornless (see for instance Skolmen 1990, Lee *et al.* 1992). Indeed, this feature of the south coast huarango, together with others that we will come across in this chapter, hints at possible deep-time human–*Prosopis* relationships on the south coast of Peru.

The Form of the Huarango

The obvious problem faced by plants and, indeed, all life in arid regions is water availability. The relatively few plants that survive in desert environments have evolved adaptations, either to find other sources of water or to make more conservative use of available water, to meet their metabolic requirements (Horton and Hart 1998). These include, for instance, the thick cuticles and specialised photosynthesis (crassulacean acid metabolism, or 'CAM') of the cacti and succulents. Trees of the genus *Prosopis*, meanwhile, are so-called 'phreatophytes'—plants with exceedingly long taproots that thereby access deep groundwater unattainable by most plant species (Simpson and Solbrig 1977, Mooney *et al.* 1980). They also have some so-called 'xerophytic' (or 'dry-loving') features and physiological responses. Indeed, as we will see here, most of the features that define the genus *Prosopis*

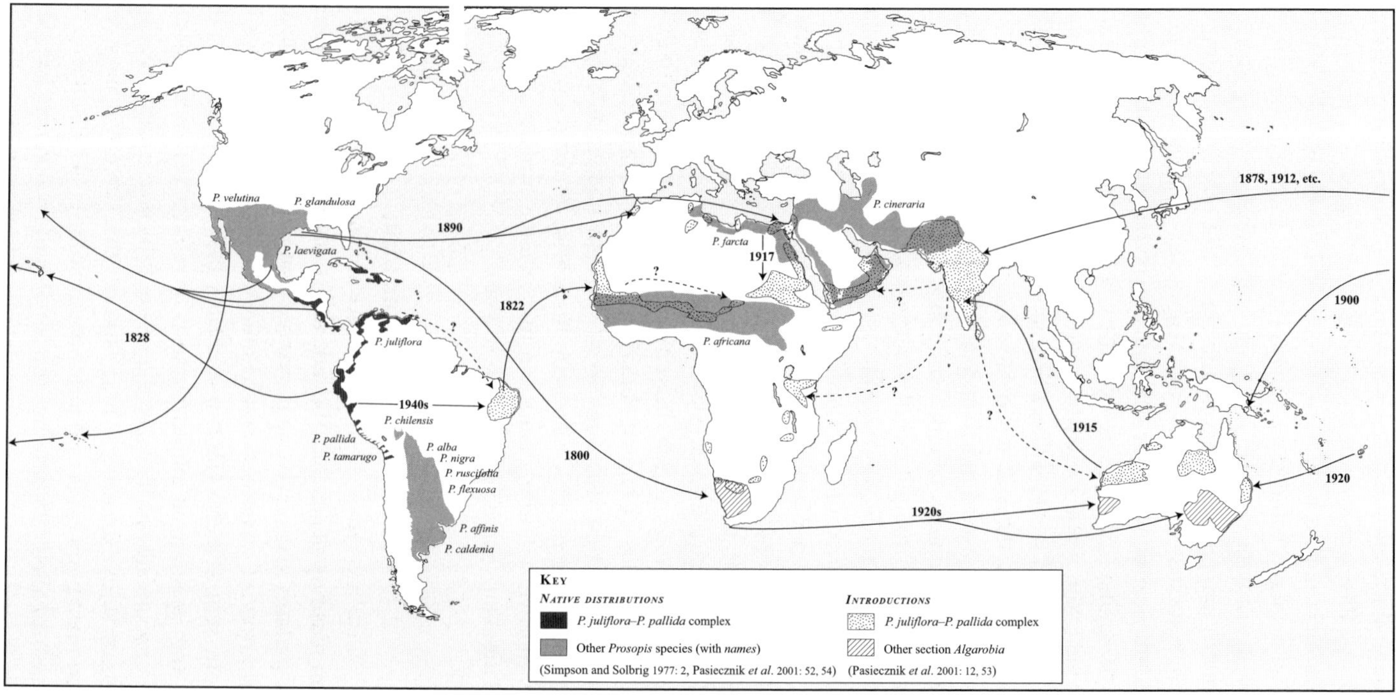

Figure 7.1. Native distributions of the genus *Prosopis* and historical introductions of New World species worldwide

and the form of the south coast huarango reflect their remarkable adaptations to their desert environment.

Root architecture

Describing the underground root architecture of a tree is obviously no easy matter. Carefully excavating an entire tree is almost impossible, and roots can be difficult to identify at any taxonomic level (Jackson *et al.* 2000). Nonetheless, records of the extents of tree roots do exist and, perhaps unsurprisingly, show the greatest measures in arid, tropical environments (Canadell *et al.* 1996). Some roots reach apparently extraordinary depths. Well-diggers in the Kalahari Desert, for instance, encountered roots at 68 metres depth, often cited as the deepest roots thus far recorded (Schulze *et al.* 1998). Stone and Kalisz (1991) survey the evidence of root depths for 211 woody plant species in 96 genera. Few exceed 20 metres in depth. The greatest they record is for *Juniperus monosperma*, encountered in a mineshaft at 61 metres. Yet, for a *Prosopis juliflora* of only modest size, at 6 metres tall, Stone and Kalisz (1991: 80) report a root depth of 53 metres and lateral radial extents of more than 19 metres.

Indeed, there are many reports of very deep *Prosopis* roots on the south coast of Peru. Galera (2000: 195; my translation) notes that the lateral roots of *P. pallida* 'develop at up to two to three times the diameter of the tree's crown', and that 'roots have been found up to 60 metres in length'. Félix Quinteros (personal communication) of Universidad de Ica, who has spent a lifetime studying the huarango of the south coast, reports living, radial roots at a horizontal distance of 81 metres from an individual *P. pallida* encountered during the digging of a well in the La Victoria district of Ica, and Oliver Whaley (personal communication) of the Royal Botanic Gardens at Kew has observed similar root dimensions. These put on record that the roots of the south coast huarango are amongst the longest and deepest of any tree species worldwide.

After germination, usually in short-lived conditions of temporary moisture, *Prosopis* roots grow very rapidly and can reach a depth of 40 centimetres in eight weeks (Garg 1998, 1999, Pasiecznik *et al.* 2001). Once mature, its root architecture becomes 'dimorphic'—two distinct systems with different hydraulic functions (see for instance Sudzuki 1985b, Gile *et al.* 1997, Galera 2000, Pasiecznik *et al.* 2001). One or two main taproots form a deep system to access permanent groundwater. These can become very thick and, as we have seen, very long (Figure 7.2D). Meanwhile, a second, shallower, radial lateral root system extends about the tree, forming a dense, complex root mat (Figure 7.2B). These roots also show 'xerophytic' adaptations, for, as Simpson and Solbrig (1977: 15) put it, they 'can extract water from soils too arid for most plant species'. Reductions in soil water under *Prosopis* have been recorded down to minus 15 bar (Mooney *et al.* 1977), enabling the tree to extract water held even under very high matric forces. As we will see in the next chapter, this extraordinarily deep and dimorphic root architecture has crucial significance, not only for the water relations of the huarango itself, but also for the entire ecosystem of which it is part.

A Transverse section of huarango bough, Usaca.
B Huarango timbers ('*horcones*') sold in Ica.
C Excavated huarango trunk and main rootbole, Ica.
D Huarango rootbole excavated by *carboneros*, Ica.
E Lateral huarango roots exposed in riverbank, Usaca.

(Photographs C and D by O. Whaley)

Figure 7.2. The roots and wood of the south coast huarango

Huarango leaves: *poña*

Yet, despite its specialised root system, *Prosopis* is still exposed to the stresses of dry desert air and it has various adaptations to reduce excessive water loss through its leaves by transpiration. Its leaves are highly variegated with an epidermal surface covered by a coating of wax. Leaf morphology is one of the main features used to distinguish species within the genus and *P. pallida* and *P. limensis* have very well-developed 'brachyblasts' — the smallest lignified leaf branches (cf. Mom *et al.* 2002) — and many more, much smaller leaves than other species. These leaves are 'bipinnate' — split into pairs of pinnae — each of which has up to twenty-nine pairs of tiny leaflets less than 7 mm long (see Figure 7.3; Burkart 1976, Díaz Celis 1995, Pasiecznik *et al.* 2001).

This mass of brachyblasts and tiny leaflets in the huarango will usually become enmeshed into 'dreadlocks' of spider-webs and dead tree litter material (Figure 7.4A and B). Whaley (personal communication) observes that this may confer twofold advantages in an arid climate. Firstly, the air within the dense brachyblast/leaflet cluster itself forms a microclimate that reduces transpiration. And secondly, these clusters create a greatly expanded surface area upon which high night-time humidity may condense and thereby be captured by the plant through mechanisms that we will examine further in Chapter 8. The highly variegated leaf canopy of the tree nonetheless allows much more sunlight to filter through than would larger, simpler leaves. And as we will also see, this has great significance for the growth of other, so-called 'understory' plants, elegantly expressed by the great Peruvian writer José María Arguedas — '*los guarangos dejan pasar el sol, pero quitándole el fuego*' (the huarangos let the sun pass, but take out its fire — my translation).

Huarango wood

Like the wood of many slow-growing desert trees, that of the huarango is extremely fine-grained, heavy, strong and hard (see Figure 7.2C). Indeed, Rogers (2000: 74) calls *Prosopis* 'one of the world's best woods'. It is also a very high-quality fuel. These characteristics, which derive from its structure and chemical constituency, underlie much of its value as a human resource and, thereby, its occurrence in the archaeological record.

Prosopis heartwood is red in colour, darkening with drying and quite distinct from the much lighter, cream sapwood (see Figure 7.2A). This is because this heartwood has more than twice the content of resins, tannins and oils of most hardwoods. These contribute both to its quality as a fuel and to its virtual invulnerability to fungi and insect attack (see for instance Goel and Behl 1996, 2001, Rogers 2000, Pasiecznik *et al.* 2001). Its growth rings are lightly distinct, irregular dark bands (Acevedo Mallque and Kikata 1994).

The mechanical properties of the tree's wood derive from its cellular structure. This is described by wood anatomists using thin sections cut as precisely as possible along three perpendicular planes, which, when considered together, describe the microscopic three-dimensional structure of wood (see for instance Schweingruber 1978). Acevedo Mallque and

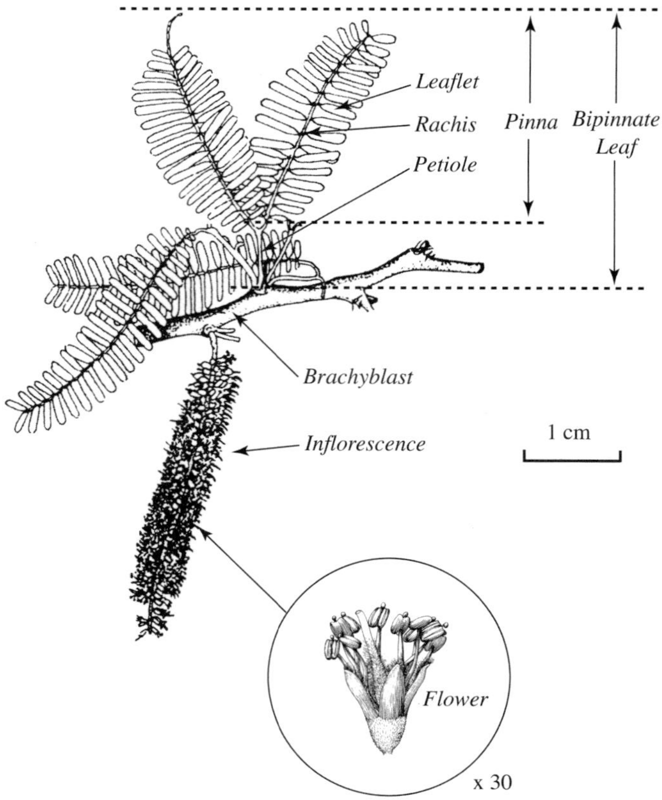

Figure 7.3. Nomenclature of *Prosopis* parts (adapted from Simpson *et al.* 1977, Solbrig *et al.* 1977 and Pasiecznik *et al.* 2001)

Kikata (1994) and Moutarde (2006) provide anatomical descriptions of *P. pallida* wood from the coast of Peru. By way of brief summary the features of huarango wood are as follows. The wood pattern is diffuse porous (meaning that the diameters and frequency of vessels are more or less the same throughout the season's growth and thus across a growth ring). Vessels (or pores, the xylem tubes of the tree's vascular system) are few, solitary and small, with simple perforation plates. Parenchyma cells (the tree's storage cells) are abundant and non-storied. Medullary rays (which give the wood structural strength in the radial plain from pith to outer cortex) are homogeneous, multiseriate and non-storied. Fibres (which give the wood its vertical structural strength) are abundant, short and non-storied with very thick walls. Gums and chambered crystals are usually present in vessels, parenchyma and rays. Together, these microscopic features—small and solitary vessels; abundant, narrow but very thick walled fibres; and numerous, multiseriate rays—mean that huarango wood is heavy and extremely hard with great tensile strength (D'Antoni and Solbrig 1977). Moreover, its timber has strength in all three dimensions and has excellent—that is, low and uniform—shrinkage

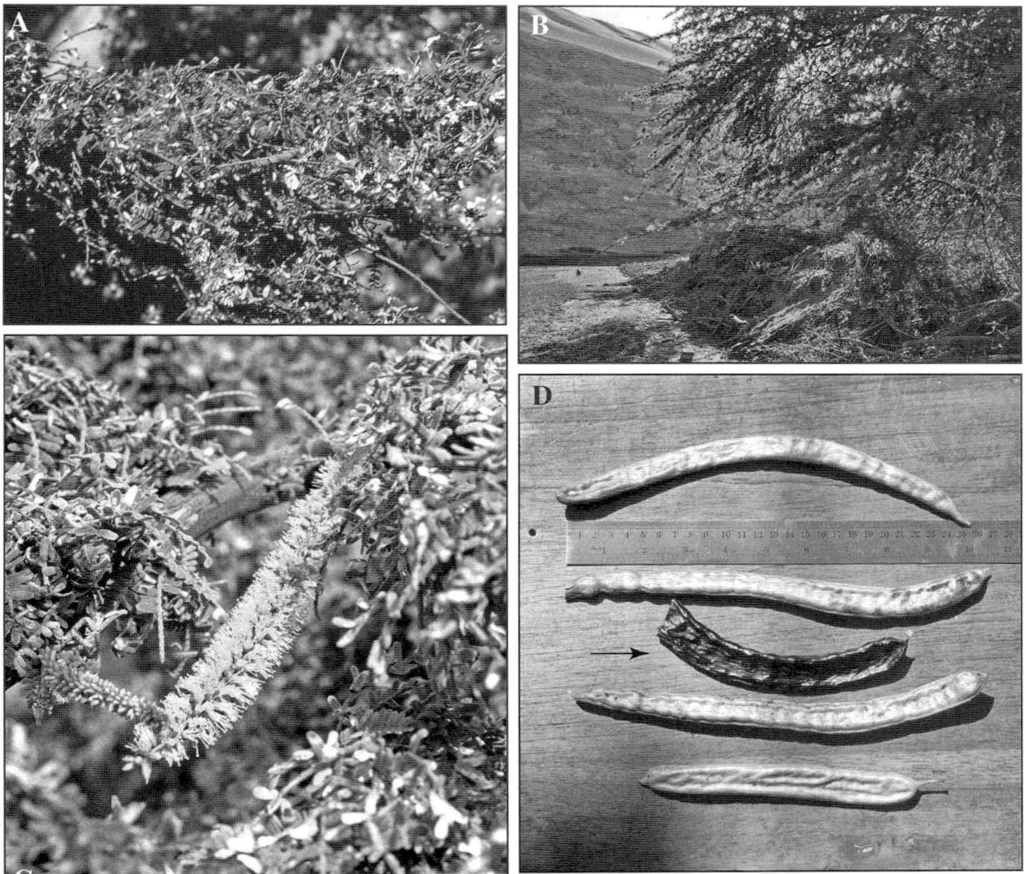

A Huarango bracyblasts and leaflet cluster, Samaca.
B 'Dreadlocked' huarango foliage, Usaca.
C Huarango inflorescence, Samaca.
D Variation in huarango pod sizes collected in the Ica Valley by Félix Quinteros, with pod of carob (*Ceratonia siliqua* – marked) for comparison.
E Pod harvest from single *P. pallida*, Samaca.

Figure 7.4. The leaves, flowers and pods of the south coast huarango characteristics (Rogers 2000). The density of wood, expressed as its specific gravity relative to water, encapsulates many of these characteristics in a single measure. They will vary, of course, with growing conditions. Within the genus, the densest woods are those of the arid Peru–Chile Desert: *P. tamarugo*, *P. chilensis* and *P. pallida* (Pasiecznik *et al.* 2001). The specific gravity of *P. pallida* from the Peruvian coast is 0.88 (Acevedo Mallque and Kikata 1994), as compared with around 0.75 for English oak. Indeed, huarango wood is over one and half times as hard as teak (*Tectona grandis*) and is much harder and stronger than oak, mahogany or walnut (Ibrahim 1992, Pasiecznik *et al.* 2001: 79).

These remarkable mechanical properties of *Prosopis* wood cannot be better illustrated than by the uses to which it has been put. In the early 1900s, timber blocks of *Prosopis* were used to pave the streets of San Antonio, Texas (Rogers 2000) and Buenos Aires, Argentina (D'Antoni and Solbrig 1977). These still underlie the asphalted road surface of many streets of these cities. Even more extraordinarily, the first shots of the Mexican war of independence were fired from a cannon that the insurrectionists, lacking artillery, made from a large hollowed-out trunk of mesquite. The wooden cannon worked well and is now an exhibit at the National Museum in Mexico City (Rogers 2000).

Its high density and tannin content also make *Prosopis* wood such an excellent fuel that it has been called 'wooden anthracite' (Pasiecznik *et al.* 2001: 4). It does not spit, spark or emit much smoke but has a very high heat of combustion with a calorific value of around 5,000 kcal/kg (Arya *et al.* 1992) and thus burns with a hot, even heat. Today, *Prosopis* wood is an important source of fuel for millions of people in arid areas worldwide (see for instance Díaz Celis 1995, Lea 1996, Pasiecznik *et al.* 2001). Its green wood burns well when freshly cut so *Prosopis* firewood does not require storage and drying (Pasiecznik *et al.* 2001). Indeed, such is its flammability that the charcoal burners (or *carboneros*) of the Peruvian south coast report that large huarangos cannot easily be felled through controlled use of fire, since it is impossible to prevent the entire tree 'exploding' into flame.

Burning *Prosopis* wood under anaerobic conditions produces a high-quality charcoal. This is lighter and less bulky to transport than firewood: around five kilograms of wood must be burned to produce one of charcoal (Pasiecznik *et al.* 2001). Today on the coast of Peru, charcoal burning provides livelihoods for those with few economic options through the supply of distant urban markets, rather than providing a domestic fuel source in the area of production itself. It is still manufactured here in traditional earth ovens. Stacks of wood cut into equally sized pieces are moistened and covered with soil to form the oven before being fired (Figure 7.5). Burning conditions within are carefully maintained over a period of about a week through the opening and closing of air holes. Once an even burn has been achieved throughout, the oven is broken open and allowed to cool, before bagging and sale to middlemen for transport and sale in Lima. And, whereas for domestic firewood small branches are preferred (Pasiecznik *et al.* 2001), for charcoal the greatest efficiencies are obtained by selecting the largest available trees and removing them in their entirety, including their main root wood, the consequences of which are written in the age profile of the huarango population of the south coast today.

A Felling huarango with chainsaws.
B Wood logged and ready for burning.
C Charcoal oven.
D Charcoal prepared and bagged.
E Aftermath.

Figure 7.5. Producing charcoal from huarango, Usaca woodland

The fruit of *Prosopis* on the south coast: *miskyhuaranga*

In a desert environment of limited and erratic water supply, *Prosopis* needs to disperse its seed away from the parent tree to locations where they may successfully germinate. To this end the huarango produces its seeds within copious quantities of sweet, highly nutritious, bean-like fruit — known as *miskyhuaranga* on the south coast. Their structure — in three distinct layers, much like the common bean — and their composition are consequences of an adaptation for dispersal by animals. For these pods — or legumes — are indehiscent, that is, covered with a thin, leathery 'exocarp', which does not split open on maturity, but instead falls from the tree as a single structure. Within this is a fleshy 'mesocarp', high in carbohydrates and proteins, within which are a number of stony 'endocarp' segments, each containing a soft, oval, brown seed. The sugars and starch in the mesocarp make the pods highly palatable and they are eaten avidly by both wild and domesticated mammals and various types of reptile, bats and birds (Mooney *et al.* 1977, Kingsolver *et al.* 1977, Ansley *et al.* 1997, Pasiecznik *et al.* 2001). The stony endocarp, meanwhile, protects the seed from animal chewing. Passage through the digestive tract then scarifies the seed, which enhances germination. In due course it is deposited in animal dung, providing an immediate source of nutrients for the young seedling. Germination occurs only upon the reception of suitable cues such as during seasonal river flows. Indeed, water itself is also an important agent of dispersal: both pods and seed endocarps float and survive extended periods, even in seawater (Pasiecznik *et al.* 2001). Desert river flows are erratic, of course, and, if necessary, *Prosopis* seed can remain dormant and viable for up to forty years (Ibrahim 1992). Once germinated, the seedling dedicates much of its initial energy to finding groundwater, thereby developing its extraordinary root system. This mechanism of dispersal likely evolved with large American mammals such as camelids, mastodons and giant ground sloths (Mooney *et al.* 1977). Most of these mega-fauna became extinct towards the end of the Pleistocene, perhaps owing to the first arrival in the Americas of human hunters (see for instance Martin 1967), and today domesticated livestock such as cattle, horses and goats are the primary agents of dispersal for *Prosopis* throughout most of its American distribution ranges (Fisher 1977, Pasiecznik *et al.* 2001). These animals are, of course, relatively recent introductions, following contact with the Old World and, as we will see, they have wrought considerable changes upon the distribution and habit of *Prosopis*.

Yet, while adaptation for animal dispersal is common to all species of *Prosopis*, there is nonetheless great variation between them in the size and composition of their legume pods. Because of their nutritional value, *Prosopis* pods have been the subject of considerable research and studies consistently note that Peruvian coastal accessions of the *P. pallida–P. juliflora* complex produce larger pods, higher in sugars, carbohydrates and proteins, in much larger numbers than do other members of the genus. Pasiecznik *et al.* (2001: 85–6), for instance, review the results of thirty-two such studies from locations worldwide of the pods of the *P. pallida–P. juliflora* complex, and conclude that these 'suggest that Peruvian *Prosopis* pods are of an inherently better quality than pods from *P. juliflora* of the northern races'. In Peru itself, research is ongoing at the Algarrobo Research Project at the Universidad de Piura, on the far north coast. Here the composition of *P. pallida* fruit-pulp is shown to be 46 per cent sucrose and 8–13 per cent protein with significant amounts of vitamins E and C and potassium, while the seeds themselves are some 36 per cent protein, one of the highest levels for any legume (Grados and Cruz 1996). Meanwhile, Lee *et al.* (1992: 11) report that in Brazil *P. pallida* of Peruvian accession have 'the longest pods we have ever observed (about 50 cm)'. Pods of the south coast huarango are between 10 and 45 cm long (Figure 7.4D).

Furthermore, Peruvian *P. pallida* trees are more productive than North American *Prosopis* species, which typically yield between 19 and 34 kilograms per mature tree per year (Ibrahim 1992). By contrast, exceptional *P. pallida* trees on the north coast of Peru yield up to 300 kilograms (Grados and Cruz 1996) and fruit productions of up to 420 kilograms are reported from *P. pallida* trees of Peruvian accession in Brazil (Pasiecznik *et al.* 2001: 93). Although *P. pallida* on the north coast of Peru produce fruit once a year in June and July (Díaz Celis 1995), on the south coast we see *P. pallida* usually producing two fruit crops in a year: once during a main season between December and March when rivers flow; and again, in a lesser production season—'*la cosecha de San Juan*'—between June and July, when winter air humidity is at its highest. Figure 7.4E shows the pod harvest from a single ten-year-old tree in the Samaca Basin at the end of the fruiting season in April 2002.

Accessing deep groundwaters *P. pallida* here produces fruit almost regardless of the highly erratic hydrology of the Río Ica (cf. Simpson *et al.* 1977). This ability to produce copious, nutritious fruit for animal fodder or human consumption, somewhat independent of short-term climatic variations, underpins the deep-time importance of the genus to humankind in arid areas of the New World. Indeed, as Felker (1981) notes, no tree legume has been more widely used as a food source.

The size and form of the huarango

How an individual *Prosopis* tree grows and attains its eventual form is, naturally, a matter both of its genetic makeup and of the environment in which it finds itself. *Prosopis* growth rates therefore vary widely between species, and within populations (see for instance Pasiecznik *et al.* 2001). Agroforestry trials using *P. pallida* trees of Peruvian accessions show faster growth rates, attaining larger sizes on maturity, than other species of the genus. Trials in Senegal, Haiti and India compare the growth of various *Prosopis* species from diverse origins in Argentina, Chile, Haiti, Mexico, Peru and the United States and record that those of Peruvian origin grew significantly faster, taller and straighter than others, including those of native origin to the trial area (Lee *et al.* 1992, Felker and Patch 1996, Harris *et al.* 1996, 2003, Harsh *et al.* 1996, Pasiecznik *et al.* 2001, Deans *et al.* 2003). Harris *et al.* (1996: 4–27), for instance, conclude that 'Peruvian genetic stock is near the top in evaluations in three distinctly different environments: Haiti, Cape Verde, and the interior deserts of India'.

Tree growth can also be greatly affected by human intervention. The practices of pruning, coppicing and pollarding have been used in the management of woodland resources for millennia. Such adjustments to tree architecture are employed to diverse ends (see Reynel and Felipe-Morales 1987 for details in Peruvian contexts), but, in general, they greatly augment the rate of production of woody biomass by placing the tree under stress. And *Prosopis* is no exception. Elfadl and Luukkanen (2003: 448) report, for instance, that heavy pruning of *P. juliflora* in the Sudan increases their wood production by up to six times.

All these studies of the growth rates of *Prosopis*, however, pertain to rather young trees. Rapid initial growth is of obvious advantage to plants seeking to establish themselves successfully in unpredictable desert environments. But data on the longer-term growth of *Prosopis* species are largely lacking and, typical of many desert hardwood trees, the huarango, as we will see shortly, can live for a very long time. Today, the form (or 'habit') of *Prosopis*, throughout its New World range, is usually of dense stands of desert shrub or shrubby trees (Figure 7.6A). And in some grassland areas it has become established as a noxious, invasive woody weed. However, conflicting perceptions of the genus in appreciation of its value, on the one hand, and intense dislike as a thorny, invasive weed, on the other, are mostly the result of relatively recent *human* disturbances. For, as *Prosopis* species of section *Algarobia* have had their distribution expanded by deliberate human introductions worldwide, so too have they extended subsequently in some new locations, through invasions. This success, of course, derives from those same features of morphological and genetic plasticity that so well adapt *Prosopis* to desert environments, or what Pasiecznik *et al.* (2001: 13) call its 'broad ecological amplitude'. Indeed, so successful is *Prosopis* that, once established in arid environments outside its native range, it can become impossible to eradicate. So Peattie (cited in Pasiecznik *et al.* 2001: 1) describes mesquite on the Texas rangelands as 'something more than a tree, it is almost an elemental force, comparable to fire—too valuable to extinguish completely and too dangerous to trust unwatched'.

On the cattle rangelands of the south-west United States and north-west Argentina, for instance, species invasions by thorny *Prosopis* scrub have spread far and wide. Ranchers have responded with attempts at mechanical and herbicide control which damage the tree but lead to heavy, multi-stemmed regrowth from the trunk base. Decades of these attempts have succeeded only in creating ever-denser thickets of shrubs (Ansley *et al.* 1997) and thousands of hectares have thereby been rendered useless for cattle grazing. Although geographically distant the Argentinean and United States rangelands share a common land-use history. Beginning around 1850, cattle numbers in these areas increased by many orders of magnitude. Along with this came overgrazing of grass cover and severe soil surface disturbance, all of which created ideal conditions for rapid invasion by *Prosopis*—often dispersed by the livestock themselves (Fisher 1977). These problems come as little surprise to agroforesters. As Felker and Patch (1996) have shown, the only secure defence against invasions by dense stands of *Prosopis* shrubs are large *Prosopis* trees. Large trees accomplish self-thinning, *intra*-specific competition, preventing encroachment by younger saplings. So, in less disturbed *Prosopis* woodland, the tree population decreases as larger and larger trees come to dominate the stand. And since mature *Prosopis* trees obtain water from deep horizons, they offer far less *inter*-specific competition than do dense stands of small trees. Indeed, as we will see in Chapter 8, they exert a host of soil (or so-called 'edaphic') effects, which combine to stimulate understory herbaceous growth, in direct proportion to the age of the *Prosopis* trees.

The coast of Peru, meanwhile, presents an entirely different environment to that of the American rangelands. Sufficient rainfall to support extensive dry forest savannah prevails only in the far north near the border with Ecuador. Elsewhere, *Prosopis* is limited to isolated riparian habitats scattered over one of the world's driest deserts. Here, as we have seen, human impact has also been dramatic, but with very different causes and effects. Indeed, there are, as Pasiecznik *et al*. (2001: 11) observe, 'no records of *P. pallida* as a weed in its native range' (2001: 11). Instead, here *Prosopis* deforestation has led often to processes of desertification. For in this hyperarid desert, human disturbance may extinguish completely even the 'elemental force'—as Peattie called it—of *Prosopis*. Or it may prevail, but with a dramatically altered age profile, dominated now by small trees and shrubs. This, in turn, has led to the oft-used term of 'scrub-forest' (or its local variant *monte*), to describe the riparian vegetation of the south coast (Figure 7.6A). Yet, just as with the *Prosopis* invasions of grasslands elsewhere in the Americas, this *monte* scrub of the south coast of Peru is an *artefact*: the product of human action. In fact, as we will see presently, given time, the huarango of the coast of Peru are enormous trees.

Relict Huarango Forms on the South Coast of Peru

Although the vast majority of its huarango population has been reduced to *monte* scrub, there are still, at the time of writing at least, some tiny fragments remaining on the Peruvian south coast of far, far more ancient *Prosopis* habits. These include scattered numbers of exceptional older, isolated trees protected by accidents of fortune; some extensively managed mature woodland fragments along stretches of the lower Río Nasca; and a single relic of what might be termed 'old-growth' *Prosopis* woodland, in the Quebrada Usaca. The *Prosopis* species of the Peru–Chile Desert, *P. pallida*, *P. juliflora, P. chilensis* and *P. tamarugo*, all may become substantial trees of between 15 and 20 metres high (Brack Egg 1999, Díaz Celis 1995, Grados and Cruz 1996). But, because of its extraordinary form, the measure of tree height quite fails to convey the true size of a mature huarango on the south coast.

As we have seen from the studies showing the superior growth and form of Peruvian coastal *Prosopis* in locations worldwide, much of its variation in habit is genetically controlled. Yet, as Harvard (cited in Pasiecznik *et al*. 2001: 59) observed in 1884, 'there is hardly any soil, if it is not habitually damp, in which mesquite cannot grow; no hill too

A Huarango-dominated monte scrub, Samaca, Río Ica.
B Prostrate-form huarango, Cahuachi, Río Nasca.
C Mature huarango in full foliage, Río Ica.
D Three-year-old sapling growing on *yapana,* Samaca, Río Ica.
E Huarango growing on rock, Río Poroma.
F Erect-form, twenty-year-old huarango, Hacienda Elias, Ica.
G Erect-form huarango, Cahuachi, Río Nasca.

Figure 7.6. The forms of the huarango on the south coast of Peru rocky or broken, no flat too sandy or saline, no dune too shifting . . . to entirely exclude it'. And this ability of the genus to persist in the most variable of sites naturally gives rise to a huge variety of tree forms (Figure 7.6). Forms also vary, of course, with maturity. While younger trees have erect branches, as the huarango gets older its boughs become ever larger and more decumbent. In time they come to evoke Calancha's 1639 description of the huarangos of old Ica as 'tall, growing sideways as contorted mountains'.

One such ancient individual tree grows near Palpa, alone on a relict river terrace of the Río Santa Cruz, some 40 metres above the current floodplain. Known locally as '*El Huarango Milenario*', its age was determined in the 1980s to be 1,064 years old by investigators from the universities of Huamanga and La Agraria, La Molina through counting growth rings on a damaged main bough (Carlos Reynel, personal communication). This tree has a short trunk of tremendous girth (14.4 metres in circumference and almost 5 metres in diameter) that divides into seven huge decumbent boughs, which extend to a maximum of 43 metres from the main trunk. As Figure 7.7 shows it is well-nigh impossible to capture a tree of such dimensions in a single photograph.

Indeed, the extraordinary seven-stemmed form of the *Huarango Milenario* has all the hallmarks of a tree subject to human interference in its youth. For it has a striking resemblance to those oldest markers of English boundaries: an ancient coppice stool (Rackham 1980). The location of this ancient huarango on the edge of the main Río Santa Cruz floodplain also marks the entrance to a narrow *quebrada* in which lies a major Late Intermediate Period settlement site: Huayuri (see for instance Mächtle *et al.* 2009). The suggestion that the form, location and even preservation of the *Huarango Milenario* may identify it as an artefact and landscape marker is of course highly speculative. Yet nonetheless, this ancient tree certainly stands as a powerful illustration of the different timescales over which human–huarango relationships need to be evaluated. For it was a sapling during the Middle Horizon which preceded the Huayuri occupation and was already old when the Inca Pachakuti Yupanqui conquered the south coast, some four hundred years later. It is still, just about, alive today.

The age of the Huarango de Huayuri also offers us a 'rule-of-thumb' for *Prosopis* growth rates on the south coast of Peru. The tree shown Figure 7.6F, for example, has a trunk diameter of half a metre and a known age of twenty years, equating to a 2.4 centimetre diameter per year growth rate (and see Felker and Patch 1996). Of course, growth rates will slow with age. The ancient trunk of the Huarango de Huayuri indicates an average growth rate over its tremendous lifespan of only 0.43 cm per year. Figure 7.8 then illustrates this expected decrease in growth rate with tree age. Obviously this estimate is very crude: an extrapolation between two points of data, which ignores any number of possible local environmental variations. Nonetheless, it may be useful, since controlled agroforestry trials, even over the thirty years that some Indian studies now approach, can of course only be conducted over *human* timescales.

Aside from scattered giants such as the Huarango de Huayuri, there are also still today some tracts of secondary huarango woodland along the lower reaches of the Río Nasca.

A Detail of main trunk.
B Tree in context; note person for scale.
C Trunk and procumbent boughs.

Figure 7.7. The Huarango of Huayuri (or the '*Huarango Milenario*'), Río Santa Cruz, Nazca

This river runs west, along the southern edge of the Nazca Pampa, famous for its concentration of geoglyphs. The Río Nasca provides a perfect example of the misleading impressions of hydrological poverty caused by surface river flows on the south coast, which we saw in Chapter 2. For on the surface it appears an unimportant tributary of the Río Grande de Nazca: comprising a mere seven per cent of its eventual total surface flow (see Table 2.4). And yet, land under irrigation today in the Río Nasca drainage is some 15,000 acres, much more than that of the Ingenio, Upper Grande and Palpa rivers combined. Its subsurface water flow is clearly very significant. The introduction of deep tube wells in the 1930s has allowed increased exploitation of this groundwater and agriculture expansion on the upper reaches of the tributaries of the Río Nasca, but archaeological investigation shows that the significance of its groundwater flow was also understood and exploited in the pre-Hispanic past (Rossel Castro 1977, Schreiber and Lancho Rojas 1995). Phreatophytic huarangos are, as we have seen, adapted to accessing these hidden water supplies. So it is unsurprising that the last vestiges of riparian woodland on the south coast are to be found precisely along the lower stretches of the Río Nasca and its tributaries. The forms of these woodlands are, however, changing fast.

Alongside the Nasca site of Cahuachi, 'the place where water appears' (Silverman 1993: 12), is a grove of huarangos of about a century in age, protected, appropriately enough, by the guardian of the archaeological site (Figure 7.6B and G). Its trees, however, have lost all foliage and may be diseased (Oliver Whaley, personal communication). Travelling further

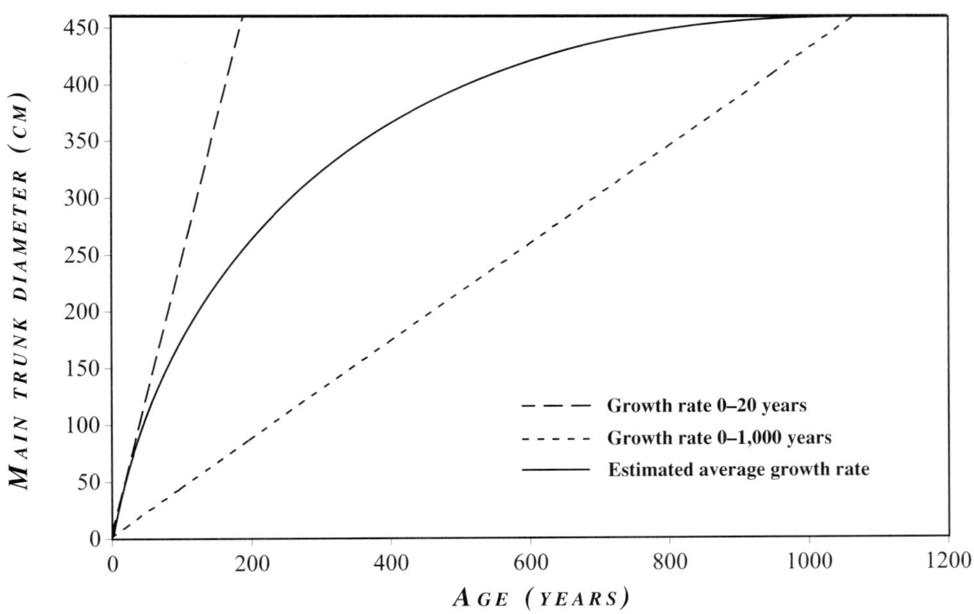

Figure 7.8. 'Rule-of-thumb' estimate of huarango growth rate on the south coast of Peru

downstream along the Río Nasca, however, there are still quite extensive stretches of secondary riparian woodland. In Majuelos and Jumana, for instance, the landscape remains dominated by woodland. As recently as the early 1990s most of these woodlands were divided between families of goat herders who, depending upon *Prosopis* fruit for their livestock, resisted the deprecations of *carboneros* and protected seedlings from their animals (Figure 7.9C). Since then, however, large areas have been cleared for cotton growing and in the long dry season they are now full of charcoal burners. The centurial tree photographed in 1995 (Figure 7.9B), for instance, no longer exists. So Jumana and Majuelos are today currently undergoing the transition, already complete on the rest of the south coast, from mixed-age secondary woodland to scrub woodland dominated by young trees and shrubs (Figure 7.9D).

A small tributary, the Río Poroma, joins the Río Nasca just upstream from Majuelos. Up this tributary in Usaca is a fragment of what might be termed 'old-growth' woodland—to our knowledge the last remaining relict of ancient woodland on the south coast of Peru. The Quebrada Usaca is a steep, narrow valley, dominated to the south by an enormous wall of dunes blown up by the winds from the mouth of the Río Grande. Along its higher edges are extensive Nasca Period cemeteries (Isla 1992). The floor of the *quebrada* is, however, covered with dense riparian woodland, which spreads up its flanks to considerable heights above the Río Poroma watercourse (Figure 7.10A). Usaca has a tiny forest fragment, perhaps 40 hectares. It is also clearly secondary woodland, considerably altered in form and composition by human activity in its environs, primarily that of goat herding. It is, nonetheless, perhaps the only and closest observable analogue left on the south coast for the riparian woodlands which once characterised the region's vegetation. Its woodland includes *Acacia* and *Salix* trees of considerable size, but it is dominated by huarango, a few of which have reached truly enormous proportions (Figure 7.10).

The largest are to be found growing along the outer edge of the woodland fragment and have main trunks of up to 7 metres in circumference—or more than 2 metres in diameter—and reach heights of around 30 metres. Their main boughs are decumbent, often draped up the steep slopes of the *quebrada*'s edge. Sometimes these vast pendulous boughs replant themselves at some distance from the main bough and have sprouted anew, such that an individual tree may sprawl across an area of well over a thousand square meters. Our 'rule-of thumb' estimate would conservatively put their ages at about four hundred years old.

Yet today, the somnolent Usaca woodlands are disturbed often by the harsh rip of the chainsaw—but one more, perhaps the last, chapter in the long story that we reviewed in Chapter 6. And the results are grim, dramatic and absolute (see Figure 7.5). When charcoal burners worked with hand axes they avoided giant trees like those in Usaca, because of the huge efforts required to fell them. The tremendously hard wood of the huarango takes its toll even on chainsaws—they require hours of resharpening after every use. But a large tree can provide several tonnes of high-quality charcoal. After centuries, the ancient giants of the Quebrada Usaca are falling, to be burnt, bagged and transported to the oblivious barbeques of faraway Lima.

A Majuelos woodland, Río Nasca, 1995.
B Century-old huarango, Marjuelos, 1995.
C Livestock herding, Marjuelos, 1995 (note protected sapling in foreground).
D Open huarango woodland, Jumana, Río Nasca, 2002.

Figure 7.9. Huarango woodland in Majuelos 1995

The Huarango: an Artefact?

Those general characteristics that we have seen appreciated by agroforesters for the *Prosopis* species of Peruvian coastal accessions, and in particular those of *P. pallida* forma *pallida*—or rather, following Mom *et al.* (2002), *P. limensis*—lead rather naturally to speculation that they could be the product of long co-evolution with humans. To recapitulate, these characteristics include faster and more erect growth to much larger sizes, the production of more copious quantities of larger, sweeter pods, and indeed the preponderance of thornless forms, when compared with the rest of the *P. juliflora–P. pallida* complex, or indeed with any of the rest of the genus *Prosopis*.

As we will see in further detail in Chapter 9, *Prosopis* is recognised as the single most valuable wild plant food resource in the ethnobotany of all American arid environments. Certainly the huarango is not a 'domesticate' or even in any strict sense a cultivar, for it requires no human intervention to persist. Nonetheless, as has been long appreciated, the control and cultivation of food sources (ultimately, agriculture) was not an 'event', but rather a protracted co-evolutionary process between humans and parts of their environment

A View south of the Quebrada Usaca, Río Poroma, Nazca.
B–D Ancient trees of the Usaca woodland.

Figure 7.10. Ancient huarango woodland, Quebrada Usaca, Río Poroma, Nazca

(Rindos 1980). The categories of 'wild' and 'cultivated' thus fall along a long continuum of plant use by humans. Some plants growing wild — such as the Brazil nut — provide foods on an industrial scale, while other cultivated food plants — such as the carrot — are rather similar to their wild progenitors (see for instance Vaughan and Geissler 2000).

This is particularly so with tree species. In the case of the olive (*Olea europaea*), for instance, the precise phenotypic or genotypic differences between wild and cultivated varieties remain unclear (see for instance Lumaret and Ouazzani 2001), except for the obvious lack of thorns in the latter — typically the initial stage in any process of plant selection by humans. This is partly because of complications arising through grafting between woody plant species that do not naturally hybridise. But it is also because the individual lifespan of an olive or *Prosopis* may begin to approach the duration of entire processes of domestication for other plants — such as the kiwifruit. So the living genotype of an ancient huarango will preserve any influence of human selection from as far back in time as the Middle Horizon.

As Pasiecznik *et al.* (2001: 5) obverve, 'human influences including intentional introduction, weedy invasions and deforestation over the last 500 years have significantly altered . . . the native range of the *P. juliflora–P. pallida* complex'. And they go on to speculate that the isolated populations along the Peruvian coast today 'may have been connected before deforestation during the last 500 years'. Deforestation within riparian ecosystems on the south coast of Peru is of course our theme here. Yet, while Pasiecznik *et al.*'s observation of greater connection between populations in the recent past may well be true over much of the range of the *P. juliflora–P. pallida* complex in semi-arid regions of the countries north of Peru, it certainly cannot be true *outside* the riparian contexts of the south coast of Peru. For these have been completely isolated by stretches of hyperarid desert over far greater time-depths. Indeed, the isolation here of *P. pallida* populations within their riparian contexts is further defined, on the one hand, by the Pacific Ocean, and on the other, by the Andes mountain range. For, as Pasiecznik *et al.* (2001: 2) note, *P. juliflora–P. pallida* is a truly tropical complex, 'killed to the ground . . . at temperatures of only −6°C'. So the range of *P. pallida* on the Peruvian coast does not extend above 1,500 m of altitude (Brack Egg 1999: 414). Furthermore, possible seed dispersals by the ocean are limited along the south coast because of its paucity of wide alluvial river deltas. Huarango populations of the riparian ecosystems of the south coast have therefore experienced particular isolation from the larger population of the *P. juliflora–P. pallida* complex far to the north. Of course, such restrictions do not present absolute barriers to *Prosopis* dispersal over the great time-depth of its botanical evolution, but they certainly do represent relative barriers to dispersal, hybridisation and backcrossing. More recently the coast of Peru has experienced five hundred years of profound changes, including the introduction of many new animal agents of seed dispersal from the Old World, the construction of transport infrastructure linking its valleys in modern times and, indeed, the fading of the importance of *Prosopis* as a food resource for humans. And yet the productive, thornless form of *P. limensis* — the huarango — of the isolated riparian systems of the Peruvian south coast remains distinct, thereby representing, perhaps, *relict* populations, whose seed germ plasm—especially of ancient trees—preserves uniquely here the effects of human selection over those past millennia during which it was far more important to human subsistence than it is today. Indeed, as Pasiecznik *et al.* (2001: 51) note, 'disjunct populations near to ancient centres of population suggest that man has also been a dispersal agent in historic and prehistoric times'. Certainly, it is remarkable that the coast of Peru—the location in which *Prosopis* varieties exhibit all those characteristics for which humans would, and still do, choose to select—is, coincidentally that location whose archaeological record reflects the longest human cultural trajectories of the entire Americas, and wherein sedentism and complex society seem to have developed in Peru (see for instance Quilter and Stocker 1983, Dillehay *et al.* 2004, Heggarty and Beresford-Jones 2010).

8. The Huarango in the Desert Riparian and Agricultural Ecosystem

While in the last chapter we used the agroforestry literature on the genus *Prosopis* and our own observations in the Ica Valley to identify those particular characteristics of the huarango of the Peruvian south coast that have made it such a valuable human resource in the past, here we will do so to different ends. For the importance of the tree to our archaeological interpretations goes far beyond its value as a human resource. We need also to consider the subtler role of *Prosopis* in underpinning a fragile desert ecology.

It is perhaps difficult to exaggerate the dominance of this genus within its desert environments, especially on the coast of Peru, where rather few tree species occur naturally. As we will see, no other desert tree has as pervasive an influence upon soil physical, chemical, biological and moisture properties; sub-canopy microclimate; neighbouring vegetation; and wildlife and insect populations. The huarango thereby integrates diverse parts of the desert ecosystem. In modifying the environmental extremes characteristic of deserts, especially one as arid as the Peruvian south coast, *Prosopis* makes what would otherwise be inhospitable lands habitable for other species, including humankind. In other words, if we are to lay bare the ecological consequences of deforestation on the south coast, we need to understand why, here, the huarango is what ecologists term a 'keystone species'.

Influence on the Soil

We begin here with soils, since they are fundamental to all life in deserts and elsewhere, although their full ecological significance is all too easily overlooked. This is because, as

Chapterhead: Detail of Nasca embroidered textile showing a llama with possibly a peanut plant (*Arachis hypogaea*) growing out of its back. Beans, peanuts pods, root vegetables and possibly maize husks are depicted inside the llama (drawing courtesy of the Brooklyn Museum).

Russell (cited in Bridges 1997: 1) observed, 'a clod of earth seems at first sight to be the embodiment of the stillness of death'. And yet, most of the land's biomass is, in fact, to be found in its soils: 'a physical, chemical and biological complex on which all of us are dependent', as Bridges (1997: 1) puts it. The term 'soil' will be used here in its straightforward agricultural sense of 'the stuff in which plants grow' (Bridges 1997: 1), although as we saw in Chapter 4, distinctions are drawn between 'soils' and 'sediments'. In deserts they are peculiar. To uncover the powerful and pervasive influence of the huarango upon them, we will need to dig into the 'rhizosphere', or root-world.

Soil stabilisation

Most obviously, in an environment such as that of the lower Ica Valley which frequently experiences winds of well over 100 kilometres per hour and extremely erratic river flows, trees with extensive root systems physically maintain soil stability. Indeed, successful agriculture is just not possible here without the protection afforded by trees. Arid areas are particularly vulnerable to wind and water erosion. Overgrazing, unsustainable agriculture and the destruction of trees for fuelwood increase this vulnerability. Consequent problems, such as what Singh and Rathod (2002: 309) call the 'menace of sand drift', are of course hardly unique to the coast of Peru.

Naturally, vegetation reduces soil loss through wind erosion: in a moderate wind regime, a vegetation cover of only 4 per cent will reduce the soil loss of bare ground by at least 15 per cent (Fryrear 1995). And the root architecture of the huarango—one of the deepest and most laterally extensive of *any* tree in *any* environment—*underpins* floodplain and river meanders, protecting other plants of the riverbank from water erosion. Indeed, *Prosopis* has been introduced to arid regions worldwide for precisely these reasons (Dutton *et al*. 1992, Sene 1996, Pasiecznik *et al*. 2001).

On the coast of Peru *Prosopis* cover is recorded as reducing the average wind speed by almost 30 kilometres per hour (see Asencio Díaz 1997, and be it parenthesised here that in the lower Ica Valley, with its continuous average wind speed of 28.8 kilometres per hour, this protection represents the difference between being able to grow almost any crop, and none at all). The huarango's importance in controlling wind erosion is illustrated dramatically by Figure 8.1, which shows the encroachment of dunes along the western edge of the middle Ica Valley over the recent past. As the trees growing along and stabilising these dunes have been chopped down the desert has begun its advance into today's agricultural heartland of the valley.

Moreover, the physical binding of soils by huarango roots is but part of how the tree stabilises soils in the face of the wind. For, as we will see, alterations to the microclimate, soil quality and moisture regimes under *Prosopis* canopies promote understory growth and less friable soils, which, in turn, further the control of soil erosion.

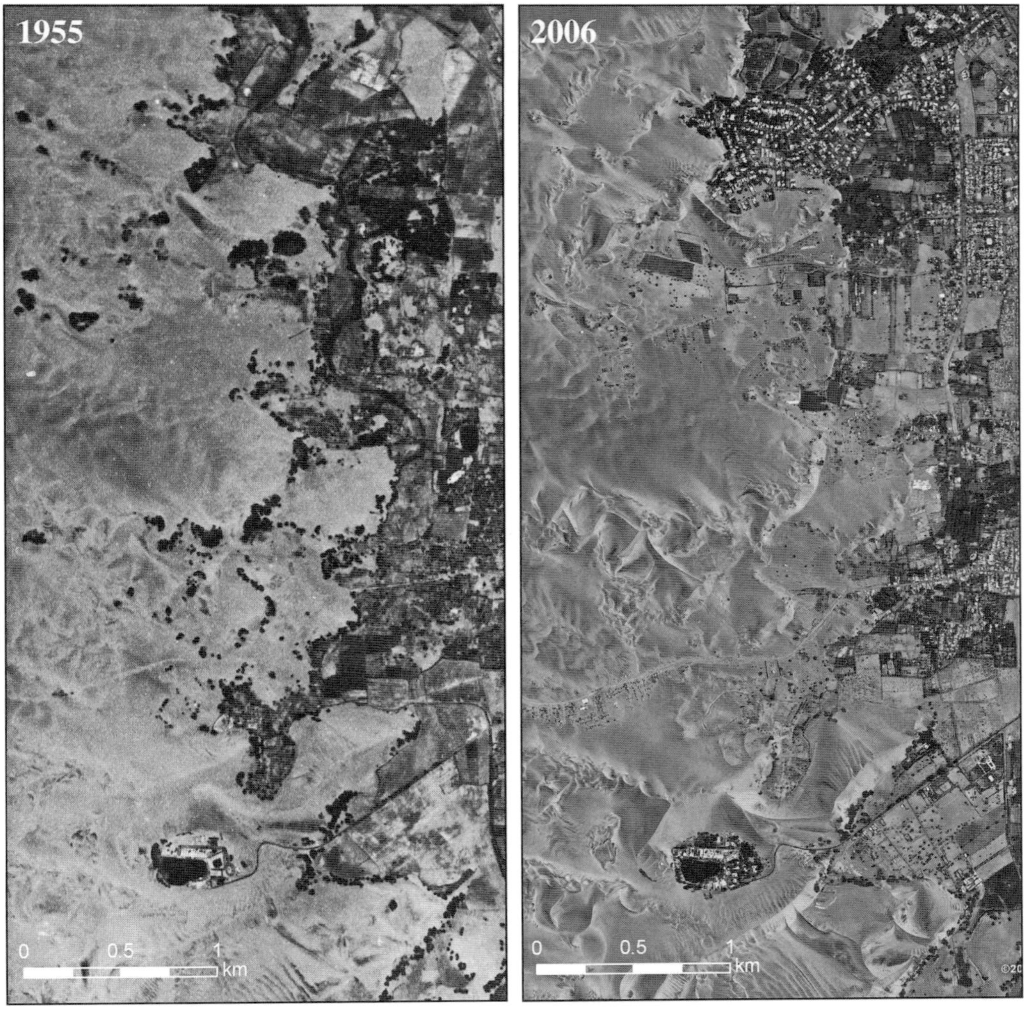

Figure 8.1. Dune encroachment and change in huarango cover from 1955 to 2006, on the western edge of the middle Ica Valley (courtesy of Justin Moat and Oliver Whaley, RBG Kew)

Soil quality

Although water availability is an obvious limiting factor in arid sub-tropical ecosystems, the amounts of organic matter in their soils may be just as, or even more important, to their productivity. For these soils have the lowest organic carbon and nitrogen contents of any soil ecosystem (Jenny 1944, Rundel *et al.* 1982, Geesing *et al.* 2000). This affects their bulk density, porosity and salt cation exchange capacities and so, the rate at which water infiltrates. Moreover, the limits of arid ecosystem soil productivity are determined by the proportions of both these components, since build-up of soil organic carbon is only possible with additions of organic matter and nitrogen (Geesing *et al*. 2000).

Desert trees, and in particular legumes such as *Acacia* and *Prosopis*, have profound effects upon the distribution of soil resources and biochemical processes., for when nutrients become limiting to biological productivity, a conspicuous concentration of vegetation occurs under these trees where the soil nutrient content is higher. These are what desert ecologists call 'islands of fertility'. As we will see, there are many records of much higher levels of nutrients, particularly nitrogen, under *Prosopis* canopies than in the open spaces between trees.

Part of the reason for this may seem obvious: *Prosopis* is a member of the legume family, whose well-known general characteristic is the ability to fix nitrogen from the air within the soil in the form of nitrates, through symbiosis with *Rhizobium* micro-organisms. Yet not all leguminous trees fix nitrogen and the amounts of fixation vary widely according to factors that are hard to assess outside artificial experimental environments and over the lengths of time during which trees influence the soil. Nonetheless, field trials — some lasting more than thirty years — are gradually yielding meaningful data on the various mechanisms by which trees moderate the physical, chemical, biological and hydrological properties of the soils on which they grow. And *Prosopis* consistently show among the most marked effects upon soil quality of all dryland species.

Fisher (1990) usefully offers five hypotheses for how trees affect soil quality, with which we can structure our discussion here of the influence of the huarango. The first two are due to tree litter fall and root turnover, which induce so-called 'nutrient pumping', whereby nutrients deep within the soil profile are accessed by tree roots and redistributed to upper soil horizons (see also Barth and Klemmedson 1982).

We have seen that the huarango produces a copious litter fall — *poña* — which carpets the desert under the tree, increasing soil humus content and supplying nitrogen, phosphorous, potassium and other nutrients as it decomposes (see for instance Garg 1992, 1998, Singh 1996, Bhojvaid and Timmer 1998, Mishra and Sharma 2003). Indeed, *poña* is gathered and used as fertiliser on the south coast of Peru by those too poor to afford commercial products. *P. juliflora* trees less than eight years old produce up to eight tonnes of dry leaf litter per hectare per year (Singh 1996, Garg 1992, 1998), yielding substantial nutrient contributions per hectare per year of 127 kilograms of nitrogen, 10 of phosphorous, 73 of potassium, 113 of calcium and 48 of magnesium, by Garg's (1992, 1998) measurements. Older trees of course produce more litter fall. *P. juliflora* of thirty years of age, for instance, produce more than 12 tonnes per hectare per year (Bhojvaid and Timmer 1998).

Root turnover also makes substantial contributions to the organic matter and nutrient content of soil (Bhojvaid and Timmer 1998), although these are naturally difficult to quantify. Yet roots also have other direct effects on soil quality. For — as we saw in the case of the lower Ica Valley — the soils of arid areas are particularly prone to the development of hard, compacted pans. And tree roots — especially ones as extensive as those of the huarango—physically disrupt and penetrate these hard pans within the soil, thereby improving its physical and hydrological properties. Infiltration rates are enhanced and run-off reduced, giving a more uniform distribution of water in the soil profile. Research at various semi-arid locations in India shows the root effects of *P. juliflora* on the physical characteristics of degraded, sodic soils: greatly increasing their porosity and water-holding capacity (Garg 1999, Mishra and Sharma 2003, Mishra *et al.* 2003). Indeed, water infiltration rates through these soils increase fivefold (Mishra and Sharma 2003: 255).

The third way suggested by Fisher (1990) by which certain, leguminous trees contribute to soil quality is through nitrogen fixation. Ever since Martin (1948) failed to locate the nodules that are characteristic of *Rhizobium* symbiosis on *Prosopis* in field settings in Texas, a vague perception prevailed for many years that the genus did not actively fix significant nitrogen. And some therefore proposed other mechanisms for the demonstrable increases in soil nutrients under *Prosopis* canopies, such as the 'nutrient pumping' we have just discussed (see for instance Barth and Klemmedson 1982). Yet it is now quite clear that the genus *does* actively fix nitrogen. Typically, the nitrogen content of the soil beneath the *Prosopis* canopy is two to seven times that in the open (Dommergues 1992, Ansley *et al.* 1997). The amounts of nitrogen fixed may vary widely according to tree species and age and environmental factors (Pasiecznik *et al.* 2001). Nonetheless, the quantities are significant: in the range of 40 to 175 kilograms of nitrogen per hectare per year (Johnson and Mayeux 1990, Abrams *et al.* 1990, Dommergues 1992, Ansley *et al.* 1997). Indeed, a recent study of *Prosopis* fixation by Geesing *et al.* (2000) is particularly striking for both its accurate methodology and results. For they record huge increases over background levels in soil organic carbon and nitrogen under *Prosopis* canopies. Moreover, these increases are correlated with tree size, offering powerful evidence that 'the trees did not fortuitously come to occupy an island of fertility' (Geesing *et al.* 2000: 166). In other words, *Prosopis* does not occur selectively on islands of fertility: it *causes* them.

Fisher's (1990) fourth hypothesis for the mechanisms by which trees affect soil quality is that of a 'rhizosphere effect', causing an increased microbial biomass (Bhojvaid and Timmer 1998). While the symbiosis between *Prosopis* and *Rhizobium* to fix nitrogen is a specific example of this plant–microbe interaction, micro-organisms play many other crucial roles in soil formation through decomposition and nutrient cycling. They also influence soil structure and contribute greatly to total soil respiration. Five groups—bacteria, actinomycetes, fungi, algae and protozoa—make up the microbial population of soils, although in most ecosystems it is composed mainly of fungi (Purohit *et al.* 2002). As Carrillo-Garcia *et al.* (1999: 322) summarise, fungi in the soil interconnect 'the root systems of adjacent plants, facilitating exchange of nutrients between them and contributing to plant growth and to soil structure because of their intimate association with the living cells within both root and soil'. In the soils of arid regions, however, all micro-organism growth is restricted by low moisture and intense solar radiation (see for instance Purohit *et al.* 2002). But many studies show the powerful influence of *Prosopis* trees upon the ecology of soil fungi and other micro-organisms in desert ecosystems.

Bhojvaid and Timmer (1998), for instance, record a nearly fivefold increase in the total soil microbial biomass under *P. juliflora* growing for thirty years on degraded sodic soils in semi-arid Haryana, India (and see also Purohit *et al.* 2002 for *P. cineraria*'s effect on fungal biomass). In the dry soils of the Mexican central highlands, Reyes-Reyes *et al.* (2002) report that the microbial biomass under the legume trees of *Prosopis* and *Acacia* is much higher than that in agricultural soils, even when those are intercropped in the traditional manner with maize and leguminous beans. Meanwhile, Carrillo-Garcia *et al.* (1999) study the 'islands of fertility' that occur about trees in the Sonoran Desert, finding that large volumes of their soil are enmeshed by arbuscular-mycorrhizal (or 'AM') fungi. The importance of AM fungi to agricultural ecosystems has long been appreciated (see for instance Bird *et al.* 2002: 446). Proliferating in a shaded microenvironment, these fungi help bind the windborne soil particles that aggregate under tree canopies in the nabkha mounds, which we saw in the archaeological record of the lower Ica Valley. As Carrillo-Garcia *et al.* (1999: 331) summarise, soil, plant and fungi form 'an autocatalytic cycle . . . fungi improve plant growth through enhanced nutrient uptake, the more vigorous plant intercepts more windborne soil, this soil is bound by the mycorrhiza into a growing mound, and the mound provides more nutrients to the plant and a growth substrate for the fungus, thus closing the cycle'. The most important of these so-called 'facultative island-formers' recorded by Carrillo-Garcia *et al.* (1999) in the Sonoran is *Prosopis articulata* (mesquite), which supports the largest number of other plants beneath its canopy. The soil of the 'islands of fertility' underneath these *Prosopis* canopies has five times the AM fungi and more than twice the bacteria content than that outside them. Consequently, these soils have better aeration, finer texture, lower pH and higher organic carbon, nitrogen and moisture contents (see also Bird *et al.* 2002). Carrillo-Garcia *et al.* (1999) thus define mesquite as the 'keystone' species for this desert.

The final mechanism suggested by Fisher (1990) by which trees affect soil quality is through the modifications that they bring about to microclimate. In deserts tree canopies moderate soil and air temperatures, greatly improving soil moisture and quality through a series of interrelated effects. Decomposition of organic matter into humus and nutrients can only occur with the presence of moisture. And, above 35 °C, any soil organic matter rather quickly becomes oxidised and degraded (Jenny 1944), exactly like that in the once organic-rich, old soil horizons buried under the climbing dune of Samaca H-13 which we saw in Chapter 4. Yet tree shading cools soil temperatures by between 5 and 12 °C (Asencio Díaz 1997, Bhojvaid and Timmer 1998, Geesing *et al.* 2000), and the 'mulching' effect of tree litter creates further microclimatic moderations at the soil surface, reducing evaporation. As we have seen, these microclimatic alterations also create congenial environments for soil micro-organisms. Conversely, at night deserts can be remarkably cold and soil temperatures under tree cover can then be up to 6 °C warmer than outside (Asencio Díaz 1997, Bhojvaid and Timmer 1998). So the moderated conditions under tree canopies in arid climates assist in building up and then maintaining soil organic matter and soil fertility.

In concert these mechanisms contribute to one of the most remarkable characteristics of the genus *Prosopis*: its ability to flourish in saline and highly alkaline soils and, over time, to ameliorate those conditions, thereby reclaiming those soils for other less-tolerant plants, including crops. For degradation of soils by accumulating salts is a vast problem, affecting almost one billion hectares of otherwise productive land in many arid parts of the world (Pessarakli and Szabolcs 1999). Saline soils are characterised by high alkalinity (or pH), low organic matter content, an excess of toxic sodium salts, high clay dispersion and hard duracrete salt-enriched horizons (or 'hard pans'), particularly of calcium carbonate—precisely as we observed in the basins of the lower Ica Valley in Chapter 4. Unsurprisingly, these cause restricted plant growth and very reduced agricultural productivity (see for instance Bhojvaid *et al.* 1996). And many of these salt-encrusted soils are caused by *human* activity.

The introduction of irrigation farming causes shallow groundwaters. Over time, and together with inadequate leaching due to limited water supply, salts become concentrated by evaporation in low-lying areas. These anthropogenic, salt-affected lands often occur in what were once the most productive agricultural parts of these arid countries. Indeed, they have been implicated in ancient agricultural collapses, as we saw in Chapter 4. Today, for instance, six million hectares or almost half of the Indus plain—the agricultural heartland of Pakistan and the font of the Harappan or Indus Valley Civilization some five thousand years ago—is afflicted by sodic soils caused by millennia of irrigation (Khanzada *et al.* 1998, Mahmood *et al.* 2001). In India around ten million hectares are affected, including the canal-irrigated agricultural lands of the Indo-Gangetic plains (Bhojvaid *et al.* 1996, Singh 1996, Singh *et al.* 1998, Mishra and Sharma 2003). So it is hardly coincidental that so much of the research cited here has been carried out in the Subcontinent—predominantly on *P. juliflora*, introduced from the New World.

Prosopis can tolerate very alkaline soils with a pH higher than 10 and can grow in a soil salinity regime equivalent to that of seawater (Singh 1996). Moreover, as the tree grows it rehabilitates lifeless, salt-afflicted soils through all those mechanisms that we have discussed—adding organic matter, initiating biological activity, reducing water evaporation loss, opening up soils with deep roots for salt leaching—and through root chemical processes. For the biological activity of roots and their associated micro-organisms increases carbon dioxide levels in the soil. With water, this forms carbonic acid, which dissolves relatively insoluble calcium carbonate. Ca^{2+} ions thus mobilised then exchange with toxic and more active Na^{+} ions in ion exchange (Bhojvaid and Timmer 1998, Garg 1999, Mishra and Sharma 2003). The result is a remarkable change in soil chemistry. Mishra and Sharma (2003), for instance, record a threefold fall in percentage calcium carbonate and a fall in toxic sodium salts of two-and-a-half times in the soil under a nine-year-old plantation of *P. juliflora*. Over twenty years, *Prosopis* reduces an initial soil pH of 10.3 to an average of 8 and increases its organic content by five times (Singh 1996). As Pasiecznik *et al.* (2001: 62) summarise, 'trees in the *P. juliflora–P. pallida* complex have the ability to . . . [reduce] high pH soils by approximately one unit every ten years'.

Over time, as these degraded soils are reclaimed by *Prosopis*, crop plants can be grown on them. Singh *et al.* (1998: 458), for instance, measure the yields of wheat and oats grown on soils collected from under various 24-year-old tree plantations grown at Karnal, India, concluding that 'the yield levels of wheat and oats achieved in the *Prosopis* soil were 4.5 and 3.5 times higher respectively, than that obtained on the farm control soil, suggesting that prolonged afforestation may restore productivity of abandoned soils much above the agricultural production levels'. Indeed, Bhojvaid and Timmer (1998: 189) observe that 'crop yield in the case of the soil collected from the 30-year-old plantation [of *P. juliflora*] even surpassed that attained on a reference non-sodic farm soil' (and see Nyberg and Högberg 1995 and Deans *et al.* 2003 for similar results in African contexts).

These many agroforestry studies on New World *Prosopis* species worldwide (and see also East and Felker 1993, Rundel *et al.* 1982, Pasiecznik *et al.* 2001, Rossi and Villagra 2003) work to explain why, as Nabhan (1985) observes of the deserts of the south-western United States, 'the soil beneath *Prosopis* grows richer, as the tree grows'. Yet we have still to elucidate fully all of the processes at play between tree and environment, and in particular the role of *Prosopis* in influencing soil moisture profiles. For water availability remains, of course, the most obvious factor limiting plant growth and production in arid ecosystems.

Unique Water Relations

As we saw in Chapter 7, plants adapted to arid environments have evolved specialised morphologies and physiologies to find other sources of water, or make more conservative use of available water, so as to minimise water stress. In the case of the genus *Prosopis*, those adaptations are both phreatophytic, that is accessing deep groundwater sources through exceedingly long taproots, and xerophytic, that is having roots capable of extracting water held under very high matric forces, and other features to control water loss through transpiration. These adaptations have implications, not just for the water relations of *Prosopis*, but also for those of the plant community and whole ecosystem of which it is part.

All plants need water in essential biochemical reactions and to maintain their cell turgidity. In order to absorb water from the soil a plant produces a lower water potential within the root than the water potential of the surrounding soil, thereby exerting a 'suction' force greater than that which binds water molecules to soil particles. Simultaneously, plants absorb carbon dioxide for photosynthesis through openings in their leaves called stomata. Since the water potential of the dry atmosphere is more negative than that within the plant tissue, water vapour is lost through the stomata at the same time (see for instance Simpson and Solbrig 1977). Water therefore moves from soil to plant to atmosphere along a 'continuum of increasingly negative water potential, flowing "downhill" thermodynamically, but "uphill" physically from root to shoot', as Jackson *et al.* (2000: 482) put it. In this way, plants transpire great volumes of water and indeed recycle more than half of the precipitation that falls over the land (Jackson *et al.* 2000).

The rate of transpiration depends upon atmospheric conditions and the resistance of leaf stomata to water loss. For plants to avoid desiccation in arid conditions, plant water conductance cannot exceed its supply rate through the roots. Even by the standards of desert-adapted trees, *Prosopis* is a remarkably efficient user of available water. Tomar *et al.*'s (2003) study of thirty-one arid-region tree species at Karnal, India reveals that, while *P. juliflora* can continue to extract water even in the driest drought months, its overall extraction was low, and its water use efficiency (calculated as the amount of biomass produced per water transpired) exceptional: more than twice that of the average of all the species evaluated (Tomar *et al.* 2003). Indeed, *P. juliflora* transpires water at only around 20 per cent and 40 per cent of the rates of *Eucalyptus* and *Acacia* species, respectively (Mahmood *et al.* 2001). Yet, while above the ground mechanisms of water conductance by vascular plants are easily observed, below the ground they are still remarkably poorly understood (see for instance Dawson 1993, Jackson *et al.* 2000).

One of the explanations invoked for the stable coexistence of trees and understory shrubs and grasses in arid environments is that, while these trees obtain water from deep within the soil, shallow-rooted plants use separate sources of soil moisture. Known as the 'two-layer' model of soil moisture resource partition (see for instance Sarmiento 1984), it has been observed in ecosystems as diverse as the savannas of southern and eastern Africa, the Patagonian steppe, semi-arid central Argentina and North American sub-tropical woodlands (Weltzin and McPherson 1997: 156). As we saw in Chapter 7, the root architecture of *Prosopis* is both deep (phreatophytic) and laterally extensive (dimorphic). Unsurprisingly, then, given the verdancy of the 'islands of fertility' that grow beneath these trees, the 'two-layer' model is frequently associated with the genus. Studies on the extraction and transpiration of groundwaters by a riparian plant community, dominated by mesquite in the San Pedro River Basin, a tributary of the Gila River in the Sonoran Desert, for instance, confirm that these trees obtain their water from much deeper within the soil profile than do grasses and shallower-rooted shrubs (see for instance Scott *et al.* 2000, 2003, and see also Toky *et al.* 1992 and Peláez *et al.* 1994 for studies on water resource partitioning by *Prosopis* species in India and Argentina, respectively).

Moreover, in the desert environment, *Prosopis* demonstrably increases the moisture content of soils immediately beneath its canopy. We have already seen some of the reasons for this: improved soil physical characteristics and cooler temperature in its shade. New research, however, is re-evaluating the proper importance of root transport to the total hydraulic conductance of plants and coining a new term—'hydraulic lift'—to describe the even more direct influence of some trees on soil moisture. And this phenomenon was first recognised in a tree growing in the Atacama Desert of northern Chile: *Prosopis tamarugo* studied by Fusa Sudzuki in the 1960s (Sudzuki 1985a, 1985b).

Hydraulic lift

P. tamarugo grows almost only on the Pampa de Tamarugal, in the Salar de Pintados Basin of the Chilean Atacama. The environment here is similar to that of the south coast of Peru: precipitation is essentially non-existent, although relative atmospheric humidity can be as high as 100 per cent at night and there are substantial groundwater sources running off the Andes to the east (Mooney *et al.* 1980, Sudzuki 1985b). *P. tamarugo* is a sizable tree and grows in places where the water table occurs up to 40 metres below the surface. Its root system is typically dimorphic, with one or more taproots to depth and a dense superficial root mass. Its leaf stomata are covered by a thick mucilaginous layer and open only at night, in direct relation to the amount of air humidity (Sudzuki 1985a, 1985b). The remarkable observation that Sudzuki made of *P. tamarugo* was, as Mooney *et al.* (1980: 178) later put it, that 'although both immediately above and below the rooting mat the soil was quite dry, the soil within the rooting mat had a considerable amount of moisture—in fact, exceeding the field capacity for that soil'. In other words, in this rainless land, the surface soil moisture profile beneath *P. tamarugo* was being influenced in a way that contradicted the simple model of tree roots absorbing available soil moisture and then transpiring it to the atmosphere.

Although various microclimate moderation factors have, as we have seen, been advanced to explain higher soil moisture beneath trees, these cannot account for soil moistures of the order of 28 per cent recorded by Sudzuki within the root mat of *P. tamarugo*. So Sudzuki and subsequent observers (Went 1975, Mooney *et al.* 1980), concluded that the tree roots were, under certain circumstances, *exuding* water in upper soil layers. And measures of soil water potentials of around minus 52 bar beneath the tree, relative to those distant from the tree's influence (of minus 15 bar), and within the tree's xylem (varying from minus 13 bar at night to minus 32 bar at noon), confirmed the likelihood of water flow from the tree roots into the soil (Mooney *et al.*1980, Sudzuki 1985b). Nonetheless, there remained considerable doubts as to what might be the source of this exuded water, and indeed what possible adaptive advantage the mechanism might confer upon the tree, so as to account for its existence.

Sudzuki herself argued that the source of this moisture was the atmosphere: that the tree absorbed water through its stomata which were open at night when relative atmospheric humidity in the Atacama approached 100 per cent and exuded it into its root mass to be later reabsorbed during the day as water stress levels rose. Indeed, by spraying the trees with isotope-labelled water, she appeared to show that this water was apparently transferred to the soil surrounding tree roots at night. Others, however, proposed alternatively that *P. tamarugo* was lifting groundwater through its deep taproots and transporting it into drier upper soil levels (Mooney *et al.* 1980). This mechanism—defined as the nocturnal movement of water from deep, relatively moist layers, to upper, drier soil layers through the conduit of a plant root system and driven by root and soil water potential gradients—has since become known as 'hydraulic lift' (see Figure 8.2; Richards and Caldwell 1987, Caldwell *et al.* 1998). But, whatever the mechanism—or indeed, combination of mechanisms — in a hyperarid desert with no precipitation, but with deep groundwater supplies and high atmospheric humidity, *P. tamarugo* greatly increases soil moisture in the upper soil horizons under its immediate influence. This moisture may then be available for other less deeply rooted, 'parasitic' plant species (Rundel *et al.* 1991: 25).

The remarkable water relations of *P. tamarugo* are sometimes presented as unique (Mooney *et al.* 1977: 35, Pasiecznik *et al.* 2001: 31). Yet it is also the only *Prosopis* species of this hyperarid coast ever studied in such detail. Moreover, a burgeoning body of research, all acknowledging academic ancestry in Mooney *et al.*'s (1980) conjectures for *P. tamarugo*, shows hydraulic lift by a wide variety of other plants (see for instance Richards and Caldwell 1987, Dawson 1993, Caldwell *et al.* 1998, Horton and Hart 1998). Indeed, as Jackson *et al.* (2000: 485) note, 'many plants with dimorphic root systems influence soil water distribution in novel ways' and hydraulic lift has now been demonstrated in nearly fifty plant species.

The quantities of water hydraulically lifted at night by some trees can be substantial — up to a quarter of their subsequent transpiration the following day (Emerman and Dawson 1996, Caldwell *et al.* 1998: 156). And tagging water with an isotope signature shows that deep waters hydraulically lifted by trees are indeed used by other 'parasitic' plants (Caldwell and Richards 1989, Dawson 1993). Jackson *et al.* (2000: 486, emphasis added) report that hydrological model simulations of hydraulic lift 'for a shrub-grassland steppe suggest that *most* vertical water movement during the growing season occurs through roots, *not* through soil capillary flow'. So those plants that can tap and then hydraulically lift deep groundwaters thereby influence the entire hydrologic balance of the plant community of which they are part (Dawson 1993: 573).

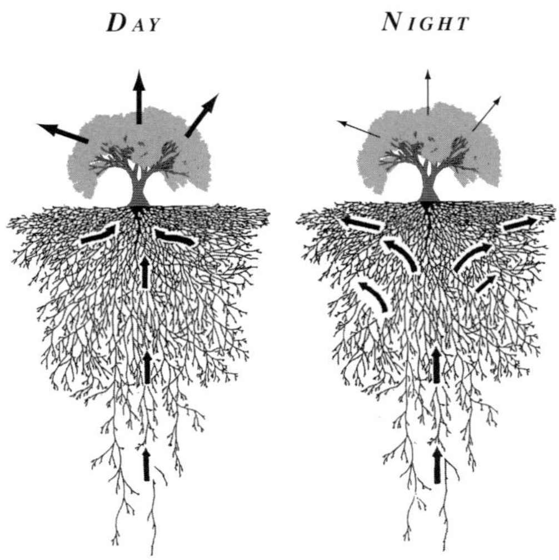

Figure 8.2. Hydraulic lift
Source: Adapted from Caldwell *et al.* 1998

Precisely why deep-rooted plants in arid regions should have evolved to give up some of their water to other plants is all part of what Caldwell *et al*. (1998: 157) call 'an emerging view that not all plant–plant interactions are necessarily negative and that facilitation is an important process in plant communities'. Clearly, in arid environments hydraulically lifted water makes a valuable buffer supply to even out water stress during the day for the lifting plant itself. There may, however, be additional benefits to giving up water to the soil and other plants, in the form of nutrient acquisition, root growth and persistence in otherwise dry soils, and the many other soil physical and biological improvements that we have discussed above (Caldwell *et al*. 1998: 159).

Atmospheric humidity resources: inverse hydraulic lift

It is an interesting coda to our consideration of the water relations of *Prosopis*—in the light of Sudzuki's argument that soil moisture beneath *P. tamarugo* arose through the absorption through its leaves of atmospheric water—that *inverse* hydraulic lift has been shown recently in plants growing in the Kalahari Desert. For it has long perplexed observers exactly how, in very arid regions, the deep roots of plants ever succeed in growing through the metres of dry soil that inevitably lie between the depth to which any surface moisture would penetrate and the deep water table. The mechanism proposed by which such deep root systems become established is 'inverse hydraulic lift' (Schulze *et al*. 1998).

Just as hydraulic lift is defined as the upward transfer of water through plant roots to drier, upper soils with more negative water potentials, so inverse hydraulic lift is the same process of water transport downwards, along an inverted water potential gradient, which occurs when upper soil layers are wetter than lower layers. As Schulze *et al*. (1998: 460) note, 'over 60 years ago, Breazeale and Crider (1934) speculated that water transfer through roots to growing root tips might assist root growth of desert plants in dry soil in Arizona'. Schulze *et al*. (1998: 460) hypothesise that inverse hydraulic lift could be a mechanism by which 'water flux through the roots and efflux into the rhizosphere could facilitate root growth'. They then demonstrate the mechanism in various deep-rooted Kalahari plant species, through the use of isotope-labelled water (and see also Smith *et al*. 1999 for a review of the phenomenon in other environments and plants).

As we have seen, Sudzuki proposed that *P. tamarugo* was able to absorb the very high atmospheric moisture of the Peru–Chile Desert nights through its leaves and exude this moisture in the soil around its roots for subsequent reabsorption during the day (and see also Went 1975). Mooney *et al*.'s (1980) proposed alternative mechanism of hydraulic lift is now widely cited in the ecological literature. And yet the 'new' mechanism of inverse hydraulic lift demonstrated in the Kalahari is, in effect, a variation of that originally proposed by Sudzuki for *P. tamarugo*.

Indeed, inverse hydraulic lift is likely to be an important process in the Peru–Chile Desert ecosystem, whether or not trees actually absorb moisture through their leaves. In *lomas* environments along the Peruvian coast, for instance, the critical importance of atmospheric humidity is widely recognised (see for instance Rundel *et al.* 1991, Dillon *et al.* 2003). Here, as we saw in Chapter 2, since ephemeral vegetation is itself a fog catcher, once its growth is established, the soil beneath receives several times more water than would have been produced on a barren slope by *garúa* processes alone. So, in these deserts vegetation acts not as a water-*consuming*, but as a water-*producing* factor in a self-increasing process.

Just as in the *lomas*, our observations lead us to believe that capture of atmospheric humidity by huarangos is likely an important process also in riparian contexts on the south coast (Whaley 2004, Beresford-Jones 2005, Whaley *et al.* 2010b). For, as we saw in the previous chapter, a particular morphological characteristic of the huarango is its well-developed brachyblasts with many, small leaves in dense clusters, a characteristic which greatly increases the surface area upon which atmospheric moisture can condense. Anyone sleeping beneath the tree becomes uncomfortably aware of this by dawn. Whether thereby directly absorbed through the leaves, or 'merely' deposited on the soil surface, inverse hydraulic lift through roots is the most plausible mechanism for the transport of ephemeral atmospheric humidity deeper into the soil profile.

A *Tillansia* 'air plant'.
B Huarangos high on dune face above Huacachina, Ica.
C *Tillansias* growing on dune huarangos, Huacachina.

Figure 8.3. *Tillansia*–huarango association on dunes near Huacachina, Ica

Figure 8.3 shows huarangos growing high on the dunes at Huacachina, in the middle Ica Valley. These relatively small trees are remarkable because they are growing at more than 85 metres above the water level of the adjacent Huacachina lagoon (an artificial level, moreover, today replenished by pumped water from Ica). Their presence, so high above groundwater, begs rather obvious questions as to how they first became established and how they persist. Certainly, this growing location is evidence either of extraordinarily deep root growth into the dry sand of the dune, through the mechanism of inverse hydraulic lift, or that the huarango endures here by absorbing atmospheric humidity through its leaves, exactly as proposed for *P. tamarugo* by Sudzuki; or indeed, a combination of both. Moreover, that atmospheric humidity is occasionally very high at this location, high on the dune ridge, is manifest in the great numbers of bromeliad plants (*Tillansia* sp.) that grow on these trees (Figure 8.3A). For these 'air plants' are typical in *lomas* ecosystems, and obtain all their water supply from the atmosphere. This *Tillansia–Prosopis* association was once more common amidst the higher dunes of the Ica Valley (Quinteros, personal communication; and see Figure 8.1).

In sum, then, we have reviewed abundant evidence that the *Prosopis* rhizosphere has a profound (pun intended) impact upon the distribution of water within the soil profile. This is driven by water potential gradients along root and soil whose direction and magnitude vary according to the time of day, the season, and the trees' growing habit and habitat. Sometimes it distributes water upwards from deep groundwater (through hydraulic lift) and at other times downwards from atmospheric humidity (through inverse hydraulic lift).

Dawson summarises the implications of hydraulic lift as follows:

> There have been a variety of previous studies that have reported improved soil water balance and development, greater soil nutrient concentrations and higher floristic diversity directly under or in close proximity to tree canopies. These observations have been attributed to modifications in the physical and chemical processes induced by a tree-modified microclimate. Alternatively, it is possible that some of the tree species investigated in these studies may be conducting hydraulic lift and contributing to the improved physical and chemical status and greater floristic diversity beneath tree canopies.
> (Dawson 1993: 573)

In other words, the 'islands of fertility' observed around *Prosopis* and other arid-region trees might, it seems, just as appropriately be termed 'islands of humidity'. This has consequences not only for land-use, irrigation and agroforestry practices today, but also for our interpretations of human–environment interactions, land-use changes and the consequences of deforestation in the past, particularly on the south coast of Peru.

The 'Keystone' Species

Our discussion here of the influence of *Prosopis* upon the stability, quality and moisture of the soil in which it grows sets the scene for our understanding of its role as the 'keystone' to the edifice of life in its native habitat: the riparian oases of arid, New World lands. For here the tree has an all-pervasive influence upon its neighbouring vegetation and, in turn, upon the wildlife and insect populations that flourish within the 'islands of fertility', brought about by its effects upon the soil and its shade from a harsh desert sun. In the Sonoran Desert, south-western United States and in semi-arid north-west Argentina, for instance, Mares *et al.* (1977) record around twice, and four-and-a-half times, respectively, the number of individuals of grasses and herbs growing under *Prosopis* than in the exposed areas between them.

The huarango produces abundant, tiny, pale-yellow or white flowers twice a year that yield copious amounts of nectar and pollen. A mature *Prosopis* tree produces some two million individual flowers a year (see Figure 7.4), with more pollen per floral-unit than any other insect-pollinated desert plant species (Simpson *et al.* 1977). It is pollinated mainly by bees, and, when in flower, the tree hums with invertebrate life. Indeed, in the Sonoran *Prosopis* is recorded as attracting more species of insect than any other plant, including more than 160 species of bees (Nabhan 1985). Unsurprisingly, apiarists rate *Prosopis* as the most valuable honey plant in the North American south-west (Ibrahim 1992). Hundreds of other insect species including flies, moths, butterflies, wasps, mantids, weevils, bruchids, beetles and crab spiders use *Prosopis* inflorescences and fruit as food, mating sites and hunting grounds (Simpson *et al.* 1977, Kingsolver *et al.* 1977). And of course *Prosopis* pods are food for a variety of animals including deer, foxes, rodents and rabbits (Ansley *et al.* 1997). Other animals are associated with the tree because other plants or insects that depend on it provide their food, or simply because it provides shade. Fifteen animal species and ninety-five bird species, including twenty-eight nesting, are recorded in a single *Prosopis* stand in the Sonoran Desert (Nabhan 1985).

So, as Whaley *et al.* (2010a: 7 my translation) observe, 'no plant is truly an island'. Rather than the keystone of an edifice, the huarango is perhaps better viewed as the centre of a web of desert life, made up of millions of connections between organisms—many of which we have yet to understand—and from which, humans are indivisible. Each connection arises through co-evolution and confers interdependence: plants cannot persist and propagate long without birds, insects, mammals and micro-organisms, which perform vital roles in pollination, seed dispersal and mechanisms of 'bio-control'. Birds and insects, such as parasitic wasps for instance, control certain other insects, which might otherwise develop into infestations that would kill the host plant. Indeed, the tree is vulnerable to such imbalances in web self-regulation (Whaley *et al.* 2010b). Removal of parts of the web weakens the whole system. Removal of its keystone may cause it to collapse entirely.

What then of the ecology of the riparian oases of the Peruvian south coast? Until recently this was sadly under-studied. The few published accounts of plant associations and distributions here are overviews (see for instance Velázquez Zea 1995, though more detailed studies of flora do exist for the north coast, in particular, Sagástegui 1973). Indeed, most botanical studies in the Peruvian coastal desert focus upon *lomas* ecosystems, perhaps because of their peculiar, endemic plant diversity. Some of these provide brief comments on the riparian ecosystems that adjoin them (Rundel *et al.* 1991, Dillon 2003). In the past these riparian strips were important corridors of life across the desert linking the diverse flora and fauna of the Andean foothills with the *lomas* formations along the Peruvian south coast (Whaley *et al.* 2010b). But they are also, of course, the location where humans chose to settle and cultivate in the millennia following the development of agriculture. Consequently, their original riparian ecology is highly fragmented. On the south coast those fragments that prevail do so only because they are remote and provide some marginal livelihood such as raising goats. None, of course, are in any sense ecologically 'pristine', nor have they been for millennia. Nonetheless, their significance as the places where people actually *lived* makes the paucity of ecological information on the south coast riparian oases all the more unfortunate.

This is now being remedied by a study co-ordinated by the Royal Botanic Gardens Kew (or 'RBG Kew') as part of the Darwin Initiative-funded project 'Habitat Restoration and Sustainable Use of Southern Peruvian Dry Forest', or the *Proyecto Huarango*, which grew out of the research described here on prehistoric human ecology. Initially we made botanical surveys and herbarium collections of seventy-eight plant species in thirty-three families, identified by botanists of the RBG Kew and the Universidad La Agraria, La Molina (Beresford-Jones 2005). The scope of these collections, however, has now been greatly widened by the *Proyecto Huarango* to cover other south coast vegetation associations and augmented to total some 480 different plant species in 64 families (Whaley *et al.* 2010b).

Nearly one-third of this recorded flora of Ica is represented by plants from the grass (Fam. Gramineae) and legume (Fam. Leguminosae) families, and more than half by these together with four other families: Compositae, Solanaceae, Malvaceae and Cyperaceae (Table 8.1). The *Proyecto Huarango* has also co-ordinated comprehensive surveys of the birds, animals and insects of the south coast riparian ecosystem (Whaley *et al.* 2010b). This information now allows for a much better understanding of the *Prosopis*-dominated riparian ecosystems, wherein human settlement and agriculture developed on the south coast of Peru. Indeed, it also provides a baseline against which to judge their changing condition today, and in the past. We will review these studies here for two, very contrasting, south coast riparian locations: the Usaca old-growth woodlands and Huerto Huamaní, in the Samaca Basin.

Usaca: old-growth woodland ecology

Usaca, on the Río Poroma, is, as we saw in Chapter 7, almost certainly the last fragment of 'old-growth', secondary woodland left on the south coast today. It is thereby a unique and partial analogue for the *Prosopis*-dominated woodlands that were once much more widespread in these riparian valleys. The Usaca vegetation may be divided according to three locations characterised by different plant associations: the riverbank, the woodland itself, and clearings within it (Figure 8.4).

Along the edges of the Río Poroma grow the most strictly 'riparian' of plants. The riverbanks are dominated by dense stands of *Tessaria integrifolia* (Fam. Compositae),

Table 8.1. A summary of the flora of the south coast of Peru

Family	Sub-family	Number of species	Percentage of total collection[a]
Gramineae		80	17
Leguminosae	Papilionoideae	27	6
	Caesalpiniaceae	13	3
	Mimosaceae	10	2
		50	10
Compositae		52	11
Solanaceae		32	7
Malvaceae		24	5
Cactaceae		14	3
Cyperaceae		13	3
Chenopodiaceae		10	2
Scrophulariaceae		10	2
Euphorbiaceae		10	2
Convolvulaceae		9	2
Cruciferae		9	2
52 other families		167	35
Total		**480**	**100**
Total endemic to Peru and southern Ecuador		**141**	**29**
Total endemic to south coast region		**55**	**10**

[a] Rounded to nearest per cent.
Source: Whaley *et al*. 2010a: 9, and elaborated by Whaley, personal communication.

known locally as 'pajaro bobo', and the giant reeds of *Gynerium*, known as 'caña' or 'carrizo'. Growing rapidly these stands are the first line of defence against riverbank erosion during floods (Figure 8.4C). Permanently damp areas and backwaters also have wetland sedges and rushes or 'juncos' such as *Cyperus* and *Bolboschoenus* (Fam. Cyperaceae) and *Typha* (Fam. Typhaceae). Sometimes, yellow-flowering wild tobacco species of *Nicotiana* (Fam. Solanaceae) may be found. Behind these along the woodland edge along the bank are large trees of 'sauce'—the South American willow, *Salix humboltiana* (Fam. Salicaceae)—typical of coastal and Andean waterways (Gentry 1996). Weberbauer (1945) recorded them as widespread on the south coast in the early 1900s but today the tree is rare outside Usaca (Whaley *et al*. 2010a). Their presence here is indicative of a healthy, moist soil regime.

Beyond lies the woodland itself, made up of a relatively small number of species, for dry forest is not noted for its high tree diversity (see for instance Grados and Cruz 1996, Whaley *et al*. 2010a). Unlike almost anywhere on the south coast today, the Usaca woodland has a true forest canopy formed from those enormous and ancient huarangos that we saw in Chapter 7. But there are also many *Acacia macracantha*, also a Mimosoideae legume tree, known as 'espino' on the south coast, and a few, large *Schinus molle*, or 'molle' trees (Figure 8.4A).

A Woodland of huarango and acacia.
B Río Poroma woodland edge.
C Río Poroma riverbank with dense stands of 'parajo bobo' (*Tessaria*).
D Clearing with 'torñuz' (*Pluchea*) extending to woodland understorey.

Figure 8.4. Different plant associations of the Usaca 'old-growth' woodland

Since, in Argueda's memorable words, 'the huarangos let the sun pass, but take out its fire', a range of understory shrubs thrive beneath the Usaca woodland canopy. Indeed some grow only there, including *Indigofera*, or 'tintillo' (which we saw in the archaeobotanical record of the lower Ica Valley), *Galvezia fructicosa* (Fam. Scrophulariaceae), or 'curi', which produces copious small purple staining berries, and *Vallesia dichotoma* (Fam. Apocynaceae), known as 'perlillo' because of its small white fruits (Figure 8.5K). Since the woodland is used for raising livestock, grasses and smaller weedy and herbaceous species, common in the Samaca and Ullujaya basins, are fewer in Usaca.

Along the woodland fringes grow many small trees or shrubs of *Parkinsonia aculeata*, or 'uña de gato'. This tremendously tough, very spiny, desert tree has green photosynthesising branches, thus minimising the water-profligacy of leaves (Figure 8.5B). These fringes also have splashes of the pale green foliages of woody shrubs such as *Lycium americanum* ('lucraco') and *Grabowskia boerhaaviaefolia* ('palo negro') and bursts of the large, red tubular flowers of *Tecoma fulva*, or 'cahuato' (Figure 8.5A).

The Usaca woods ring with the call of the 'chaucato'—or long-tailed mockingbird (*Mimus longicaudatus*). But it is full of other birds too: ornithologists for the *Proyecto Huarango* record some thirty-two species. Three types of hummingbirds, the oasis, amazilia and Peruvian sheartail (*Rhodopis vesper*, *Amazilia amazilia* and *Thaumastura cora* respectively), dart in brilliant flashes among the red *Tecoma* flowers (Figure 8.6B). This tiny woodland fragment has at least seventy breeding pairs of the black-necked woodpecker (*Colaptes atricollis*, Figure 8.6A). Testament to its insect abundance, insectivores are legion among Usaca's glades, including Peruvian miners (*Geositta peruviana*), nighthawks (*Chordeiles acutipennis*), tyrant fly-catchers (*Elaenia albiceps* and *Camptostoma obsoletum*), bran-coloured fly-catchers (*Myiophobus fasciatus*) and beautiful vermillion fly-catchers (*Pyrocephalus rubinus*, Figure 8.6E). Other Usaca birds have intimate association with the seasonal riparian water sources. The Amazon kingfisher (*Chloroceryle americana*) bides time in the boughs that overhang and shade the summer pools, while the great egret (*Ardea alba*) stalks across them, both seeking river crayfish. The white-collared swift (*Streptoprocne zonaris*) swoops low over the water surface to catch hatching midges (Figure 8.6F). At least two species of raptor frequent Usaca, hunting small mammals of the forest floor: the harris hawk (*Parabuteo unicinctus*) and the great horned owl (*Bubo virginianus*). This large owl is elsewhere rare on the south coast (Figure 8.6D). Even more remarkably, Usaca is home to at least sixty breeding pairs of the slender-billed finch (*Xenospingus concolor*, Figure 8.6J), a species endemic to the riparian habitats of the Peru–Chile Desert, but today, owing to the fragmentation of that habitat, classed as vulnerable to extinction on the IUCN's 'Red List' (Whaley *et al*. 2010a).

And Usaca has a rich variety of other fauna, including amphibians like the coast toad (*Bufo limensis*), reptiles such as the endemic lizards (*Microlophus thoracicus* and *Dicrodon heterolepis*, see Figure 8.6H) and snakes of the genus *Alsophis* (Figure 8.6I) and the venomous desert lancehead (*Bothrops pictus*). Insects are abundant and diverse including many scorpions and a huge and primitive beetle (Figure 8.6K). Aside from many small

A Cahuato (*Tecoma fulva*). Usaca woodland clearings.
B Uña de gato (*Parkinsonia aculeata*), open scrubland, Samaca.
C Tomatillo (*Solanum pimpinellifolium*), open scrubland, Samaca.
D Chlico (*Baccharis salicifolia*), open scrubland, Samaca.
E *Sesuvium* sp., field edges, Huerto Huamaní, Samaca.
F Espino (*Acacia macracantha*), Usaca woodland.
G Leche leche (*Alternanthera hamifolia*), field edges, Huerto Huamaní, Samaca.
H Torñuz (*Plucheae chingoyo*), open scrubland, Samaca.
I Summer landscape of *Sesuvium* and *Alternanthera*, Samaca.
J Zapallo (*Cucurbita maxima*) harvest, Huerto Huamaní, Samaca.
K Perillo (*Vallesia dichotoma*), Usaca woodland understorey.

Figure 8.5. Selected flora of the south coast riparian ecosystem (photographs A, D, F, H and K courtesy of Oliver Whaley; photographs B, C, E, G, J and I courtesy of Claudia Lüthi)

A Black-necked woodpecker (*Colaptes atricollis*), Usaca.
B Amazilia hummingbird (*Amazilia amazilia*), Usaca.
C Hueraqueque (*Burhinus superciliaris*), Samaca.
D Great horned owl (*Bubo virginianus*), Usaca.
E Vermillion fly-catcher (*Pyrocephalus rubinus*), Usaca.
F White-collared swift (*Streptoprocne zonaris*), Usaca.
G Tyrant fly-catchers (*Elaenia albiceps*), Usaca.
H Lizard (*Microlophus thoracicus*), Usaca.
I *Alsophis* sp. snake, Usaca woodland.
J Slender-billed Finch (*Xenospingus concolor*), Usaca.
K Unidentified beetle, Usaca.

Figure 8.6. Selected fauna of the south coast riparian ecosystem (all photographs courtesy of Oliver Whaley) rodents of the genera *Phyllotis* and *Peromyscus*, mammals in Usaca include the Andean fox (*Pseudalopex culpaeus*) and the small feline the pampas cat (*Lynchailurus colocolo*, with Syn. *Felis colocolo* or *Oncifelis colocolo*), which is very shy and difficult to see on the south coast and consequently poorly studied (Garcia-Perea 1994, Villalba 2006). Much of this fauna is clearly and accurately depicted in all its rich variety in the naturalistic iconography of Early Nasca Period, including felines and foxes, hummingbirds, and all the creatures of the river and its banks such as swifts, egret, crayfish, frogs, catfish, tadpoles and even the wasps that gather mud at the river's edge (Silverman and Proulx 2002: 147). Indeed, as Whaley *at al*. (2010b) perceive, the Early Nasca artistic canon proclaims a truly 'riparian consciousness'.

Within the woodland are many clearances where trees have been chopped down by *carboneros*, or for small market gardens and orchard *huertos*. The natural floristic composition of these clearances is quite distinct from the woodland itself. With no mature trees to compete with, it is dominated by two types of large, woody shrubs, both of the Asteraceae Family: *Baccharis salicifolia*, known locally as 'chilco', and *Pluchea chingoyo*, known as 'torñuz' (Figures 8.5D and H). *Heliotropium* sp. (Fam. Borginaceae) and thorny *Scutia spicata* (Fam. Rhaminaceae), or 'lloque', are also common.

The Usaca *huertos* meanwhile are, of course, sown with crop plants—usually the traditional maize/bean intercrop. The edges of their small fields are lined with fruit trees, some of which are exotic to the south coast including mango, key lime and date palms. Many, however, are cultivated native fruit trees including *Inga feuillei*, or 'pacay', another Mimosoideae tree legume, whose large (to 50 cm) pods contain a fairly dry, sweet, white pulp which surrounds large, hard black seeds; *Psidium guajava*, or 'guava'; *Cordia lutea*, or 'membrillo', which produces small, very hard fruits; and of course, the huarango. In Chapter 5 we saw the remains of all these, except *Cordia*, recorded in the ancient rubbish middens of the lower Ica Valley. The flora of these clearances thus lie along a continuum of ecological change, between the old-growth Usaca woodland and the degraded riparian basins of the lower Ica Valley, which we will examine next.

Samaca and Ullujaya: degraded woodland ecology

Today, as we have seen, the active river floodplain of the Samaca and Ullujaya basins is much reduced from its original extent by river down-cutting, and its vegetation altered greatly by its history of deforestation. Indeed, these degraded riparian associations are typical of almost the entire lower Ica Valley. In 1994, however, Alberto Benavides founded a smallholding in Samaca called Huerto Huamaní (Benavides 2004), growing a wide range of traditional south coast cultivars according to necessary practice for organic certification by the Soil Associations of both Peru and Spain. Huerto Huamaní's *raison d'être* is self-sufficiency, and Samaca is of course distant from the agricultural heartland and markets of the middle Ica Valley. But, for precisely these reasons, Huerto Huamaní is a rather unusual experiment in traditional land management and offers a useful analogue for pre-Hispanic agricultural practice in the lower Ica Valley. We therefore made plant collections amid its anthropogenic landscape of fields and hedgerows, as well as from the areas of degraded *monte* scrub that make up the rest of these basins.

The fauna of these basins is generally similar to that of Usaca, albeit in greatly reduced numbers and diversity. Yet some bird species prefer the open areas of Samaca and at night, after the winds die down, tall thin-legged huerequeques (*Burhinus superciliaris*) scurry in close pairs across the empty relict river terraces (Figure 8.6C) and the tiny burrowing owl (*Athene cunicularia*) makes its home amid the expanses of caliche.

Farming practice in Huerto Huamaní stands in sharp contrast to that of most of today's agriculture in the middle Ica Valley, carried out by Peruvian and international agro-industries growing a number of monocultures—notably asparagus, tomatoes and cotton—on vast scales. These can be extremely lucrative, depending upon the vagaries of market prices. In 2006, for instance, asparagus destined for European and US markets might earn profits after operating and capital costs of US$10,000 per hectare. These industries use fossil water supplies pumped from very deep tube wells, but as we saw in Chapter 2 these supplies are being depleted faster than they are being replenished by several orders of magnitude. The Ica agro-industry thus has all the hallmarks of those high-return, short-term, extractive businesses that have long earned Peru's economic elites quick yet ephemeral fortunes.

In Huerto Huamaní meanwhile, fields are created, tilled and sown largely by hand and are therefore small—not more than half a hectare in area. The word 'traditional' can be all too carelessly taken to infer praxis immemorial. But on the south coast we have every reason to assume that agriculture has indeed been carried out for millennia in small *huertas* (and *huertos*—both words connoting combinations of market gardens and orchards). For it was this landscape of *huertas* amid woodlands that invoked the delight of Cieza de León and other early Spanish writers that we saw in Chapter 6. And pockets of *huerta* farming, often providing subsistence to individual families, can still be seen today in parts of the middle Ica Valley in San Juan de Bautista, Substanjalla and along sections of the Achirana and Mochica irrigation canals in Cachiche, Huamangilla, Aquiqes, Pueblo Nuevo and Santiago (see Figure 8.7 and Whaley *et al.* 2010a: 43). Above all, this is small-scale, sustainable farming.

Traditional *huertas* are watered using a range of techniques across the 'continuum of hydrostatic manipulations' (Nabhan 1979: 246) from floodwater farming to canal irrigation—all forms of 'spate agriculture' (Whaley *et al.* 2010a: 41). As seasonal water arrives—'*agua nueva*' or '*agua de avenidas*'—it is diverted into canals (or *asequias*), along small channels ('*surcos*'), into convoluted swales (or '*caracoles*') and sunken fields ('*hoyadas*') (Figures 8.8B and E). These annual inundations bring with them huge quantities of the fine alluvial silts—the *yapana* 'top-ups'—which, we saw in Chapter 4, are very fertile and, being so fine, dry out so slowly that crops can be sown, cultivated and at length harvested upon them. Fields in Huerto Huamaní, for instance, are embanked about their edges to a height of some three metres to retain these seasonal floodwaters. Huarango-dominated *monte* scrub is left along these embankments, creating hedgerows (Figure 8.8C and D). These are

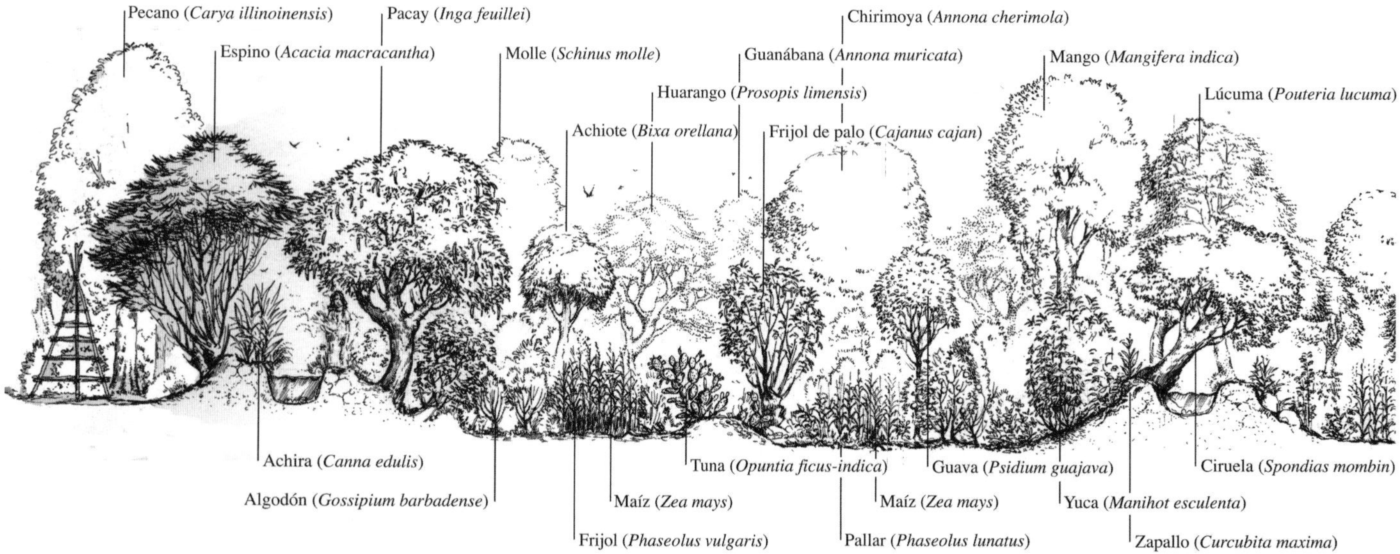

Figure 8.7. Traditional *huerta* agriculture of the south coast—and its major economic plant associations. Mango, pecano and ciruela are Old World introductions. (Drawing courtesy of Oliver Whaley.)

windbreaks essential to any agriculture in an environment with such an extremely strong and persistent wind regime. And they are also sources of fuelwood, through judicious coppicing, and of copious pods for livestock and preparation of sweet *huarangina* syrup for human consumption (Figure 8.8A; and see Reynel and Felipe-Morales 1987 for similar traditional agroforestry practices, still widespread in parts of the Andes). Since Huerto Huamaní fields are maintained without machinery and without the use of commercial pesticides or herbicides, their open, disturbed areas include a disproportionately high number of weeds, grasses and other so-called 'agrestal' plants growing together with sown cultivars.

The variety and quantity of crops grown in the 25 hectares under cultivation at Huerto Huamaní is quite surprising, and more than sufficient for the small community that grow them. In 2001, for example, this produce included three varieties of maize (*Zea mays*), maíz blanco, morado and de gallina; five varieties of beans, including nine tonnes of pallares (*Phaseolus lunatus*) and one and half tonnes of frijol panamito (*Phaseolus vulgaris*); together with pumpkins and squash (various *Cucurbita* sp.), including 'three truck loads' of enormous zapallos (*C. maxima*, Figure 8.5J). These three crops are of course the famous triumvirate of American domesticates that together provide an almost complete nutritional balance. Other food cultivars grown in Huerto Huamaní include various varieties of chilli (*Capsicum annum*) and starch-rich tubers such as the Andean potato (*Solanum tuberosum*), achira (*Canna edulis*) and jícama (*Smallanthus sonchifolius*). Important exotic crops grown in Huerto Huamaní include alfalfa and the sunflower (*Helianthus* sp.). Native and exotic fruit trees such as those described in the *huertos* of Usaca are rather few in Huerto Huamaní because of the area's winds and the time it takes to grow them and to establish hedgerows.

Before turning to the weed species associated with these cultivars, it is worth noting that the distinction between so-called 'volunteer' weed species and cultivars in Huerto Huamaní fields is often rather blurred. Many cultivated plants such as zapallo will grow and propagate freely without human intervention and they rapidly come to dominate the embankments between fields and underneath the huarango hedgerows in Huerto Huamaní (Figure 8.8C). Moreover, these fields have a great variety of some twenty-three species of weedy herbaceous species and at least seven grass species, including various members of the Amaranthus and Chenopodiaceae families (Figure 8.9E and F), from which several important so-called 'pseudo-cereal' crops have been domesticated in the Andes, namely kiwicha (*Amaranthus caudatus*), quinoa (*Chenopodium quinoa*) and kaniwa (*C. pallidicaule*). Weeds such as mat-grass Panadero (*Phyla* Syn. *Lippia canescens*) and the semi-succulent halophyte *Sesuvium portulacastrum* (or *Portulaca portulacastrum*), which are widespread throughout arid sub-tropical America, are common in Huerto Huamaní fields (Figure 8.5F and I). There are also various fruiting, prostrate shrubby weeds of the Solanum Family including *Lycium* sp. and three species of 'tomatíllo', two of which (*Solanum pimpinellifolium* and *S. peruvianum*) produce copious, tiny red or yellow fruit with a delicious, intense tomato flavour (Figure 8.5C).

Indeed, these are precisely those agrestal weeds which we have noted in the archaeobotanical record of the lower Ica Valley in Chapter 5, and, as we will see shortly, the use by humans

A Huarango coppiced for fuelwood in field of beans (*Phaseolus vulgaris*).
B Spate agriculture – seasonal water ('*agua nueva*') being channelled for agriculture (photo courtesy Oliver Whaley).
C *Prosopis* hedgerow atop a field edge embankment with 'volunteer' weeds of *Amaranthus*, *Chenopodiaceae* and pumpkins (*Cucurbita maxima*), providing wind protection for a field of sunflowers and maize/bean intercrop.
D *Prosopis* hedgerow about an embanked bean field.
E *Prosopis* and *Acacia* growing along a small canal bank.

Figure 8.8. Huerto Huamaní agricultural landscapes

A Maize and bean intercrop with huarango coppice.
B Bean (*Phaseolus vulgaris*).
C Zapallo pumpkin (*Cucurbita maxima*).
D Extra-long staple cotton (*Gossipium barbadense*).
E *Chenopodium* sp. agrestal weed.
F *Amaranthus spinosus* agrestal weed.

Figure 8.9. Some cultivars and agrestal weeds of the Huerto Huamaní fields of almost all these 'wild' plant species is recorded in the ethnobotany of the North American Sonoran Desert. This invokes a striking analogy between Huerto Huamaní, traditional agriculture of the North American Sonoran Desert, and our archaeological evidence from the lower Ica Valley, which we will explore further in the next chapter.

The Huarango in Historical Ecology

Before exploring that analogy, it may be worth recapitulating very briefly those themes that our discussion over the preceding two chapters has tried to develop. We have seen that *Prosopis* has a profound role in modifying desert environmental extremes and underpinning fragile New World desert ecologies. And we have extended this understanding into the riparian valleys of the Peruvian south coast, which are still under-studied despite their significance as the places where human settlement and cultivation took place. Indeed, here in its native environment, we have noted that the form of *Prosopis* — the *huarango* — belies perceptions elsewhere of the genus as an invasive pest. On the contrary, we have seen that this form, conveying such utility as a resource, shows signs of long co-evolution with humans. Moreover, the huarango's significance to human agro-ecology extends deep into the unseen rhizosphere and its subtle and gradual influence upon soil quality and moisture. So does C.V. Konda Reddy describe the effect of the introduction of New World *P. juliflora* into Arandha Pradesh, India a century ago thus:

> The rebellious sands are subdued and the inhospitable soils are colonised. The dreary scene of dry districts is changed to that of green belts. The bleak tree-less landscape is painted with splashes of brown, green and yellow. The monotony is broken for the traveller and the sheep and goats munch and crunch happily on the proteinous pods. The rural folk, whose lands were getting buried under drifting sands are grateful to the Forester and Prosopis, and the poor folk who have no fuel to burn in their hearths now have Prosopis. (Reddy 1978, cited in Pasiecznik et al. 2001: 1)

These chapters then are far more than an ecological digression from, or mere 'background' to, our archaeological theme. For we simply cannot begin to understand the consequences of deforestation, or trace an ever-changing relationship between people and their environment — historical ecology — without this detail. Today, for instance, thousands of tourists come away from Nazca fascinated by the 'Nazca Lines', those great ceremonial pathways etched upon the deserted pampa. And yet flying over the lines is a peculiarly disembodied experience as Silverman (1992: 11) points out. Indeed, the impression left by this vast empty ritual space and by the dusty modern towns and wide fields of agro-industry is, in a fundamental sense, quite misleading of the ancient world of the south coast. For it overlooks those few, delightful remaining pockets of *huertas* and fragments of old-growth huarango woodland in which people actually *lived*, and out of which sprang the 'riparian consciousness' so celebrated by the beautiful Early Nasca artistic canon.

9. The Sonoran Desert:

An Ethnoecological Analogue?

In light of the information that we have reviewed for what makes *Prosopis* a useful human resource, and for its role in modifying desert environmental extremes, it is hardly surprising that the relationship between humans and this genus in the arid lands of the New World is almost as ancient as human occupation itself. We turn now to explore this in one particular part of these American drylands: the Sonoran Desert of the south-western United States or, to be more specific, within the riparian basins of the Salt and Gila rivers of that desert. For here, a more recent human ecology — or 'ethnoecology' as Martin (2004) calls it — may offer us an analogue for the far deeper time-depths of the Peruvian south coast.

In the Sonoran, and elsewhere in the United States, several species of section *Algarobia* of the *Prosopis* genus are known collectively as 'mesquite', a name deriving from the Nahuatl name for the tree of *misquitl*, which means the 'bark that tans', deriving from its high content of tannins (Pasiecznik *et al*. 2001: 7). Mesquite is the one of the most common plants along the washes of North American arid lands and, as we will see, was a vital resource for its peoples. Moreover, although peoples of the Sonoran had sustained contact with Europeans from the time of the first Jesuit missions in 1687, for various reasons it was only by the end of the nineteenth century that Anglo-Hispanic impact there finally became inexorable. So there exists for the Sonoran a rich body of ethnological, linguistic and ethnobotanical commentary, which has long influenced interpretations of the region's archaeology. By contrast, a much earlier history of European domination erased many such details from the ethnographic record of the south coast of Peru.

We ought to embark with care upon any analogy between the historical Sonoran and the ancient south coast of Peru, for they are of course separated by vast gulfs of both time and space. The dangers of glib ethnographic analogy in archaeological interpretation have been widely discussed (see for instance Gould 1980, Hodder 1982, Cunningham 2003), and consequently such 'comparative analogies' have become rather unfashionable. Yet analogy

Chapterhead: Detail of Nasca embroidered textile depicting hummingbirds around a flower (source: Peters 1991).

itself remains intrinsic to interpretation—for how else would we recognise an archaeological site at all? As Wylie (1985) and others have pointed out, the problem is not analogy per se, but the ways in which it is applied. As we will see, properly justified inferences from Sonoran *Prosopis*–human relationships hold the power to illuminate a 'missing' ethnoecology for the ancient Peruvian south coast.

Of course, such comparisons are often usefully invoked in ecology. Ever since the time of von Humboldt, it has been recognised that processes of parallel and convergent evolution can give rise to remarkable similarities in the ecologies of distant regions with similar physical environments. As Simpson and Solbrig (1977: 3) note, 'as a consequence of this similarity, many ecologists have hypothesized that most other biological properties of such ecosystems should also be similar'. This offers a way of justifying our analogy on independent grounds. Hodgson (2001: 2, emphasis added) defines ethnobotany as the study of 'how people perceived and interacted with *each and all* of the plants within their environs'. So, if we can verify similarity between the two, distant riparian contexts of the Sonoran and the south coast of Peru, at the broad level of the totality of their two ecologies, we might invoke an analogy that rests upon the *homologous* roles of *Prosopis* within those two ecologies.

Yet cultural similarities cannot be so certainly ascribed. Wylie (1985), for instance, usefully distinguishes between 'formal analogies', which rely on the comparison between contexts of certain elements in deriving conclusions about other elements, and much stronger 'relational analogies', which rely on cultural and natural connection between two contexts. There is of course no direct prehistoric continuity between the south coast of Peru and the Sonoran Desert (or at least none since the earliest peopling of the Americas). So, following Wylie (1985), we will use analogy here only to propose a hypothesis—in ecological terms, hardly audacious—that *Prosopis* was for the inhabitants of the ancient south coast of Peru, just as it was for the native cultures of the North American south-west, what Felger (1977: 175) calls the 'staff of life'.

Justification of an Ethnoecological Analogue

Papaguería or 'Oasis America'

Although the vast North American south-west encompasses a great diversity of Native American cultures, topography, biodiversity and climate, it is generally arid to semi-arid country with rather few permanent rivers: 'Arid America' as Kirchhoff (cited in Woodbury 1979) calls it. Much of 'Arid America' is composed of the so-called 'Basin and Range Province'—the Sonoran Desert—that extends across southern Arizona and New Mexico in the United States, and Sonora, Baja California and Chihuahua in Mexico. Within these drylands lies what Kirchoff calls 'Oasis America': the riparian oases that stretch along the Gila and Salt rivers. The Spanish called this country *Papaguería* and it is the homeland of the Pima (or O'odham) nation and their ancient predecessors, the Hohokam.

Just like the Peruvian south coast then, the Sonoran is a so-called 'basin-range' desert. As we saw in Chapter 2, these are rare among the world's deserts and, having topographies dominated by alternating mountains and basins, are characterised by enclosed drainage systems. Those basins make for convenient landscape units within which to define an ethnoecology. The Sonoran stretches along the Pacific coast of the Gulf of California up eastwards into the Arizona uplands and the mountains of the Sierra Madre Occidental. Rivers such as the Gila and its tributary, the Salt River, drain down from these highlands along steep, short outwash slopes (known as *bajadas*) and emerge into floodplain basins (see for instance Fontana 1983b). Castetter and Bell describe the course of the Gila:

> [It] rises in the mountainous country of western New Mexico . . . and emerges from the mountain region of eastern Arizona. Here it enters upon the detrital plains of the Basin Range Province, and, throughout its westward course, except at a few places, winds over deep deposits of alluvium in broad valleys between short mountain ranges. Over its lower course it has cut a very shallow valley. The Gila is an interrupted river, that is having a permanent flow over short distances of its entire course throughout the year, and along these stretches there have been more or less permanent settlement and irrigation. (Castetter and Bell 1942: 13)

The western edge of the Sonoran Desert is very dry. Rain here is scarce, varying between none and 1,000 mm per year, although all of this falls in a few storms (Castetter and Bell 1942, Fontana 1983b). This is insufficient to support agriculture and so here, as on the Peruvian south coast, life depends on seasonally flooding rivers, arising in distant eastern highlands. These floods continually restore the fertility of these river basins through deposits of deep alluvium. Not only, then, do the Sonoran geomorphology and climate invite close comparison with those of the Peruvian south coast, so too do their respective river hydrologies. For the average annual stream flows of the Salt and Gila rivers of 1,100 and 297 million m^3 (Masse 1991) compare well with those for the combined Rio Grande de Nazca drainages and Ica River of 764 and 257 million m^3 per year (see Table 2.4). Moreover, these Sonoran rivers are also extremely erratic (see for instance Gregory 1991). Within the great diversity of the North American south-west then, it is specifically in these river basins of Kirchoff's 'Oasis America' — or *Papaguería* — that we might seek an ethnoecological analogy with the south coast of Peru.

Sonoran flora

To Anglo and Hispanic eyes perfunctory impressions of the Sonoran *Papaguería* were of an arid and inhospitable land. Font's (cited in Castetter and Bell 1942: 18) first reaction in 1775 was typical: 'in short, in all this land of Papaguería which we passed through, I did not see a single thing worthy of praise'. Much later in 1894 Gaillard's (cited in Nabhan 1986b: 43) was similar: 'the entire region is a hopeless desert, and few if any [white] Americans reside in it. It is unadapted for agriculture, yet when the July rains commence, the Indians forsake their *rancherías* [villages] and hasten to their *temporales*, where they plant crops of corn, pumpkins, melons, squashes, etc.'

Yet these were ignorant opinions as Howard (cited in Nabhan 1986b: 43), the Indian agent in *Papaguería*, came to understand, observing in 1887, 'place the same number of whites on a barren, sandy desert such as they live on, and tell them to subsist there; the probability is that in two years they would become extinct'. They are belied by two important features of the Sonoran which we will explore further here: firstly, the rich potential of its river floodplains which, in the time of the ancient Hohokam, were exploited through an irrigation system so vast that it is the largest pre-Colombian artefact in North America; and secondly, its desert flora, which provides an extraordinary 540 edible plant species. Indeed, fully *one-fifth* of all the Sonoran Desert's plants can provide useful foods for humans, a far higher proportion than in other, more verdant lands (Hodgson 2001).

A complete account of Sonoran plant diversity plainly lies beyond my means or purpose here (see Simpson and Solbrig 1977, Mares *et al.* 1977, Fontana 1983a for vegetation inventories of the Sonoran *bajadas*; Castetter and Bell 1942, Nabhan 1979, 1986a, Scott *et al.* 2000 and Yepez *et al.* 2003 for the Sonoran riparian floodplains; and Felger and Moser 1985 and Hodgson 2001 for excellent Sonoran ethnobotanical studies). But we can make a broad ecological comparison between the major northern Sonoran riparian and *bajada* plant associations and the riparian flora of the south coast of Peru, which we saw in the last chapter. And such a comparison, shown in Appendix 1, reveals some striking similarities between the major plant associations of these two, distant New World riparian arid ecosystems.

Both are dominated by species of *Prosopis* of the section *Algarobia*. Castetter and Bell (1942: 21) observe of the Gila and Salt river courses that, 'wherever deep alluvial soils have been built up and subterranean water is available, dense forests of mesquite formerly were, and to some extent still are, to be found'. Other than mesquite, the most common trees of the fragmented Gila riparian woodlands are cottonwood (*Populus* sp.) and black willow (*Salix* sp.). The vegetation is also characterised by many other shrubby trees of the legume family, including catsclaw and white thorn (*Acacia*), paloverde (*Caesalpinia*), ironwood (*Olneya*) and Jerusalem thorn or Mexican paloverde (*Parkinsonia aculeata*), shrubs of saltbush and chamiso (*Atriplex* species of Chenopodiaceae), and dense thickets of arrow weed (*Pluchea sericea*). As we saw in Chapter 8, the riparian woodland of the south coast of Peru is also characterised by tree legumes other than *Prosopis*, including the genera *Acacia, Caesalpinia* and *Parkinsonia*, and by *Salix* trees. And the open spaces of both regions are dominated by dense stands of the woody shrubs of the Asteraceae family (*Pluchea* and *Baccharis*).

Grasses too are important in both desert ecosystems. In the Sonoran *Distichlis* is locally dominant in low, saline washes and *Sporobolus wrightii* in riparian bottoms. Grasses of the genera *Chloris*, *Bouteloua*, *Eragrostis*, *Leptochloa*, *Panicum* and *Pleuraphis* are also found (Mares *et al.* 1977). The composition of the grass family in the riparian habitats of south coastal Peru is very similar, with *Distichlis* and *Sporobolus* genera also locally dominant and the genera *Chloris*, *Eragrostis* and *Leptochloa* also present. Likewise, herbs of the families Chenopodiaceae, Amaranthaceae, Solanaceae, Aizoaceae, Verbenaceae, Portulaceae and Polgonaceae are also important components of both ecosystems. Indeed, some plants of the same species grow in both regions, including *Baccharis salicifolia*, various *Chenopodium* sp., various *Cyperus* sp. and *Parkinsonia aculeata*. The invasive species *Cynodon dactylon* and *Tamarix* sp. are exotic to, but now firmly established in, the riparian bottoms of both deserts. Slightly higher on the Sonoran *bajadas*, paloverde interspersed with various perennial cactus species become the common vegetation association. And the cactus family is also well represented in the *quebradas* of the lower Andean foothills and in the *lomas* formations of the Peruvian south coast (Whaley *et al*. 2010a).

Outside its riparian corridors, the Sonoran landscape is frequently covered in vegetation. Almost all of this, however, is one of the most widespread drought-enduring xerophytes of New World deserts, the creosote bush (*Larrea* sp.), which provides no source of food for humans (Simpson and Solbrig 1977, Fontana 1983b: 128). Of course, on the hyper-arid south coast of Peru there is no vegetation outside the riparian corridors. Yet, and uniquely throughout all Peru, Ecuador and Colombia, in the *quebradas* of the lower Andean slopes of the south coast, *Larrea* does grow (Gentry 1996: 851).

Indeed, the comparison shown in Appendix 1 of the major, representative plants of the Sonoran Desert (seventy-six genera in thirty-one families) and those of the Peruvian south coast (seventy genera in twenty-eight families) proves illuminating. For this shows that the overall desert flora diversity of the two regions is remarkably similar. Twenty-five plant families, or more than 80 per cent of the total number of families in each region, are shared by both. Within these families, the two regions share a total of thirty-eight genera, or more than half of the total genera listed for each. Most significantly, however, sixteen of these shared genera, or 40 per cent of them, are those of plants that are recorded as ‘frequent’ or ‘dominant’ in both regions, and which together thereby represent the majority of their plant cover. Unsurprisingly, given this similarity in wild flora, the suite of plant cultivars grown by people in the two regions, to which we will return shortly, also shows remarkable coincidence. Of course, this broad similarity of the floras of these two New World arid ecosystems derives from those similarities in their geomorphological and hydrological characters noted earlier. And it is against this background of physical and ecological comparability that the limited use of analogy drawn from the rich ethnobotany of the Sonoran Desert, and more specifically the role of the genus *Prosopis*, within these two regions, becomes meaningful for our purposes here.

Prosopis in the Ethnoecology of the Sonoran

Mesquite was one of the first plants noted by the Europeans in North America. In 1527 disaster befell the Narváez expedition on the Texas coast of the Gulf of Mexico and left only four survivors, one of whom was Álvar Núñez Cabeza de Vaca. For eight years he wandered the south-west, becoming familiar with the native languages and eventually coming to be regarded as an itinerant medicine man by the many societies through which he moved. In time he was reunited with his countrymen moving north from Mexico, and later appointed governor of the newly founded Buenos Aires, a position from which he was shortly dismissed for his excesses of sympathy with its natives. Cabeza de Vaca's (1993 [1542]: 91) extraordinary chronicle of the years of his journey across the south-west is a *sui generis* account of life there before the European arrival and he makes many references to 'mesquite . . . a fruit like the carob . . . sweet and good to eat'. He describes the preparation of mesquite pod flour and its association with 'great celebration . . . a banquet, which is a great one for them'. Cabeza de Vaca (1993 [1542]: 65) also notes that mesquite was used for 'medicinal purposes and for dances and festivals', and indeed observes that 'this is the thing they value the most'.

Later in 1540, Fr. de Niza's fabrications of gold and cities larger than Mexico excited the Coronado expedition into the south-west region (Plog 1997). Its dreams of fortune and glory proved empty, but one of its party, Hernando de Alarcón, diverted through *Papaguería* and was presented there with gifts of 'cakes of maize and a loaf of *mizquiqui*' —bread made from *Prosopis* flour (Hodgson 2001: 179). The futility of the Coronado expedition left the Spanish with little interest in the region for the next century and a half, before the remarkable Jesuit, Eusebio Kino, entered the Sonoran in 1687. Kino lived, and died in 1711, among the people of *Papaguería*, introducing wheat, horses and cattle to the region (see for instance Castetter and Bell 1942, Fontana 1983a, Nabhan 1986b, Hodgson 2001).

The assignment of the Company of Jesus to proselytise in *Papaguería* was fortuitous for our ethnoecological purpose, for—in contrast to the Pope's stormtroopers, the Franciscan and Dominican orders—the scholarly Jesuits were, as Massey (1949: 273) puts it, 'notably acute in recording tribal and linguistic information'. Their meticulous documentation of Native American lifeways prior to their expulsion from all the Americas in 1767 has, as Castetter and Bell (1942: 3) observe, 'given us a better understanding of this area than any other part of New Spain' (and we benefited from this same Jesuit perspicacity in those accounts of Cobo in Peru and Lozano in Argentina in Chapter 6). The Jesuits carried out the first recorded manipulation of *Prosopis* distributions, by introducing *P. glandulosa* to the Baja California peninsula, as Fr. Miguel del Barco describes in the mid-1700s:

> In Yaqui and other parts of that coast these seeds [of mesquite] have a good flavour, and the people eat them. But in [Baja] California they are all bitter, and that is why only beasts eat them. In Loreto and in one other mission some sweet mesquites can be found, but these came originally from the area of the Yaquis, or from that coast. They were taken from there to [Baja] California either as seed or when they were very small and grew there fairly well.
>
> (Fr. Miguel del Barco cited in Hodgson 2001: 180)

> And these same mesquites, now very large trees, still stand in front of the church in Loreto
>
> (Hodgson 2001: 180).

Jesuit observations, particularly those of Kino, are one of Edward Castetter and Willis Bell's main historical sources in their 1942 book, *Pima and Papago Indian Agriculture*, which offers inimitable detail on which to draw here. It is revealing in itself that this book makes forty references to mesquite use by the peoples of *Papaguería*, as compared with only twenty-three to that pre-eminent crop of the Americas, maize. By contrast, accounts of ancient agriculture on the Peruvian south coast make few, if any, references to the huarango.

The peoples of Papaguería

The Sonoran Desert was, and still is, a region of great cultural diversity. Hodgson (2001: Figure I) shows fifty-eight distinct indigenous peoples with historical distributions in its environs. These peoples followed many lifeways occupying a continuum of subsistence strategies, from nomadic hunter-gatherers to those with sophisticated dryland agricultural systems. Of these, the people whom Kino encountered in the riparian basins of the Gila and Salt rivers were the Pima nation.

There is also diversity within the Pima nation (for more detail, see Felger 1977, Fontana 1983b, Hodgson 2001). Fontana (1983b: 125) observes that, 'in modern times, the Gila River Pimans call themselves '*ákimel o'odham* ("river people") as distinct from the *tóhono o'odham* ("desert people"), their Papago neighbours to the south'. Yet they share the same Piman language (Fontana 1983b) and, in Kino's day, there was much intercourse between them (Castetter and Bell 1942). Indeed, as Ezell (1983: 149) observes, 'the terms Pima and Papago have come to connote ethnic differences beyond what the people themselves perceive; they have not forgotten . . . that they were both parts of a larger Pima nation'. Both the Pima and Papago were agriculturalists, though to differing degrees, the Pima dwelt in the lush riparian basin bottoms, while the Papago farmed the smaller *bajadas* away from the main rivers.

The Gila and Salt river basins have a rich archaeological heritage. The Pima called their predecessors the 'Hohokam', or 'those who have gone' (Plog 1997: 73), a name now used by archaeology to describe the prehistoric culture that flourished in the area from around 300 BC, reaching its apogee around AD 1000, and then apparently collapsing by around 1450. We will return to the reasons for that collapse later, since it is instructive for our purpose here. The Hohokam lived in many small villages along the river courses and a few, larger agglomerations such as the site of Snaketown on the Gila River, with buildings of adobe brick and distinctive ballcourts, all linked by a vast irrigation system. And most scholars see continuity between the Hohokam and the modern Pima, for as Haury (cited in Ezell 1983: 149), puts it, 'to assert that there was no connection between the Piman people and the Hohokam requires the removal of the latter from the area by about AD 1450 and the introduction of the Pimans with an impressively similar lifeway almost immediately'. Historical Piman lifeways are therefore frequently invoked to inform archaeological interpretations of the Hohokam.

Among the diverse cultures of the Sonoran Desert, then, it is the Pima nation, and specifically the farmers of the Gila and Salt river basins—the *Akimel O'odham*, or 'River People'—and their forebears the Hohokam, in whom we might seek an ethnoecological analogue with the south coast of Peru. Bahr (1983: 187) notes that 'all Pimans used a set of five patrilineal clan names that were grouped in turn into a pair of patrilineal moieties', while Hackenberg (1983: 177) observes that their social structures worked through the decentralisation of authority, acting 'to preserve the undivided interest of its ancestral families in community resources against both enterprising residents and outsiders'. There are striking resonances here with the traditional Andean *ayllu* structures, which have been used to interpret the archaeological record of the south coast of Peru.

Akimel O'odham agriculture

In these drylands, Piman agriculture was founded upon the skilful manipulation and conservation of ephemeral water sources, rising largely outside the Sonoran. A great variety of water management systems have been described for the arid North American south-west, ranging from simple floodwater farming, to various techniques of 'water harvesting', to complex canal irrigation. As Doolittle (2000) and others have noted, although it is convenient to categorise these techniques for the purpose of description, they are parts of what Nabhan (1979: 246) properly terms 'a continuum of hydrostatic manipulations', and he offers a useful summary:

> Floodwater-based agro-ecosystems function via (1) hydrostatic manipulations of the physical environment, and (2) synecological manipulations of the plant community. Agronomically productive hydrostatic conditions have been developed by geomorphological manipulations of the floodplain, including canals, terraces, grids, spreaders, and weirs . . . Traditional floodwater farming in arid America has depended upon ephemeral, drought avoiding and heat tolerant genotypes. In addition, native Americans manipulate the wild and weedy flora of floodwater fields by discouraging or protecting and harvesting selected species. (Nabhan 1979: 245)

Whereas the Tohono O'odham relied upon varieties of water harvesting, the Akimel O'odham relied nearly exclusively upon canal irrigation (Doolittle 2000). Moreover they, and their Hohokam predecessors, are renowned as the quintessential irrigators of North America. As Doolittle (2000: 364) puts it, 'the Akimel O'odham seem to have irrigated for as long as there is a written record, and . . . earlier'. Certainly, when Kino first encountered the Pima on the Gila River they were carrying out agriculture by means of canal irrigation, and many early Europeans were deeply struck by the extent and success of Pima irrigation and agriculture in this seemingly unprepossessing landscape. Manjes (cited in Doolittle 2000: 355), who first accompanied Kino into *Papaguería* in 1687, observed for instance that these were 'good lands for agriculture and sowing with many canals for their irrigation'.

Kino brought with him to *Papaguería* an Old World cereal—wheat—which quickly became popular as an 'off-season' crop, since it ripened after the full harvest of corn and pumpkins had been exhausted (Castetter and Bell 1942). And by the time that Garcés and Font (cited in Castetter and Bell 1942: 38) travelled through *Papaguería* in 1775, they observed that 'in all these pueblos they raise large crops of wheat, some of corn, cotton, calabashes, etc.' Font's description is precise:

> In the afternoon I went . . . to see the fields. These milpas are enclosed by stakes, cultivated in sections, with five canals or draws, and are excessively clean. They are close by the town on the banks

> of the river, which is large only in the season of the freshets. At that time the water was so low that an Indian who entered and crossed it had the water but halfway up his leg. From what they have told me, this is the reason that they had not yet made their sowing, for inasmuch as the river was so low the water could not enter the canals. They also told me that to remedy this need they were all anxious to come together for a council, and had already thought of sinking many stakes and branches into the river to raise the water so that it might enter the drains; this industry on their part is a proof of their devotion to toil and shows that they are not restless and nomad like other races, for to maintain themselves in their towns with their fields they themselves have contrived to hold and control the river. (Font 1775 cited in Russell 1908: 29)

Much later, Emory (1848, cited in Castetter and Bell 1942: 156) was 'impressed with the beauty, order and disposition of the arrangements for irrigation and draining of the land'. For Emory (1848, cited in Castetter and Bell 1942: 38), 'these Indians were further advanced in the art of agriculture and were surrounded with more comforts than any uncivilised tribe he had ever seen'. Bartlett (1854, cited in Castetter and Bell 1942: 38) likewise observed that 'the Pima made agriculture more of a system than did the Colorado tribes . . . and their crops were larger and very luxuriant'. War Department documents (Castetter and Bell 1942: 39) record that in 1862 the Pima provided 'over a million pounds of wheat, as well as pinole, chickens, green peas, green corn, pumpkins and melons, supplying the entire California column'.

The archaeological record of the Gila and Salt river basins reveals that the irrigation systems of their Hohokam ancestors were, if anything, even more extensive. Canal irrigation was, as Doolittle (2000: 369) puts it, 'a hallmark characteristic of the ancient Hohokam culture'. At their peak, around AD 700, Hohokam canals extended for hundreds of kilometres (see for instance Gumerman and Haury 1979, Crown 1991, Plog 1997). Indeed, they are, as Turney (1924:5, cited in Doolittle 2000: 369) puts it, 'the greatest exploit of ancient man in [North] America'. Within that great network of canals, the traces can be recognised of that same 'continuum of hydrostatic manipulations' noted ethnographically by Nabhan and others for the O'odham (see in particular Fish 2000).

Just as on the south coast of Peru, the controlled use of river floodwater continually replenished fields with mineral and organic nutrients. Castetter and Bell (1942: 172) observe that 'the fact that the Piman fields were under cultivation for hundreds of years, producing sustained yields without the addition of manures or other fertilizers, is evidence that considerable plant nutrients were carried by the waters used for irrigation in the Gila Basin'. So there was no need for the Pima to use fallow cycles or crop rotation to preserve fertility. McGee observed of their agriculture in 1898:

> The location of the temporale [floodwater field], like all other things human in the desert, is determined primarily by the occurrence of water, and secondarily by character of soil. A favourite situation is the seaward terminus of the arroya on whose middle reach the ranchería is located; thither flows the unevaporated residue of the winter storm floods, soaking the soil and fertilising it with a veneer of fine mud, just as the valley of the Nile is fertilised by the Nilotic flood; and even if the storm freshet fails on the surface, its waters penetrate the subsurface sands within reach of the roots. (McGee 1898: 367 cited in Nabhan 1986b: 49)

Nabhan also cites H.V. Clotts who studied O'odham water harvesting in 1915 and was greatly impressed by how precisely they placed their water control features. Clotts warned future Indian agents that they should not try to disrupt the traditional farming system:

> The Papago Indians, by several hundred years of desert experience, are thoroughly conversant with the conditions in their country, and with consummate judgement have so located their charcos and fields as to secure maximum results from the limited water available. We cannot go into their country with the idea of teaching them farming or irrigation as we find them in other parts of the country. Any attempt to introduce modern farming methods, as we understand them from elsewhere, would result in disaster. The most we should do for these people is first protect them in possession of the land which they have beneficially used for hundreds of years.
>
> (Clotts 1917: 42 cited in Nabhan 1986b: 54)

All these observations of agriculture in the Gila and Salt river basins are very evocative of the 'spate-agriculture' described in the previous chapter for the south coast of Peru today, and, indeed, make for apposite comparisons with the archaeological record of the lower Ica Valley. Moreover, the suite of arid-adapted domesticated plants cultivated in O'odham (and Hohokam) fields—maize, beans, pumpkins, squash and cotton—is more or less the same suite of cultivars that were and are grown on the south coast of Peru. The domesticated variety of chilli (*Capsicum annum*) was introduced to the Sonoran from the south by Kino (Castetter and Bell 1942), although the wild variety (var. *glabrissculum* or 'chilepín') had been gathered as part of the Sonoran diet for more than eight thousand years (Hodgson 2001). The only major cultivar of the prehistoric Sonoran not also grown on the south coast of Peru was tobacco (var. *Nicotiana* sp.). And yet here again our comparison proves abiding for, as we saw in Chapter 8, wild species of *Nicotiana* grow in the Usaca woodland fragment.

What then of the importance of *Prosopis*? The remarkable fact is that, despite their peerless skill in dryland agriculture and the frequent munificence of their produce, the Pima and their Hohokam ancestors were always reliant upon the wild plant foods of the Sonoran. And pre-eminent among these was the fruit of mesquite.

The importance of wild plant foods and mesquite

Gathered, wild plant foods remained vital to the Pima because of, as Hackenberg (1983: 162–3) puts it, 'the unpredictability of the yield of plant and animal foods from year to year' in an arid land of erratic river hydrology. Moreover, as we have seen, a remarkable one-fifth of the Sonoran Desert flora is edible.

The full extent of Piman reliance upon gathered, wild foods is set forth plainly by Castetter and Bell:

> The conclusion we are forced to draw from our own field studies, as well as historical accounts as to the ancient basis of Pima subsistence, is that, before white contact radically disturbed the economic pattern, the Pima cultivated crop in average years comprised about 50 to 60 per cent of the total food supply, wild plants and animals constituting the remainder; thus food gathering was absolutely necessary to supplement the inadequate cultivated crop. (Castetter and Bell 1942: 56–7)

As Castetter and Bell (1942: 56) note, their estimate thus confirms Russell (1908: 74) and Whittemore's (1893: 54) observations 'that mesquite beans were the principal article of Pima food'. Recall that these assessments apply to those pre-eminent agriculturalists of the Sonoran—the Akimel O'odham ('River People'). So they represent the absolute *minimum* of dependence upon wild foods amongst all the diverse peoples of the region. The Tohono O'odham ('Desert People'), for instance, relied upon wild foods for around three-quarters of their food supply (Castetter and Bell 1942, Hackenberg 1983). Indeed, the Tohono would exchange wild foods gathered in the greater Sonoran with the agricultural produce of their cousins, the Akimel, and Russell (1908) lists the rich content of this barter exchange.

Nabhan (1979: 252) observes that, in the mixed cropping practised in traditional Sonoran floodwater fields, rather than ploughing or weeding an entire field, 'farmers traditionally cleared only the vegetation surrounding each crop plant that would be in competition with it'. These fields therefore would carry a rich community of plants, which Nabhan (1979: 253) notes would be 'tolerated, protected or encouraged, rather than being eliminated, due to their cultural value as supplemental foods, fibres and medicines. Many of these volunteering species are opportunistic agrestals or plants which are adapted to open, disturbed field soils.'

A brief inventory of the major wild foods collected by the Pima includes the seeds, buds, fruits and joints of various cacti, chiefly saguaro fruit (*Carnegiea* sp.) and chollas and prickly pear fruit (*Opuntia* sp.); the seeds of ironwood (*Olneya* sp.), paloverde (*Parkinsonia* sp.), amaranth (*Amaranthus* sp.), saltbush (*Atriplex* sp.), lambsquarter (*Chenopodium* sp.), wild mustard (*Brassica* sp.—introduced), wild tepary bean (*Phaseolus* sp.), honey mesquite (*Prosopis glandulosa*), screwbean (*Prosopis pubescens*); the greens of lambsquarter, saltbush, cañaigre (*Rumex* sp.), amaranth, poverty-weed (*Monolepis* sp.) and pigweed (*Trianthema portulacastrum*); roots and bulbs of the sandfood (*Pholisma* sp.) and covena (*Dichelostemma* sp.); and yucca (*Yucca* sp.) fruit (for further details see, especially, Hodgson 2001).

It is revealing to compare this list with the general compilation of Sonoran and Peruvian south coast floras shown in Appendix 1. For of the nineteen edible parts, of plants of fourteen genera, that make up the major Piman wild foods listed, thirteen plants of eight genera *also* occur on the south coast of Peru, or 68 and 57 per cent respectively (excluding *Brassica* sp., which was introduced to the New World in historical times). Moreover, of the twelve agrestal 'volunteer' genera tolerated within traditional O'odham fields of 'definite historical use' (Nabhan 1979: 252), eight are also recorded in our plant collections made in the fields of Huerto Huamaní in the lower Ica Valley.

It is also clear from the archaeological data that wild plant foods were a major component of ancient Hohokam diets (see for instance Bohrer 1970, Gumerman and Haury 1979, Masse 1991). Wild plant foods, particularly *Prosopis* beans, *Amaranthus*, *Chenopodium* and *Boerhaavia* sp. seeds and cactus fruit remains have been found in significant amounts in Hohokam sites ever since the first excavations (see for instance Castetter and Bell 1942, Bohrer 1970, Fish 2000). Pollen samples from prehistoric agricultural contexts reveal a rich weedy flora alongside crops (Fish 1985, 2000). Fish (2000: 259) concludes that 'the

Hohokam likely followed ethnographic south-western practices of permitting desirable weeds to remain in fields and sometimes even scattering seeds to ensure a sufficient supply'. Masse (1991: 206) likewise notes that 'wild plant resources were critical for the Hohokam diet and for a variety of other purposes. Many edible plants were collected by the Hohokam, chief among them being mesquite pods, a major staple of the Hohokam diet.' Fish (2000: 258) goes on to speculate that 'destruction of leguminous trees, the most common desert species, was likely minimised in deference to the dietary importance of their abundant and nutritious beans'.

Indeed, as concerns mesquite, Castetter and Bell continue their assessment cited above of the importance of wild foods to the Akimel O'odham as follows:

> Our estimate is supported by Russell's statement made forty years ago [1908: 74] that mesquite constituted nearly, if not quite, the chief native article of Pima diet in primitive times; also by that of Whittemore that mesquite beans were the principal article of Pima food. Mesquite was a dependable crop and the Pima ate it in abundance every year. (Castetter and Bell 1942: 56)

When Kino first arrived among the Pima in 1678 he recorded that, having no cornmeal because of a recent flood, they offered him mesquite instead (Russell 1908: 38). Depending upon the season, many early visitors to *Papaguería* came away convinced that mesquite was the main food of the Pima (Hackenberg 1983). Baegert (cited in Russell 1908), for instance, writes in 1863 that 'the gathering of this fruit may be considered as the harvest of the native inhabitants'. Felger (1977: 155) usefully defines two categories of wild edible plants in arid lands: 'facultative crops', which depend upon short-term climatic conditions to thrive; and 'unfailing crops', which can always be relied upon, independent of short term climatic fluctuation. And he observes that mesquite was the single most important 'unfailing crop' of the Sonoran.

Prosopis is called *haas* by the Seri and *kui* by the O'odham and Pima peoples. According to Felger (1977: 155) these terms are impossible to analyse, that is, each is a single root in the language, and cannot be broken down into smaller component units of meaning. As such, they represent the 'simple' sub-type of 'primary name' in botanical nomenclature (Martin 2004: 211). Provided one can exclude an origin as loanwords from external sources, such word forms typically denote a relatively long established presence in the language, in which many would see implication of cultural antiquity and significance (Paul Heggarty personal communication). In view of our discussion of the complications in its taxonomy, it is noteworthy that those distinctions recognised by botanists between the species in the genus *Prosopis* are *not* made by native North American peoples (Felger and Moser 1985). Instead, a single monotypic folk genus is recognised among each tribe. This is quite contrary to what Felger (1977: 152) calls the 'axiomatic tendency in folk taxonomy to over classify economically important species where consistently recognisable differences can be identified'. So the latest trend in *Prosopis* taxonomy to reduce apparent over-classification under 'complexes' (Pasiecznik *et al.* 2001) is, effectively, a return to the original taxonomic treatment of native peoples.

Both Felger (1977) and Hodgson (2001) use the term 'tree of life' to describe the role mesquite played within the lives of the Pima 'River People'. Such was its importance that two months in the Akimel O'odham calendar are named by reference to the mesquite lifecycle: 'mesquite leaves moon' and 'mesquite flowers moon' (Rea 1997). Hodgson (2001: 184) observes that 'trees were once so abundant and fruited so prolifically that people could selectively collect the thickest, sweetest pods from the ground'. As huge quantities of pods ripened during a relatively short time, runners notified outlying districts and people converged on the mesquite groves. Evenings were spent there, 'singing, dancing, playing games and making love' (Felger 1977: 154)—the banquets first described by Cabeza de Vaca.

Gathered pods were stored in basketry granaries made of arrow-weed (*Pluchea* sp.) and willow (*Salix* sp.). These basket granaries were a distinctive feature of the roofs of O'odham houses, and provided sustenance until cultivated maize could be harvested (Felger 1977, Hodgson 2001). Russell (1908) described the process of 'pit-cooking' the pods by the River Pima. They placed the pods in pits lined with arrow-weed. This mass was then covered with earth and left to stand for three or four days, after which the pods were removed and dried for use or for storage in the basket bins on the tops of houses. Dried pods were pounded on a mortar into a fine flour. This was eaten as pinole or used to prepare fermented, beer-like drinks and cakes and breads (Hodgson 2001). Early travellers in *Papaguería* saw enormous conical cakes of up to 60 pounds each, which were stored in grass-lined pits (Felger 1977: 162).

Beyond their significance to the Pima agriculturalists, mesquite pods were the 'staple of life' to the Mohave, Kamia, Maricopa, Quechan, Cocopa, Cahuilla, Kumeyaay, Yaqui, Seri and Eudeve of the Greater Sonoran (Felger and Moser 1985, Hodgson 2001). Many of these south-western desert peoples had clans or lineages named for mesquite, which had totemic significance (Felger 1977). Where mesquite grew was often a determining factor in the choice of settlement sites and its pods were an important item of barter between peoples, particularly at its geographic limits (Hodgson 2001: 179). It was also used for a variety of medicinal purposes, usually in the form of a tea prepared with leaves, bark or sap. Pounded mesquite roots were used to prepare strong cordage of many kinds. Black dyes were prepared from bark and sap was used for face paints and decorating pottery and baskets. And of course mesquite wood served for weapons, agricultural and fishing tools, and house posts and beams, and provided an important source of fuel (Felger 1977, Felger and Moser 1985). Felger and Moser conclude a review of more than four hundred 'ethno-species' of Sonoran desert flora with:

> Mesquite was the single most important resource to the diverse peoples of the arid and semi-arid regions of southwestern North America . . . used as a primary resource for food, fuel, shelter, weapons, tools, fibre and medicine. Every part of the tree was used. Its use was ubiquitous amongst agriculturists and nomadic hunter-gatherers. (Felger and Moser 1985: 151)

Yet the importance of mesquite extended beyond its value as a human resource. The agriculturists of the Sonoran such as the Akimel O'odham would leave large *Prosopis* trees amid their fields and in dense hedgerows about them (Castetter and Bell 1941, Rea 1981).

Leaf litter from these trees was dug into the soil around their crops (Nabhan 1985). In 1897 the Indian agent to the O'odham, McGee (cited in Nabhan 1986b: 50), observed that 'fields are often 5–10 acres in extent; associated with them are temporary shelters or bowers erected around mesquite trees in the fields or near their living fences'. Sonoran farmers were, it seems, very well aware of those effects of *Prosopis* upon soil quality and moisture that we reviewed in Chapter 8. Rea (1981, 1983, 1997) records how Pima field edges and hedgerows consisted of herbaceous and woody plants which were selectively spared in clearing so that they might furnish firewood and other resources, while harbouring a supply of small game. And of the ancient Hohokam, Fish writes that:

> Numerous combinations of happenstance and design are embodied by the array of noncultigens now thought to have been productively enhanced or concentrated in anthropogenic vegetation by the Hohokam. Among this group are plants such as mesquite that may have been differentially spared in field clearing, become dense in hedgerows, thrived on canal seepage, or been tended and selectively harvested in adjacent natural settings. (Fish 2000: 260)

Yet mesquite was not considered holy or venerated by the peoples of the Sonoran despite, or rather, *because* of, its all-pervading importance in their lives. For it was ubiquitous in the desert environment and, unlike cultivated crops, required no human intervention for virtually unfailing provision of fruit and material.

Implications of a Sonoran Ethnoecological Analogy

How then might we summarise the implications of this historical Sonoran analogy for the ancient south coast of Peru? These are twofold.

Firstly, what we have seen of Akimel O'odham subsistence sharpens our awareness and appreciation of the continued importance of gathered wild foods to agriculturalists. Archaeology's long concern with tracing how hunter-gatherers gradually 'evolved' into agriculturalists is understandable enough, for of course civilisation itself was founded upon the changes in food production that come with plant and animal domestication. Yet, too often still, it comes at the cost of a proper accounting of how important wild foods continued to be. This is true everywhere, but nowhere more so than in the drylands of the New World.

For here a much higher proportion of the total flora is edible than in more lush ecologies. The evolutionary origins of this would seem plain: with less vegetation comes less need to deter the attentions of voracious herbivores through mechanisms of toxicity. On the contrary, there is all the more need to entice seed dispersal by relatively fewer fauna. Along with this comes relatively fewer insect pests and, indeed, competition for human agricultural efforts. Ever since Lathrap (1970) there has been a widely held conviction that the origins of plant domestication in the New World lie in its moist tropical lowlands. And yet in the Andes at least the first truly agricultural societies, and thus the origins of complex society itself, lay along the fertile floodplains of the rivers that cross their desert coast. Many of the most important New World domesticates such as squash, beans, cotton and even maize turn out to be well-adapted to those drylands. But for all their fertility these river systems are relatively unpredictable. Thus here, exactly as we have seen in the ethnoecology of the North American south-west, there was always a continued reliance upon gathered wild foods.

The archaeology of the Tehuacán Valley caves, at Puebla, in the semi-arid, central Mexican highlands provides an excellent case in point. Excavations there yielded long sequences of a host of important domesticated plant remains. Maize remains from Tehuacán famously became central to the story of domestication of this pre-eminent food crop of the Americas (see for instance Flannery 1968, 1973, Smith 1995). And yet, amid the hubbub over Tehuacán's domesticated plants, what often goes unnoticed is that analyses of its human coprolites — obviously direct evidence of human diet — reveal that 'the *second most* important dietary component . . . in *all* cultural phases after 3500 BC and no doubt in earlier phases too' (Callen 1969: 239, emphasis added, and see also Smith 1967: 241) was mesquite pods.

Quite simply, neither in the plant remains data from Tehuacán, nor in *any* other archaeobotanical data set from arid and semi-arid America, including the south coast of Peru, is there ever *any* evidence of any eventual replacement by domesticated plant foods of wild plant resources, chief among which was the fruit of *Prosopis*. In the case of the Akimel O'odham and the Hohokam — those quintessential agriculturalists and builders of the largest canal system in North America — gathered wild foods accounted for about *half* of the total overall diet. Thus judicious application of a Sonoran ethnoecological analogy — in full agreement with the archaeological data presented here for the lower Ica Valley, and indeed, with all other archaeobotanical data from the region — argues for a considerable change in emphasis for the importance of gathered wild plant resources (and in particular *Prosopis*) to the ancient agriculturalists of the south coast of Peru.

The second implication of our analogy unfolds from the more recent history of *Papaguería*. For the story of the Pima through the nineteenth century is a desperate one of decline and the unravelling of tribal society, initiated by Apache hostilities, and then brought to its nadir by the inexorable pressure of European settlement. Russell (1908) relates how, too proud to beg or steal, many Pima simply chose to starve to death, as scarce water resources were appropriated by white settlements upstream. By 1887, a decade after Russell lived among the Pima, the Indian Agent Howard was reporting that:

> The county is fast filling up with cattlemen (whites), and now at almost every spring or well some white man has a herd of cattle, and the inevitable result follows, the Indian is forced to leave and the 'superior race' usually enforces such an order . . . I have travelled one hundred miles over a desert to secure an Indian the privilege of taking water from a well that he had dug himself. The mesquite wood is rapidly being exhausted, being cut to supply mining camps and towns, thus depriving them of mesquite beans, which have always been one of their principal articles of food.
>
> (Howard 1887: 6, cited in Nabhan 1986b: 47)

We have already seen the dramatic changes wrought by the introduction of vast numbers of cattle on the form of mesquite, now widely recognised as an invasive shrubby tree throughout the North American south-west.

For Pima agriculture an almost complete collapse was precipitated by extreme climatic perturbations that began in 1868 with disastrous floods that wiped out villages and entire canal systems and caused river down-cutting. This was followed by the onset of the driest conditions in six hundred years in the Gila watershed (Hackenberg 1983). Agent Grossman (cited in Hackenberg 1983: 170) reported that 'by 1870 less than 3,000 acres (20 per cent of the area farmed in 1859) were cultivated by the Pima'. In *Papaguería* such was the severity of the collapse that eventually even the 'unfailing crop' of mesquite failed. By 1873 Agent Stout (cited in Hackenberg 1983: 171) recorded that 'the mesquite trees above and below the Casa Blanca district had been consumed as fuel by two steam flour mills operated during the boom years'. The Casa Blanca floodplain, a breadbasket in former times and the provider of bumper crops merely a decade earlier, was abandoned and became a 'dry barren waste . . . The crop of *mesquit* beans . . . has been an entire failure.'

The soils of *Papaguería*, just like those of other arid regions that require irrigation for agriculture, were vulnerable to the problems of salt encrustation (Castetter and Bell 1942: 122–3). In the 1920s one of the pioneers of geomorphology, Kirk Bryan, published seminal investigations as to the causes and effects of landscape degradation that he had been witnessing in the Gila Basin ever since the 1870s. Bryan described the phenomenon of 'arroyo cutting', which had catastrophic consequences for the landscape and for irrigation and floodwater farming (Nabhan 1986b). As Hackenberg (1983: 162) explains, 'living streams with narrow channels, ideal for irrigation with primitive tools, became intermittent flood channels with crumbling and widening banks — impossible to control'. Arroyo cutting in the south-west has subsequently received considerable attention in geomorphology (see for instance Cooke and Reeves 1976, Graf 2002), and it involves a complex interplay between what Cooke *et al.* (1993: 160) term 'self-enhancing feedback mechanisms' of human-induced and climatic effects. Yet its origins lie in the gradual removal of riparian vegetation from the river floodplain, particularly the deep-rooted genus *Prosopis*. We have already seen the geomorphological record for the same process at play in the basins of the lower Ica Valley and we return to it again in our interpretations in the next chapter. But it will be salutary for our purposes to recall that in the Sonoran drylands, the *agricultural* collapse of the Akimel O'odham 'River People', while precipitated by climatic perturbation, was caused primarily by the *cultural* changes and ecological degradation that followed Apache and Anglo-Hispanic incursions into the riparian basins of the *Papaguería*. Moreover, precisely such a fatal combination of human-induced environmental impacts in the form of salinisation and river entrenchment, cultural changes and extreme climatic perturbations of floods and droughts has been put forth as an explanation for the collapse of the ancient Hohokam (see for instance Redman 1999: 148–56) — 'those who have gone', as the Pima called them.

10. Putting the Tree Back into the Landscape

This book began with the archaeology of the Ullujaya and Samaca basins of the lower Ica Valley on the south coast of Peru. As we have seen, vast areas of these basins are today depopulated and largely bereft of cultivation, and yet their archaeological remains attest to substantial pre-Hispanic populations. The lower Ica Valley thus presents a *prima facie* case for dramatically changed ecological and landscape conditions. The archaeological investigations described here were therefore undertaken to answer the following questions. Were these basins ever significantly more productive and vegetated landscapes? If so, when and how did change take place, and why? And how did these ecological and landscape changes correlate with cultural ones?

The second part of the book conducted a thorough review of the botanical and agroforestry literature, together with our own observations, on the ecological *keystone* species of the region, the huarango—a tree of the genus *Prosopis*—to show how important a role this genus plays in the desert ecosystem of the south coast of Peru. It also reviewed references to the huarango in the wider archaeological literature for the south coast and traced the history of riparian woodland deforestation here during more recent times. Finally, it attempted to define and justify a limited analogy with the rich ethnoecological record of the Sonoran Desert.

This twofold structure reflects the design that underlies the research presented here: (1) to gather as multi-proxy an archaeological dataset as practicable; and (2) to analyse that dataset against a thorough understanding of the physical landscape of the south coast—both its riparian and agricultural ecologies in general, and its most important individual component, the genus *Prosopis*. This concluding chapter will seek to achieve a synthesis between these two parts to offer answers to those aforementioned questions posed by today's austere landscape of the lower Ica Valley. In so doing, it will propose a model for geomorphological, ecological

Chapterhead: Detail of Nasca embroidered textile showing a monkey carrying beans and root crops (drawing courtesy of Ann Peters).

and land-use changes through time for the basins of the lower Ica Valley. It will also aim to relate this model to cultural trajectories.

This is a novel approach to the archaeology of the south coast of Peru, for the huarango rarely achieves footnote status in the archaeological literature, and then almost invariably in reference to its use as a construction material. The riparian dry forests of the south coast of Peru are almost gone. And the implications for the region's landscape can only be appreciated in the context of the biological information presented here on *Prosopis* and on its importance in modifying desert environmental extremes and in maintaining the complexity of its sensitive ecosystem, humans included. Yet, this has not been incorporated into archaeological interpretations of the south coast, which remain coloured by a twenty-first-century landscape of lowered water tables, the wide fields of agro-industry, degraded alkali and saline soils, shifting dunes and *monte* scrub. The physical landscape of the south coast of Peru is not an unchanging background canvas, upon which to elaborate our archaeological interpretations.

This attempt to synthesise the archaeological record with ecological data takes as its premise that if we wish to understand properly the impact humans have on their environment, then we are perforce required to understand the components of that environment: the perspective of 'historical ecology', advocated by Balée (1994), among others. We are, as Hodgson simply puts it, 'part of the natural ecosystem, whether we like it or not' (2001: 2). Such a premise does *not* necessarily make our interpretations environmentally deterministic. On the contrary, it allows for more informed discrimination between human agency and environmental response. For answering the questions posed by this research requires proper consideration of the actions of human beings. The myth of the 'ecologically noble savage' (Lentz 2000: 2), living within an effectively static ecological landscape, only intermittently impacted by large magnitude catastrophic climatic events, continues to pervade our south coast archaeological interpretations. It is contradicted by the evidence from the lower Ica Valley case study presented here.

No less interestingly, however, this case-study also appears to record correlations between changes in society and degrees of human ecological impact. This may allow us to begin to reconcile the apparent contradictions between the popularly held view that New World peoples preserved the wilderness of the Americas—a view lent some substance by detailed contemporary anthropologies of Amazonia and the ethnohistory of the Andes and other parts of the New World—and much archaeological evidence, including that of the lower Ica Valley. Achieving this reconciliation will require us to distinguish those particular ecological and cultural circumstances in which significant human impacts occurred.

Was the Lower Ica Valley A Productive Landscape?

This first question seems almost rhetorical in the light of the many relict tree trunks visible today across the barren expanses of the Ullujaya and Samaca basins (see Cook 1999: 65).

Almost four hundred of these *in situ*, relict huarango tree trunks have been surveyed, stretching over the barren terraces of these basins (see Figure 5.1). Many are very far from the current vegetated river floodplain and some lie high above the current groundwater level. Yet, as we have seen, this tree has a very deep root system and larger isolated trees are occasionally to be seen growing high upon relict terraces, dunes or even rock outcrops, well above and beyond the extent of other riparian vegetation. The large number, local groupings and varied sizes of the relict trunks recorded make it unlikely that they represent, *in toto*, the historical occurrence of only very deep-rooted, isolated individuals. Still, the answer that these conspicuous macrofossils proffer to whether these relict terraces were once a productive, vegetated landscape is not obvious without some further contextual and taphonomic consideration.

Many other *Prosopis* fossils were recorded across Samaca and Ullujaya. These include *in situ* roots and desiccated huarango macrofossils including tree litter (*poña*), seeds, and masticated pod fragments in human coprolites, identified from the flotation of excavated archaeological contexts. Heavy, entomophilous *Prosopis* pollen was identified in extractions from certain of these contexts. Indeed, huarango macro- and microfossils were the single common denominator of the lower Ica Valley excavations. Some huarango trunks seen amid the upturned contexts of the looted cemeteries of the Ullujaya Basin are of far larger proportions than those seen in the scrub forest remnants of the lower Ica Valley today. And, on a truly basin-wide scale, the edges of these duracrete horizons themselves are often seen to be composed of dense, extremely fragile, calcium carbonate pseudomorphs of distinctive *poña* tree litter (see Figure 5.2).

Certainly, all these data may represent trees growing at different times. Yet, since the natural lifespan of the huarango exceeds a millennium, together these fossils are relicts of vegetation covering deep and overlapping time periods. Indeed, the dimensions of some of these relict trunks indicate that they were alive for many hundreds of years, encompassing entire cultural periods. Concerning the huarango, we are in what Annales School historians call the *longue durée*. Or, looked at another way, in the sense of their implication for ecological change, huarango fossils, in effect, 'compress time'. So taken together these many, highly wind-abraded, relict tree trunks and numerous other *Prosopis* fossils and pseudomorphs across these barren river terraces strongly suggest that they were once vegetated with more than isolated trees.

Furthermore, as we have also seen, above groundwater levels, desiccated organic remains enjoy remarkable preservation in these hyperarid conditions, and many other plant macro- and microfossil assemblages were extracted and identified from the excavation contexts of these basins. Many of these were from midden contexts whose anthropogenic assemblages do not necessarily perfectly mirror the ecology of their immediate surroundings. Yet specific elements—such as the quantities of desiccated *poña* in the excavations of midden mound 23 on Samaca H-13—certainly do represent local vegetation cover. These, and the plant data from the contexts of ancient, buried land surfaces such as Test Pits 1, 1/030 and 1/031 on Samaca H-13, are relevant to measuring the degree and extent of vegetation change across the Samaca and Ullujaya basins. And these included many plants from the riparian dry forest ecosystem, agricultural and disturbed areas, and even of obligate wetland status.

Geomorphological data corroborate the picture of landscape change presented by archaeobotanical remains. The western edge of the current river floodplain in both the Ullujaya and Samaca basins is delineated by a steep embankment incised by the river at some point in the past. We examined a deep profile of this embankment (Section 1/013) because it represents the terrace history prior to the deposition of the archaeological remains on its surface. Analyses of this section strongly suggest a very different environment of sediment deposition in those deeper time contexts, both from its upper layer proximate to archaeological remains, and indeed from those that persist today atop these terraces. Since a relict canal system is recorded across the surface of these terraces, this geomorphological distinction can be interpreted quite straightforwardly as the imposition by humans of a regime of control, agriculture and pedogenesis, upon the river floodplain and its underlying history of high-energy episodic clastic sediment deposition.

Preserved surfaces dating to archaeological time periods are scarce across these basins owing to the effects of wind deflation. Yet they are encountered buried and sealed beneath the deposits of the climbing dune anchored along the western flank of the Samaca Basin by its unimodal wind regime. And micromorphological analysis has demonstrated the occurrence of ancient buried organic *soils* in the contexts beneath these dune deposits.

These different contexts, and the different associations in which plant fossils occur, all have further implications for interpretations of how and why change occurred in the basins of the lower Ica Valley, to which we will return shortly. But all these data demonstrate quite unequivocally that the past landscape of Ullujaya and Samaca was quite different from its present state of windswept desolation. The measure of the extent of this change is most clearly illustrated by Figure 4.5A: a view of the context of Test Pit 1 on Samaca H-13 in the midst of a landscape devoid of any vegetation, half a kilometre distant from, and some five metres above, the edge of today's vegetated, riparian Río Ica floodplain. Among the buried soils, occasional roots and other plant macro- and microfossil data that this excavation revealed was the plainest and most poignant evidence of landscape change: a remarkably preserved footprint in once moist silt, buried and preserved beneath its covering of dune.

When Was It A Productive Landscape?

Archaeology provides a means of dating the processes of landscape change in the lower Ica Valley. Many hundreds of pottery sherds covering time periods from the Early through to the Middle Horizon were recorded in our survey and excavation of the Samaca and Ullujaya contexts. Although aeolian deflation has destroyed most of the original stratigraphy of the exposed relict terraces of Ullujaya and Samaca, it has also, in effect, excavated vast expanses to leave heavier archaeological materials scattered in multi-period palimpsests upon today's land surface. Our first observation from the numerous archaeological remains recorded over the expanses of the relict terraces of H-13 in Samaca and G8/9 in Ullujaya is the conspicuous absence of almost any material on them from the later periods of prehistory, despite the presence of the two large Late Intermediate sites (H-8 and H-9) in the lower Samaca Basin. So we conclude that these were abandoned landscapes *prior* to those periods. Further archaeological data helped refine that conclusion.

The profound effect that duracreted horizons have upon the extant form of the H-13 and G8/9 terrace surfaces, and the effects of aeolian deflation of this surface, have created a classic inversion of relief, whereby features such as the canals that were once cut into the land surface are preserved by their duracrete enrichment to stand today above the deflated surrounding landscape (see Figure 3.10). The precise dating of features such as canals that were in use over considerable periods of time is acknowledged to be problematic. Yet the evidence strongly suggests that these relict canal fragments were once part of a contemporary system, which can be dated accurately, but not precisely, by artefact data to a *terminus ante quem* at the end of the Early Nasca Period. Those data included ceramic finds in excavations of the canal courses themselves, survey data allowing extant fragments of canals to be matched together, and also instances of the construction of Late Nasca platforms over their courses. The question of when this system was first built is, of course, even more difficult to answer. But calcrete concretion beneath the courses of relict primary canals to a depth of more than three metres is evidence at least that these were in operation, prior to their abandonment, for a very long period of time (and see Hesse and Baade 2008).

The occurrence of the aforementioned relict tree trunks across the terraces of the lower Ica Valley is clearly associated with areas of duracrete exposed by wind deflation (see for instance Figure 10.2 below). The great majority were surveyed in a tight range of altitudes between 220.0 and 220.5 m a.s.l.—corresponding to those surfaces. Sherds from Early Horizon Ocucaje Phases through to the Late Nasca Period, covering more than a millennium of time-depth, were encountered in mixed scatters upon these deflated duracrete surfaces. The relict trunks themselves show the effects of long wind abrasion. In the hyperarid conditions of the south coast huarango wood can be preserved over centuries, for, as we have seen, it is very dense and hard. Yet the extant forms of these relict trunks are quite distinct from the huarango posts (*horcones*) in the Late Intermediate site of H-8, exposed to the same wind regime, but which exhibit far fewer wind erosion effects (see Figure 6.2C). On various bases then, these relict trunks can be interpreted as the remains of trees that met their demise at some time prior to the Late Intermediate Period.

Finally, the predominant mound in the H-13 landscape, mound 23, dates to the Middle Horizon. While its upper contexts were of a Middle Horizon midden, below these, at depth, its character—with tree throws and fine sands full of desiccated *poña*—established it to be a relict nabkha, formed by wind deposition beneath the canopy of a large tree. The extant form of the mound standing amid its surrounding deflated duracreted landscape, covered with mixed pottery sherds from earlier epochs, is a consequence of its later age, the binding effects of nabkha formation, and the sheer density of heavy Middle Horizon ceramic and lithic midden materials on its surface.

Flotations of the mound 23 midden contexts yielded well-preserved desiccated plant assemblages which included coca seeds together with remains of the fruit trees pacay and guava. Coca leaf, the useful part of the plant, first becomes visible in the south coast archaeobotanical record from Late Nasca Phases to the Middle Horizon. The presence of coca seeds in this conjunction of plant remains may be noteworthy because historically, and until recently, a specific variety of the plant (*Erythroxylum novogranatense* var. *truxillense*) was grown on the Peruvian coast—always under shade trees of pacay and guava. Be that as it may, these archaeobotanical remains suggest dramatically altered ecological conditions because neither coca nor the large, simple-leafed fruit trees of pacay and guava can persist anywhere today in the wind regime of this part of the lower Ica Valley.

Together, these data show that the now desolate Samaca H-13 and Ullujaya G8/9 terraces were vegetated until the Middle Horizon Period, but that they became denuded and abandoned prior to the Late Intermediate Period. Still closer examination of these data offers important clues to the answer of the third question posed: how did this change occur over time?

How did Change Occur?

Punctuated equilibrium

A characteristic of Andean archaeological interpretation is its focus upon catastrophic events in the form of El Niño flood and/or La Niña drought events (alias the Southern Oscillation Index, or 'ENSO'). The history of these events has naturally become a matter of great interest and the subject of studies using various datasets. Some of those studies have provided data that have been set alongside the archaeological record to offer insights into cultural change evident in that record. Ice cores, for instance, taken from the Quelccaya ice cap on Mt Ausangate, near Cuzco (Thompson *et al.* 1985), have been used to postulate correlations of major climatic perturbations with archaeological interpretations of a so-called 'punctuated equilibrium' in culture change at various places along the Peruvian coast (see for instance Moseley 1992, Shimada *et al.* 1991, Shimada 1994, Silverman and Proulx 2002, but especially Silverman 2002: 23–5 for the south coast). Why this model of 'punctuated equilibrium' has become so important to archaeological interpretation is reflected by some of the data from the lower Ica Valley context that we have seen here.

For, as we have seen, a thick fluvial layer, 'S.U. 19' in the excavation of mound 43, Samaca H-13 (see Figure 4.8), is one of several remaining fragments of a sheet flood deposit—*yapana*—up to 60 centimetres deep, which once covered much of the area of a second relict river terrace lying just below the main area of H-13. Fluvial deposits cannot per se be taken as indicators of past El Niño events, although in Chapters 2 and 4 arguments have been advanced, based upon historical data and our observations in the lower Ica Valley during the 1997/8 El Niño event, to justify precisely such an association in the specific case of the S.U. 19 layer. The significance of S.U. 19 lies in both its position in the landscape — some 6.5 metres above today's Río Ica thalweg — and its approximate dating: this flood layer directly caps midden contexts containing Nasca 5 pottery sherds.

The effects of any El Niño event vary widely from one coastal valley to the next. On the south coast the magnitude of floods they may cause derive from distant rainfall on the Andean foothills far to the west of the coastal floodplains themselves. As we have seen, the 1997/8 El Niño event was particularly severe in the Ica Valley. It flooded the city of Ica to a depth of more than 2 metres, and further downstream in the Samaca Basin destroyed much of the substantial Late Intermediate archaeological site of 'H-9' (Figure 2.6). This was therefore the greatest flood in the lower Ica Valley for at least the past millennium.

Yet this flood appears a relatively minor affair, in its spatial effects upon the upper Samaca Basin, in comparison with the event that deposited S.U. 19. The surveyed altitudes of preserved fragments of S.U. 19 conservatively imply a sheet flood some 3.5 metres higher than the maximum river level during the 1997/8 El Niño, across the equivalent profile in the Samaca Basin. This is illustrated in Figure 10.1, which uses a digital elevation model (DEM) of the basin's current topography to project a theoretical sheet flood at the level of the S.U. 19 deposit. Indeed, there are some striking apparent correlations between the projected extents of the S.U. 19 event and the extant form of archaeological and landscape features of Samaca H-13.

The original primary canal operating across the Samaca and Ullujaya basins during the Early Nasca Period is today preserved in two fragments, Features 40 and 34, separated by the incursion of the river floodplain, which coincides precisely with the simulated incursion of the S.U. 19 flood into H-13 (Figures 10.1 and 3.11D). A secondary relict canal, Feature 33, running alongside mound 43, was completely submerged by this flood event. As we have seen, the edges of the relict Ullujaya and Samaca terraces are defined by a 5 metre deep embankment: the result of river down-cutting. And the steepest and sharpest part of that embankment edge on H-13 today is the one that occurs along the edge parallel to the river's direction where Section 1/013 was recorded. It would be here that the erosive force of the river would have been at its strongest during the postulated flood. Moreover, downstream from this embankment edge there are a series of 2 metre high, relict braided channel banks composed of very large river cobbles deposited by the river in spate (Feature 18 on Figure 10.1).

This all stands as evidence of a major flood event occurring at some time towards the end of the Early Intermediate Period, which spread a 60 centimetre deep horizon of *yapana* across the Samaca Basin, and caused the river to cut down into its floodplain by some 5 metres. It had catastrophic effects upon the Early Nasca canal system of H-13, which can still be noted in its extant form. So our research records, for the lower Ica Valley, those wider-scale observations of the likely catastrophic effects major El Niño events have had along the coast of Peru.

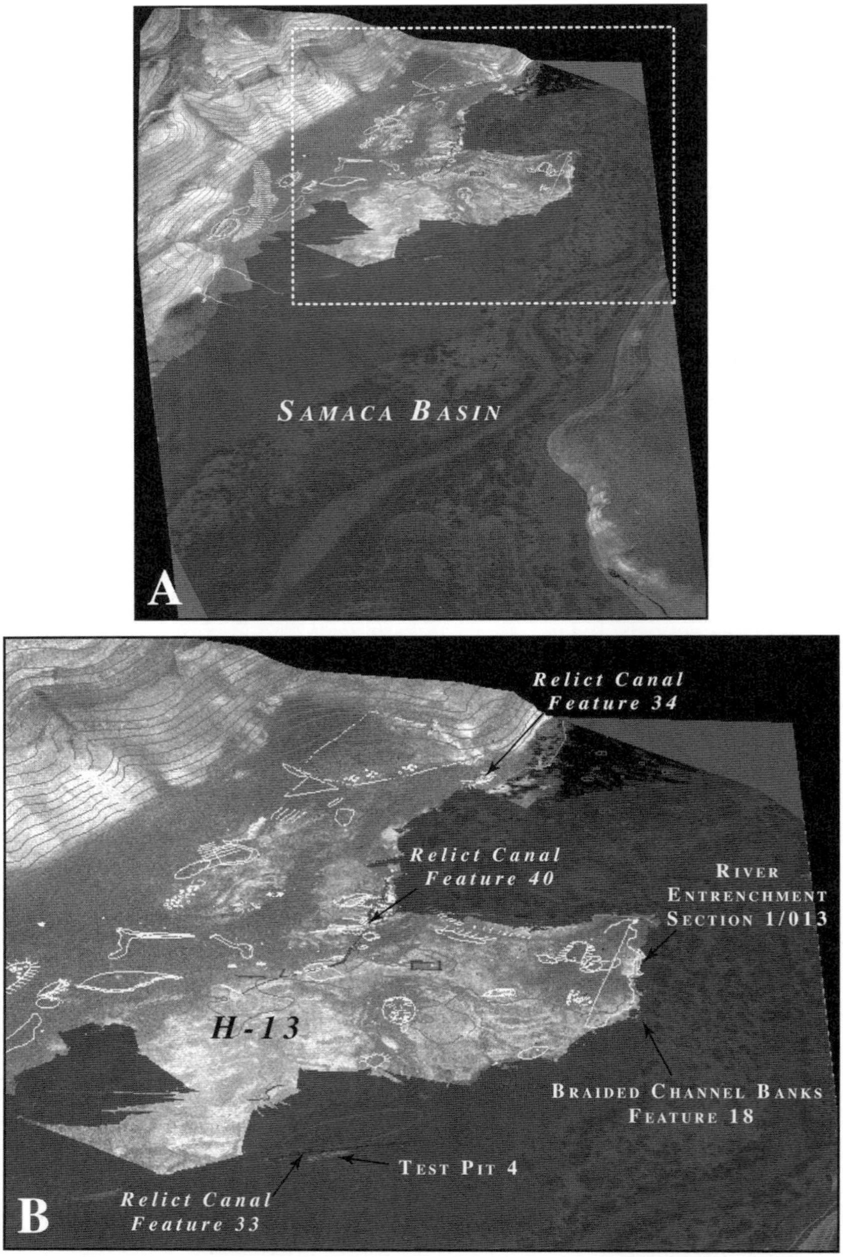

A Isometric view north of Samaca Basin DEM simulating the S.U. 19 flood event.

B Inset detail of A with archaeological and geomorphological features affected or caused by the S.U. 19 flood event marked.

Figure 10.1. A digital elevation model recreation of the ancient S.U. 19 flood event in the Samaca Basin

And yet it may be simplistic merely to posit Figure 10.1 as the answer to the question of how change occurred in these basins. For the S.U. 19 event shown has, of course, been projected on to the Samaca Basin's existing topography. Conceivably, this conflates the effects of several high-energy flood events. More certainly however, it renders doubtful the topographical basis for the comparison between the relative magnitudes of the 1997/8 El Niño and S.U. 19 flood events. Indeed, as we will see shortly, there is strong evidence that the ancient course of the Río Ica in these basins is not the same as it is today. A more satisfying explanation of their landscape change will thus require consideration of two related factors: riparian vegetation changes and river down-cutting.

Riparian vegetation

Cooke *et al.* observe that:

> It is a mistake to assume that because riparian vegetation is generally less dense in deserts than elsewhere, it is of no consequence. In fact phreatophytes . . . which draw their sustenance from groundwater at depth—can significantly influence channel geometry by increasing bank resistance to erosion, inducing deposition and increasing roughness. (Cooke et al. 1993: 153)

The pre-eminent native phreatophyte of arid American riparian ecosystems is the genus *Prosopis*, which has one of the deepest and most laterally extensive root systems of any tree in any environment. Huarango roots are typically two to three times the diameter of the tree's crown, access water tables up to 25 metres deep and have been recorded at well over 60 metres in length. This root architecture 'underpins' floodplain and river meanders, providing the edaphic conditions for a rich riverbank assemblage of other species. The combined, heterogeneous root architecture and vegetation cover of this riparian plant association makes for a robust, erosion-resistant system.

The effect of changes in the density of riparian vegetation on channel form and process has been the subject of studies by William Graf (2002) on the drainage of the Gila River, a North American arid land river whose hydrology and ecology are, in many important respects, analogous to those of the Río Ica. Graf's studies on the Gila show how channel width decreases, and channel sinuosity increases, with increasing phreatophyte density, because of the effects of their root systems. The corollary of these influences upon channel form is increased overbank discharge during flood events, giving rise to standing flood deposits like those represented by S.U. 19.

The apparently much greater extent of the S.U. 19 flood shown in Figure 10.1 compared with that of the 1997/8 El Niño event may therefore be a reflection not so much of differences in river flow between the two events, but rather of a much greater density of riparian vegetation in the floodplain when the S.U. 19 event occurred. Given the sheer magnitude of the 1997/8 event—demonstrably the largest for the past millennium—this would seem to be a rather likely explanation for the some of the apparent differences in magnitude between these events. Moreover, the other factor of topographic change, intimately related to riparian vegetation cover, is river down-cutting.

River down-cutting

Plant macrofossils enjoyed excellent preservation in the deposits beneath S.U. 19, making it very likely that this was a rare, or perhaps unique, inundation at this point in the landscape of the Samaca Basin. Indeed, it is difficult to see why the Early Nasca inhabitants would have gone to the trouble of constructing canal 33 perpendicular to the river direction within the usual, active river floodplain. The Río Ica is therefore unlikely to have significantly altered its course laterally in the Samaca Basin since the S.U. 19 event. That it has likely entrenched downwards, however, by at least some five metres, is evidenced by the aforementioned terrace embankment described as Section 1/013.

Moreover, there is even stronger evidence for the extent of river down-cutting in the Ullujaya Basin, where the edge of the G-8/9 terrace is also marked by a steep incision. And, in this wider basin, it would seem that as well as down-cutting, the river has also altered its course laterally. For an original thalweg can still be traced today, high up on the surface of relict terrace G-8/9 (Figure 10.2). We cannot be certain precisely when that lateral alteration took place. Yet, since the evidence would seem to tie the S.U. 19 event to river down-cutting in the Samaca Basin at some time after the Early Nasca Period, at least one straightforward explanation would have the same event as being responsible for both the river's lateral alteration in the Ullujaya Basin and its down-cutting in both basins. In any case, down-cutting by the river will, by definition, diminish its floodplain area, changing the relationship between river flood volume and the extent of a resulting sheet flood, and thus rendering unalike the bases of the comparison between the S.U. 19 and the 1997/8 events.

In a seminal study of north coast irrigation systems, Moseley *et al.* (1983) noted precisely such river down-cutting as the likely cause of a progressive abandonment of canal systems in the Moche Valley. To maintain a given area under canal irrigation following down-cutting, canal intakes have to be extended further and further upstream. Water loss in unlined canals exposed to high evaporation sets a limit on how far extensions can be taken, thus eventually causing abandonment of the canal system. Moseley *et al.* postulated tectonic uplift as the agent prompting river entrenchment, based upon the occasionally uphill course followed by the famous Late Intermediate Chicama–Moche inter-valley canal. Further investigations, however, have shown that this canal system never actually carried water along its whole length and its sometime uphill course has since been interpreted as engineering failure rather than subsequent tectonic uplift (Pozorski and Pozorski 1982, 2003a). Furthermore, there is little geomorphological evidence that the Andean north coast has experienced significant uplift during archaeological time periods (Cooke *et al.* 1993, Wells 1990, Wells and Noller 1999). Indeed, Moseley *et al.* (1983: 323) explicitly recognise another possible explanation, noting that 'in theory, if such land supported a more erosion-resistant vegetation cover when under irrigation than when left abandoned, then a corollary of highland irrigation collapse could be "deforestation" and consequent erosion that could exacerbate river down cutting, leading to intake stranding of the coastal canal systems'. We have explored the 'erosion resistance' of *Prosopis* in some detail here.

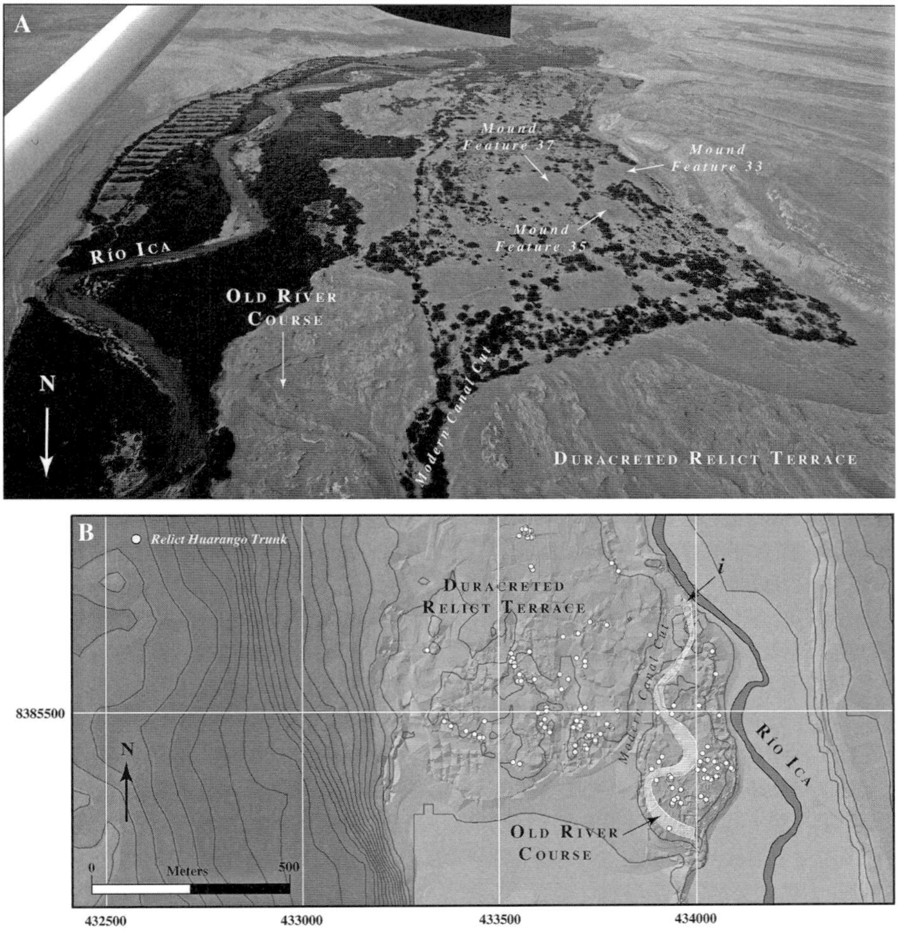

A Aerial photograph of the Ullujaya Basin showing an old river course high on the duracreted surface of relict terrace G-8/9. A modern canal cut from attempts to grow cotton here in the twentieth century lies in the foreground and various archaeological features are also indicated.

B Digital elevation model from a survey of the same area with the old river course marked, together with relict huarango trunks.

C The old river course visible in section at the edge of relict terrace G-8/9 at i. on B.

Figure 10.2. The ancient river course in the Ullujaya Basin

Moreover, as we have seen, the geomorphologist Kirk Bryan described the rapid degradation in the Gila River Basin in the 1920s through the phenomenon of 'arroyo cutting'. This had catastrophic consequences for the landscape and for irrigation and floodwater farming in the region. Hackenberg summarises the process:

> The major environmental damage occurs through loss of vegetation whose root structures formerly held the banks of streams and rivers in place. Removal of these plants causes the rapid runoff following heavy rains to widen the channels with breathtaking speed. The runoff velocity itself is accelerated by denuding of vegetation on the watershed resulting from aridity and erosion. Widened channels are cut deeper by subsequent rapid runoff, and the result is an arroyo, a deep trench cut to a depth of 50 feet or more into the terrain. These trenches in turn lower the groundwater level by draining soil moisture from the adjoining terrain. (Hackenberg 1983: 162)

The causes of arroyo cutting—a complex interplay between 'self-enhancing feedback mechanisms' Cooke *et al.* (1993: 160) of human-induced and climatic effects—have subsequently received considerable attention (Cooke and Reeves 1976, Graf 2002, Cooke *et al.* 1993). I suggest that, analogous to the North American south-west, the river entrenchment noted in the Samaca and Ullujaya basins (and perhaps elsewhere on the Peruvian coast) is the result, not of tectonic uplift, but of ongoing diminution of riparian vegetation in the river floodplain, and in particular of *Prosopis*. We might then account for the apparent difference between the extent of the S.U. 19 event and the 1997/8 El Niño flood event in the lower Ica Valley by, firstly, much denser riparian vegetation in the river floodplain at the time of the S.U. 19 event than today, and secondly, river entrenchment during that and perhaps subsequent flood events, caused by gradual, ongoing removal of that riparian vegetation from the floodplain.

Nonetheless, S.U. 19 represents an enormous flood event—the result of a so-called 'super' El Niño, comparable to that of 1997/8 (see Beresford-Jones *et al.* 2009a)—that damaged and submerged parts of the Early Nasca canal system in the lower Ica Valley. Grodzicki (cited in Orefici and Drusini 2003: 128) identifies roughly contemporary effects of a major El Niño flood around AD 600, including river down-cutting and a narrowing of the vegetated floodplain, at the major Nasca Period site of Cahuachi on the Río Nazca. Subsequently, the Quelccaya ice core appears to show a long drought between AD 570 and 610 (see Thompson *et al.* 1985). The Quelccaya ice sheet lies, however, at a distance of more than 400 kilometres from the south coast on the eastern Andean watershed, and rainfall during 'normal' years on western Andean slopes derives from overspill of Intertropical Convergence Zone weather systems over Amazonia to the east. So while the Quelccaya ice core's record of drought years might be correlated with years of poor river hydrology in coastal rivers with some confidence, its use as a record of prehistoric El Niño flood events—which originate from perturbations to Pacific weather systems —should perhaps be treated with much more caution.

The point here is not to deny the significance of these chaotic climatic fluctuations, but rather to observe that their effects would be precipitated by ongoing processes of gradual change, causing them to breach critical desert geomorphic thresholds, particularly through river down-cutting. A more complete picture of how change occurred emerges from superimposing processes of *gradual* change upon the punctuated equilibrium of El Niño/drought impacts. Indeed, that these relict terraces did not suddenly become denuded of vegetation following the S.U. 19 event, or until long after, is evidenced by several lines of data, including for instance, the identification of the Middle Horizon mound 23 as a relict nabkha. Archaeobotanical and geomorphological data offer further insights into that process of gradual change across the Samaca and Ullujaya basins.

Gradual change

Pollen data, interpreted according to context and taphonomic considerations and together with comparisons with plant macrofossil data, helps to elaborate that history of gradual change in the lower Ica Valley. As we have seen, good pollen concentrations were extracted from certain Samaca H-13 contexts, most notably a sequence from Test Pit 1/031, in which Early Nasca pottery provided us with a rough time framework. This location was an effective trap for wind-borne pollen blown across H-13 and for heavy entomophilous pollen deposited in its immediate vicinity—such as maize, *Prosopis* and most other riparian tree species—with limited possibilities for non-local contamination (Figure 5.9). In due course it was buried and sealed by the graded aeolian deposits of the climbing dune.

That pollen sequence showed a gradual replacement of woodland by cultivation and anthropogenic disturbance on H-13. A rich, huarango-dominated pollen assemblage recorded for the bottom of the sequence was almost directly comparable to that observed from the modern forest floor of the last remaining old-growth woodland fragment on the south coast at Usaca. Desiccated leaf litter macrofossils also dominated these contexts. Both provide powerful evidence of trees growing close to this location, today distant from the vegetated river floodplain (Figure 4.5A). *Prosopis* pollen and *poña* macrofossils declined steadily up through the sequence as pollen from domesticated plants such as maize, cotton and possibly beans appeared and increased. Maize pollen reached a maximum in the Early Nasca Period layer of 76–80 cm, the same period in which the canal system on H-13 was in operation. As *Prosopis* pollen declined up the 1/031 sequence, chenopods and amaranths ('Cheno-Ams'), those halophytic pioneers of open ground that are markers of human disturbance and agriculture, and also of degraded riparian vegetation, increased. They dominated entirely the pollen assemblage of the Middle Horizon contexts of 1/030, while huarango, other arboreal species, maize and cotton all but disappeared.

And this pollen sequence mirrors the picture presented by the archaeobotanical macrofossil data which we saw summarised in Table 5.1. The earliest contexts—dating the Early Horizon—showed no evidence of agriculture other than cotton, also the first cultivar to be recorded in our pollen sequence. In contrast, by the Late Nasca Period rubbish middens contained a complete suite of south coast domesticates including maize, beans, pumpkin, peanuts, achira, chilli peppers and the fruit trees of guava and pacay. Today these latter two plants cannot be grown easily in the Samaca and Ullujaya basins because of their wind regime. *Indigofera*, a plant that thrives along watercourses and in the shade of riparian woodland and also is not found today in the lower Ica Valley, was present in earlier archaeological contexts but disappeared from later ones. Indeed, just like the pollen sequence, the plant macrofossil record showed a clear trend of increasing intensity of agrestal weeds such as chenopods and amaranths, through the various archaeological periods analysed. At the same time those other indicators of open-area disturbance to riparian woodland—grasses and shrubs—also increased steadily. Meanwhile, *Sesuvium*, another classic halophyte and particularly well adapted to saline conditions, increased markedly in the plant macrofossil record, which may well reflect a gradual increase in salinity, often a consequence of long-term irrigation. Increases in dissolved salts were also noted in the geomorphological sequences of Section 1/013. In short then, our archaeological record bears witness to a gradual increase in the amount of agriculture being carried out over time in these basins.

But, by the Middle Horizon—the last time period analysed in Table 5.1—human subsistence in the lower Ica Valley would seem to have turned a full circle, back to the subsistence regime of the Early Horizon, almost two millennia earlier. For Middle Horizon rubbish middens contained few obvious food plant cultivars. Rather, they were full of marine and land molluscs from distant locations, in conjunction with a plant assemblage dominated by those wild plant foods whose importance to human diet we have noted in other, analogous, arid American environments. The consumption of the most important of these, the fruit of the huarango, was evident in human coprolites from those Middle Horizon middens. Moreover, the identification of mound 23 as a relict nabkha is, in and of itself, indicative of gradual environmental change (Figure 3.4), for only land surfaces that are *already* subject to considerable wind erosion give rise to nabkha formation. Nabkhas can be seen in many parts of the south coast, and in particular in the degraded Callango Basin of the lower Ica Valley, today composed mostly of multiple nabkha formations. These are not environments in which successful cultivation of tall maize plants is possible, because of the very strong winds that prevail in the region.

By the time of the Middle Horizon, when human occupants of the valley used mound 23 as a sheltered spot to consume a diet of largely gathered, wild foodstuffs, the surrounding area had already undergone and was still undergoing gradual change from the stable, productive agricultural landscape that had prevailed during the preceding Early Intermediate Period. The strong unidirectional wind regime of the region was entraining particles from a dry surface, some of which were being deposited in a few isolated nabkha formations like that of mound 23. The rest were moved across the relict terraces until they become anchored in the climbing dune that gradually built up along the western flank of the basin. The aeolian deflation of the H-13 and G-8/9 terrace surfaces had begun. At some point prior to the Late Intermediate even the large individual huarangos, about which nabkha mound 23 had formed, had died or been used for firewood or construction. By then gradual ecological change on the relict terraces of the lower Ica Valley had ceased—while geomorphological change was accelerating. With no vegetation to impede the wind, the process became irreversible. Wind deflation of land surfaces increased. No significant cultural materials from this, or any later cultural phases, are noted across the great expanses of desolate terraces in the lower Ica Valley.

Today, some one thousand years after the Middle Horizon, the surfaces of these relict terraces, with their canal systems thrown into inverted relief, their mixed scatters of pottery sherds from various time epochs and their relict tree trunks and other fossil evidence sealed beneath climbing dunes, stand in testimony to this story of gradual biophysical change. Some of the answers to the final, and most difficult, question posed in this research are already implicit in this model of gradual change—and they have to do with human agency.

Why Did Change Occur?

This model for when and how geomorphological and ecological change happened in the basins of the lower Ica Valley argues that a significant factor in change was diminution of riparian vegetation in general and of huarango in particular. Understanding the effects of changes in woodland cover, and answering the question of why change occurred, requires a proper incorporation of the profound role the huarango plays within the wider ecology of the south coast of Peru, of which humans and their other food sources are a part. It also requires us to consider the changes in human decisions and actions that underlie the story of change evoked by the model. Put simply: only humans remove large trees.

Putting the tree back into the landscape

The model presents a story of a gradual shift from relatively undisturbed old-growth woodland—for which a partial modern analogue on the south coast survives today only in the Quebrada Usaca—to a controlled, irrigated agricultural landscape during the Early Nasca Period. This was doubtless a gradual process with considerable time-depth.

The earliest occupation yet recorded in these basins of the lower Ica Valley is a few settlements dating to the Early Horizon. The largest of these, Feature 1004 (Plate 1), likely dating to the Late Ocucaje period (Phases 9/10), lies high up the edge of the Samaca Basin at over 300 m a.s.l. This location—far above the traces of later settlements and well over a hundred metres above the current river floodplain—suggests a radical change in the geomorphology of the basin and diminution of the vegetation extent within it since this ancient time. Aside from this, there are only the smallest vestiges of occupation such as that excavated alongside midden mound 21 on Ullujaya G8/9, which date back to the Chavín Early Horizon (Ocucaje Phases 3 and 4) at around 750 BC. Those ancient rubbish remains contain no evidence of domesticated food plants, but only sea urchin and other marine molluscs gathered from the Pacific Ocean some 25 kilometres distant. They do contain some plant remains, including gathered wild foods such as huarango beans, typical of riparian woodland. This evidence suggests that, at this early date, the occupants of the Ullujaya Basin were not subsisting on any form of agriculture. They seem to have been living in, and inflicting little impact upon, the natural dry forest ecology of these basins.

By the subsequent Early Intermediate Nasca Period, some eight hundred years later, midden and pollen data tell a story of a changed, farmed landscape. Importantly, however, this model of gradual change still envisages a landscape largely dominated by trees. For, apart from the multiple lines of evidence that we have reviewed, it is quite simply impossible to carry out successful agriculture in the environment of the lower Ica Valley *without* underpinning by huarango. With it, on the other hand, the landscape has the potential for some of the most productive agriculture in the world.

Agricultural practices of this time evoke the analogues of Huerto Huamaní in the lower Samaca Basin and the North American Sonoran Desert. Maize, cotton, beans, pumpkin and other domesticated plants are grown in small fields, with raised edges to maintain irrigation water, together with all the other components of spate-agriculture, or Nabhan's (1979: 246) 'continuum of hydrostatic manipulations'. Dense huarango hedgerows grow on these banks. Yet wild plants — including, most notably, huarango — still constitute perhaps *half* of people's total food source, especially between harvests. This is in line with both the Sonoran analogue and *all* the available Peruvian south coast archaeobotanical data (see for instance Silverman 1993, Piacenza 2005, Roque *et al.* 2003), even if rarely explicitly acknowledged in the interpretation of those data. Indeed, the importance of *Prosopis* went far beyond its provision of what Felger (1977: 155), in the context of the Sonoran, calls its 'unfailing crop' of highly nutritious pods. Through the botanical and agroforestry literature and our own observations, we have also seen the role that the tree plays as a 'keystone' species in the south coast desert ecosystem and agro-ecology. Consequently, any truly satisfactory interpretation of landscape change must incorporate the effects of changes in riparian woodland. For no other desert tree has a more pervasive influence upon neighbouring vegetation, soils, sub-canopy microclimate, and wildlife and insect populations.

As we have seen, the wind regime of the lower Ica Valley is extremely strong and extraordinarily unidirectional — from the south with an overall continuous average wind speed of no less than 28.8 kilometres per hour. Most obviously then, in an environment of very high winds and extremely erratic river flows, tree canopies protect other plants, whilst extensive root systems physically maintain soil stability. The microclimate beneath the tree canopy maintains stable, cooler soil and air temperatures, convivial to micro-organisms and the decomposition of litter fall. The huarango produces copious amounts of this *poña,* which carpets the desert under the tree, increasing soil humus content and contributing nutrients as it decomposes. *Poña* is still used today on the Peruvian south coast as a fertilizer. Litter 'mulching' further enhances microclimatic alterations at the soil surface. Together these make the soil less friable, further decreasing the effects of wind erosion.

Nitrogen shortage is the single most limiting factor in plant growth, particularly in arid regions. And the quantities of nitrogen and other nutrients added to the soil by the leguminous *Prosopis* are highly significant. In the rhizosphere, through 'autocatalytic relationships' with bacteria and fungi, *Prosopis* fixes nitrogen in the soil, and improves soil structure and respiration. *Prosopis* in the Sonoran Desert with only a 30 per cent canopy cover is recorded as fixing 40 to 50 kilograms of nitrogen per hectare per annum. Soil fertility and nitrogen contents beneath *Prosopis* are much greater than among agricultural intercrops, even when these include leguminous beans, as shown in semi-arid Mexico. Rhizosphere biological activity increases carbon dioxide partial pressures that contribute to the dissolution of insoluble calcium carbonate, the calcrete whose wide extension in the basins of the lower Ica Valley today is evidence both of past irrigation and of long standstill condition. The high pH of lower Ica Valley groundwaters is counteracted by the 'remarkable' effects of the genus on soil pH and salinity. Through all these influences the 'soil beneath *Prosopis* grows richer as the tree grows', as Nabhan (1985) puts it.

Archaeological interpretations of the south coast are replete with observations of the 'limitations' and 'restrictions' of its environment (see for instance Kroeber 1944, Menzel *et al*. 1964, Kosok 1965, Paul 1990, Silverman 1991, 1993, Sawyer 1997, Kroeber and Collier 1998, Silverman and Proulx 2002). Yet, given the protection from strong winds afforded by the huarango, the region's 350 days of sunshine per year and annually replenished alluvial soils are extremely productive, and can yield several harvests a year. Today, Chilean agro-industrial concerns in the middle Ica Valley attain production levels of tomatoes, for instance, which are among the highest in the world.

The region's most obvious limitation would appear to be water availability. Archaeological interpretations frequently invoke the perceived hydrological poverty of south coast rivers (Menzel *et al*. 1964, Craig and Psuty 1968, Silverman 1993, Sawyer 1997, Silverman and Proulx 2002), relative to the coastal valley systems to their north. Yet again, as we have seen, surface flows may be quite misleading. The Río Ica and the Río Grande de Nazca do indeed have very different configurations to the broad fan-shaped delta complexes of most of the major Peruvian westward flowing coastal rivers, because their access to the sea is blocked by the uplifted formations of the Tablazo de Ica and the ancient batholith of the Coastal Cordillera (Figure 2.1). But this same topographic peculiarity creates a vast natural dam, preserving high groundwater levels and sub-surface flows. Consequently, these rivers *lose* little water to the sea. Estimated sub-surface flows for the Río Ica total more than 155 per cent of average surface flow. Thanks to groundwater pumping, the middle Ica Valley today actually sustains a greater population and more hectares under cultivation than do its northern neighbours (Table 2.4).

Furthermore, *Prosopis* influences soil moisture, especially in a region characterised by zero rainfall, high night-time air humidity and a predominantly sub-surface groundwater hydrology. Its deep dimorphic root system accesses water at great depth and deposits some of that water amid its dense upper root mat through the process of 'hydraulic lift'. Moreover, the huarango contributes to the moisture of upper soil horizons by capturing atmospheric humidity on the huge surface area of its brachyblasts/leaflet clusters. In these ways the tree creates 'islands of fertility and moisture', which influence agriculture and other plants of the basins of the lower Ica Valley—all part of 'an emerging view that not all plant–plant interactions are necessarily negative and that facilitation is an important process in plant communities' as Caldwell (1998: 157) puts it.

In this landscape most El Niño years are *not* great catastrophes. On the contrary, they are years of abundance. River channel forms are preserved by dense riparian vegetation, most significantly by huarango phreatophytes. High-energy, potentially erosive flow is maintained in narrower river channels and irrigation systems are left unaffected. Groundwater levels are replenished. Dense riparian growth around the river thalweg prompts low-energy, standing floods over extensive areas that deposit huge amounts of rich alluvial sediments, whose fine particle sizes preserve their moisture content from evaporation as waters subside, and which support highly productive floodplain agriculture. This much is evident in the Quechua etymology of the name for these silts—*yapana*—'top-ups' of fertility and moisture.

By the subsequent Middle Horizon the picture is very different. Gradual woodland removal has undermined all the influences described above: benefits to soil structure, quality and moisture; floodplain protection; and microclimatic amelioration of the effects of strong wind and sunshine. The loss of riparian vegetation from the floodplain has permitted high-energy lateral instability in river channel form and down-cutting, and ecological thresholds are likely breached by the occurrence of 'super El Niño' events—like that of S.U. 19. Irrigation systems have been both damaged in the short term by the resultant flood events, and rendered inoperative over the long term by the river's entrenchment. Incipient wind erosion deposits material on nabkha mounds forming around large, isolated huarangos whose deep root systems still access groundwaters. Agriculture has been abandoned across the relict terraces of the Samaca and Ullujaya basins. Instead, people's diets are entirely composed of food resources gathered from distant sea and *lomas* locations, supplemented by wild plant foods including, notably, huarango beans. Once critical geomorphological and ecological thresholds are breached, land degradation accelerates and soon becomes irreversible. Although chaotic fluctuations in the climate like El Niño and La Niña are the likely tipping points—causing the thresholds to be finally breached—the seeds of sudden instability were sown long before through processes of gradual, human-induced change. By the Late Intermediate Period ecological change is complete and, on the relict terraces of the lower Ica Valley, the role of the huarango removed from the model .

The hand of human endeavour, or what Doolittle (2000: 6) properly calls 'anthropogenic geomorphology', is evident throughout this model of change: from the hydrostatic manipulations of water sources, including the canal systems that converted riparian dry forest into agricultural lands—or more accurately, agroforestry—to the gradual destruction of the keystone riparian species, the huarango, and its consequent impact upon the lower Ica Valley landscape. Answering our final question of why change occurred requires of us a careful consideration of *cultural* changes that caused shifts in the human–huarango relationship, and the human decisions which underlay these changes.

Putting the tree back into cultural change

The fine-scale picture of gradual and punctuated ecological degradation from the Early through to the Middle Horizon recorded here for the basins of the lower Ica Valley is, of course, only one part of a much wider archaeological record for the south coast of Peru. Great cultural changes are evident in this record over these time periods — changes that can be juxtaposed interestingly with the smaller-scale story of the Samaca and Ullujaya basins.

The iconography on the pottrey finds from the earliest occupation that we have thus far documented for the Ullujaya and Samaca basins shows a direct relationship with that of the monumental site of Chavín de Huántar, in the distant central Andes (see Figure 3.12). While the precise nature and duration of the Early Horizon may still be debated, this material in the Ica Valley likely represents almost the southernmost extent of this 'Chavín Horizon' — the first time the wider archaeological record clearly reflects a pan-Andean dissemination of people and/or ideas (see for instance Burger 1992, 1993).

With the passing of time through the various later Ocucaje Phases on the south coast, the archaeological record reflects the florescence of a new material culture which, while drawing upon earlier Chavinoid themes, is regionally constrained to the river valleys of the south coast (see for instance Menzel *et al.* 1964). There still remain many detailed uncertainties and chronological imprecisions surrounding the social interactions that underlie the transition from the later Ocucaje (or 'Paracas') Early Horizon to the subsequent, 'Nasca', Early Intermediate Period (Silverman 1991, Hecht 2009, Unkel and Kromer 2009). Yet such is the similarity between 'Paracas' and 'Early Nasca' that many believe that any distinction between the two is 'essentially arbitrary', as Menzel *et al.* (1964: 2) put it. While, as we have seen, some uncertainties also linger over the details of the Dawson Nasca ceramic seriation, for our purposes of attempting to establish correlations with broad changes in human ecology, it suffices simply to subsume the Nasca Phases 2 to 5 under the common — and happily uncontroversial — grouping of 'Early' (or 'Monumental') Nasca (see Kroeber and Collier 1998). Early Nasca as defined here thus endured on the south coast for at least the first four hundred years of the Common Era (Figure 3.3).

The iconography of Paracas and Early Nasca beautifully depicts the fecundity of nature and agriculture on the south coast (see any of the illustrations on this book's chapter opening pages), and is usually interpreted — in the context of the arid environment — as reflecting concern with agricultural fertility associated with the abundance of life forms and the ritual control of 'fundamental fertility factors such as the life-giving power of water, the growth potential of seeds, and the productivity of plants', as Silverman (1993: 323) puts it (see also Sawyer 1961, 1979, 1997, Peters 1991, Reinhard 1993). Much of the fauna and flora of the south coast riparian woodland in all its rich variety is clearly and accurately depicted in the naturalistic iconography of the Nasca Period, including felines and foxes, hummingbirds and all the creatures of the river and its banks such as swifts, egret, crayfish, frogs, catfish, tadpoles and even the wasps that gather mud at the river's edge. Indeed, the Nasca artistic canon truly proclaims a 'riparian consciousness'. Its conservative conventions of technique and expression are, moreover, an example of what Moseley (1992: 73, 190) terms a 'corporate style'; or, as he puts it, 'individuality—with cultural coherence, but without large scale or integrated power—were hallmarks of Nasca society'. Thus can iconographic style be used to make inferences about the societies that underlie them—a point to which we shall return shortly.

Although some see the tree depicted in one of the Nazca pampa geoglyphs, the huarango is not generally displayed explicitly on ceramics and textiles in the manner of cultivated crops such as maize, peppers and beans. I suggest—again invoking the analogue of the role of mesquite in the lives of the peoples of the Sonoran—that this was precisely

Figure 10.3. The forms of the *huarangal*

because of its all-pervading importance in their lives. For it was ubiquitous in the desert environment and, unlike cultivated crops, required no human intervention for a virtually unfailing provision of fruit and material. Instead, the forms of the *huarangal* woodland, with its distinctive, contorted growth, subtly pervade the *entire* Nasca artistic canon during this period (see Figure 10.3). And there are other, more speculative hints of more extensive woodlands in Early Nacsa iconography.

Monkeys and felines, or rather human impersonators of them, are frequently depicted in Paracas and Early Nasca iconography. Monkeys, or simian prehensile feet are very commonly depicted in the Nasca geoglyphs and on ceramics (see the illustration on the opening page of this chapter). As Peters (1991: 284) observes, monkeys are not found on the coast today and it is not clear whether any species were native to the 'scrub forest' of the south coast. Consequently she speculates that these figures indicate contacts across the Andes to the far eastern rainforests. Yet, as we have seen, 'scrub forest' is not an appropriate description for the tiny fragments of old-growth huarango forest that still persist, and monkey species are well known for their very wide range of habitat adaptations. Meanwhile, feline and human feline impersonator images sometimes carry human trophy heads. The archaeological literature has identified these images with the 'pampas cat' (*Felix colocolo* according to Dwyer 1979, Sawyer 1979, Paul 1990, Peters 1991, but likely a syn. for *Oncifelis colocolo*): 'a feline the size of a large house cat, still today the largest predator on the south coast of Peru', as Paul (1990: 79) describes. This very elusive and poorly studied animal is indeed associated with agricultural fertility rituals in Bolivia today (Villalba 2006). But its unlikely relationship with human prey in some Nasca feline iconography is explained by Peters (1991: 249) as being a south coast adaptation of 'primal Andean mythological roles generated by the earlier Chavín interaction sphere'. In other words, like the monkey, this feline iconography also derives from distant eastern rainforests. There are, however, historical references of much larger cats on the coast of Peru. Rostworowski (1981: 57), for example, cites a *relación* of the city of Piura as late as 1885 stating that many wild animals inhabit the algarrobo woods in its vicinity, including deer, wild pigs, bears '*y hasta tigueres*' ('and even tigers'). Indeed, Vázquez de Espinosa describes the woodlands of Ica in 1629 'with many savage wild animals' (1942 [1629]: 485). Interestingly, Felger and Moser (1985: 50) report that the Seri of the Sonoran, today also distant from modern-day ranges of larger felines, 'had knowledge of, and names for, both the spotted and black phases of jaguar', and for the puma. Moreover, a large puma lived in the lower Ica Valley during six months in 1998, feeding upon goats and dogs until it was finally shot in Ocucaje. Its corpse weighed around 80 kilograms. It seems unlikely therefore that in the ancient forested valleys of the south coast these animals were not more common. If so, they doubtless served as a more likely inspiration for the sometime feline predator in Early Nasca iconography than the humble pampas cat.

Cahuachi—manifestly the most important Early Nasca site—was constructed at this time on the Río Nasca (see Figure 2.2). As we have seen Cahuachi was a sacred pilgrimage and burial place serving a number of independent societies participating in and sharing a single Nasca cultural religious tradition. Yet, while the site is certainly very large, covering some 150 hectares, archaeological investigations indicate that it had no significant urban population. In striking contrast to the huge, contemporary adobe pyramids constructed by the Moche society on the Peruvian north coast, Cahuachi was also 'monumentally unmonumental', as Silverman puts it (1993: 324), being constructed upon natural hills. Where exactly the people who visited Cahuachi and who were buried in the vast cemeteries that surround it actually lived was for some time unclear. Yet, as we have seen exemplified in our lower Ica Valley case-study, this turns out to be because habitation sites were small, dispersed and built of ephemeral materials. Archaeological survey work has since revealed hundreds of unobtrusive Nasca habitation sites along the drainages of the south coast. Few are greater in area than 4 hectares, and they show little size hierarchy between sites, and almost no internal differentiation within them (Silverman 2002, Silverman and Proulx 2002). The growth of Cahuachi but lack of evidence for a large residential population there is thus explained by this abundance of Early Nasca habitation sites throughout the Rio Grande and Rio Ica drainages at the time during which the ceremonial centre reached its apogee (Silverman 1993). Returning to Early Nasca iconography, and again in quite distinct contrast to Moche, we note no clear depiction of noticeably differentiated individuals. In fact, the Early Nasca canon hardly ever shows scenes of interaction between individuals at all. Furthermore, although most Nasca tombs have been looted rather than excavated, the limited mortuary data that we do have show little evidence of unambiguous social hierarchy (see especially Silverman and Proulx 2002: chapter 10).

The archaeological record for the subsequent Late Nasca Period (Nasca 6 and 7, *c*. AD 450–600) reflects great changes in the society of the south coast. Cahuachi was abandoned and its decline was mirrored by a dramatic decrease in habitation sites and rearrangements in settlement patterns (Silverman 1993, 2002, Silverman and Proulx 2002). Schreiber (1999: 167) observes that 'most people moved from a series of closely spaced small villages into a very small number of very large sites spaced more widely apart'. The conservative iconographic canon of Early Nasca fractured into (at least) three sub-styles, and dramatic new iconography appeared including voluptuous seated naked women figurines and an increased prevalence of trophy-head taking and other militaristic themes. The depictions of naturalistic themes that so distinguish earlier Nasca iconography become rare (Silverman and Proulx 2002, Hecht 2009).

Silverman and Proulx (2002: 252) argue that these themes reflect an increased concern with fertility in the face of major climatic perturbations, specifically droughts evidenced by the Quelccaya ice core record, and that the break-up of the coherent Nasca iconographic style is a 'tangible reflection of competing worldviews following the breakdown of the Cahuachi cosmological hegemony'. It is here then, towards the end of the Late Nasca Period, that we might look to see the first repercussions of the gradual process of landscape change that we have traced in the archaeology of the lower Ica Valley. The scene was being set for a 'tipping point', which may well then have come in the form of climatic perturbations like that of the S.U. 19 flood. Perhaps this set loose the dogs of internecine 'resource wars'. Indeed, we have glimpsed hints of these convulsions gripping society around this time in the Late Nasca archaeological record of the lower Ica Valley itself. And the emergence of new social formations in Late Nasca also coincides with the rise in the adjacent Ayacucho highlands of one of the largest ancient urban centres in the Americas, Huari, and the dawning of the Wari Middle Horizon. For, as its name implies, the Middle Horizon (*c.* AD 600–1000) once again represents a wide extension of ideas and/or people across much of Peru. And this Ayacuchano Horizon reverberates particularly strongly in the archaeological record of the neighbouring south coast.

Other data substantiate the hypothesis that environmental conditions were deteriorating at this time. Tomasto's (2009) osteology of south coast skeletons reports much higher incidences of spongiosclerosis—frequently related to anaemia—in Middle Horizon as opposed to Nasca Period individuals. Her Middle Horizon sample is very small, yet Kellner (2002, cited in Tomasto 2009: 156) reports the same. Moreover, Drusini *et al.*'s (2001) study of 582 human skeletons from mortuary contexts in the Nasca Valley indicates that whilst the infant mortality rate during the Early Intermediate Nasca Period was 33 per 1,000, it reached 105 per 1,000 in the subsequent Middle Horizon. Moreover, overall life expectancy also fell from 38–43 years during the Nasca Period to 31–36 years during the Middle Horizon. Drusini *et al.* (2001: 157) conclude that these data confirm 'worse conditions of the Wari population in comparison with the previous Nasca people'.

The model presented here for the ecological changes wrought on the basins of the lower Ica Valley shows correlation with these wider changes. Based upon the evidence discussed I argue that huarango woodlands were once a far more widespread and indeed dominant feature of the Early Intermediate Period riparian landscape on the south coast of Peru. I also argue that the ecological importance of the *huarango*, and its gradual diminution, are just as critical to an understanding of these changes as are major climatic perturbations. Taken together, the many lines of archaeological data we have discussed here combine to paint a detailed picture of Early Nasca society within a dry forested landscape that we shall return to shortly in attempting to answer the hardest question of all: why did humans decide to chop down trees to an extent that caused irreversible environmental change? And, in the context of the popular myth of Native Americans as 'ecologically noble savages', what more specific inferences might we draw from this archaeological record about those social and ecological contexts in which significant human environmental impacts in the New World did, and did not, arise? Because, not only was the ensuing environmental change in the Samaca and Ullujaya basins in large part *human-induced*, but it also coincides with the impact of the Middle Horizon on the south coast.

Changes in human–huarango relationships

We have reviewed here direct and circumstantial archaeological, ethnohistorical and ethnographic evidence that identifies the huarango as a 'staff of life' for south coast inhabitants, just as it was for the inhabitants of the Sonoran Desert. For it provided a host of invaluable resources: shade, fruit that were processed into flour, bread, syrups and alcoholic beverages, fodder for camelids, black dyes, adhesives, fibre for cordage and medicines. Indeed, no other plant played an older or more important role in south coast human–plant interactions. Here, in its native range, the tree has none of those features which have caused exotic *Prosopis* introductions to come to be regarded as an invasive pest in some parts of the world. On the contrary, its morphological features—thornlessness, pod size and production—and tree growth characteristics hint at a long process of co-evolution with humans as an essential resource. Uniquely, these characters of *P. pallida* forma *pallida* (or *P. limensis*, as preferred here) may have been preserved within the relative isolation of the riparian oases of the south coast from the subsequent dispersal, hybridisation and backcrossing that has taken place elsewhere, as its relative importance as a human resource declined. Moreover, over the *longue durée* of huarango lifespans, we may still see these features in living trees—trees that were saplings during the Middle Horizon. Silverman's (1993) thesis, that the tree was a totem, a symbolic representation of the south coast ayllu society, is lent considerable weight by the biological, ecological and ethnohistorical evidence presented here. The inhabitants of the south coast, like those of the Sonoran, may have named their lineages after the tree. It was essential to sustainable agroecology in the riparian basins of the south coast. Yet the time-depth and importance of this human–huarango relationship begs the obvious question of why people would so deplete woodland cover in the lower Ica Valley basins so as to induce irreversible environmental change?

Of course, the huarango also provided wood for weapons and tools, fine-quality timber for construction and a high-temperature steady-burning fuel for households, the firing of ceramics and the smelting of metals. Huarango wood likely provided fuel for the many 'fired-earth pits' surveyed in Samaca and Ullujaya that were used to fire ceramics. Plainly, its use in these respects could result in a diminution of woodland cover and the age profile of the tree population. Unfortunately, however, human consumption of woodland is not susceptible to rude estimation. For trees of course are a renewable resource—their exploitation can be managed. Human manipulation through pollarding and coppicing can increase the production of *Prosopis* woody biomass by up to six times. Given the sophistication of agriculture in the Andes in its better-known aspects, and indeed its long tradition of agroforestry techniques (see Reynel and Felipe-Morales 1987), it seems highly improbable that such woodland management was not practised during pre-Hispanic times on the south coast of Peru. Any attempt to determine the impact of fuel consumption on woodland is rendered meaningless in the absence of evidence for or against such management practices. Furthermore, wooden construction artefacts endure in the hyperarid climate of the south coast and are consequently still reused today. Indeed, the analogy with the North American Sonoran would suggest the value of *Prosopis* as a resource in these respects likely contributed to its preservation and proliferation on the ancient south coast, rather than vice versa. Rather, the most obvious way in which humans would likely influence woodland cover would be through its clearance for increased agriculture. And, as we have seen, precisely such a gradual change is recorded in the archaeobotanical data for the lower Ica

Valley. Moreover, serious impact upon woodland cover in the basins of the lower Ica Valley would appear to coincide with the social and cultural changes wrought widely on the south coast of Peru by the Middle Horizon.

The archaeological record for the Wari Middle Horizon persuades most archaeologists that it was precipitated by an expansionist state, likely the first truly 'state-level' society in the Andes (see for instance Lumbreras 1974, Isbell and Schreiber 1978, Isbell 1988, 2001, Isbell and McEwan 1991, Schreiber 1992, D'Altroy and Schreiber 2004). The Wari heartland lay in the Ayacucho highlands of the south-central Andes, centred on the eponymous urban centre there. The consensus would have Wari expanding rapidly out of this region during its so-called Epoch 1B, to control directly vast swathes of the central and southern coasts, and the Peruvian highlands over an even greater extent, from Cuzco to Ancash. At its apogee around AD 800, its capital at Huari was vast, covering some 15 square kilometres. It remains to this day the largest archaeological site in South America (see Isbell *et al.* 1991: 24). Indeed, its size, complexity and poor state of preservation have defied comprehensive archaeological survey to date (Isbell 1988: 167). Speculative population estimates for the city range between 50,000 and 100,000 (Benavides 1991: 56), or 20,000 and 34,000 (Isbell 1988: 173). Whatever, it was by any measure an enormous ancient city—even five hundred years later, Venice, the largest city in Europe, had a population of less than 50,000 (McEvedy 1992: 75). Survey data indicate how populations in surrounding areas gradually became drawn into the vast agglomeration that was Wari (Schreiber 1992: 88, Isbell and Vranich 2004: 177). And the evidence for Wari's early domination of the south coast during this period is particularly strong—after all, the Ayacucho highlands are its immediate hinterland. Indeed, as Rowe (1956: 148) observed more than fifty years ago, the Middle Horizon 'apparently marks the virtual replacement of one culture by a radically different one on the south coast'.

It may be interesting, therefore, to ponder the environmental changes at this time in the basins of the lower Ica Valley in light of the striking assemblage of plant fossils from the midden context of S.U. 32 in the Middle Horizon mound 23 on Samaca H-13. These included coca seed in association with evidence for pacay (*Inga* sp.) and guava (*Psidium* sp.) fruit trees (see Figure 5.8). As we have seen, this conjunction of plant fossils resonates with the history of coca plantations on the coast of Peru in association with precisely these shade trees. Schreiber (1999, 2001) has argued that Middle Horizon expansion on to the south coast may have been driven in part by an ambition to seek new sites for the production of coca, which does not grow at the altitudes of the Wari Ayacucho heartland. The lower Ica Valley lies at the lower end of the suitable range defined by Rostworowski (1989: 245–6) for the coastal variety of coca—*Erythroxylum novogranatense* var. *truxillense*. Moreover, the historical documentation that Rostworowski reviews also describes coca being grown together with cotton, for which we have abundant evidence in the same midden contexts in the form of fibre, seeds, capsule fragments and leaves. Indeed, looted Middle Horizon funerary contexts in the lower Ica Valley contain extraordinary quantities of raw cotton. Anecdotally at least, this suggests that these basins may have been given over to producing vast amounts of that 'industrial' cultigen. Just like coca, cotton also does not grow in the Ayacucho highlands, but it was much sought after for textile manufacture, not least to make the strong warps that define the corpus of famous Wari shirts (see for instance Stone-Miller 1992).

While their mixed agroecology was sustained in part by huarango woodland, dense hedgerows and trees left standing amid its small fields, the basins of the lower Ica Valley might have appeared ideal for conversion to monocrops of cotton and coastal coca in the shade of large-leafed fruit trees. Decisions to impose such a conversion may have made by people exotic to, or even remote from, this area, perhaps as part of some state-imposed Middle Horizon policy to serve distant urban markets. It would therefore have been contrary to the traditional practices of the lower Ica Valley inhabitants and in ignorance of the prevailing biophysical characteristics that gave rise to those practices. That such a conversion would have had short lived and disastrous results if carried out on any scale is implicit in all the above discussion of the role of the tree in maintaining the viability of the agroecosystems in this environment. Broad-leafed plants such as *Inga* and *Psidium* (and of course coca) cannot be propagated in the wind regime of these basins today. This suggestion is, of course, for now speculative and based upon limited data. Yet, whatever the anecdotal evidence for the role of monocultures of coca and/or cotton production in explaining woodland reduction in the lower Ica Valley, these are but symptomatic details in a larger-scale picture of huge cultural changes on the south coast at this time.

Reconciling Contradictions?

There is overwhelming archaeological evidence from various parts of the New World, including the lower Ica Valley case study here, which gives the lie to the popular myth that Native Americans preserved the wilderness of the Americas, with 'barely perceptible human disturbance'. This 'myth of the ecologically noble savage', as Lentz (2000: 2) calls it, is rather naturally viewed from the perspective of archaeology with perplexity. Yet, on the other hand, there is also abundant evidence that much Native American land stewardship did indeed entail extremely sophisticated conservationism. We see as much in the detailed contemporary anthropologies of Amerindian societies in Amazonia and the ethnohistories of the Andes and other parts of the New World, including the ethnoecological analogue invoked here of the Sonoran Desert. As demonstrated so eloquently by the Amazonian ethnoecologies of Descola (1994), Balée (1994) and others, our very bifurcation between 'nature' and 'culture' lies within our own philosophical tradition, and not that of the worldviews of those societies. Indeed, it is perhaps this very bifurcation that has led to archaeological interpretation without proper regard for the complexity of dynamic ecological context. It also obstructs our understanding of human ecology by obscuring the continuum between 'domesticated' and 'wild' plant use, which we have been at such at pains to avoid here.

There are a number of seemingly glaring differences between these contemporary Amazonian contexts and those of the south coast of Peru, although these are perhaps less obvious on closer inspection. The perspective of historical ecology used by Balée (1994), for example, shows the modern Ka'apor to be depauperate residues of a once much larger agricultural society. Over time, they have become progressively less dependent on domesticated plants, and more on foraging for wild plants: a human–ecology continuum which echoes that of the archaeobotanical record for the Middle Horizon in the lower Ica Valley. We are not, then, simply making inappropriate comparisons between 'agricultural' and 'hunter-gatherer' extremes. There are also, of course, stark contrasts between Amazonian and arid American ecologies. Indeed, they appear to lie at opposite ends of an environmental spectrum dictated by rainfall. Nonetheless, it has long been appreciated that initial impressions conveyed by the verdant fecundity of Amazonia are misleading. The soil formations of the Amazonian lowlands (so-called 'acrisols' and 'plinthsols') have low natural fertility and weak structures. When cleared for agriculture these soils are subject to severe erosion or hardening with limited root penetration when cleared (see Bridges 1997). So, just like arid ecosystems, those of the Amazon turn out to be remarkably fragile and vulnerable to human impact. Moreover, the Sonoran Desert ethnoecology—which we went to some lengths to justify as an analogue for the south coast of Peru—also shows what one might term this 'ecological sophistication' in thinking. Meanwhile, the view from the Andes themselves might most eloquently be summarised in Rostworowski's (1981: 55; my translation) citation of the melancholic reflections of Pizarro's companion in arms, Mancio Serra de Leguizamo, on the lost 'order and harmony' of the Inca Empire, and upon how well its people had managed its 'lands and mountains and mines and pastures and households and woodlands'.

How are we to reconcile these apparently contradictory views of pre-Hispanic land stewardship? The answer of course lies in clearing a path through the polemic by seeking to be much more precise about the circumstances in which environmental impacts did, and did not, occur. One way of doing this is to test those hypotheses that, as we saw, Butzer drew from his detailed historical ecology of the Mediterranean (1996, 2005), against our model for ecological and culture change in the lower Ica Valley. In fact, a satisfactory interpretation of the archaeological record there requires us to draw more specific inferences about exactly what social and ecological contexts might result in significant human environmental impacts, 'regardless of any ethos of harmony with nature' as Butzer (1996: 142) puts it.

Firstly then, for the Mediterranean, Butzer (1996: 146) observes that 'agrosystems evolve through trial and error; early agriculture was experimental in nature, and initial technostrategies were exploitative, and often ephemeral'. Indeed, this rather well describes the archaeological record we have seen here for the lower Ica Valley during the Early Horizon Chavín Period of Ocucaje Phases 3 and 4.

Secondly, Butzer (1996: 46) hypothesises that 'cumulative experience should select for conservationist strategies'. Diamond (1994: 57) likewise observes that 'it is still true that small, long-established, egalitarian societies tend to evolve conservationist practices'. The archaeological record for the lower Ica Valley and for the wider south coast that we have reviewed here for the Early Nasca Period describes a regionally constrained society with deep roots back into its ancient past in the Chavín Horizon. It shows little evidence of social hierarchy. Its settlements are small and scattered throughout a landscape, which, whilst certainly agricultural, retains dominant elements of 'natural' riparian woodland ecology. The material culture of this society shows the highest standards of craftsmanship, and these are reflected across all parts of that society. Its iconographic canon is extremely conservative: imbued with and commingling agri-'cultural' and 'natural' themes. Indeed, it is hard to imagine an art style that better mirrors the term 'domestic nature', as coined by Descola to 'capture the Achuar socialisation of nature and naturalisation of the social' as Pollock (1996: 159) puts it. I have argued here that the distinctive forms of the riparian woodland pervade the entire Early Nasca canon and that its iconography proclaims a riparian consciousness. Thus, the picture painted by the various lines of archaeological data presented here supports the view that the Early Nasca Period on the south coast conformed to Butzer's second inference, which of course also pertains to the Amazonian case studies and to Sonoran ethnoecology.

Finally, Butzer (1996: 146–7) observes that in the Mediterranean case expansion and intensification of agricultural production were linked to the development of urban centres, and that 'at some point urban demand and high rural populations could place the ecosystem under stress, triggering periods of degradation'. Expansions into new ecozones also lead him to infer that 'prior environmental experience cannot be transplanted without initial damage', and that 'political instability and rural insecurity will reduce incentives for conservationist management of resources'. In a similar vein, Diamond (1994: 57) notes that 'damage is likely to occur when people suddenly colonise an unfamiliar environment', and, 'is also likely in centralised states that concentrate wealth in the hands of rulers who are out of touch with their environment'. We have seen here the subsequent fracture of the Nasca style during the Late Nasca Period and the very different nature of Middle Horizon society as reflected in the archaeological record. This was unequivocally a period of great social change in the prehistory of the Andean region and there is rather good evidence that it also represents the first formation of a so-called 'state-level' urban society in the southern sierra, which subsequently expanded and imposed its control over a huge swathe of modern Peru, including the south coast. It is this period that coincides with the major landscape changes noted in the archaeological record of the lower Ica Valley and which resonates, therefore, with these last inferences that Butzer derives from the Mediterranean.

There remains one final specific observation to make here about the precise contexts in which one might foresee significant human environmental impacts: the obvious, or as Diamond (1994: 57) puts it, 'almost banal' observation that they are more likely in more vulnerable ecologies. Many of the archaeological cases for human damage in pre-Hispanic times occurred in areas with dry climates. Nowhere does this apply more strongly than on the coast of Peru. Today these valleys bear little resemblance to those first descriptions in

1553 by Cieza de León, as 'fresh and luxuriant as sprigs of basil, with woods and glades full of birds of many types . . . and many deer' (1995 [1553]: 203). Nor can those early descriptions be explained by environmental recovery following population collapse: one of the origins of the 'myth of the ecologically noble savage' elsewhere in the Americas. For Cieza's evocations follow on the very heels of conquest. And the huarango is a very slow-growing desert hardwood. Its lifespan is measured in centuries and it takes many of these for it to reach the stature of the last ancient giants of Usaca. Following contact with the Old World, the native population collapsed on the south coast of Peru as badly as it did anywhere in the New World. Doubtless, significant cycles of environmental recovery took place — ironically enough for instance, until the twentieth century, in the long abandoned lower Ica Valley. But, since the riparian dry forest ecology of the south coast recovers very slowly from depredation, and because the ecological and geomorphic thresholds of this coastal desert are peculiarly critical, the course that we have traced through the Spanish chronicles, administrative records and recent memory on the south coast is a generally inexorable one of deforestation. On the south coast in particular, the story is now all but complete.

Deforestation of the middle Ica Valley reached vertiginous rates during the twentieth century. The *huarangals* that once surrounded the city of Ica — described by Vázquez de Espinosa as 'impenetrable at many points', and 'so thick that the highway is the only way to get through them and one sees nothing but woods and sky' (1942 [1629]: 485) — are long gone. They are replaced by a modern landscape of urban shanty sprawl, fallen water tables, degraded saline soils, the broad fields of agro-industry, shifting dunes and *monte* scrub — which has unduly coloured our archaeological interpretations. As we saw in the last chapter, very similar environmental changes were wrought in relatively recent history by Anglo-Hispanic incursion into the riparian basins of the North American south-west. It is salutary for our purpose here that the seeds of all these major environmental changes were sown, not by the impact of any El Niño, but by the *cultural* cataclysms that followed European conquest.

Yet, in the basins of the lower Ica Valley, the case presented here is that long *before* European arrival, the Middle Horizon too had already brought comparably catastrophic and — in the main — human-induced environmental change. Ultimately, despite (or perhaps because of) the preponderance of ecological argument and data presented here, I argue for a less environmentally determined interpretation of changes in south coast cultural trajectories. Ancient south coast lifeways need to be viewed within landscapes very different from those that prevail today. Early Nasca artistic manifestations are justifiably renowned for celebrating the abundance of south coast nature and agriculture. They offer us glimpses of their riparian woodland consciousness. Reconstructing these lifeways, so distant in time and ecological space, calls for considerable imagination. As Anatole France himself put it, 'history is not science, it is an art, and man succeeds in it only by his imagination'. To stimulate our imaginations, however, we should rely on a more complete *scientific* understanding of the environmental and ecological contexts in which these unique lifeways unfolded.

A final coda to this archaeological story is its powerful contemporary resonance. For today, the last remaining 'old-growth' riparian forest relicts on the south coast resound to the chainsaws of illegal charcoal-burning operations. Over the past thirty years, populations on the Peruvian coast have exploded as people have left the Andean sierra to seek easier lives on the coast or to escape terrorism. More than three-quarters of the population of Ica are recent immigrants from Ayacucho. Indeed, a new 'Horizon' is unfolding before our eyes. Today, more than 80 per cent of modern Peru's GDP and population are concentrated along the coast. The consequences of this are tremendous pressures upon water resources, agricultural production and the fragile biomes of the riparian desert and *lomas* — all of which increases vulnerability to climatic perturbations such as El Niño. Tragically for our understanding of prehistory, yet almost incidentally in a country with one of the lowest per capita GDPs in Latin America, those pressures extend inevitably to its rich archaeological heritage.

Moreover, the problems of fragile arid ecosystems, degraded alkali soils and high population densities experienced today on the Peruvian coast are representative of a wider global phenomenon. One-fifth of the world's poorest inhabitants live in arid lands (Barker and Gilbertson 2000) and almost one billion hectares of these have suffered human-induced degradation (Pessarakli and Szabolcs 1999). We are more aware than ever that the course of our current relationship with our environment is unsustainable. And we have important lessons to learn from rediscovering past human relationships with their environments through different social structures, and — the particular object of this study — the role of huarango woodlands for sustaining human ecology within arid environments. For, as the ethanobotanist Wade Davis (1995: 43) puts it, 'the character of a people's relationship with the plant world is . . . one means of approaching an understanding of the cognitive foundations of a culture'.

Appendix

A comparison of Sonoran Desert and South Coast Peru Flora

Family	Sonoran Desert Flora						South Coast Peru Flora					
	Plant	Common Name	Habit	Main Habitat	Occurrence	Source	Plant	Common Name	Habit	Main Habitat	Occurrence	Source
Agavaceae	***Various*** *Agave* ***sp.***	Agave / maguey	Sub-shrub	Dry flats / upper bajadas	Frequent	5, 6, 9, 11						
	Various *Yucca* ***sp.***	Yucca	Sub-shrub	Dry flats / upper bajadas	Frequent	9, 11						
Aizoaceae	*Trianthema portulacastrum*	Desert horse-purlsane	Herb	Dry flats / lower riparian	Frequent - possibly exotic	9, 11	*Trianthema portulacastrum*	Verdolaga	Herb	Dry flats / lower riparian	Frequent - possibly exotic	14
							Sesuvium portulacastrum (Syn. Portulaca portulacastrum)		Herb	Dry flats / lower riparian	Frequent	12, 14
Amaranthaceae	*Amaranthus fimbriatus*	Fringed amaranth	Herb	Upper & lower bajadas	Present	3, 9, 11	*Amaranthus spinosus*	Yuyu macho	Herb	Field weed	Frequent	12, 14
	Amaranthus palmeri	Carelessweed	Herb	Upper & lower bajadas	Frequent	3, 4, 9, 11						
	Tidestromia lanuginosa	Wooly tidestromia	Herb	Upper & lower bajadas	Frequent	2, 3, 11	*Alternanthera halimifolia*	Leche-leche	Herb	Field weed	Present	12, 14
Anacardiaceae	*Rhus trilobata*	Skunkbush / sumac	Shrub	Riparian floodplains	Present	1, 9, 11	*Schinus molle*	Molle	Tree	Riparian woodland	Present	13, 15, 16
Arecaceae	*Phoenix dactylifera*	Date palm	Palm tree	Riparian floodplains	Frequent - exotic	6, 11	*Phoenix dactylifera*	Date palm	Palm tree	Riparian floodplains	Present - exotic	12, 13
	Washingtonia filifera	Calinornia fan palm	Palm tree	Riparian floodplains	Present	6, 11						
Asteraceae	Various *Ambrosia* sp.	Burrobush	Shrub / sub-shrub	Dry flats	Frequent	2, 3, 4, 9, 11	*Ambrosia artemisiodes*		Herb	Lomas	Frequent	15
	Baccharis salicifolia	Mules fat	Shrub	Riparian floodplains	Frequent	1, 8, 11	*Baccharis salicifolia*	Chilco	Shrub	Open spaces riparian floodplain	Frequent	12, 13, 14
	Bidens sp.	Bur-marigold	Herb	Upper and lower bajadas	Present	9, 11	*Tessaria intergrifolia*	Pajaro bobo	Graminoid/ shrub	Riparian edge	Frequent	12, 13, 14
	Encelia farinosa	Brittlebush	Sub-shrub / shrub	Upper bajadas	Present	2, 11	*Encelia canescens*		Shrub	Lomas	Present	14, 15
	Helianthus **sp.**	Wild sunflowers	Herb	Upper & lower bajadas	Present	9, 11						

	Isocoma tenuisecta	Burroweed	Sub-shrub / Herb	Riparian floodplains	Present	6, 11	*Grindelia glutinosa*			Lomas	Dominant	15
	Pectis papposa	Chinchweed	Herb	Upper & lower bajadas	Frequent	2, 3, 9, 11						
	Pluchea sericea	Arrow weed	Shrub	Riparian floodplains	Dominant	1, 11	*Pluchea chigoyo*	Torfluz	Shrub / sub-shrub	Open spaces riparian floodplain	Frequent	12, 13, 14
	Various Sonchus sp. (including *S. oleraceus*)	Sow-thistle	Herb	Upper & lower bajadas	Frequent - exotic	9, 11	*Sonchus oleraceus*	Cerraja	Herb	Field weed	Frequent - exotic	14
Borginaceae							*Heliotropium curassavicum*		Herb / vine	Dry open areas of riparian floodplain	Present	12, 13
							Heliotropium pilosum			Lomas	Present	15
Buxaceae	*Simmondsia chinensis*	Jojoba	Shrub	Upper bajadas	Present	1, 2, 11						
Cactaceae	*Carnegiea gigantea*	Saguaro	Columunar cactus	Upper bajadas	Frequent	1, 2, 5, 6, 9, 11	*Various Haageocereus* sp. (some with Syn. *Cereus*)		Columunar / shrub cactus	Dry Andean foothill quebradas & *lomas*	Frequent	18, 19
	Mammillaria sp.	Chollita	Columunar cactus	Upper bajadas	Present	9, 11	*Eryocise* sp. (Syn. *Neoporteria, Echinocactus*)		Columunar / shrub cactus	Dry Andean foothill quebradas & *lomas*	Frequent	18, 19
	Various *Opuntia* sp. (some Syn. *Cylindropuntia*)	Cholla / prickly pear	Shrub cactus	Upper & lower bajadas	Frequent	1, 2, 5, 6, 9, 11	*Opuntia* sp.	Tuna	Shrub cactus	Cultivated - riparian floodplain	Present	16, 17
	Various *Stenocereus* sp.	Organ pipe cactus	Columunar cactus	Upper & lower bajadas	Present	1, 6, 8, 9, 11	*Neoraimondia* sp. (Syn. *Cereus*)		Tree cactus	Dry Andean foothill quebradas & *lomas*	Present	16, 18, 19
							Cleistocactus sp.		Shrub cactus	Dry Andean foothill quebradas & *lomas*	Present	18, 19
							Echinopsis (Syn. *Trichocereus*)	San Pedro	Columunar cactus	Cultivated - riparian floodplain	Present	16, 17
Capparaceae	*Koeberlina spinosa*	Allthorn	Shrub	Riparian floodplains	Present	1, 11						

Family	Sonoran Desert Flora						South Coast Peru Flora					
	Plant	Common Name	Habit	Main Habitat	Occurrence	Source	Plant	Common Name	Habit	Main Habitat	Occurrence	Source
Chenopidaceae	Various *Atriplex* sp.	Chamiso / saltbush	Shrub	Riparian floodplains / dry flats	Present / dominant	1, 9, 11	*Atriplex* sp.		Shrub	*Lomas*	Frequent	15
	Allenfolfea occidentalis	Iodine-bush	Shrub	Riparian salt marsh	Dominant	1, 9						
	Various *Chenopodium* sp.	Goosefoot / lambsquarter	Herb	Upper & lower bajadas	Frequent	4, 9, 10, 11	*Chenopodium* sp.		Herb	Field weed	Frequent	12
							Chenopodium ambrosiodes	Paicco / Yerba del gallianzo	Herb	Field weed	Frequent	12, 14
							Chenopodium sp.	Yerba blanca	Shrub	Riparian floodplain	Present	12
	Monolepis sp.	Poverty-weed	Herb	Riparian floodplains	Present	4, 6, 9, 11						
Convolvulaceae	Ipomoea sp.	Morning glory	Vine / subshrub	Upper & lower bajadas	Frequent	3, 4, 9, 11	*Ipomoea alba*		Vine	Riparian woodland	Present	13, 14
Cucurbitaceae	Various *Cucurbita* sp.	Gourd / calbaza	Vine / herb	Upper & lower bajadas	Present	4, 5, 9, 11	*Curcurbita pepo* (syn. *maxima*)	Zapallo	Vine / Subshrub	Field edges	Frequent	12
							Luffa operarculata	Jabón de pobre	Sub-shrub / shrub	Dry areas of riparian floodplain	Frequent	12
Cyperaceae	Various *Cyperus* sp.	Flat-sedge	Graminoid	Riparian floodplains	Frequent	9, 11	*Cyperus articulatus*		Graminoid	Riparian margins	Frequent	12, 14
							Cyperus oderatus		Graminoid	Riperian margins	Frequent	13, 14
	Various Schoenoplectus sp. (Syn. *Scripus*)	Club-rush	Graminoid	Riparian floodplains	Frequent	6, 9, 11	*Schoenoplectus maritimus* (Syn. *Scirpus*)	Piri piri	Graminoid	Open well margins	Present	12, 14
Ephedraceae	Various Ephedra sp.	Mormon tea / joint tea	Shrub / subshrub	Riparian floodplains	Present	8, 9, 11	*Ephedra americana*		Shrub	*Lomas*	Present	15
Euphorbiaceae	Various *Chamaesyce* sp.	Sandmat	Herb	Upper & lower bajadas	Present	3, 11	*Croton alnifolius*		Herb	*Lomas*		15
	Various *Cnidoscolus* sp.	Mala mujer	Herb	Upper & lower bajadas	Present	3, 9, 11						
	Various *Euphorbia* sp.	Spurge	Herb	Upper & lower bajadas	Frequent	2, 3, 11						

	Jatropha cardiophylla	Limberbush	Shrub	Upper & lower bajadas	Present	2, 11						
Fouquieriaceae	*Fouquieria* sp.	Ocotillo	Shrub	Upper & lower bajadas	Present	2, 4, 11						
Leguminosae	*Acacia constricta*	White thorn	Tree	Riparian floodplains	Present	1, 2, 8, 9	*Acacia macracantha*	Espino	Tree	Riparian woodland	Frequent	12, 13, 15, 16
	Acacia greggi	Cat Claw	Tree	Riparian floodplains	Present	1, 2, 4, 5, 6, 8, 9						
	Crotalaria sp.	Rattlebox	Herb	Lower bajadas / riparian floodplains	Present	9, 11	*Croataria incana*		Herb	Field weed	Present	12, 14
	Olneya tesota	Desert ironwood	Tree	Upper bajadas	Present	1, 2, 5, 6, 9, 11	*Inga feuillei*	Pacae	Tree	Edge of fields	Present	13
	Parkinsonia aculeata	Jerusalem thorn / Mexican palo verde	Tree / shrub	Upper bajadas	Present	4, 9, 11	*Parkinsonia aculeata*	Uña de gato / palo verde	Shrub / tree	Dry edges riparian woodland	Frequent	12, 13, 15
	Parkinsonia florida (Syn. *Cercidium floridum*)	Palo verde	Tree / shrub	Upper bajadas	Dominant	1, 2, 5, 6, 9, 11						
	Parkinsonia microphyllum (Syn. *Cercidium microphyllum*)	Yellow palo verde	Tree / shrub	Upper bajadas	Dominant	1, 2, 5, 6, 9, 11						
	Psorothamnus spinosus	Smoke tree	Tree	Riparian floodplains	Present	6, 11						
	Various *Caesalpinia* sp.	Holdback	Tree / shrub	Lower arroyos	Present	9, 11	*Caesalpinia gilliesii*	Uña de gato	Shrub / tree	Riparian woodland	Present	13
	Prosopis glandulosa	Honey mesquite	Tree	Riparian floodplains	Dominant	1, 5, 9	*Prosopis pallida* forma *armata*	Huarango (macho)	Tree	Riparian woodland	Present	12, 13
	Prosopis pubescens	Screwbean	Tree	Riparian floodplains	Present	1, 5, 9	*Prosopis pallida* forma *pallida*	Huarango (hembra)	Tree	Riparian woodland	Dominant	12, 13
	Prosopis veluntina	Velvet mesquite	Tree	Lower bajadas / riparian floodplains	Frequent	2, 3, 4, 5, 8, 9, 10						
	Phaseolus acutifolius	Tepary bean	Herb	Dry margins	Frequent	6, 9	*Indigofera truxillensis*		Herb / subshrub	Riparian woodland	Present	12
							Vigna luteola		Herb	Field weed	Present	12
							Adesmia sp.		Herb	Field weed	Present	12

Family	Sonoran Desert Flora						South Coast Peru Flora					
	Plant	Common Name	Habit	Main Habitat	Occurrence	Source	Plant	Common Name	Habit	Main Habitat	Occurrence	Source
Malvaceae	Various *Rhychosida* sp.	Buffpetal	Herb	Upper & lower bajadas	Present	3, 11	*Anoda* sp.		Herb	Field weed	Present	12
	Various *Sphaeralcea* sp.	Globemallow	Herb	Upper & lower bajadas	Frequent	2, 11						
Nyctaginaceae	*Allinonia incarnata*	Trailing windmills	Herb	Upper & lower bajadas	Frequent	3, 11						
	Various *Boerhavia* sp.	Spideling	Herb	Upper & lower bajadas	Present	3, 9, 11	Various *Boehavia* sp.	Pega-pega	Herb		Present	14
							Argemone subfusilormis		Herb	Dry, open areas riparian floodplain & fields	Present	12
Passifloraceae	Various *Passiflora* sp.	Passion flower	Vine	Riparian floodplains	Present	9, 11	*Passiflora foetida*		Vine	Riparian woodland	Present	13
Poaceae (Gramineae)	*Chloris virgata*	Feather fingergrass	Graminoid	Upper & lower bajadas	Present	3, 11	*Chloris virgata*		Graminoid /vine	Floodplain woodland near irrigation canal	Present	12, 14
							Chloris radiata		Graminoid /vine	Between fields	Present	12, 14
	Various *Bouteloua* sp.	Needle grama	Graminoid	Upper & lower bajadas	Frequent	2, 3, 11	*Echinochloa colona*		Graminoid	Field weed	Present	12
	Distichlis sp.	Salt grass	Graminoid	Riparian salt marsh	Dominant	9, 11	*Distichlis spicata*		Graminoid	Disturbed low areas	Present	12, 14
	Eragrostis sp.	Love grass	Graminoid	Upper & lower bajadas	Present	3, 11	*Eragrostis ciliaris*		Graminoid	Field weed	Present	12, 14
							Eragrostis pilosa		Graminoid	Field weed	Present	12, 14
	Leptochloa sp.		Graminoid	Upper & lower bajadas	Present	3, 11	*Leptochloa uninervia*		Graminoid	Between fields	Frequent	12, 14
Poaceae (Gramineae)	*Cynodon dactylon*	Bermuda grass	Graminoid	Riparian floodplains	Dominant exotic	9, 11	*Cynodon dactylon*	Grama dulce	Graminoid /vine	Riparian woodland	Frequent - exotic	12, 14
	Panicum obtusum	Vine-mesquite grass	Graminoid	Riparian floodplains	Frequent	3, 8, 9, 11	*Cenchrus echinatus*	Pega pega	Graminoid	Dry, open areas riparian floodplain	Present	12, 14
	Phragmites sp.	Reeds	Graminoid	Lower riparian	Frequent	9, 11	*Setaria verticillata*		Graminoid	Riparian woodland	Present	12, 14

	Pleuraphis mutica	Tobosa grass	Graminoid	Riparian floodplains	Present	8, 11	*Arundo donax*	Caña	Graminoid	Riparian margins	Present	12, 14
Poaceae (Gramineae) *(cont.)*	*Sporobolus wrightii*	Giant sacaton	Graminoid	Riparian floodplains	Frequent	1, 8, 9, 10, 11	*Sporobolus virginicus*		Graminoid	Between fields	Present	12, 14
							Gynerium sagittatum	Caña Brava	Graminoid	Riparian margins	Dominant	12, 14
							Eleusine indica		Graminoid	Field weed	Present	12, 14
Polygonaceae	*Rumex crispus*	Curly dock / legua de vaca	Herb	Riparian floodplains / field weed	Frequent	1, 4, 9, 11	*Rumex crispus*	Lengua de vaca	Herb	Field weed	Present	14 cf. 16
	Rumex hymenosepalus	Sand dock / cañaigre	Herb	Riparian floodplains / field weed	Frequent	1, 4, 6, 9, 11						
Rhamnaceae	*Condalia* sp.	Snakewood	Shrub	Riparian floodplains	Frequent	6, 9, 11	*Scutia spicata*	Lloque Shrub		Riparian woodland	Present	12, 13, 14
	Ziziphus obtusifolius	Lotebush / jujube	Shrub	Riparian floodplains	Frequent	9, 11						
Salicaceae	*Salix gooddingii*	Willow	Tree	Riparian floodplains	Frequent	1, 8, 9	*Salix humboltiana*	Sauce	Tree	Riparian margins	Present	12, 13, 14
	Populus fremontii	Cottonwood	Tree	Riparian floodplains	Dominant	1, 8, 9						
Scrophulariaceae							*Galvesia fructiosa*		Shrub	Usaca riparian woodland	Present	12, 15
Solanaceae	*Capsicum annum*	Tabsaco pepper / wild chile	Herb	Dry flats	Frequent	9, 11	*Capsicum annum*	Ají	Herb	Samaca Cultivar	Cultivar	12
	Various *Lycium* sp.	Squawberry / tomatillo /	Shrub	Riparian floodplains	Frequent	6, 9, 11	Various *Lycium* sp.		Herb / shrub	Riparian woodland	Present	12
	Various *Physalis* sp.	Ground cherry / tomatillo	Herb	Upper & lower bajadas	Present	3, 9, 11	*Datura inoxia*		Herb	Dry, open areas riparian floodplain	Present	12
							Datura stramonium	Chamico	Herb	Dry, open areas riparian floodplain	Present	12, 14
	Nicotiana trigonophylla	Wild tobacco	Shrub	Riparian floodplains	Present	1, 4, 11	*Nicotiana paniculata*			Lomas		3
							Solanum nigra	Yerba mora	Herb	Dry, open areas riparian floodplain	Present	12, 14

Family	Sonoran Desert Flora						South Coast Peru Flora					
	Plant	Common Name	Habit	Main Habitat	Occurrence	Source	Plant	Common Name	Habit	Main Habitat	Occurrence	Source
							Solanum pimpinellifolium	Tomatillo	Herb	Dry, open areas riparian floodplain	Present	12, 14
							Solanum peruvianum	Tomatillo	Herb	Dry, open areas riparian floodplain	Present	12, 14
Sterculiaceae							*Waltheria ovata*	Lucraco	Herb	Dry, open areas riparian floodplain & fields	Present	12
Tamaricaceae	*Tamarix* sp.	Salt cedar	Tree	Riparian floodplain	Dominant - exotic	1, 11	*Tamarix* sp.		Tree	Riparian floodplains	Dominant	12
Typhaceae	*Typha domingensis*	Cattail	Graminoid	Riparian marshland	Frequent	6, 11						
Verbenaceae	*Phyla* sp. (syn. *Lippia* sp.)	Oregano	Herb	Upper & lower bajadas	Present	9, 11	*Phyla canescens*	Pandero	Herb	Dry, open areas riparian floodplain	Present	12, 14
Ulmaceae	Various *Celtis* sp.	Hackberry	Shrub	Riparian floodplains	Present	1, 9, 11						
Zygophyllaceae	Various *Kallstroemia* sp.	Caltrop	Herb	Bajadas and riparian floodplains	Frequent	2, 11	*Bulnesia retamo*		Shrub / subshrub	Riparian floodplain	Present	12, 15
	Larrea tridentata	Ceosote bush	Shrub	Dry flats	Dominant	1, 2, 5, 9, 11	*Larrea* sp.		Shrub	Lower Andean slopes	Present	16

SOURCES:
1 Castetter & Bell 1942
2 Simpson & Solbrig 1977
3 Mares et al. 1977
4 Nabhan 1979
5 Fontana 1983a
6 Nabhan 1986a
7 Felger & Moser 1985
8 Scott et al. 2000
9 Hodgson 2001
10 Yepez et al. 2003
11 USDA, NRCS 2004
12 South Coast Reference Collection – Samaca Basin (see Beresford-Jones 2005)
13 South Coast Peru Reference Collection – Usaca Woodland (see Beresford-Jones 2005)
14 Sagastegui Awa 1973
15 Rundel et al. 1991
16 Gentry 1996
17 Calderon, personal communication
18 Tropicos 2004

K EY: Shared flora

References

Abrams, E.M. and D.J. Rue 1988 The causes and consequences of deforestation among the prehistoric Maya. *Human Ecology* 16(4): 377–395.

Abrams, M.M., W.M. Jarrell, H.A. Smith and P.R. Clark 1990 Nitrogen accretion in soil and biomass by three *Prosopis* species. *Agroforestry Systems* 10: 93–97.

Acevedo Mallque, M. and Y. Kikata 1994 *Atlas of Peruvian Woods*. National Agrarian University, La Molina, Peru and Nagoya University, Japan.

Alpers, C.N. and G.H. Brimhall 1988 Middle Miocene climatic change in the Atacama Desert, northern Chile: evidence from supergene mineralisation at La Escondida. *Geological Society of America Bulletin* 100: 1640–1656.

Ansley, R.J, J.A. Huddle and B.A. Kramp 1997 Mesquite ecology. In *Brush Sculptors: Innovations for Tailoring Brushy Rangelands to Enhance Wildlife Habitat and Recreational Value. Proceedings of a Conference*, edited by D. Rollins, D.N. Ueckert and C. G. Brown. TAMU Agricultural Research and Extension Centre, San Angelo, Texas. Available from Texas Natural Resource Server: http://texnat.tamu.edu/symposia/sculptor/8.htm.

Arnold, D.Y. and C.A. Hastorf 2008 *Heads of State: Icons, Power, and Politics in the Ancient and Modern Andes*. Left Coast Press, Walnut Creek, CA.

Arya, S., O.P. Toky, B.P. Bisht and R. Tomar 1992 Potential of *Prosopis cineraria* (L.) Druce in arid and semi-arid India. In *Prosopis Species: Aspects of their Value, Research and Development. Proceedings of the Prosopis Symposium, Centre for Overseas Research and Development, University of Durham*, edited by R.W. Dutton, M. Powell and R.J. Ridley, pp. 61–70. FAO, Rome.

Asencio Díaz, F.W. 1997 *La Producción de Algarroba de los Bosques Secos: Economía y Medio Ambiente en la Región Grau*. CBC, Central Peruana de Servicios, Piura, Peru.

Bahr, D.M. 1983 Pima and Papago social organization. In *Handbook of North American Indians, Vol. 10, The Southwest*, edited by W.C. Sturtevant, pp. 178–192. Smithsonian Institution, Washington, DC.

Balée, W.L. 1994 *Footprints in the Forest. Ka'apor Ethnobotany—The Historical Ecology of Plant Utilization by an Amazonian People*. Columbia University Press, New York.

Barker, G.W.W. and D.D. Gilbertson 2000 Living at the margin: themes in the archaeology of drylands. In *The Archaeology of Drylands*, edited by G.W.W. Barker and D.D. Gilbertson, pp. 3–19. Routledge, London.

Barth, R.C. and J.O. Klemmedson 1982 Amount and distribution of dry matter, nitrogen and organic carbon in soil–plant systems of Mesquite and Palo Verde. *Journal of Range Management* 35: 412–418.

Bartlett, J.R. 1854 *Personal Narrative of Explorations and Incidents in Texas, New Mexico, California, Sonora, and Chihuahua (Vols. 1 and 2)*. Appleton, New York.

Benavides Ganoza, A. 2004 El templo de la soledad. In *Desiertos Vivos*, edited by J. Barrón and A. Balaguer, pp. 37–104. Colección APU. AFP Integra, Lima, Peru.

Benavides, M. 1991 Cheqo Wasi, Huari. In *Huari Administrative Structure*, edited by W.H. Isbell and G.F. McEwan, pp. 55–70. Dumbarton Oaks, Washington, DC.

Bengtsson, L. and M. Enell 1986 Chemical analysis. In *Handbook of Holocene Palaeoecology and Palaeohydrology*, edited by B. Berglund, pp. 423–451. J. Wiley and Sons, Chichester.

Bennett, K.D., W.D. Simonson and S.M. Pelgar 1990 Fire and man in postglacial woodlands of eastern England. *Journal of Archaeological Science* 17: 635–642.

Bentham G. 1875 Revision of the suborder Mimoseae. *The Transactions of the Linnean Society of London* 30: 335–664.

Beresford-Jones, D.G. 2005 Pre-Hispanic Prosopis-Human Relationships on the South Coast of Peru: Riparian Forests in the Context of Environmental and Cultural Trajectories of the Lower Ica Valley. Ph.D. thesis, University of Cambridge (available on-line at www.arch.cam.ac.uk/dgb27/).

Beresford-Jones, D.G., S. Arce Torres and C. Grimaldo 2004 Informe de los Trabajos Realizados Durante la Primera Temporada 2002 Presentada ante la Comisión Técnica de Arqueología. Unpublished report to the Instituto Nacional de Cultura del Perú, Lima, Peru.

Beresford- Jones, D.G., H.A. Lewis and S. Boreham 2009a Linking cultural and environmental change in Peruvian prehistory: geomorphological survey of the Samaca Basin, south coast Peru. *Catena* 78(3): 234–249.

Beresford-Jones, D.G., S. Arce Torres, O.Q. Whaley and A.J. Chepstow-Lusty 2009b The role of *Prosopis* in ecological and landscape change in the Samaca Basin, lower Ica Valley, south coast Peru from the Early Horizon to the Late Intermediate Period. *Latin American Antiquity* 20: 303–332.

Berglund, B.E. and M. Ralska-Jasiewiczowa 1986 Pollen analysis and pollen diagrams. In *Handbook of Holocene Palaeoecology and Palaeohydrology*, edited by B. Berglund, pp. 455–484. J. Wiley and Sons, Chichester.

Betancourt, J.L. and T.R. Van Devender 1981 Holocene vegetation in Chaco Canyon, New Mexico. *Science* 214: 656–658.

Betancourt, J.L., J.S. Dean and H.M. Hull 1986 Prehistoric long-distance transport of construction beams, Chaco Canyon, New Mexico. *American Antiquity* 51: 370–375.

Bird, S.B., J.E. Herrick, M.M. Wander and S.F. Wright 2002 Spatial heterogeneity of aggregate stability and soil carbon in semi-arid rangeland. *Environmental Pollution* 116: 445–455.

Bhojvaid, P.P., V.R. Timmer and G. Singh 1996 Reclaiming sodic soils for wheat production by *Prosopis juliflora* (Swartz) DC. Afforestation in India. *Agroforestry Systems* 34: 139–150.

Bhojvaid, P.P. and V.R. Timmer 1998 Soil dynamics in an age sequence of *Prosopis juliflora* planted for sodic soil restoration in India. *Forest Ecology and Management* 106: 181–193.

Böhlke, J.K., G.E. Ericksen and K. Revesz 1997 Stable isotope evidence for an atmospheric origin of desert nitrate deposits in northern Chile and southern California, USA. *Chemical Geologist* 136: 135–152.

Bohrer, V.L. 1970 Ethnobotanical aspects of Snaketown, a Hohokam village in southern Arizona. *American Antiquity* 35: 413–430.

Brack Egg, A. 1999 *Diccionario Enciclopédico de Plantas Útiles del Perú*. Centro Regionales Andinos Bartolomé de las Casas, Cuzco, Peru.

Brako, L. and J. Zarucchi 1993 *Catálogo de las Angiospermas y Gimnospermas del Perú*. Missouri Botanical Garden, St Louis, Missouri.

Breazeale, J.F. and F.J. Crider 1934 Plant association and survival, and the build-up of moisture in semi-arid soils. *Technical Bulletin of the University of Arizona* 53: 95–123.

Bridges, E.M. 1997 *World Soils*. Cambridge University Press, Cambridge.

Browman, D.L. 1983 Tectonic movement and agrarian collapse in prehispanic Peru. *Nature* 302: 568–569.

Brugnoli, P.B. and Soledad H.G.C. 1991 Análisis de un textil pintado Chavín. *Boletín del Museo Chileno de Arte Precolombino* 5: 67–80.

Bullock, P., N. Fedoroff, A. Jongerius, G. Stoops, T. Tursina and U. Babel 1985 *Handbook for Soil Thin Section Description*. Waine Research Publications, Wolverhampton.

Burger, R.L. 1992 *Chavin and the Origins of Andean Civilisation*. Thames and Hudson, London.

Burger, R.L. 1993 The Chavin Horizon: stylistic chimera or socioeconomic metamorphosis? In *Latin American Horizons*, edited by D.S. Rice, pp. 41–82. Dumbarton Oaks, Washington, DC.

Burger, R.L. and L.C. Salazar 2008 The Manchay Culture and the coastal inspiration for highland Chavín civilization. In *Chavín: Art, Architecture and Culture*, edited by W.J. Conklin and J. Quilter, pp. 85–106. Cotsen Institute of Archaeology Monograph 61. Cotsen Institute of Archaeology, Los Angeles, California.

Burger, R.L., K. Schreiber, M.D. Glasock and J. Ccencho 1998 The Jampatilla obsidian source: identifying the geological source of Pampas Type obsidian artifacts from southern Peru. *Andean Past* 5: 225–240.

Burkart, A. 1976 A monograph of the genus *Prosopis* (Leguminosae subfam. Mimoisoideae). Catalogue of the recognised species of *Prosopis*. *Journal of the Arnold Arboretum* 57: 219–249 (Part 1) and 450–525 (Part 2).

Burkart, A. and B.B. Simpson 1977 The genus *Prosopis* and annotated key to the species of the world. In *Mesquite. Its Biology in Two Desert Ecosystems*, edited by B.B. Simpson, pp. 201–215. US/IBP Synthesis Series 4. Dowden, Hutchinson and Ross, Stroudsburg, Pennsylvania .

Butterfield, R. 1996 *Prosopis* in the Sahelian forestry projects: a case study from Niger. In *Prosopis: Semiarid Fuelwood and Forage Tree. Building Consensus for the Disenfranchised*, edited by P. Felker and J. Moss, pp. 1-3–1-27. Centre for Semi-Arid Forest Resources, Kingsville, Texas.

Butzer, K.W. 1982 *Archaeology as Human Ecology*. Cambridge University Press, Cambridge.

Butzer, K.W. 1992 The Americas before and after 1492: an introduction to current geographical research. *Annals of the Association of American Geographers* 82 (3): 345–368.

Butzer, K.W. 1996 Ecology in the long view: settlement histories, agrosystemic strategies and ecological performance. *Journal of Field Archaeology* 23 (2): 141–150.

Butzer, K.W. 2005 Environmental history in the Mediterranean world: cross-disciplinary investigation of cause-and-effect for degradation and soil erosion. *Journal of Archaeological Science* 32: 1773–1800.

Cabeza de Vaca, A.N. 1993 *The Account: Álvar Núñez Cabeza de Vaca's Relación (1542)*, translated by M.A. Favata and J.B. Fernández. Arte Público Press, Houston, Texas.

Caldwell, M.M. and J.H. Richards 1989 Hydraulic lift: water efflux from upper roots improves effectiveness of water uptake by deep roots. *Oecologia* 79: 1–5.

Caldwell, M.M., T.E. Dawson and J.H Richards 1998 Hydraulic lift: consequences of water efflux from the roots of plants. *Oecologia* 113: 151–161.

Callen, E.O. 1969 Diet as revealed by coprolites. In *Science in Archaeology. A Comprehensive Survey of Progress and Research*, edited by D.R. Brothwell and E. Higgs, pp. 186–194. Basic Books, New York.

Canadell, J., R.B. Jackson, J.R. Ehleringer, H.A. Mooney, O.E. Sala and E.-D. Schulze 1996 Maximum rooting depth of vegetation types at the global scale. *Oecologia* 108: 583–595.

Carrillo-Garcia, A., J.L. León de la Luz, Y. Bashan and G.J. Bethlenfalvay 1999 Nurse Plants, Mycorrhizae, and plant establishment in a disturbed area of the Sonoran Desert. *Restoration Ecology* 7 (4): 321–335.

Carrillo-Garcia, A., Y. Bashan, E. Díaz Rivera and G.J. Bethlenfalvay 2000 Effects of resource island soils, competition, and inoculation with Azospirillum on survival and growth of *Pachycereus pringlei*, the giant cactus of the Sonoran Desert. *Restoration Ecology* 8 (1): 65–73.

Castetter, E.F. and W.H. Bell 1942 *Pima and Papago Indian Agriculture*. University of New Mexico Press, Albuquerque, New Mexico.

Catalano, A.S., J.C. Vilardi, D. Tosto and B.O. Saidman 2008 Molecular phylogeny and diversification history of *Prosopis* (Fabaceae: Mimosoideae). *Biological Journal of the Linnean Society* 93: 621–640.

Cerrón-Palomino, R. 2008 *Voces del Ande: Ensayos Sobre Onomástica Andina*. Fondo Editorial de la Pontificia Universidad Católica del Perú (PUCP), Lima, Peru.

Chepstow-Lusty, A.J. and M. Winfield 2000 Inca agroforestry: lessons from the past. *Ambio* 29 (6): 322–328.

Chepstow-Lusty A.J., K.D. Bennett, J. Fjeldså, A. Kendall, W. Galiano and A. Tupayachi Herrera 1998 Tracing 4,000 years of environmental history in the Cusco area, Peru, from the pollen record. *Mountain Research and Development* 18 (2): 159–172.

Cieza de León, P. de, 1995 *La Crónica del Peru* (1553), Part I, 3rd edn. Fondo Editorial de la Pontificia Universidad Católica del Perú (PUCP), Lima, Peru.

Clotts, H.V. 1917 History of the Indians and Irrigation on Indian Reservations. Unpublished report for the US Indian Service, Los Angeles, California.

Cobo, B.S.J. 1956 *Historia del Nuevo Mundo, Capítulo XXI (1653). Obras del Padre Bernabé Cobo. Vol 1.* Estades Artes Gráficas, Madrid.

El Comercio 1999 Huaqueros depredan antiguo cemetario de la cultura Wari. Report in Peru Section A, *El Comercio*, 11 February. Lima, Peru.

Conklin, W.J. 2008 The culture of Chavín textiles. In *Chavín: Art, Architecture and Culture*, edited by W.J. Conklin and J. Quilter, pp. 261–278. Cotsen Institute of Archaeology Monograph 61. Cotsen Institute of Archaeology, Los Angeles, California.

Conrad, G.W. and A.A. Demarest 1984 *Religion and Empire: The Dynamics of Aztec and Inca Expansionism.* Cambridge University Press, Cambridge.

Cook, A.G. 1994 Invesitigaciones de Reconocimiento Arqueologico en la Parte Baja del Valle de Ica. Informe Final (1988–1990). Unpublished report to the Instituto Nacional de Cultura, Lima, Peru.

Cook, A.G. 1999 Asentamientos Paracas en el Valle Bajo de Ica, Perú. *Gaceta Arqueologica Andina* 25: 61–90.

Cook, A.G. 2004 Wari art and society. In *Andean Archaeology*, edited by H. Silverman, pp. 146–166. Blackwell Press, Oxford.

Cook, A.G. and N. Parrish 2005 Gardens in the desert: archaeobotanical analysis from the lower Ica Valley, Peru. *Andean Past* 7: 135–156.

Cook, N.D. 1981 *Demographic Collapse: Indian Peru, 1520–1620.* Cambridge University Press, Cambridge.

Cooke, R.U. and R.W. Reeves 1976 *Arroyos and Environmental Change in the American Southwest.* Oxford University Press, Oxford.

Cooke, R.U., A. Warren and A.S. Goudie 1993 *Desert Geomorphology*. University College London Press, London.

Craig, A.K. 1982 Ambiente costero del norte de Chile. *Chungara* 9: 4–20.

Craig, A.K. and N. Psuty 1968 *The Paracas Papers: Studies in Marine Desert Ecology.* Occasional Publication No. 1, Department of Geography. Florida Atlantic University, Boca Raton, Florida.

Crown, P.L. 1991 The Hohokam: current views of prehistory and the regional system. In *Chaco and Hohokam: Prehistoric Regional Systems in the American Southwest*, edited by P.L. Crown and W.J. Judge, pp. 135–158. School of American Research Press, Santa Fe, New Mexico.

Cunningham, J.J. 2003 Transcending the 'obnoxious spectator': a case for processual pluralism in ethnoarchaeology. *Journal of Anthropological Archaeology* 22: 389–410.

Dagar, J.C., G. Singh and N.T. Singh 2001 Evaluation of forest and fruit trees used for rehabilitation of semi-arid alkali-sodic soils in India. *Arid Land Restoration and Ecology* 15: 115–133.

D'Antoni, H.L. and O.T. Solbrig 1977 Algarrobos in South American cultures: past and present. In *Mesquite. Its Biology in Two Desert Ecosystems*, edited by B.B. Simpson, pp. 189–199. US/IBP Synthesis Series 4. Dowden, Hutchinson and Ross, Stroudsburg, Pennsylvania.

D'Altroy, T.N. and K. Schreiber 2004 Andean empires. In *Andean Archaeology*, edited by H. Silverman, pp. 255–279. Blackwell Press, Oxford.

Davis, E.W. 1995 Ethnobotany: an old practice, a new discipline. In *Ethnobotany: Evolution of a Discipline*, edited by R. Schultes and S. von Reis, pp. 40–51. Dioscorides Press, Portland, Oregon.

Dawson, T.E. 1993 Hydraulic lift and water use by plants: implications for water balance, performance and plant–plant interactions. *Oecologia* 95: 565–574.

Dean, W.E. 1974 Determination of carbonate and organic matter in calcareous sediments and sedimentary rocks by loss on ignition: comparison with other methods. *Journal of Sedimentary Petrology* 44: 242–248.

Deans, J.D., O. Diagne, J. Nizinski, D.K. Lindley, M. Seck, K. Ingleby and R.C. Munro 2003 Comparative growth, biomass production, nutrient use and soil amelioration by nitrogen-fixing tree species in semi-arid Senegal. *Forest Ecology and Management* 176: 253–264.

DeLeonardis, L. 1997 Paracas Settlement in Callango, Lower Ica Valley, 1st Millennium BC, Peru. Unpublished PhD thesis, Catholic University of America, Washington, DC.

DeLeonardis, L. 2005 Early Paracas cultural contexts: new evidence from Callango. *Andean Past* 7: 27–55.

DeLeonardis, L. and G.F. Lau 2004 Life, death and ancestors. In *Andean Archaeology*, edited by H. Silverman, pp. 77–115. Blackwell Press, Oxford.

Denevan, W.M. 1992 The pristine myth: the landscape of the Americas in 1492. *Annals of the Association of American Geographers* 82 (3): 369–385.

Descola, P. 1994 *In the Society of Nature*. Cambridge University Press, Cambridge.

DeVries, T.J. 1987 A review of geological evidence for ancient El Niño activity in Peru. *Journal of Geophysical Research* 92 (C13): 14471–14479.

DeVries, T.J. and L.E. Wells 1990 Thermally-anomalous Holocene molluscan assemblages from coastal Peru: evidence for paleogeographic, not climatic change. *Palaeogeography, Palaeoclimatology, Palaeoecology* 81: 11–31.

DeVries, T.J., L. Ortlieb, A. Díaz, L. Wells and C. Hillaire-Marcell 1997 Determining the early history of El Niño. *Science* 276: 965–966.

Diamond, J. 1994 Ecological collapses of past civilizations. *Proceedings of the American Philosophical Society* 138: 363–370.

Diamond, J. 2005 *Collapse: How Societies Choose to Fail or Survive*. Allen Lane, London.

Díaz Celis, A. 1995 *Los Algarrobos*. CONCYTEC, Lima, Peru.

Dillehay, T.D., D. Bonavia and P. Kaulicke 2004 The first settlers. In *Andean Archaeology*, edited by H. Silverman, pp. 16–34. Blackwell Press, Oxford.

Dillehay, T.D., J. Rosen, T. Andres and D.E. Williams 2007 Preceramic adoption of peanut, squash and cotton in NOrthern Peru. *Science* 316: 1890–1893.

Dillon, M.O., M. Nakazawa and S.L. Gonzáles 2003 The *lomas* formations of coastal Peru: composition and biogeographic history. In *El Niño in Peru: Biology and Culture over 10,000 years*, edited by J. Haas and M.O. Dillon, pp. 1–9. Fieldiana Botany New Series 43. Field Museum of Natural History, Chicago.

Dommergues, Y. 1992 Maximising nitrogen fixation in *Prosopis* spp. In *Prosopis Species: Aspects of their Value, Research and Development. Proceedings of the Prosopis Symposium, Centre for Overseas Research and Development, University of Durham*, edited by R.W. Dutton, M. Powell and R.J. Ridley, pp. 207–218. FAO, Rome.

Donaire Vizarreta, J. 1998 [1959] *Campiña Iqueña. Aspectos Folklóricos* (1941). 4th edn. Ital Perú, Lima, Peru.

Doolittle, W.E. 2000 *Cultivated Landscapes of Native North America*. Oxford University Press, Oxford.

Drusini, A.G., N. Carrara, G. Orefici and M.R. Bonati 2001 Palaeodemography of the Nasca Valley: reconstruction of the human ecology in the southern Peruvian coast. *Homo* 52 (2): 157–172.

Dunbar, R.B., P.A. Baker, R.C. Marty and J. Cruzado 1990 *Pisco Basin Guidebook. Geologic Setting, Stratigraphy, and Biogenic Sediments of the Pisco Basin, Peru*. Earth Systems Institute, Rice University, Houston, Texas and Petróleos del Perú, Lima, Peru.

Dutton R.W. 1992 *Prosopis* spp: a justification for their future research and development. In *Prosopis Species: Aspects of their Value, Research and Development. Proceedings of the Prosopis Symposium, Centre for Overseas Research and Development, University of Durham*, edited by R.W. Dutton, M. Powell and R.J. Ridley, pp. 33–40. FAO, Rome.

Dwyer, J.D. 1979 The chronology and iconography of Paracas-style textiles. In *The Junius B. Bird Pre-Columbian Textile Conference 1973*, edited by A.P. Rowe, E.P. Benson and A.L. Schaffer, pp. 129–160. The Textile Museum and Dumbarton Oaks, Washington, DC.

East, R.M. and P. Felker 1993 Forage production and quality of four perennial grasses grown under and outside canopies of mature *Prosopis glandulosa* Torr. Var. *glandulosa* (Mesquite). *Agroforestry Systems* 22: 91–110.

Eitel, B., S. Hecht, B. Mächtle, G. Schukraft, A. Kadereit, G.A. Wagner, B. Kromer, I. Unkel and M. Reindel 2005 Geoarchaeological evidence from desert loess in the Nazca-Palpa Region, southern Peru: palaeoenvironmental changes and their impact on Pre-Columbian cultures. *Archaeometry* 47 (1): 137–158.

Eitel, B. and B. Mächtle 2009 Man and environment in the eastern Atacama Desert (southern Peru): Holcene climate changes and their impact on Pre-Columbian cultures. In *New Technologies for Archaeology:*

Multidisciplinary Investigations in Palpa and Nasca, Peru, edited by M. Reindel and G.A. Wagner, pp. 17–38. Springer, Berlin.

Elfadl, M.A. and O. Luukkanen 2003 Effect of pruning on Prosopis juliflora: considerations for tropical dryland argoforestry. *Journal of Arid Environments* 53: 441–455.

Emerman, S.H. and T.E. Dawson 1996 Hydraulic lift and its influence on the water content of the rhizosphere: an example from sugar maple, *Acer saccharum*. *Oecologia* 108: 273–278.

Emory, W.H. 1848 *Notes of a Military Reconnoissance from Fort Leavenworth in Missouri to San Diego, California*. Wendell and Van Benthuysen, Washington, DC.

Engel, F.-A. 1980 *Prehistoric Andean Ecology: Man, Settlement and Environment in the Andes. Atlas of Archaeological Sites in the Central Andes*. Abstracts of the Archives of the Centre for Arid Land Studies (CIZA), National Agrarian University of Peru. Humanities Press, City University of New York, New York.

Engel, F.-A. 1981 *Prehistoric Andean Ecology: Man, Settlement and Environment in the Andes. The Deep South*. Abstracts of the Archives of the Centre for Arid Land Studies (CIZA), National Agrarian University of Peru. Humanities Press, City University of New York, New York.

Ezell, P.H. 1983 History of the Pima. In *Handbook of North American Indians, Vol. 10, The Southwest*, edited by W.C. Sturtevant, pp. 149–160. Smithsonian Institution, Washington, DC.

Fagg, C.W. and J.L Stewart 1994 The value of *Acacia* and *Prosopis* in arid and semi-arid environments. *Journal of Arid Environments* 27: 3–25.

Farrington, I.S. 1974 Irrigation and settlement pattern: preliminary research results from the north coast of Peru. In *Irrigation's Impact on Society*, edited by T.E. Downing and M. Gibson, pp. 83–94. University of Arizona Press, Tuscon, Arizona.

Felger, R.S. 1977 Mesquite in Indian cultures of southwestern North America. In *Mesquite. Its Biology in Two Desert Ecosystems*, edited by B.B. Simpson, pp. 151–176. US/IBP Synthesis Series 4. Dowden, Hutchinson and Ross, Stroudsburg, Pennsylvania.

Felger, R.S. and M.B. Moser 1985 *People of the Desert and the Sea: Ethnobotany of the Seri Indians*. University of Arizona Press, Tucson, Arizona.

Felker, P. 1981 Uses of tree legumes in semi-arid areas. *Economic Botany* 35 (2): 174–186.

Felker, P. 1998 The value of mesquite for the rural Southwest: fine lumber and soil improvement. *Journal of Forestry* 96: 16–21.

Felker, P. and N. Patch 1996 Managing coppice, sapling and mature *Prosopis* for firewood, poles and lumber. In *Prosopis: Semiarid Fuelwood and Forage Tree. Building Consensus for the Disenfranchised*, edited by P. Felker and J. Moss, pp. 4-35–4-48. Centre for Semi-Arid Forest Resources, Kingsville, Texas.

Ferreyra, R. 1987 *Estudio Sistemático de los Algarrobos de la Costa Norte del Perú*. Dirección de Investigación Forestal y de Fauna, Lima, Peru.

Fish, S.K. 1985 Prehistoric disturbance floras of the lower Sonoran Desert and their implications. *American Association of Stratigraphic Palynologists, Contributions Series* 16: 77–88.

Fish, S.K. 2000 Hohokam impacts on Sonoran Desert environment. In *Imperfect Balance: Landscape Transformations in the Precolumbian Americas*, edited by D.L. Lentz, pp. 251–280. Columbia University Press, New York.

Fisher, C.E. 1977 Mesquite and modern man in southwestern North America. In *Mesquite. Its Biology in Two Desert Ecosystems*, edited by B.B. Simpson, pp. 177–187. US/IBP Synthesis Series 4. Dowden, Hutchinson and Ross, Stroudsburg, Pennsylvania.

Fisher, R.F. 1990 Amelioration of soil by trees. In *Sustained Productivity of Forest Soils*, edited by S.P. Gessell, D.S. Lacate, G.F. Weetman and R.F. Powers, pp. 290–300. Faculty of Forestry, University of British Columbia, Vancouver.

Flannery, K.V. 1968 Archaeological systems theory and early Mesoamerica. In *Anthropological Archaeology in the Americas*, edited by B.J. Meggars, pp. 67–87. Anthropological Society Washington, Washington, DC.

Flannery, K.V. 1973 The origins of agriculture. *Annual Review of Anthropology* 2: 271–310.

Fontana, B.L. 1983a History of the Papago. In *Handbook of North American Indians, Vol. 10, The Southwest*, edited by W.C. Sturtevant, pp. 137–150. Smithsonian Institution, Washington, DC.

Fontana, B.L. 1983b Pima and Papago: Introduction. In *Handbook of North American Indians, Vol. 10, The Southwest*, edited by W.C. Sturtevant, pp. 125–136. Smithsonian Institution, Washington, DC.

French, C. 2003 *Geoarchaeology in Action*. Routledge, London.

Fryberger, S.G. and G. Dean 1979 Dune forms and wind regime. In *A Study of Global Sand Seas*, edited by E.D. McKee, pp. 305–397. USGS Professional Paper 1052. US Government Printing Office, Washington, DC.

Fryrear, D.W. 1995 Soil losses by wind erosion. *Soil Science Society of America Journal* 59: 668–682.

Galan de Mera, A. 1996 Relación entre los suelos y la vegetación del Perú. *Arnaldoa* 4: 87–94.

Galan de Mera, A., 1999 La clases fitosociologicas de la vegetación del Perú. *Boletín de Lima* 117: 84–94.

Galera, F.M. 2000 *Los Algarrobos: Las Especies del Género Prosopis (Algarrobos) de América Latina con Especial Énfasis en Aquellas de Interés Económico*. FAO/Universidad Nacional de Córdoba. Graziani Gráfica, Córdoba, Argentina.

Galen Smith, S., H.A. Kantrud, J. Browning and K.D. Gordon-Gray 2004 *The Alkali (Scirpus maritimus L.) and Saltmarsh (S. Robustus Pursh) Bulrushes: A Literature Review*. USGS. Northern Prairie Wildlife Research Center (available online at www.npwrc.usgs.gov/resource/literatr/bulrush).

Garcia-Perea, R. 1994 The Pampas Cat group (Genus *Lynchailurus* Servertzov, 1858) (Carnivora: Felidae), a systematic and biogeographic review. *American Museum Novitates* 3096: 1–36.

Garg, V.K. 1992 Litter production and its nutrient concentration in some fuelwood trees grown on sodic soil. *Biomass and Bioenergy* 3 (3): 323–328.

Garg, V.K. 1998 Interaction of tree crops with a sodic soil environment: potential for rehabilitation of degraded environments. *Land Degradation and Development* 9: 81–93.

Garg, V.K. 1999 Leguminous trees for the rehabilitation of sodic wasteland in northern India. *Restoration Ecology* 7 (3): 281–287.

Garg, V.K. and R.K. Jain 1991 Influence of fuelwood trees on sodic soils. *Canadian Journal of Forestry Research* 22: 729–735.

Geesing, D., P. Felker and R.L. Bingham 2000 Influence of mesquite (*Prosopis glandulosa*) on soil nitrogen and carbon development: implications for global carbon sequestration. *Journal of Arid Environments* 46: 157–180.

Gentry, A.H. 1996 *A Field Guide to the Families and Genera of Woody Plants of Northwest South America (Colombia, Ecuador, Peru) with Supplementary Notes on Herbaceous Taxa*. University of Chicago Press, Chicago.

Gilbertson, D.D., C.O. Hunt, N.R.J. Feller and G.W.W. Barker 1994 The environmental consequences and context of ancient floodwater farming in the Tripolitanian pre-desert. In *Environmental Change in Drylands: Biogeographical and Geomorphological Presepectives*, edited by A.C. Millington and K. Pye, pp. 229–251. J. Wiley and Sons, Chichester.

Gile, L.H. 1966 Coppice dunes and the Rotura Soil. *Soil Science Society of America, Proceedings* 30: 657–660.

Gile, L.H., R.P. Gibbens and J.M. Lenz 1997 The near-ubiquitous pedogenic world of mesquite roots in an arid basin floor. *Journal of Arid Environments* 35: 39–58.

Goel, V.L. and H.M. Behl 1996 Fuelwood quality of promising tree species for alkaline soil sites in relation to tree age. *Biomass and Bioenergy* 10 (1): 57–61.

Goel, V.L. and H.M. Behl 2001 Genetic selection and improvement of hard wood tree species for fuelwood production on sodic soils with particular reference to *Prosopis juliflora*. *Biomass and Bioenergy* 20: 9–15.

Goldberg, P. and R.I. Macphail 2006 *Practical and Theoretical Geoarchaeology*. Blackwell Press, Malden, UK.

Goudie, A.S. 1973 *Duricrusts in Tropical and Sub-Tropical Landscapes*. Clarendon Press, Oxford.

Goudie, A.S. 1983 Calcrete. In *Chemical Sediments and Geomorphology*, edited by A.S. Goudie and K. Pye, pp. 93–131. Academic Press, London.

Gould, R.A. 1980 *Living Archaeology*. Cambridge University Press, Cambridge.

Grados, N. and G. Cruz 1996 New approaches to industrialization of algarrobo (*Prosopis pallida*) pods in Peru. In *Prosopis: Semiarid Fuelwood and Forage Tree. Building Consensus for the Disenfranchised*, edited by P. Felker and J. Moss, pp. 3-25–3-42. Centre for Semi-Arid Forest Resources, Kingsville, Texas.

Graf, W.L. 2002 *Fluvial Processes in Dryland Rivers*. Reprint of 1988 1st edn. The Blackburn Press, Caldwell, New Jersey.

Gregory, D.A. 1991 Form and variation in Hohokam settlement patterns. In *Chaco and Hohokam: Prehistoric Regional Systems in the American Southwest*, edited by P.L. Crown and W.J. Judge, pp. 159–194. School of American Research Press, Santa Fe, New Mexico.

Gumerman, G.J. and E.W. Haury 1979 Prehistory: Hohokam. In *Handbook of North American Indians, Vol. 9, The Southwest*, edited by W.C. Sturtevant, pp. 75–90. Smithsonian Institution, Washington, DC.

Gunn, C. and C. Ritchie 1988 Identification of disseminules listed in the Federal Noxious Weed Act. *US Department of Agriculture Technical Bulletin* 1719: 1–313.

Hackenberg, R.A. 1983 Pima and Papago ecological adaptations. In *Handbook of North American Indians, Vol. 10, The Southwest*, edited by W.C. Sturtevant, pp. 161–177. Smithsonian Institution, Washington, DC.

Harlan, J.R. 1975. *Crops and Man*. American Society of Agronomy, Madison, Wisconsin.

Harris, G.A. and G.S. Campbell 1981 Morphological and physiological characteristics of desert plants. In *Water in Desert Ecosystems*, edited by D.D. Evans and J.L. Thames, pp. 59–74. US/IBP Synthesis Series 11. Dowden, Hutchinson and Ross, Stroudsburg, Pennsylvania.

Harris, P.J.C., N.M. Pasiecznik, M.T. Vera-Cruz and M. Bradbury 1996 *Prosopis* genetic improvement trials in Cape Verde. In *Prosopis: Semiarid Fuelwood and Forage Tree. Building Consensus for the Disenfranchised*, edited by P. Felker and J. Moss, pp. 4-3–4-20. Centre for Semi-Arid Forest Resources, Kingsville, Texas.

Harris, P.J.C., N.M. Pasiecznik, S.J. Smith, J.M. Billington and L. Ramírez 2003 Differentiation of *Prosopis juliflora* (Sw.) DC and *P. pallida* (H. & B. ex. Willd.) H.B.K. using foliar characters and ploidy. *Forest Ecology and Management* 180: 153–164.

Harsh, L.H., J.C. Tewari and N.K. Sharma 1996 Performance of *Prosopis* species in arid regions of India. In *Prosopis: Semiarid Fuelwood and Forage Tree. Building Consensus for the Disenfranchised*, edited by P. Felker and J. Moss, pp. 4-21–4-29. Centre for Semi-Arid Forest Resources, Kingsville, Texas.

Hather, J.G. 2000 *Archaeological Parenchyma*. Archetype Publications, London.

Hayes A.C., D.M. Brugge and W.J. Judge 1981 *Archaeological Surveys of Chaco Canyon, New Mexico*. National Park Service, Publications in Archaeology 18A. Chaco Canyon Studies. US Department of the Interior, Washington, DC.

Hecht, N. 2009 Of layers and sherds: a context-based relative chronology of the Nasca Style Pottery from Palpa. In *New Technologies for Archaeology: Multidisciplinary Investigations in Palpa and Nasca, Peru*, edited by M. Reindel and G.A. Wagner, pp. 207–230. Springer, Berlin.

Heggarty, P. and D.G. Beresford-Jones 2010. Agriculture and language dispersals: limitations, refinements, and an Andean exception? *Current Anthropology* 51: 163–191.

Hesse, R. and J. Baade 2008 Irrigation agriculture and the sedimentary record in the Palpa Valley, southern Peru. *Catena* 77: 119–129.

Hodder, I. 1982 *The Present Past*. Batsford, London.

Hodell, D.A., J.H. Curtis and M. Brenner 1995 Possible role of climate in the collapse of Classic Maya civilization. *Nature* 375: 392–394.

Hodgson, J.M. 1974 *Soil Survey Field Handbook*. Soil Survey Technical Monographs 5. Soil Survey of England and Wales, Harpenden, UK.

Hodgson, W.C. 2001 *Food Plants of the Sonoran Desert*. University of Arizona Press. Tuscon, Arizona.

Holden, T.G. 1991 Evidence of prehistoric diet from northern Chile: coprolites, gut contents and flotation samples from the Tulán Quebrada. *World Archaeology* 22 (3): 320–331.

Holden, T.G. and L. Núñez 1993 An analysis of the gut contents of five well-preserved human bodies from Tarapacá, Northern Chile. *Journal of Archaeological Science* 20: 595–611.

Horton, J.L. and S.C. Hart 1998 Hydraulic lift: a potentially important ecosystem process. *Tree* 13 (6): 232–235.

Howard, E.A. 1887 *Reports of Agents in Arizona: Pima Agency, 1887. Annual Reports of Commissioner for Indian Affairs to the Secretary of Interior.* US Government Printing Office, Washington, DC.

Hubbard, R.N.L.B. and A. Clapham 1992 Quantifying macroscopic plant remains. *Review of Palaeobotany and Palynology* 73: 117–132.

Ibrahim, K.M. 1992 *Prosopis* species in the southwest United States: their utilisation and research. In *Prosopis Species: Aspects of their Value, Research and Development. Proceedings of the Prosopis Symposium, Centre for Overseas Research and Development, University of Durham*, edited by R.W. Dutton, M. Powell and R.J. Ridley, pp. 83–115. FAO, Rome.

Isbell, W.H. 1988 City and state in Middle Horizon Huari. In *Peruvian Prehistory*, edited by R.W. Keatinge, pp. 164–189. Cambridge University Press, Cambridge.

Isbell, W.H. 1997 *Mummies and Mortuary Monuments: A Postprocessual Prehistory of Central Andean Social Organization*. University of Texas Press, Austin, Texas.

Isbell, W.H. 2001 Represando el Horizonte Medio: el caso de Conchopata, Ayacucho, Perú. In *Huari y Tiwanaku: Modelos vs. Evidencias*, edited by P. Kaulicke and W.H. Isbell, pp. 9–68. Boletín de Arqueología PUCP 4, Fondo Editorial de la Pontificia Universidad Católica del Perú, Lima, Peru.

Isbell, W.H. and G.F. McEwan 1991 A history of Huari studies and introduction to current interpretations. In *Huari Administrative Structure*, edited by W.H. Isbell and G.F. McEwan, pp. 1–17. Dumbarton Oaks, Washington, DC.

Isbell, W.H. and K. Shreiber 1978 Was Huari a state? *American Antiquity* 43: 372–389.

Isbell, W.H. and A. Vranich. 2004 Experiencing the cities of Wari and Tiwanaku. In *Andean Archaeology*, edited by H. Silverman, pp. 167–182. Blackwell Press, Oxford.

Isbell, W.H., C. Brewster-Wary and L.E. Spickard 1991 Architecture and spatial organization at Huari. In *Huari Administrative Structure*, edited by W.H. Isbell and G.F. McEwan, pp. 19–54. Dumbarton Oaks, Washington, DC.

Isla, J. 1992 La ocupación Nasca en Usaca. *Gaceta Arqueológica Andina* 22: 119–151.

Isla, J. 2009 From hunters to regional lords: funerary practices in Palpa, Peru. In *New Technologies for Archaeology: Multidisciplinary Investigations in Palpa and Nasca, Peru*, edited by M. Reindel and G.A. Wagner, pp. 119–140. Springer, Berlin.

Jackson, R.B., J.S. Sperry and T.E. Dawson 2000 Root water uptake and transport: using physiological processes in global predictions. *Trends in Plant Science* 5 (11): 482–488.

Jacobsen, T. and R.M. Adams 1958 Salt and silt in ancient Mesopotamian agriculture. *Science* 128: 1251–1258.

Jenny, H. 1944 *Factors of Soil Formation*. McGraw-Hill, New York.

Jett, S.C. and J.S. Wood 1992 Museum exhibit and book review of Seeds of Change: 500 Years of Encounter and Exchange, an exhibit of the National Museum of Natural History, Smithsonian Institution, Washington, DC and Seeds of Change: a Quincentennial Commemoration, edited by H.J. Viola and C. Margolis. *Annals of the Association of American Geographers* 82 (3): 566–568.

Johnson, A. and T. Earle 1987 *The Evolution of the Human Society*. Stanford University Press, Palo Alto, California.

Johnson, H.B. and E.B. Mayeux 1990 *Prosopis glandulosa* and the nitrogen balance of rangelands: extent and occurrence of nodulation. *Oecologia* 84: 176–186.

Jones, M. K. 2009 Moving north: archaeobotanical evidence for plant diet in Middle and Upper Palaeolithic Europe. In *The Evolution of Hominid Diets: Integrating Approaches to the Study of Palaeolithic Subsistence*, edited by M.P. Richards and J.-J. Hublin, pp. 171–180. Springer, London.

Kaur B., S.R. Gupta and G. Singh 2002 Bioamelioration of a sodic soil by silvopastoral systems in northwestern India. *Agroforestry Systems* 54: 13–20.

Kautz, R.R. 1980 Palynology of coprolites from sites in northern Chile. In *Prehistoric Trails of the Atacama: Archaeology of Northern Chile*, edited by C.M. Meighan and D.L. True, pp. 205–213. Monumenta Archaeologica 7. Institute of Archaeology, University of California, Los Angeles.

Keefer, D.K., S.D. DeFrance, M.E. Mosely, J. Richardson, D.R. Satterlee and A. Day-Lewis 1998 Early maritime economy and El Niño events at Quebrada Tacahuay, Peru. *Science* 281: 1833–1835.

Kellner, C.M. 2002 Coping with Environmental Stress and Social Challenges in Prehistoric Peru: Bioarchaeological Analysis of Nasca Populations. Unpublished PhD thesis, University of Santa Barbara, California.

Kembel, S.R. and J.W. Rick 2004 Building authority at Chavín de Huántar: models of social organization and development in the Initial Period and Early Horizon. In *Andean Archaeology*, edited by H. Silverman, pp. 51–76. Blackwell Press, Oxford.

Khanzada, A.K., J.D. Morris, R. Ansari, P.G. Slavich and J.J. Collopy 1998 Groundwater uptake and sustainability of *Acacia* and *Prosopis* plantations in southern Pakistan. *Agricultural Water Management* 36: 121–139.

Kingsolver, J.M., C.D. Johnson, S.R. Swier and A.Teran 1977 *Prosopis* fruits as a resource for invertebrates. In *Mesquite. Its Biology in Two Desert Ecosystems*, edited by B.B. Simpson, pp. 108–121. US/IBP Synthesis Series 4. Dowden, Hutchinson and Ross, Stroudsburg, Pennsylvania.

Kosok, P. 1965 *Life, Land and Water in Ancient Peru*. Long Island University Press, Brooklyn.

Kroeber, A.L. 1944 *Peruvian Archaeology in 1942*. Viking Fund Publications in Anthropology 4. Viking Fund, New York.

Kroeber, A.L. and D. Collier 1998 *The Archaeology and Pottery of Nazca, Peru. Alfred Kroeber's 1926 Expedition*, edited by P. Carmichael. AltaMira Press, Walnut Creek, California.

Lancho Rojas, J. 1998 El Huarango en el proceso histórico de Nasca. *Umbral* 10: 16–19.

Lathrap, D.W. 1970 *Upper Amazon*. Thames and Hudson, London.

Layme Pairumani, Félix, 1997 *Diccionario bilingüe – Aimara – castellano Castellano – aimara*, 2nd edition. Secretaría Nacional de Educación, La Paz, Bolivia.

Lea, J.D. 1996 A review of the literature on charcoal in Haiti. In *Prosopis: Semiarid Fuelwood and Forage Tree. Building Consensus for the Disenfranchised*, edited by P. Felker and J. Moss, pp. 2-33–2-44. Centre for Semi-Arid Forest Resources, Kingsville, Texas.

Lee, S.G., E.J. Russel, R.L. Bingham and P. Felker 1992 Discovery of thornless, non-browsed, erect, tropical *Prosopis* in 3-year-old Haitian progeny trials. *Forest Ecology and Management* 48: 1–13.

Lentz, D.L. 2000 Introduction: definitions and conceptual underpinnings. In *Imperfect Balance: Landscape Transformations in the Precolumbian Americas*, edited by D.L. Lentz, pp. 1–12. Columbia University Press, New York.

Lovell, W.G. 1992 'Heavy shadows and black night': disease and depopulation in Colonial Spanish America. *Annals of the Association of American Geographers* 82 (3): 426–443.

Lumaret, R. and N. Ouazzani 2001 Ancient wild olives in Mediterranean forests. *Nature* 413: 700.

Lumbreras, L.G. 1974 *The Peoples and Cultures of Ancient Peru*, translated by B. Meggers. Smithsonian Institution Press, Washington, DC.

MacBride, J.F. 1943 Flora of Peru – family Leguminosae. *Botanical Series, Field Museum of Natural History* 13: 108–110.

McCauley, J.F., C.S. Breed and M.J. Grolier 1977 Yardangs. In *Geomorphology in Arid Regions*, edited by D.O. Doehring, pp. 233–272. Allen and Unwin, Boston.

McEvedy, C. 1992 *The Penguin Atlas of Medieval History*. Penguin, London.

McGee, W.J. 1898 Papaguería. *National Geographic* 9: 345–371.

Machette, M.N. 1985 Calcic soils of the southwestern United States. In *Soils and Quaternary Geology of the Southwestern United States*, edited by D.L. Weide, pp. 1–21. Geological Society of America Special Paper 203. Boulder, Colorado.

Mächtle, B., B. Eitel, A. Kadereit and I. Unkel 2006 Holocene environmental changes in the northern Atacama Desert, southern Peru (14°30'S) and their impact on the rise and fall of Pre-Columbian Cultures. *Z. Geomorph N.F. Supplementary* 142: 47–62.

Mächtle, B., B. Eitel, G. Schukraft and K. Ross 2009 Built on sand: climatic oscillation and water harvesting during the Late Interemdiate Period. In *New Technologies for Archaeology: Multidisciplinary Investigations in Palpa and Nasca, Peru*, edited by M. Reindel and G.A. Wagner, pp. 39–48. Springer, Berlin.

McKay, C.P., E.I. Friedmann, B. Gómez-Silva, L. Cáceres-Villanueva, D.T. Andersen and R. Landheim 2003 Temperature and moisture conditions for life in the extreme arid region of the Atacama Desert: four years of observations including the El Niño of 1997–1998. *Astrobiology* 3 (2): 393–406.

Mahmood K., J. Morris, J. Collopy and P. Slavich 2001 Groundwater uptake and sustainability of farm plantations on saline sites in Punjab Province, Pakistan. *Agricultural Water Management* 48: 1–20.

Mainguet M. 1996 *Desertification. Natural Background and Human Mismanagement.* Springer-Verlag. Berlin.

Maizels, J.K. 1988 Palaeochannels: Plio-Pleistocene raised channel systems of the western Sharqiyah. *Journal of Oman Studies Special Report* 3: 95–112.

Marcus, Joyce 2008 *Excavations at Cerro Azul, Peru: The Architecture and Pottery.* Cotsen Institute of Archaeology Monograph 62. Cotsen Institute of Archaeology, Los Angeles.

Mares, M.A., F.A. Enders, J.M. Kingsolver, J.L. Neff and B.B. Simpson 1977 *Prosopis* as a niche component. In *Mesquite. Its Biology in Two Desert Ecosystems*, edited by B.B. Simpson, pp. 123–149. US/IBP Synthesis Series 4. Dowden, Hutchinson and Ross, Stroudsburg, Pennsylvania.

Martin, G.J. 2004 *Ethnobotany: A Methods Manual.* Earthscan, London.

Martin, M.P. 1948 *Observations on the Nodulations of Leguminous Plants of the Southwest.* US Department of Agriculture, Soil Conservation Service, Plant Study Series 4. Regional Bulletin 107, Washington, DC.

Martin, P.S. 1963 *The Last 10,000 Years: A Fossil Pollen Record of the American Southwest.* University of Arizona Press, Tuscon, Arizona.

Martin P. S. 1967 Prehistoric overkill. In *Pleistocene Extinctions: The Search for a Cause,* edited by P.S. Martin and H.E. Wright, pp. 75–120. Yale University Press, New Haven, Connecticut.

Martin, A.C. and W.D. Barkley 1961 *Seed Identification Manual.* University of California Press, Berkeley, California.

Masse, W.B. 1991 The quest for subsistence sufficiency and civilisation in the Sonoran Desert. In *Chaco and Hohokam: Prehistoric Regional Systems in the American Southwest*, edited by P.L. Crown and W.J. Judge, pp. 195–223. School of American Research Advanced Seminar Series, Santa Fe, New Mexico.

Massey, S.A. 1991 Social and political leadership in the lower Ica Valley: Ocucaje Phases 8 and 9. In *Paracas Art and Architecture*, edited by A. Paul, pp. 349–416. University of Iowa Press, Iowa City.

Massey, W. 1949 Tribes and languages of Baja California. *Southwestern Journal of Anthropology* 5 (3): 272–307.

Menzel, D. 1967 Style and time in the Middle Horizon. In *Peruvian Archaeology Selected Readings*, edited by J.H. Rowe and D. Menzel, pp. 146–164. Peek Publications, Palo Alto, California.

Menzel, D. 1976 *Pottery Style and Society in Ancient Peru. Art as a Mirror of History in the Ica Valley, 1350–1570.* University of California Press, Berkeley and Los Angeles.

Menzel, D., J.H. Rowe and L.E. Dawson 1964 *The Paracas Pottery of Ica: A Study in Style and Time.* University of California Press, Berkeley.

Miller, D.R., J.D. Lin and Z.N. Lu 1991 Some effects of surrounding forest canopy architecture on the wind effects in small clearings. *Forest Ecology and Management* 45: 79–91.

Mishra, A. and S.D. Sharma 2003 Leguminous trees for the restoration of degraded sodic wasteland in eastern Uttar Pradesh, India. *Land Degradation and Development* 14: 245–261.

Mishra, A., S.D. Sharma and M.K. Gupta 2003 Soil rehabilitation through afforestation: evaluation of the performance of *Prosopis juliflora*, *Dalbergia sissoo* and *Eucalyptus tereticornis* plantations in a sodic environment. *Arid Land Research and Management* 17: 257–269.

MOLAS 1994 *Archaeological Site Manual*, 3rd edn. Museum of London Archaeological Service, London.

Mom, M.P., A.D. Burghardt, R.M. Palacios and L. Alban 2002 Los algarrobos Peruanos: *Prosopis pallida* y su delimitación. *Arnaldoa* 9 (1): 39–48.

Monsalve, J.G. 1985 A pollen core from the Hacienda Lusitania. *Pro Calima* 4, edited by W. Bray. Periodic publication of Pro Calima Project, Basel.

Mooney, H.A., B.B. Simpson and O.T. Solbrig 1977 Phenology, morphology, physiology. In *Mesquite. Its Biology in Two Desert Ecosystems*, edited by B.B. Simpson, pp. 26–43. US/IBP Synthesis Series 4. Dowden, Hutchinson and Ross, Stroudsburg, Pennsylvania .

Mooney, H.A., S.L. Gulmon, R.W. Rundel and J. Ehleringer 1980 Further observations on the water relations of *Prosopis tamarugo* of the northern Atacama Desert. *Oecologia* 44: 177–180.

Moseley, M.E. 1975 *The Maritime Foundations of Andean Civilization*. Cummings Archaeological Series. Cummings, Menlo Park, California.

Moseley, M.E. 1992 *The Incas and their Ancestors, the Archaeology of Peru*. Thames and Hudson, London.

Moseley, M.E., R.A. Feldman and C.R. Ortloff 1981 Living with crises: human perception of process and time. In *Biotic Crises in Ecological and Evolutionary Time*, edited by M. Nitecki, pp. 231–267. Academic Press, New York.

Moseley, M.E., R.A. Feldman, C.R. Ortloff and A. Narvaez 1983 Principles of agrarian collapse in the Cordillera Negra, Peru. *Annals of Carnegie Museum*, Vol. 52, Article 13, pp. 299–327. Carnegie Museum of Natural History, Pittsburgh, Pennsylvania.

Moutarde, Fanny 2006 L'évolution du couvert ligneux et de son exploitation par l'homme dans la vallée du Lurín (côte centrale du Pérou), de l'Horizon Ancien (900–100 av. J.-C.) à l'Horizon Tardif (1460–1532 ap. J.-C.). Approche anthracologique. Volume II: Atlas anthracologique. Unpublished Ph.D. thesis, Université Paris I.

Moy, C.M., G.O. Seltzer, D.T. Rodbell and D.M. Anderson 2002 Variability of El Niño/Southern Oscillation activity at millennial timescales during the Holocene epoch. *Nature* 420: 162–165.

Munsell 2000 *Munsell Soil Colour Charts*. Gretag Macbeth, New York.

Murphy, C.P. 1986 *Thin Section Preparation of Soils and Sediments*. AB Academic Publishers, Berkhamsted.

Nabhan, G.P. 1979 The ecology of floodwater farming in arid south-western North America. *Agro-Ecosystems* 5: 245–255.

Nabhan, G.P. 1985 *Gathering the Desert*. University of Arizona Press, Tuscon, Arizona.

Nabhan, G.P. 1986a 'Ak-ciñ 'Arroyo Mouth' and the environmental setting of the Papago Indian fields in the Sonoran Desert. *Applied Geography* 6: 61–75.

Nabhan, G.P. 1986b Papago Indian desert agriculture and water control in the Sonoran Desert, 1697–1934. *Applied Geography* 6: 43–59.

Nabhan, G.P., C. Weber and J. Berry 1979 Legumes in Papago-Pima Indian diet and ecological niche. *Kiva* 44: 173–190.

Netherly, P.J. 1988 From event to process: the recovery of Late Andean organizational structure by means of Spanish colonial written records. In *Peruvian Prehistory*, edited by R.W. Keatinge, pp. 257–278. Cambridge University Press, Cambridge.

Nials, F.L., E.E. Deeds, M.E. Mosely, S.G. Pozorski, T.G. Pozorski and R.A. Feldman 1979 El Niño: the catastrophic flooding of coastal Peru. *Bulletin of the Field Museum of Natural History* 50 (7): 4014 (Part I) and (8): 4–10 (Part II).

Nyberg, G. and P. Högberg 1995 Effects of young agroforestry trees on soils in on-farm situations in western Kenya. *Agroforestry Systems* 32: 45–52.

O'Hara, S.L., F.A. Street-Perrott and T. P. Burt 1993 Accelerated soil erosion around a Mexican lake caused by Prehispanic agriculture. *Nature* 362: 48–51.

ONERN 1971 *Inventario, Evaluación y Uso Regional de los Recursos Naturales de la Costa. Cuenca del Río Ica*, Vols. 1 and 2. Oficina Nacional de Evaluación de Recursos Naturales (ONERN), Lima, Peru.

Orefici, G. and A. Drusini 2003 *Nasca: Hipótesis y Evidencias de Desarrollo Cultural. Documentos e Investigaciones 2*. Centro Italiano Studi e Ricerche Archeologiche Precolombiane, Lima, Peru.

Ormeño Iglesias, C. 1995 *Misterios y Simbolismos de la Cultura Nasca*. Delgado Villanueva Editores, Lima, Peru.

Ortlieb, L. and G. Vargas 2003 Debris-flow deposits and El Niño impacts. In *El Niño in Peru: Biology and Culture over 10,000 years*, edited by J. Haas and M.O. Dillon, pp. 24–51. Fieldiana Botany New Series 43. Field Museum of Natural History, Chicago.

Ortloff, C.R., M.E. Moseley and R.A. Feldman 1982 Hydraulic engineering aspects of the Chimu Chicama–Moche intervalley canal. *American Antiquity* 47: 572–595.

Paez, M.M., F. Schäbitz and S. Stutz 2001 Modern pollen – vegetation and isopoll maps in southern Argentina. *Journal of Biogeography* 28: 997–1021.

Park, C.C. 1983 Water resources and irrigation agriculture in Pre-Hispanic Peru. *The Geographical Journal (Royal Geographical Society)* 149 (2): 153–166.

Parker Gay, S. Jr. 1999 Observations regarding the movement of Barchan sand dunes in the Nazca to Tacna Area of southern Peru. *Geomorphology* 27: 279–293.

Pasiecznik, N.M., P. Felker, P.J.C. Harris, L.N. Harsh, G. Cruz, J.C. Tewari, K. Cadoret and L.J. Maldonado 2001 *The Prosopis juliflora–Prosopis pallida Complex: A Monograph*. HDRA, Coventry.

Paul, A. 1990 *Paracas Ritual Attire*. University of Oklahoma Press, Norman, Oklahoma.

Pearsall, D.M. 1980 Pachamachay ethnobotanical report: plant utilization at a hunting base camp. In *Prehistoric Hunters of the High Andes*, edited by J.W, Rick, pp. 191–232. Academic Press, London.

Pearsall, D. and D.R. Piperno 1998 *The Origins of Agriculture in the Lowland Neotropics*. Academic Press, San Diego, California.

Peláez, D.V., R.A. Distel, R.M. Bóo, O.R. Elia and M.D. Mayor 1994 Water relations between shrubs and grasses in semi-arid Argentina. *Journal of Arid Environments* 27: 71–78.

Pessarakli, M. and I. Szabolcs 1999 Soil salinity and sodicity as particular plant/crop stress factors. In *Handbook of Plant and Crop Stress*, edited by M. Pessarakli, 2nd edn, pp. 1–16. Marcell Dekker, New York.

Peters, A.H. 1991 Ecology and society in embroidered images from the Paracas Necropolis. In *Paracas Art and Architecture*, edited by A. Paul, pp. 349–416. University of Iowa Press, Iowa City.

Petrov, M.P. 1976 *Deserts of the World*. J. Wiley and Sons, New York.

Pezzia Assereto, A. 1968 *Ica y El Perú Precolombino. Tomo I. Arqueología de la Provincia de Ica*. Empresa Editora Ojeda, Ica, Peru.

Piacenza, L. 2005 Evidencias botánicas en asentamientos Nasca. *Boletín del Museo de Arqueología y Antropolgía* (UNMSM) 5: 3–13.

Plog, S. 1997 *Ancient Peoples of the American Southwest*. Thames and Hudson, London.

Plowman, T. 1979 The identity of Amazonian and Trujillo coca. *Botanical Museum Leaflets* 27: 45–68.

Plowman, T. 1984 The origin, evolution and diffusion of coca, *Erythroxylum* spp., in South and Central America. In *Pre-Columbian Plant Migration*, edited by D. Stone. *Papers of the Peabody Museum of Archaeology and Ethnology* 76: 125–163.

Pollock, D. 1996 The rise of Amazonia: a book review essay. *American Anthropologist* 98: 157–161.

Pozorski, S. and T. Pozorski 1982 Reassessing the Chicama–Moche intervalley canal: comments on the hydraulic engineering aspects of the Chicama–Moche intervalley canal. *American Antiquity* 47: 851–868.

Pozorski, S. and T. Pozorski 1987 *Early Settlement and Subsistence in the Casma Valley, Peru*. University of Iowa Press, Iowa City.

Pozorski, S. and T. Pozorski 2003a The impact of the El Niño phenomenon on prehistoric Chimú irrigation systems of the Peruvian coast. In *El Niño in Peru: Biology and Culture over 10,000 years*, edited by J. Haas and M.O. Dillon, pp. 71–89. Fieldiana Botany New Series 43. Field Museum of Natural History, Chicago.

Pozorski, S. and T. Pozorski 2003b Paleoenvironment at Almejas: an early exploitation of estuarine fauna on the north coast of Peru. In *El Niño in Peru: Biology and Culture over 10,000 years*, edited by J. Haas and M.O. Dillon, pp. 52–70. Fieldiana Botany New Series 43. Field Museum of Natural History, Chicago.

Prohaska, F.J. 1973 New evidence on the climatic controls along the Peruvian coast. In *Coastal Deserts: Their Natural and Human Environments*, edited by D.H.K Amiran and A.W. Wislon, pp. 91–107. University of Arizona Press, Tuscon, Arizona.

Proulx, D.A. 1968 *Local Differences and Time Differences in Nasca Pottery*. University of California Press, Berkeley and Los Angeles.

Proulx, D.A. 2006 *A Sourcebook of Nasca Ceramic Iconography. Reading a Culture through its Art*. University of Iowa Press, Iowa City.

Purohit, U., S.K. Mehar and S. Sundaramoorthy 2002 Role of *Prosopis cineraria* on the ecology of soil fungi in Indian desert. *Journal of Arid Environments* 52: 17–27.

Quilter, J. 1989 *Life and Death at Paloma*. University of Iowa Press, Iowa City.

Quilter, J. and T. Stocker. 1983 Subsistence economies and the origins of Andean complex societies. *American Anthropologist* 85(3): 545–562.

Rackham, O. 1980 *Ancient Woodland: Its History, Vegetation and Uses in England*. Edward Arnold, London.

Raghavan, R., C. Gaillard and S.N. Rajaguru 1991 Genesis of calcretes from the calc-pan site of Singi Talav near Didwana, Rajasthan, India: a micromorphological approach. *Geoarchaeology* 6: 151–168.

Rea, A.M. 1981 The ecology of Pima fields. *Environment Southwest* 485: 8–15.

Rea, A.M. 1983 *Once a River: Bird Life and Habitat Changes on the Middle Gila*. University of Arizona Press, Tuscon, Arizona.

Rea, A.M. 1997 *At the Desert's Edge: An Ethnobotany of the Gila River Pima*. University of Arizona Press, Tuscon, Arizona.

Reddy, C.V.K., 1978 *Prosopis juliflora*, the precocious child of the plant world. *Indian Forester* 104: 14–18.

Redman, C.L. 1999 *Human Impact on Ancient Environments*. University of Arizona Press, Tuscon, Arizona.

Reinhard, J. 1993 *The Nazca Lines*. Editorial Los Pinos, Lima, Peru.

Reyes-Reyes, G., L. Baron-Ocampo, I. Cuali-Alvarez, J.T. Frias-Hernandez, V. Olalde-Portugal, L. Varela Fregoso and L. Dendooven. 2002 C and N dynamics in soil from the central highlands of Mexico as affected by mesquite (*Prosopis* spp.) and huizache (*Acacia tortuoso*): a laboratory investigation. *Applied Soil Ecology* 19: 27–34.

Reynel, C. and C. Felipe-Morales 1987 *Agroforestería Tradicional en los Andes del Perú*. Ministerio de Agricultura, Instituto Nacional Forestal y de Fauna, y FAO, Lima, Peru.

Rice, D.S., P.M. Rice and E.S. Deevey, Jr. 1985 Paradise lost: Classic Maya impact on a lacustrine environment. In *Prehistoric Lowland Maya Environment and Subsistence Economy*, edited by M. Pohl, pp. 91–105. Harvard University, Peabody Museum of Archaeology and Ethnology, Cambridge, Massachusetts.

Richards, J.H. and M.M. Caldwell 1987 Hydraulic lift: substantial nocturnal water transport between soil layers by *Artemisi tridentate* roots. *Oecologia* 73: 486–489.

Rick, J.W. 2008 Context, construction, and ritual in the development of authority at Chavín de Huántar. In *Chavín: Art, Architecture and Culture*, edited by W.J. Conklin and J. Quilter, pp. 3–34. Cotsen Institute of Archaeology Monograph 61. Cotsen Institute of Archaeology, Los Angeles, California.

Rindos, D. 1980 Symbiosis, instability, and the origins and spread of agriculture: a new model. *Current Anthropology* 21: 751–72.

Roe, P.G. 2008 How to build a raptor: why the Dumbarton Oaks 'Scaled Cayman' Callango textile is really a Chavín jaguaroid Harpy Eagle. In *Chavín: Art, Architecture and Culture*, edited by W.J. Conklin and J.

Quilter, pp. 181–216. Cotsen Institute of Archaeology Monograph 61. Cotsen Institute of Archaeology, Los Angeles, California.

Rogers, K.E. 2000 *The Magnificent Mesquite*. University of Texas Press, Austin, Texas.

Rollins H.B, J.B. Richardson and D.H. Sandweiss 1986 The birth of El Niño: geoarchaeological evidence and implications. *Geoarchaeology* 1 (1): 3–15.

Roque J., A. Cano and A. Cook 2003 Restos vegetales del sitio arqueológico Casa Vieja, Callango (Ica). *Revista Peruano de Biología* 10 (1): 33–43.

Rossel Castro, A.P. 1954 *Caciques y Templos de Ica*. Talleres de la Penitenciaria de Lima, Lima, Peru.

Rossel Castro, A.P. 1968 *Historia Regional de Ica*. Editorial Universo, Lima, Peru.

Rossel Castro, A.P. 1977 *Arqueología Sur del Perú*. Lima: Editorial Universo, Lima, Peru.

Rossi, B.E. and P.E. Villagra 2003 Effects of *Prosopis flexuosa* on soil properties and the spatial pattern of understory species in arid Argentina. *Journal of Vegetation Science* 14: 543–550.

Rostworowski de Diez Canseco, M. 1970 Mercaderes del valle de Chincha en la época prehispánica: un documento y unos comentarios. *Revista Española de Antropología Americana* 5: 135–177.

Rostworowski de Diez Canesco, M. 1981 *Recursos Naturales Renovables y Pesca*, Siglos XVI y XVII. Instituto de Estudios Peruanos, Lima, Peru.

Rostworowski de Diez Canesco, M. 1989 *Costa Peruana Prehispanica*. Instituto de Estudios Peruanos, Lima, Peru.

Rowe, J.H. 1946 Inca culture at the time of the Spanish conquest. In *Handbook of South American Indians, Vol. 2: The Andean Civilisations*, edited by J.H. Steward, pp. 183–330. Bureau of American Ethnology 143, Vol. 2, US Government Printing Office, Washington, DC.

Rowe, J.H. 1956 Archaeological explorations in southern Peru, 1954–55. *American Antiquity* 22 (2): 1 35–151.

Rowe, J.H. 1959 Archaeological dating and cultural process. *Southwestern Journal of Anthropology* 15: 317–324.

Rowe, J.H. 1963 Urban settlements in ancient Peru. *Ñawpa Pacha* 1: 1–27.

Rowe, J.H. 1967 An interpretation of radiocarbon measurements on archaeological samples from Peru. In *Peruvian Archaeology: Selected Readings,* edited by J.H. Rowe and D. Menzel, pp. 16–30. Peek Publications, Palo Alto, California.

Rundel, P.W., E.T. Nilsen, M.R. Sharifi, R.A. Virginia, W.M. Jarrell, D.H. Kohl and G.B. Shearer. 1982 Seasonal dynamics of nitrogen recycling for a *Prosopis* woodland in the Sonoran Desert. *Plant and Soil* 67: 343–353.

Rundel, P.W., M.O. Dillon, B. Plama, H.A. Mooney, S.L. Glumon and J.R. Ehleringer 1991 The phytogeography and ecology of the coastal Atacama and Peruvian Deserts. *Aliso* 13 (1): 1–49.

Russell, F. 1908 *The Pima Indians*. 26th Annual Report of the Bureau of American Ethnology. Smithsonian Institution, Washington, DC.

Sagástegui Alva, A. 1973 *Manual de las Malezas de la Costa Norperuana*. Universidad Nacional de Trujillo, Trujillo, Peru.

Samuels, M.L. and J.L. Betancourt 1982 Modelling the long-term effects of fuel wood harvests on pinyon-juniper woodlands. *Environmental Management* 6: 505–515.

Sánchez Elías, J.E. 1957 *Cuarto Siglos de Historia Iqueña*. Editorial Victoria, Lima, Peru.

Sandweiss, D.H., J.B. Richardson, E.J. Reitz, H.B. Rollins and K.A. Maasch 1996 Georachaeological evidence from Peru for a 5,000 years BP onset of El Niño. *Science* 273: 1531–1533.

Sandweiss, D.H., H. Mc Iennis, R.L Burger, A. Cano, B. Ojeda, R. Paredes, M. de C. Sandweiss and M.D. Glasock 1998 Quebrada Jaguay: early South American maritime adaptations. *Science* 281: 1830–1832.

Sarmiento, G. 1984 *The Ecology of Neotropical Savannas*. Harvard University Press, Cambridge, Massachusetts.

Sawyer, A. 1961 Paracas and Nazca iconography. In *Essays in Pre-Columbian Art and Archaeology*, edited by S.K. Lothrop, pp. 269–298. Harvard University Press, Cambridge, Massachusetts.

Sawyer, A. 1979 Painted Nasca textiles. In *The Junius B. Bird Pre-Columbian Textile Conference 1973*, edited by A.P. Rowe, E.P. Benson and A.L. Schaffer, pp. 129–160. The Textile Museum and Dumbarton Oaks, Washington, DC.

Sawyer, A. 1997 *Early Nasca Needlework*. Lawrence King, London.

Schlesinger, W.H. 1985 The formation of caliche in soils of the Mojave Desert, California. *Geochimica et Cosmochimica Acta* 49: 57–66.

Schreiber, K.J. 1992 *Wari Imperialism in Middle Horizon Peru*. Anthropological Papers 87. University of Michigan, Museum of Anthropology, Ann Arbor, Michigan.

Schreiber, K.J. 1998 Nasca research since 1926. In *The Archaeology and Pottery of Nazca, Peru. Alfred Kroeber's 1926 Expedition*, edited by P. Carmichael, pp. 261–270. AltaMira Press, Walnut Creek, California.

Schreiber, K.J. 1999 Regional approaches to the study of prehistoric empires: examples from Ayacucho and Nasca, Peru. In *Settlement Pattern Studies in the Americas: Fifty Years since Virú*, edited by B.R. Billman and G.M. Feinman, pp. 160–171. Smithsonian Institution Press, Washington, DC.

Schreiber, K.J. 2001 Los wari en su contexto local: Nasca y Sondondo. In *Huari y Tiwanaku: Modelos vs. Evidencias*, edited by P. Kaulicke and W.H. Isbell, pp. 425–448. Boletín de Arqueología PUCP 4. Fondo Editorial de la Pontificia Universidad Católica del Perú, Lima, Peru.

Schreiber, K.J. and J. Lancho Rojas 1995 The puquios of Nasca. *Latin American Antiquity* 6 (3): 229–254.

Schultes, R.E. 1972 Hallucinogens in the Western Hemisphere. In *Flesh of the Gods: The Ritual Use of Hallucinogens*, edited by P.T. Furst, pp. 3–54. Waveland Press, Prospect Heights, Illinois.

Schulze, E.-D., M.M. Caldwell, J. Candell, H.A. Mooney, R.B. Jackson, D. Parson, E. Scholes, O.E. Sala and P. Trimborn 1998 Downward flux of water through roots (i.e. inverse hydraulic lift) in dry Kalahari sands. *Oecologia* 115: 460–462.

Schumm S.A. 2003 *The Fluvial System*, reprint of 1977 1st edn. The Blackburn Press, Caldwell, New Jersey.

Schweingruber, F.H. 1978 *Mikroskopische Holzanatomie*. Swiss Federal Institute of Forestry Research, Birmensdorf, Switzerland.

Scott, R.L., W.J. Shuttleworth, D.C. Goodrich and T. Maddock 2000 The water use of two dominant vegetation communities in a semiarid riparian ecosystem. *Agricultural and Forest Meteorology* 105: 241–256.

Scott, R.L., C. Watts, J. Garatuza Payan, E. Edwards, D.C. Goodrich, D. Williams and W.J. Shuttleworth 2003 The understory and overstory partitioning of energy and water fluxes in an open canopy, semi-arid woodland. *Agricultural and Forest Meteorology* 114: 127–139.

SENAMHI-Ica 1997 *Boletín Meteorológico*. Servicio Nacional de Meteorología e Hidrología, Ica, Peru.

SENAMHI-Ica 1998 *Boletín Meteorológico*. Servicio Nacional de Meteorología e Hidrología, Ica, Peru.

Sene, E.H. 1996 The potential of *Prosopis* in the conservation and development of drylands: the FAO perspective. In *Prosopis: Semiarid Fuelwood and Forage Tree. Building Consensus for the Disenfranchised*, edited by P. Felker and J. Moss, pp. 6–53–6–59. Centre for Semi-Arid Forest Resources, Kingsville, Texas.

Shetler, S. 1991 Three faces of Eden. In *Seeds of Change: A Quincentennial Commemoration*, edited by H.J. Viola and C. Margolis, pp. 225–247. Smithsonian Institution Press, Washington, DC.

Shimada, I. 1991 Pachacamac archaeology: retrospect and prospect. An introduction. In *Pachacamac*, by M. Uhle, pp. xv–lxviii. A reprint of the 1903 edition. Philadelphia University Museum, University of Pennsylvania, Philadelphia.

Shimada, I. 1994 *Pampa Grande and the Mochica Culture*. University of Texas Press, Austin, Texas.

Shimada, M. and I. Shimada 1985 Prehistoric llama breeding and herding on the north coast of Peru. *American Antiquity* 50: 3–26.

Shimada, I., C. Schaaf, L. Thompson and E. Mosely-Thompson 1991 Cultural impacts of severe droughts in the prehistoric Andes: application of a 1,500-year ice core precipitation record. *World Archaeology* 22 (3): 247–265.

Shougang 2004 Shougang Hierro Peru website (www.shp.com.pe/).

Silverman, H. 1991 The Paracas problem: archaeological perspectives. In *Paracas Art and Architecture*, edited by A. Paul, pp. 349–416. University of Iowa Press, Iowa City.

Silverman, H. 1992 The Nazca Lines: sacred geography and cult archaeology. In *Broken Images: The Figured Landscape of Nazca*, photographed by D. Parker. Cornerhouse Publications, Manchester.

Silverman, H. 1993 *Cahuachi in the Ancient Nasca World*. University of Iowa Press, Iowa City.

Silverman, H. 2002 *Ancient Nasca Settlement and Society*. University of Iowa Press, Iowa City.

Silverman, H. and D.A. Proulx 2002 *The Nazca*. Peoples of the Americas Series. Blackwell Press, Oxford.

Simpson, B.B., J.L. Neff and A.R. Moldenke 1977 *Prosopis* flowers as a resource. In *Mesquite. Its Biology in Two Desert Ecosystems*, edited by B.B. Simpson, pp. 84–107. US/IBP Synthesis Series 4. Dowden, Hutchinson and Ross, Stroudsburg, Pennsylvania.

Simpson, B.B. and O.T. Solbrig 1977 Introduction. In *Mesquite. Its Biology in Two Desert Ecosystems*, edited by B.B. Simpson, pp. 1–25. US/IBP Synthesis Series 4. Dowden, Hutchinson and Ross, Stroudsburg, Pennsylvania.

Singh, G. 1996 The role of *Prosopis* in reclaiming high-pH soils and in meeting firewood and forage needs of small farmers. In *Prosopis: Semiarid Fuelwood and Forage Tree. Building Consensus for the Disenfranchised*, edited by P. Felker and J. Moss, pp. 1–3–1–27. Centre for Semi-Arid Forest Resources, Kingsville, Texas.

Singh, G. and T.R. Rathod 2002 Plant growth, biomass production and soil water dynamics in a shifting dune of Indian desert. *Forest Ecology and Management* 171: 309–320.

Singh G., H. Singh and P.P. Bhojvaid 1998 Amelioration of sodic soils by trees for wheat and oats production. *Land Degradation and Development* 9: 453–462.

Skolmen, R.G. 1990 *Prosopis pallida*. In *Silvics of North America*,Vol. 2, edited by R.M. Burns and B.H. Honkala, pp. 583–586. Agriculture Handbook 654. US Department of Agriculture, Forest Service, Washington, DC.

Smith, B.D. 1995 *The Emergence of Agriculture*. Scientific American Library, New York.

Smith, C.E. 1967 Plant remains. In *The Prehistory of the Tehuacan Valley, Vol.1, Environment and Subsistence*, edited by D.S. Byers, pp. 220–255. University of Texas Press, Austin, Texas.

Smith, D.M., N.A. Jackson, J.M. Roberts and C.K. Ong 1999 Reverse flow of sap in tree roots and downward siphoning of water by *Grevillera robusta*. *Functional Ecology* 13: 256–264.

Solbrig, O.T., K. Bawa, N.J. Carman, J.H. Hunziker, C.A. Naranjo, R.A. Palacios, L. Poggio and B.B. Simpson 1977 Patterns of variation. In *Mesquite. Its Biology in Two Desert Ecosystems*, edited by B.B. Simpson, pp. 44–60. US/IBP Synthesis Series 4. Dowden, Hutchinson and Ross, Stroudsburg, Pennsylvania.

Stone, E.L. and P.J. Kalisz 1991 On the maximum extent of tree roots. *Forest Ecology and Management* 46: 59–102.

Stone-Miller, R. 1992 *To Weave for the Sun: Ancient Andean Textiles in the Museum of Fine Arts, Boston*. Thames and Hudson, London.

Strong, W.D. 1957 *Paracas, Nasca and Tiahuanacoid Cultural Relationships in South Coastal Peru*. Memoirs of the Society for American Archaeology 13. Salt Lake City, Utah.

Strong, W.D. and C. Evans 1952 *Cultural Stratigraphy in the Virú Valley, Northern Perú*. Columbia Studies in Archaeology 4. Columbia University Press, New York.

Strong, W.D., G.R. Willey and J.M. Corbett 1943 *Archaeological Studies in Peru*. Columbia University Press, New York.

Sudzuki, F. 1985a Environmental influence on foliar anatomy of *Prosopis tamarugo* (Phil.). In *The Current State of Knowledge on Prosopis tamarugo. Papers presented by the International Round Table, Arica, Chile*, edited by M.A. Habit, pp. 295–310. FAO, Rome.

Sudzuki, F. 1985b Environmental moisture utilization by *Prosopis tamarugo* (Phil.). In *The Current State of Knowledge on Prosopis tamarugo. Papers presented by the International Round Table, Arica, Chile*, edited by M.A. Habit, pp. 33–48. FAO, Rome.

Tahal Consulting Engineers 1969 Recursos de Aguas Subterráneas del Departamento de Ica. Unpublished report to CRYDI-Ica, Tel Aviv, Israel.

Taltasse, P. 1973 Distinctive hydrological characteristics of some pampas of the Peruvian coastal llain. In *Coastal Deserts: Their Natural and Human Environments*, edited by D.H.K. Amiran and A.W. Wilson, pp. 109–110. University of Arizona Press, Tuscon, Arizona.

Thompson, L.G., E. Mosely-Thompson, J.F. Bolzan and B.R. Koci 1985 A 1,500-year record of tropical precipitation in ice cores from the Quelccaya ice cap, Peru. *Science* 229: 971–973.

Thompson, L.G., E. Mosely-Thompson, M.E. Davis, P-N. Lin, K.A. Henderson, J. Cole-Dai, J.F. Bolzan and K.-B. Liu 1995 Late Glacial stage and Holocene tropical ice core records from Huascarán, Peru. *Science* 269: 46–48.

Toky, O.P., S. Ayra and R.P. Bisht 1992 Ecological perspectives of *Prosopis cineraria* (L.) druce in arid and semi-arid India. In *Prosopis Species: Aspects of their Value, Research and Development. Proceedings of the Prosopis Symposium, Centre for Overseas Research and Development, University of Durham*, edited by R.W. Dutton, M. Powell and R.J. Ridley, pp. 301–309. FAO, Rome.

Tomar, O.S., P.S. Minhas, V.K. Sharma, Y.P. Singh and Raj F. Gupta 2003 Performance of 31 tree species and soil conditions in a plantation established with saline irrigation. *Forest Ecology and Management* 177: 333–346.

Tomasto Cagigao, E. 2009 Talking bones. In *New Technologies for Archaeology: Multidisciplinary Investigations in Palpa and Nasca, Peru*, edited by M. Reindel and G.A. Wagner, pp. 141–158. Springer, Berlin.

Towle, M. 1961 *The Ethnobotany of Pre-Columbian Peru*. Viking Fund Publications in Anthropology 30. Viking Fund, New York.

Tropicos W^3 2004 Missouri Botanical Gardens VAST (VAScular Tropicos) Database (http://mobot.mobot.org/W3T/), Missouri.

Turney, O.A. 1924 *The Land of the Stone Hoe*. Arizona Republican Print Shop, Phoenix, Arizona.

Unkel, I. and B. Kromer 2009 The clock in the corn cob. In *New Technologies for Archaeology: Multidisciplinary Investigations in Palpa and Nasca, Peru*, edited by M. Reindel and G.A. Wagner, pp. 231–244. Springer, Berlin.

Urton, G. 1990 Andean ritual sweeping and the Nazca Lines. In *The Lines of Nazca*, edited by A.F. Aveni, pp. 173–206. American Philosophical Society, Philadelphia.

USDA, NRCS 2004 Plants Database, US Department of Agriculture, Natural Resources Conservation Service (available online at http://plants.usda.gov).

Vaughan, J.G. and C.A. Geissler 2000 *The New Oxford Book of Food Plants*. Oxford University Press, Oxford.

Vaughan, J-L., E. Badal García and E. Grau Almero 1985 Pollen stratigraphy of two cores from the Petén Lake district. In *Prehistoric Lowland Maya Environment and Subsistence Economy*, edited by M. Pohl, pp. 73–89. Harvard University, Peabody Museum of Archaeology and Ethnology, Cambridge, Massachusetts.

Vaughn, K.J. 2010 *The ancient Andean village: Marcaya in Prehispanic Nasca*. University of Arizona Press, Tucson, Arizona.

Vázquez de Espinosa, Antonio de 1942 [1629] *Compendium and Description of the West Indies*, translated by C. Upson Clark. Smithsonian Miscellaneous Collections 102. Smithsonian Institution, Washington, DC.

Velázquez Zea, V. 1995 Los montes ribereños del Río Ica. *Boletín de Lima* 99: 67–76.

Vildoso, C. 1996 *Apuntes Sobre El Huarango*. Centro de Estudios para el Desarrollo y Participación (CEDEP), Lima, Peru.

Villalba, L. 2006 Ecology and behaviour of two sympatric felids, the Andean cat (*Oreailurus jacobita*) and pampas cat (*Oncifelis colocolo*) in Khastor (southern Bolivia). Available from World Conservation Union, Cat Specialist Group. www.catsg.org./catsgportal/project-o-month/O2_webarchive/webarchive.htm

Villegas Kau, D. 1998 Huarangos o algarrobos? *Umbral* 10: 41–44.

Von Hagen, V.W. 1961 *Realm of the Incas*. New American Library, New York.

Vreeland, J.M. and A. Cockburn 1980 Mummies of Peru. In *Mummies, Disease and Ancient Cultures*, edited by A. Cockburn and E. Cockburn, pp. 135–174. Cambridge University Press, Cambridge.

Weberbauer, A. 1945 *El Mundo Vegetal de los Andes Peruanos*. Estación Experimental Agrícola La Molina, Lima, Peru.

Weir, G.H. and H.H. Eling Jr. 1986 Pollen evidence for economic plant utilization in pre-Hispanic agricultural fields of Jequetepegue Valley, northern Peru. In *Andean Archaeology, Papers in Memory of Clifford Evans*, edited by R. Matos, S.A. Turpin and H.H. Eling Jr. Monograph XXVII. Institute of Archaeology, University of California, Los Angeles.

Wellmann, A.P. 1998 Catastro de Recursos Naturales Renovables en el Departamento de Ica. Unpublished Thesis, Pontificia Universidad Católica de Chile, Santiago, Chile.

Wells, L.E. 1987 An alluvial record of El Niño events from northern coastal Peru. *Journal of Geophysical Research* 92 (C13): 14463–14470.

Wells, L.E. 1990 Holocene history of the El Niño phenomenon as recorded in flood sediments of northern coastal Peru. *Geology* 18: 1134–1137.

Wells, L.E. and J.S. Noller 1999 Holocene coevolution of the physical landscape and human settlement in northern coastal Peru. *Geoarchaeology* 14 (8): 755–789.

Weltzin, J.F. and G.R. McPherson 1997 Spatial and temporal soil moisture resource partitioning by trees and grasses in a temperate savannah, Arizona, USA. *Oecologia* 112: 156–164.

Weng, C., M.B. Brush and A.J. Chepstow-Lusty 2004 Holocene changes of Andean alder (*Alnus acuminata*) in highland Ecuador and Peru. *Journal of Quaternary Science* 19 (7): 685–691.

Went, F.W. 1975 Water vapour absorption in *Prosopis*. In *Physiological Adaptation to the Environment*, edited by F.J. Vernberg, pp. 67–75. Intext Educational Publishers, New York.

Westengen, O.T., Z. Huáman and M. Heun 2005 Genetic diversity and geographic pattern in South American cotton domestication. *Theoretical Applied Genetics* 110: 392–402.

Whaley, O.Q. 2004 *Proyecto Huarango*: conservation of dry forest ecosystems on the south coast of Peru. Unpublished MSc Thesis. Birkbeck College, University of London.

Whaley, O.Q. and D.G. Beresford-Jones 2004 The Secret Desert Forests of Peru. Lecture to the Anglo-Peruvian Society, Canning House, London, 25 May.

Whaley, O.Q., A. Orellana, E. Pérez, M. Tenorio, F. Quinteros, M. Mendosa and O. Pecho 2010a *Plantas y Vegetación de Ica, Perú. Un recurso para su restauración y conservación. Icamanta Yurakuna Qurakuna*. Royal Botanic Gardens, Kew.

Whaley O.Q., D.G. Beresford-Jones, W. Milliken, A. Orellana, A. Smyk and J. Leguia 2010b An Ecosystem approach to restoration and sustainable management of dry forest in Southern Peru. *Kew Bulletin* 65 (4): 1–29.

Whittemore, I.T. 1893 *Among the Pimas: The Mission to the Pima and Maricopa Indians*. Albany, New York.

Woodbury, R.B. 1979 Prehistory: Introduction. In *Handbook of North American Indians, Vol. 9, The Southwest*, edited by W.C. Sturtevant, pp. 22–30. Smithsonian Institution, Washington, DC.

Wylie, A. 1985 The Reaction against Analogy. In *Advances in Archaeological Method and Theory, Vol. 8*, edited by M. Schiffer, pp. 68–112. Academic Press, London.

Yacovleff, E. and F.L. Herrera 1934 El mundo vegetal de los antiguos Peruanos. *Revista del Museo Nacional* 3 (3): 243–322.

Yepez, E.A., D.G. Williams, R.L. Scott and G. Lin 2003 Partitioning overstory and understory evapotranspiration in a semi-arid savannah woodland from the isotopic composition of water. *Agricultural and Forestry Meteorology* 119: 53–68.

Zuidema, R.T. 1972 Meaning in Nazca art. Iconographic relationships between Inca-, Huari-, and Nazca cultures in southern Peru. Göteborgs Ethnografiska Museum. *Artstryck* 1971: 35–54.

Zumbühl, H. 1979 *Tintes Naturales para Lana de Oveja*. Kamaq Maki, SEPAS, Huancayo, Peru.

Index